COMMERCIAL ARBITRATION

The Scottish and International Perspectives

COMMERCIAL ARBITRATION

The Scottish and International Perspectives

HONG-LIN YU, Ph.D.
Reader in Law, University of Stirling

DUNDEE UNIVERSITY PRESS
2011

Published in Great Britain in 2011 by
Dundee University Press
University of Dundee
Dundee DD1 4HN

www.dundee.ac.uk/dup

Copyright © Hong-Lin Yu

ISBN 978-1-84586-107-0

All rights reserved. No part of this publication may be reproduced, stored or transmitted in any form, or by any means, electronic, mechanical or photocopying, recording or otherwise, without the express written permission of the publisher.

The right of Hong-Lin Yu to be identified as the author of this work has been asserted in accordance with the Copyright, Designs and Patents Act 1988.

To avoid distraction to the reader, DUP's house style invokes the Interpretation Act 1978, so that the maculine forms "he", "him" and "his" are used throughout: all such references are intended to be read as gender-neutral.

No natural forests were destroyed to make this product; only farmed timber was used and replanted

British Library Cataloguing-in-Publication data
A catalogue for this book is available on request from the British Library.

Typeset by Waverley Typesetters, Warham, Norfolk
Printed by Bell & Bain Ltd, Glasgow

CONTENTS

Foreword		vii
Table of Cases		ix
Table of Legislation		xvii
1	Legal Development in Scotland	1
2	Features of the Arbitration (Scotland) Act 2010	9
3	Confidentiality	19
4	Arbitration Agreement	39
5	Party Autonomy and its Restrictions	67
6	Commencement of Arbitration Proceedings and Constitution of Tribunal	97
7	Arbitrators	105
8	Procedural Law	147
9	Choice of the Proper Law	169
10	Arbitral Proceedings	225
11	The Relationship between the Courts and Arbitration	239
12	Arbitral Awards	245
13	Arbitration Expenses	281
Appendix: Arbitration (Scotland) Act 2010		293
Index		349

FOREWORD

The passing of the Arbitration (Scotland) Act 2010 has brought about a revolution in dispute resolution law in Scotland. Until now, indeed for centuries, most of the law relating to arbitration has had to be found in judicial decisions, many of considerable antiquity, not all of which were sensible, and which left large gaps in a variety of places. Now, thanks to the new Act, there is a coherent and sensibly structured statutory scheme which will enable users and practitioners to see what can be done by arbitration, and to provide a new, straightforward and generally comprehensive service. To be effectively operated, the new regime requires to be properly understood and it is clear that all those liable to be involved in arbitration will have to undertake a study of the new Act and its effect on the conduct of arbitration in the future. In her book, Dr Hong-Lin Yu undertakes a splendidly focused examination of the whole. In clear and simple language she looks closely at the various aspects of the law and practice which must be appreciated for efficient operation of the system, and provides precisely the means to enable one to carry out the sort of study which is required. The book will be an invaluable tool for the arbitrator, the practitioner and the student alike.

The Hon Lord Dervaird
November 2010

TABLE OF CASES

A v B [2007] 1 All ER (Comm) 591 168
— v — (No 2) [2007] Bus LR D 59 168
A S Rampell, Inc v Hyster Co, 165 NY 2d 475 (1957) 174
Adriatic, The [1931] PD 241 181
Aggeliki Charis Compania Maritima SA v Pagnan SpA (The Angelic
 Grace) [1995] 1 Lloyd's Rep 87 57
Aïta v Ojjeh Rev Arb (1986) 583 28
AKSA v Norsolor, judgment of 9 December 1980, Cour d'appel,
 Paris (1980), [1981] RevArb 306 .... 161, 164, 266, 270
Ali Shipping Corp v Shipyard Trogir [1998] 2 All ER 136; [1998]
 1 Lloyd's Rep 643 .... 22, 23, 25, 26
American Independent Oil Co Inc (AMINOIL) v Government of
 the State of Kuwait International (1982) 21 ILM 976; reprinted
 in (1984) IX YBCA 71 199
American Safety Equipment Corp v J P Maguire & Co, 391 F 2d 821
 (2nd Cir 1968) 62
Amin Rasheed Shipping Corp; Al Watab, The v Kuwait Insurance Co
 [1984] AC 50 .... 175, 182
AMINOIL case see American Independent Oil Co Inc (AMINOIL) v
 Government of the State of Kuwait International
Annefield, The [1971] 1 Lloyd's Rep 1 58
ANR Coal Co v Cogentrix of North Carolina, Inc, 173 F 3d 493
 (4th Cir 1999) 11, 122
Arab African Energy Corp Ltd v Olieprodukten Nederland BV [1983]
 2 Lloyd's Rep 419 55
ARAMCO case see Saudi Arabia v Arabian American Oil Company
Arenson v Casson Beckman Rutley & Co [1977] AC 405 .... 136, 137,
 138, 139, 140
Associated Electric & Gas Insurance Services Ltd v European
 Reinsurance Company of Zurich [2003] UKPC 11 25
Assunzione, The [1954] AC 224 .... 180, 181

AT&T Corp v Saudi Cable Co [2000] 2 All ER 625 (Comm) 116, 117, 118
Atlantic Underwriting Agencies v Compagnia di Assicurazione di Milano SpA [1979] 2 Lloyd's Rep 240 181
Aughton Ltd v MF Services Ltd (1991) 57 BLR 1 58

Bachvhan v India Abroad Pub Inc, 1992 WL 110403 (NY SCt, 13 April 1992) 177
Baker Marine (Nig) Ltd v Chevron (Nig) Ltd, 91 F 3d 194 (2nd Cir 1999) 272
Bank Mellat v Helliniki Techniki SA [1984] QB 291 166
Benson v Eastern Bldg & Loan Assn, 174 NY 83, 66 NE 627 (1903) .. 53
Blalock v Perfect Subscription Co, 458 F Supp 123 (SD Ala 1978) ... 177
Bleustein et autres v Société True North et société FCB International, 2003, p 373 29
Boissevain v Weil [1949] 1 KB 482 174
Bonython v Commonwealth of Australia [1951] AC 201 180
Bowen v Amoco Pipeline Co, 254 F 3d 925 (CA10 2001) 277, 278
Bradford v McLeod 1986 SLT 244 110
Bradley v Fisher US (13 Wall) 335, 20 L Ed 646 (1872) 141, 142
British Petroleum Co Ltd v Government of the Libyan Arab Republic (1979) 46 ILR 297, reprinted in (1980) v YBCA 143 .... 194, 196
Bruce v Kordula (2001) APP L R 05/15 55
Bulgarian Foreign Trade Bank v AI Trade Finance Inc 27 October 2000, Supreme Court of Sweden 27

Caledonian Rly Co v Greenock & Wemyss Bay Rly Co (1872) 10 M 892 127
Calzarano v Liebowitz, 550 F Supp 1389; 1982 US Dist, 97 Lab Cas (CCH) P10, 136 145
Cereals SA v Tradax Export SA [1986] 2 Lloyd's Rep 301 131
Channel Tunnel Group Ltd v Balfour Beatty Construction Ltd [1993] AC 384, [1993] 2 WLR 262 .... 168, 217
Chicago Typographical Union v Chicago Sun-Times, Inc, 935 F 2d 1501 (7th Cir 1991) 277
Christopher Brown Ltd v Genossenschaft Oesterreichischer Waldbesitzer [1954] 1 QB 8 129
Chromalloy Aeroservices Inc v Arab Republic of Egypt, 939 F Supp 907 (DDC 1996) 266, 267, 268, 270, 271, 272
Commonwealth Coatings Corp v Continental Casualty Co, 393 US 145 (1968) 118, 119, 120, 121, 122, 123
Compagnie Financière du Pacifique v Peruvian Guano Co (1882) 11 QBD 55 21
Compagnie Tunisienne de Navigation SA v Compagnie d'Armement Maritime SA [1971] AC 572 .... 181, 184

Cook Industries, Inc v C Itoh & Co (America) Inc, 449 F 2d 106,
   107–8 (2nd Cir 1971), cert denied, 405 US 921, 92 S Ct 957,
   30 L Ed 2d 792 (1972) 120
Cooper v O'Connor, 69 App DC 100, 99 F 2d 135 at 141 (DC Cir
   1938) 143
Coppeé Lavalin v Ken-Ren [1994] 2 WLR 631 (HL) 167
Corbin v Washington Fire and Marine Insurance Co, 278 F Supp 393,
   1968 US Dist 143, 144
Corey v New York Stock Exchange, 691 F 2d 1205 .... 141, 145
Craviolini v Scholer & Fuller Associated Architects, 89 Ariz 24,
   357 P2d 611 at 613 (1960) 143
Cruden Construction Ltd v Commission for the New Towns [1995]
   2 Lloyd's Rep 387 57

Davis v Jointless Fire Brick Co, 300 F 2d 1 (9th Cir 1924) 177
Dean Witter Reynolds Inc v Byrd, 470 US 213 (1985) 279
Deutsche- und Tiefbohrgesellschaft v Ras Al Khaimah National Oil
   Co and Shell International Petroleum Co Ltd (DST v Rakoil)
   [1990] 1 AC 295, [1987] 3 WLR 1023 216
Dolling-Baker v Merrett [1990] 1 WLR 1205 .... 20, 21, 22, 25, 26
Don v Lippmann Cl & Fin 1, 7 Eng Rep 303 (1837) 165
Doughboy Indus Inc, In re Application of, 233 NYS 2d 488 (1962) . 185

Eco Swiss China Time Ltd v Benetton International NV [1999] ECR
   I–3055 .... 61, 63
Egerton v Brownlow 10 ER 359, (1853) 4 HL Cas 1 77
Ellerine Brothers (Pty) Ltd v Klinger [1982] 1 WLR 1375 57
Emmott v Michael Wilson & Partners Ltd [2009] EWHC 1 (Comm),
   [2008] EWCA Civ 184 .... 20, 23, 48
Empresa Exportadora de Azucar v Industria Azucarera Nacional SA
   (The Playa Larga and Marble Islands) [1983] CLY 411, [1983] 2
   Lloyd's Rep 171 57
Esso Australia Resources Ltd v Plowman [1995] HCA 19; (1995)
   128 ALR 391; (1995) 69 ALJR 404; (1995) 183 CLR 10 (7 April
   1995) 26, 27, 30

Farrans (Construction) Ltd v Dunfermline District Council 1988
   SC 120 246
Federconsorzi (C–88/91) [1992] ECR I–4035 63
Fergusson v Fyffe (1841) 2 Rob 267 180
Fiona Trust & Holding Corp v Privalov [2007] UKHL 40, [2008]
   1 Lloyd's Rep 254 .... 58, 59
Försäkringsaktiebolaget Skandia v Riksgäldskontoret, K Hobér, "In
   search for the centre of gravity-applicable law in international
   arbitration in Sweden" (1994) Swedish Intl Arb 7 187
Fray v Blackburn 3 Best & Smith 576 141

Gahn v International Union Ladies' Garment Workers' Union, 311 F
  2d 113 (3rd Cir 1962) 141, 143, 145
Garnett v Ferrand (1827) 6 B & C 611, [1824–34] All ER 244 135
Gateway Technologies, Inc v MCI Telecommunications Corp, 64 F
  3d 993 (CA5 1995) 278
General National Maritime Transport Company v Götaverken
  Arendal AB Decision of 21 Feb 1980, Court of Appeal, Paris,
  107 (1980) JDI 660, [1980] RevArb 524, reprinted in (1981)
  20 ILM 883 .... 161, 162, 164, 266, 270, 272
General Trading Company (Holdings) Ltd v Richmond Corporation
  Ltd [2008] EWHC 1479 (Comm), [2008] 2 Lloyd's Rep 475 58
Grampian Regional Council v John G McGregor (Construction) Ltd
  1994 SLT 133 246

Hall Street Associates, LLC v Mattel, Inc, 128 S Ct 1396, 552 US 576
  (2008) 278, 279
Halpern v Halpern [2007] EWCA Civ 291 202
Hamlyn v Talisker Distillery [1894] AC 202 .... 183, 184
Harbour Assurance Co (UK) Ltd v Kansa General International
  Insurance Co Ltd [1993] QB 701, [1993] 3 WLR 42, [1993] 3 All
  ER 897, [1993] 1 Lloyd's Rep 455 60
Hassneh Insurance Co of Israel v Mew [1993] 2 Lloyd's Rep 243 21,
                                                                            22, 26
Hawkins v Clayton [1989] 164 CLR 539 27
Helbert Wagg & Co Ltd, Re [1956] Ch 323 181
Heyman v Darwins Ltd [1942] AC 356 59
Hilmarton, Cour d'appel, Paris, December 1991 .... 266, 267, 268,
                                                                         270, 271
Hiscox v Outhwaite [1992] AC 562 247
Hohensee v Goon Squad, 171 F Supp 562 143
Hoosac Tunnel, Dock and Elevator Co v O'Brien, 137 Mass 424
  (1984) 141, 142, 143

Industrie, The [1894] PD 58 (CA) 181
International Tank and Pipe SAK v Kuwait Aviation Fuelling Co
  KSC [1975] 1 QB 224 165

Jacada (Europe), Ltd v International Marketing Strategies, Inc, 401 F
  3d 701 (CA6 2005) 278
Jacobs v Credit Lyonnais (1884) 112 QBD 589 (CA) 181

Konkar Indomitable Corp v Fritzen Schiffsagentur und
  Bereederungs GmbH, 80 Civ 3230 (SDNY) 185
K/S Norjarl A/S v Hyundai Heavy Industries Co Ltd [1992] QB 863,
  [1991] 1 Lloyd's Rep 524 (CA) 131, 282

Kulukundis Shipping Co v Amtorg Trading Corp, 126 F 2d 978 62
Kuwait Airways Corp v Iraqi Airways Company (Nos 4 and 5) [2002]
    2 AC 883 80
Kyocera Corp v Prudential-Bache Trade Services, Inc 341 F 3d 987
    (CA9 2003) 277, 279, 280

Laker Airways Inc Fls Aerospace Ltd and Burnton Fls Aerospace Ltd
    v Laker Airways Inc [1999] 2 Lloyd's Rep 45 .... 114, 115
LaPine Technology Corp v Kyocera Corp, 130 F 3d 884 (9th Cir
    1997) 277
Lena Goldfield Arbitration (1950–51) 36 Cornell LQ 31 193
LIAMCO case *see* Libyan American Oil Company (LIAMCO) v
    Government of the Libyan Arab Republic
Libyan American Oil Company (LIAMCO) v Government of the
    Libyan Arab Republic (1982) 62 ILR 140; reprinted in (1981)
    VI YBCA 89 198
Locabail (UK) Ltd v Bayfield Properties Ltd [2000] QB 451, [2000]
    2 WLR 870 113

Mechema Ltd v SA Mines, Minerais et Metaux, Ad hoc Arbitration,
    Award of 3 November 1977; reprinted in (1982) VII YBCA 77
    at 79 213
Merak, The [1964] 2 Lloyd's Rep 527 (CA) 58
Merit Ins Co v Leatherby Ins Co, 714 F 2d 673 (7th Cir 1983), cert
    denied, 464 US 1009 (1983) 121, 122, 123
Metamorphosis, The [1953] 1 WLR 543 181
Millar v Dickson 2001 SLT 988 110
Miramar, The [1984] 2 Lloyd's Rep 129, [1984] AC 676 (HL) 58
Mitchell v Cable (1848) 10 D 1297 240
Mitsubishi Motors Corps v Soler Chrysler Plymouth Inc, 473 US 614,
    105 S Ct 3346 (1985) 62, 77
Modern Building (Wales) Ltd v Limmer & Trinidad Co Ltd [1975]
    1 WLR 1281, [1975] 2 Lloyd's Rep 318 58
Morelite Constr Corp v New York City District Council Carpenters
    Benefit Fund 748 F 2d 79 (2nd Cir 1984) 122, 123
Motorola Credit Corp v Uzan (4P 198/2005) unreported, 31 October
    2005, Bundesgericht 275
Mount Albert Borough Council [1938] AC 224 (PC) 186
M/S Bremen v Zapata Off-Shore Co, US 1, 32 LEd 2d 513 54
Musawi v R E International (UK) Ltd & Others [2007] EWHC
    2981 202
Muschany v United States, 324 US 49 (1945) 176
Myanmar Yaung Chi Oo Co Ltd v Win Win Nu [2003] SGHC 124 24

NAFIMCO v Foster Wheeler, Paris Cour d'appel, 22 January 2004 ... 29

Nashua River Paper Co v Hammermill Paper Co, 223 Mass 8, 111 NE 678 (1916)... 53
National Equipment Rental Ltd v Szukhent, 375 US 311, 11 L Ed 2d 354, 84 S Ct 411 (1964) 55
Naviera Amazonica Peruana SA v Compania International de Seguros del Peru, unreported, Court of Appeal, 10 November 1987 167
New York Life Ins Co v Cravens, 178 US 389 (1900)...................... 177
Njegos, The [1936] PD 90 181
Norske Atlas Co Ltd v London General Insurance Co Ltd [1927] 2 Lloyd's Rep 104 184
Nute v Hamilton Mutual Ins Co, 72 Mass (6 Gray) 174 (1856).......... 53
NV Handel Maatschappij J Smits v English Exports (London) Ltd [1955] 2 Lloyd's Rep 69.. 181
NV Kwik Hoo Tong Handel Maatschappij v James Finlay and Co Ltd [1927] AC 604 181

Oxford Shipping Co Ltd v Nippon Yusen Kaisha [1984] 2 Lloyd's Rep 373.. 64

Pabalk Ticaret Ltd Sirketi v Norsolor, ICC case no 3131, 26 October 1979.. 214
Palacath Ltd v Flanaga [1985] 2 All ER 161, 274 EG 143, [1985] 1 EGLR 86 138
Parsons & Whittemore Overseas Co v RAKTA, United States Court of Appeals for the Second Circuit, 23 December 1974, 508 F 2d 969 .... 78, 79
Petroleum Developments Ltd v Ruler of Abu Dhabi (1951) 18 ILR 141 193
Pilkington plc v PPG Industries Inc, unreported, 1 November 1989 115
Pittalis v Sherefettin [1986] QB 868, [1986] 2 All ER 227................... 56
Pollich v Heatley 1910 SC 469... 246
PPG Industries Inc v Pilkington plc, Libbey-Owens-Ford Co, 825 F Supp 1465; 1993 US Dist LEXIS 9524; 1993–2 Trade Cas (CCH) P70, 368.. 115
— v —, 1994 US App (9th Cir) LEXIS 14427 115
President of India v La Pintada Compania Navigation SA [1985] 1 AC 104.. 166
Puerto Rico Tel Co v US Phone Mfg Corp, 427 F 3d 21 (CA1 2005). 278

R v Gough [1993] AC 646 117
— v International Trustee for the Protection of Bondholders [1937] AC 500 .... 73, 173, 181
Richardson v Mellish (1824) 2 Bingham 229, 130 ER 294................. 77

Roadway Package System, Inc v Kayser, 257 F 3d 287 (CA3
   2001) 278
Rossano v Manufacturers Life Insurance Co [1962] 2 All ER 214 179
Royal Aquarium and Summer and Winter Garden Society v
   Parkinson [1892] 1 QB 431, [1891–4] All ER 429 136
Ruler of Qatar v International Marine Oil Co Ltd (1953) 20 ILR
   534 193

Sanderson v Armour 1909 SC 146 117 43
Sapphire International Petroleums Ltd v National Iranian Oil
   Company, arbitral award of 15 March 1963, (1968) 35 ILR
   136 .... 192, 193
Saudi Arabia v Arabian American Oil Company (1960) 27 ILR
   117 194
Scherk v Alberto-Culver Co US 506 (1974) 62, 185
Science Research Council v Nasse [1980] AC 1028 21
Scottish Provident Institution v Cohen & Co (1888) 16 R 112 180
SEEE case see Société Européene d'Etudes et d'Entreprise (SEEE) v
   Yugoslavia
Serbian Loans [1929] PCIJ Series A, no 14, p 5, 11 WC 340
   (1929) 190
Siboti K/S v BP France SA [2003] EWHC 1278 (Comm), [2003]
   2 Lloyd's Rep 364 57
Sirros v Moore [1975] QB 118, [1974] 3 All ER 776, [1974] 3 WLR
   459, 139 JP 2 135
Société Européene d'Etudes et d'Entreprise (SEEE) v Yugoslavia
   (1959) JDI 1074 .... 161, 266, 270
Société PT Putrabali Adyamulia v Société Rena Holding et Société
   Mnogutia Est Epices (2007) Revue de l'Arbitrage 507 .... 269, 270
Soleimany v Soleimany [1999] QB 785 43
Spier v Calzaturificio Tecnica, 71 F Supp 2d 279, 77 F Supp 2d 405
   (SDNY 1999) 272
Splosna Plovba of Piran v Agrelak Steamship Corp, 381 F Supp
   1368 185
SPP (Middle East) Ltd, Hong Kong and Southern Pacific Properties
   Ltd, Hong Kong v Arab Republic of Egypt and Egyptian
   General Company for Tourism and Hotels, ICC case no 3493,
   16 February 1983 200
Sutcliffe v Thackrah [1974] AC 727 .... 136, 137, 138, 139, 140
Syncor International Corp v McLeland, 120 F 3d 262 (1997) 278

T W Thomas & Co Ltd v Portsea Shipping Co Ltd [1912]
   AC 1 (HL) 58
Texaco Overseas Petroleum Co and California Asiatic Co v
   Government of the Libyan Arab Republic (1978) 17 ILM 3. 196, 197

Tote Bookmakers Ltd v Development & Property Holding Co Ltd
 [1985] Ch 261 57
Tournier v National Provincial and Union Bank of England [1924]
 1 KB 461 26
Tradax International SA v Cerrahogullari TAS (The M Eregli) [1981]
 2 Lloyd's Rep 169 57
Trygg Hansa Insurance Co Ltd v Equitas Ltd [1998] 2 Lloyd's Rep
 439 58
Tzortzis v Monark Line A/B [1968] 1 WLR 406 .... 174, 184

UHC Management Co v Computer Sciences Corp, 148 F 3d 992
 (1998) 276
Union of India v McDonnell Douglas Corp [1993] 2 Lloyd's
 Rep 48 167
United Railways of the Havana and Regla Warehouses Ltd, Re
 [1960] Ch 52 .... 180, 181
United States v Panhandle Eastern Corp (D Del 1988) 118 FRE
 346 27

Vita Food Products Inc v Unus Shipping Co Ltd [1939] AC 277 73,
 173, 175, 177
Volt Info Sciences, Inc v Stanford University, 489 US 468 277

Whitaker v Spiegel, Inc, 623 P 2d 1147 (Wash 1981) 177
Whitworth Street Estates (Manchester) Ltd v James Miller and
 Partners [1970] AC 583 (HL) 73, 165, 173, 174, 180, 186
Wilko v Swan, 346 US 427 (1953), 98 L Ed 168, 74 S Ct 182 ..... 54, 279
Williamson v Taylor (1845) 8 D 156 180
Wimbledon case [1926] PCIJ Series A, no 1, p 25 190
World Pride Shipping Ltd v Daiichi Chuo Kisen Kaisha (The Golden
 Anne) [1984] 2 Lloyd's Rep 489 64

TABLE OF LEGISLATION

Australia

1989	International Arbitration Act	30
	s 23	30
	s 24(1)	66
	(4)	66
	(5)(a)	66
	(b)	66
2005	Australian Centre for International Commercial Arbitration (ACICA) Rules	
	Art 18	35

Austria

1895	Code of Civil Procedure	
	Art 595(6)	81
	Art 616(2)	28, 30
1978	International Private Law Act	
	Art 35	81
2006	Rules of Arbitration and Conciliation of the International Arbitral Centre of the Austrian Federal Economic Chamber (VIAC) (Vienna Rules)	37, 291
	Art 3(6)	37
	Art 5(3)	37
	Art 7(4)	37
	Art 20(4)	37
	Art 22(1)	235
	Art 31	292
	Art 32	291
	Art 33(1)	291

Belgium

| 1998 | Judicial Code | 30, 159, 266, 273 |
| | Sixth Part | 130, 160, 265 |

1998	Judicial Code (*cont*)	
	Art 1697(1)	130
	(2)	43
	Art 1717	159, 160, 265
	(4)	159, 160, 273
2000	Belgian Centre for Mediation and Arbitration (CEPANI) Rules	35
	Art 17.5	35
	Appendix 2, point 9	35

China

1994	Arbitration Act	30
2004	China International Economic and Trade Arbitration Commission Rules	35
	Art 43(1)	35
	Art 44(2)	35

Costa Rica

	Code of Ethics of the International Center for Conciliation and Arbitration of Costa Rica	
	Art 15	31
1997	Arbitration Law (No 7727 of 1997)	31

Dominican Republic

2008	Commercial Arbitration Law (No 489–08)	
	Art 22	31

Dubai

2007	Dubai International Arbitration Centre (DIAC) Rules	35
	Art 41(1)	35
2008	Law No 1	31

Ecuador

1997	Law on Arbitration and Mediation (No 000 RO/145 of 1997)	
	Art 34	31

England and Wales

1889	Arbitration Act (52 & 53 Vict c 49)	60
1979	Arbitration Act (c 42)	166
1996	Arbitration Act (c 23)	3, 10, 15, 16, 20, 28, 30, 41, 58, 98, 117, 139, 166, 223, 235, 237, 248, 262, 285

1996 Arbitration Act (c 23) (*cont*)
- s 1 .... 9, 40
  - (a) 10
  - (b) 10
  - (c) 10
- s 2(1) 263
- s 3 148
- s 4 69
  - (1) 263
  - (2) 72
  - (3) 72
- s 5 41
- ss 5–8 44
- s 6(1) 57
  - (2) 57, 58
- s 7 .... 43, 59
- s 8 149
- s 9 44
- s 14 46
  - (1) 98
  - (3) 98
  - (4) 99
  - (5) 99
- s 15(2)–(3) 47
  - (3) 101, 107
- ss 15–21 105
- s 16 100
  - (1) 47, 106
  - (3) 100
  - (3)–(4) 47, 107
  - (4) 100
  - (5) 100
  - (6) 100
- s 17 108
- ss 17–18 .... 83, 107, 151
- s 19 101
- s 23 .... 47, 151
  - (3) 103
- ss 23–24 124
- s 24 .... 53, 85, 103, 125
  - (1) 47, 103
    - (a) 53, 95, 117, 154
  - (4) 53, 110
- s 25(1) 86, 104, 124, 126, 152
  - (3) 126, 152

1996 Arbitration Act (c 23) (cont)
- s 25(4) 86, 126, 152
- (5) 126, 152
- s 26 96
- (1) 124, 133
- s 27 .... 47, 127
- s 28 283
- (2) 283
- s 29 .... 94, 134, 135, 139, 140
- (1) 139
- s 30 .... 86, 127, 129
- (2) 86, 128, 253
- s 31 .... 86, 128
- s 32(2) 129
- (4) 128
- s 33 .... 87, 109, 152
- (1) 95, 154
- (a) 53
- s 34 .... 49, 226
- s 35 .... 50, 64, 237
- s 36 .... 49, 229
- s 37 49
- (1) 230
- (2) 230
- s 38(3) 233
- (4) 49, 233
- (5) 233
- (6) 233
- s 41(3) 50, 234
- (4) 50, 234
- (5) 235
- (5)–(7) 50
- (6) 235
- (7) 235
- s 43 .... 88, 152, 242
- (2) 242
- (3) 242
- s 44 50
- s 45(1) 239
- (2) 87, 152
- s 46 .... 172, 223
- (1) 51, 245
- (a) 173
- (b) 202, 217, 221, 223
- (3) 245

1996 Arbitration Act (c 23) (*cont*)
 s 47 .... 89, 152, 248
 s 48(4) 88, 152, 246
  (5) 51, 246
 s 49 .... 152, 247
 s 50 88
 s 51 .... 51, 250
 s 52 .... 51, 247
 s 55 248
 s 56 .... 89, 153, 249, 284
 s 57 51
  (3) 249
  (4) 249
  (5) 249
 s 58(1) 250
  (2) 251
 s 59 .... 52, 90, 132, 153, 281
 s 60 .... 132, 153, 285
 s 61 285
  (1) 52, 132
 s 62 285
  (2) 52, 132
 s 63 281
  (3)(a) 285
   (b) 285
  (4)(a) 285
   (b) 285
 s 64 .... 52, 285
  (1) 285
  (1)–(2) 132
  (2) 286
 s 65 52
  (1) 285
  (2) 285
 s 66 252
 s 67 .... 91, 153, 251
 s 68 .... 91, 153, 252
  (3)(a) 94, 153
 s 69(1) 52
  (2) 92
  (4) 92
  (7) 92
   (c) 94, 153
  (8) 92
 ss 69–70 153

1996 Arbitration Act (c 23) (*cont*)
 s 70 93
  (2) 251
  (3) 251
 s 72(1) 254
  (2) 254
 s 73 .... 95, 153
 s 74 .... 94, 134
 s 76 53
 ss 89–91 .... 1, 12, 41
 s 100 .... 13, 255
 s 101 .... 13, 256
 s 102 13
 s 103 .... 13, 257
 s 104 260
 Sch 3 1
 Sch 4 1

Finland

1992 Arbitration Act 32

France

1804 Code Napoléon 218
1806 Code of Civil Procedure 218
1981 Decree of 12 May 160, 161, 265
 Title V 265
 Title VI 265
 Arts 1492–1507 265
 New Code of Civil Procedure 28, 61, 160, 173, 187, 189
  Book IV 28, 187
  Art 3 82
  Art 1466 130
  Art 1469 32
  Art 1495 130
  Art 1496 187
   (1) 173
  Art 1497 221
  Art 1502 .... 265, 267, 268
   (5) 80, 267
  Art 2059 61
  Art 2060 61
   (2) 61

Germany

1900	Code of Civil Procedure	
	s 549(1)–(3)	62
	s 1030	61
	(1)	61
	(2)	61–62
	(3)	62
1998	Arbitration Act	
	s 1029(2)	43
	German Institution of Arbitration (DIS) Rules	35
	Art 43(1)	35

Greece

1968	Code of Civil Procedure VII	107
	Art 871	107

Hong Kong

1997	Arbitration Ordinance	32
	Chap 341	131
	(6B)	65–66
	s 2	29, 32
	s 13B	130
	Sch 5	130
2008	Hong Kong International Arbitration Centre (HKIAC) Rules	35
	Art 39(1)	35

Iran

1997	International Commercial Arbitration Act	32
2005	Tehran Regional Arbitration Centre (TRAC) Rules	37
	Art 4	37
2007	Iran Chamber of Commerce Rules	35
	Art 43, para E	35

Ireland

1954	Arbitration Act	32
2010	Arbitration Act	32

Italy

1942	Code of Civil Procedure	
	Art 744	33
	Arts 806ff	32
2003	Legislative Decree of 30 June	
	Art 52, para 6	33

2004 Milan Chamber of Arbitration Rules 35
          Art 43(1) 35
          Art 44(2) 35

Japan

2003 Arbitration Law No 138 33
2008 Japan Commercial Arbitration Association (JCAA) Rules
          r 40(2) 36

Kuwait

1977 Decree Law No 124 200

Libya

1954 Civil Code
          Art 1 199
1970 Nationalisation Law (Law No 115) 194

Malaysia

1998 Kuala Lumpur Regional Centre for Arbitration (KLRCA) Rules
          r 9 36

Netherlands

1986 Arbitration Act 65, 187
          Art 1045(1) 65
          Art 1054(2) 187
              (3) 221
          Art 1903 43
          Code of Civil Procedure (amended 2004)
          Art 1046(1) 65
2001 Netherlands Arbitration Institute (NAI) Rules
          Art 55(2) 36

New Zealand

1996 Arbitration Act 32
          Art 14 33
2007 Arbitration Amendment Act 33

Nicaragua

2005 Arbitration and Mediation Law (Law 540) 33
          Art 3 33

Norway

          General Provisions
              Chap 1, Section 5 33
2007 Stockholm Chamber of Commerce (SCC) Rules 36

Peru

2008 Legislative Decree No 1071
    Art 51 33

Russian Federation

    International Arbitration Court of the Chamber of Commerce
    and Industry of the Russian Federation (ICAC) Rules 35
    Art 25 35

Scotland

1695 Articles of Regulation
    25th Act 1, 310
1894 Arbitration (Scotland) Act (57 & 58 Vict c 13) 1, 14
    s 2 56
1972 Administration of Justice (Scotland) Act (c 59) 1
    s 1 .... 50, 242
    s 3 .... 14, 240
1990 Law Reform (Miscellaneous Provisions) (Scotland) Act (c 40) .. 2
    s 17 14
    s 66 .... 2, 14
    Sch 7 .... 2, 14
2000 Adults with Incapacity (Scotland) Act (asp 4) 107
    s 1(6) 83, 100, 151
2010 Arbitration (Scotland) Act (asp 1) 1, 4, 5, 9, 11, 12, 16,
                                      44, 45, 55, 69, 82, 97, 105, 107, 124,
                                      147, 148, 150, 151, 154, 157, 225,
                                      240, 246, 248, 254, 255, 293–347
    s 1 .... 9, 16, 40, 56, 69, 149, 239, 298
        (c) 239, 253
    s 2 .... 10, 99, 298–299
        (1) 10, 11, 105, 106
            (a) 10
            (b) 10
            (c) 10
    ss 2–3 10
    s 3 .... 11, 16, 99, 148, 299
        (1)(a) 148
            (i)–(iii) 148
        (b) 148
        (2) 11, 147
    s 4 .... 16, 40, 42, 299
    s 5 .... 16, 43, 299
        (1) 43
        (2) 43
        (3) 43

2010 Arbitration (Scotland) Act (asp 1) (*cont*)
- s 6 .... 43, 44, 82, 299–300
- s 7 .... 17, 45, 82, 300
- ss 7–9 17
- s 8 .... 17, 82, 149, 300
  - (1) 69
  - (3)(a) 69
    - (b) 69
  - (4)(a)(i) 69
    - (ii) 69
    - (iii) 69
    - (b) 69
- s 9 .... 17, 44, 69, 149, 301
  - (1) 149
  - (2) 46, 69, 149
  - (3) 69
    - (a) 46
    - (b) 46
  - (4) 149
    - (a)(i) 46
    - (ii) 16, 46
    - (iii) 46
    - (b) 46
- s 10 .... 17, 44, 45, 301–302
  - (1)(a) 44
    - (b) 44
    - (c) 44
    - (d)(i) 45
    - (ii) 45
    - (e) 44, 56
  - (2) 45
  - (3) 45
- s 11 .... 17, 254, 302
  - (1) 250
  - (2) 250
- ss 11–15 .... 245, 250
- s 12 302–303
  - (1) 252
  - (2)(a) 252
    - (b) 252
    - (c) 252
  - (3) 253
  - (5) 253
  - (6) 253
  - (8) 252

2010 Arbitration (Scotland) Act (asp 1) (*cont*)
 ss 12–15 17
 s 13 303
  (1) 253
  (2) 253
  (3) 253
  (4) 253
 s 14 303–304
  (1) 254
   (a) 254
   (b) 254
 s 15 .... 19, 304
  (1) 254
  (2)(a)(i) 254
   (ii) 254
   (b) 254
   (c) 254
   (d) 255
  (3) 254
 s 16 .... 12, 304–305
  (3) 12
  (4) 12
  (5) 12
  (6)(a) 12
   (b) 12
   (c) 12
 ss 16–17 .... 12, 17
 s 17 305
 s 18 .... 13, 305
  (1) 13, 255
  (2) 255
 ss 18–22 .... 13, 17, 245, 255
 s 19 305–306
  (1) 13, 256
  (2) 13, 256
 s 20 .... 13, 257, 259, 306–307
  (2) 257, 259
   (a) 257
   (b) 257
   (c) 258
    (i) 258
    (ii) 258
   (d)(i) 258
    (ii) 258
  (3) 259

2010 Arbitration (Scotland) Act (asp 1) (*cont*)

s 20(3)(a)	258
(b)	258
(c)	259
(d)	259
(4)	259
(5)	259
(6)(a)	259
(b)	259
(7)	259
s 21	256, 307
(1)	13
(2)	14
s 22	260, 302
s 23	307–308
s 24	17, 106, 308–309
(1)	101
(2)	101
ss 24–25	105
s 25	17, 309
s 26	14, 17, 309
(1)	16
(2)	16
s 27	310
s 28	310
s 29	14, 17, 255, 310
s 30	61, 310
s 31	310–311
s 32	311–312
s 33	312
s 34	312
s 35	312–313
s 36	313
(6)	106
s 37	313
Sch 1 (Scottish Arbitration Rules)	5, 10, 11, 12, 16, 17, 34, 45, 46, 47, 69, 70, 82, 85, 91, 94, 95, 96, 99, 103, 124, 125, 149, 153, 247, 248, 250
Pt 1	17, 46, 70, 97, 314–319
r 1	46, 97, 98, 314
r 2	46, 47, 99, 106, 314
(a)	106
(a)–(d)	99
(b)–(c)	106
(d)	106

2010	Scottish Arbitration Rules (*cont*)	
	rr 2–18	105, 106
	r 3	82, 83, 100, 107, 150, 151, 314
	r 4	82, 83, 96, 100, 107, 124, 150, 314
	(a)	100, 107, 151
	(b)	100, 107, 151
	r 5	46, 47, 100, 107, 314
	r 6	46, 47, 99, 101, 107, 127, 314–315
	(a)	99, 107
	(b)(i)	99, 107
	(ii)	99, 107
	r 7	82, 83, 96, 99, 101, 102, 107, 127, 150, 315–316
	(1)	83, 107
	(a)	101
	(b)	101
	(2)	83, 101, 108, 151
	(3)	83, 101, 108
	(4)	101, 108
	(a)	83, 102
	(b)	83, 102
	(5)	102, 108
	(a)	84
	(b)	84
	(6)	151
	(a)	84, 102, 108
	(b)	84, 102, 108
	(c)	84, 102, 108
	(7)	84, 108
	(8)	84, 102
	(a)	84, 101, 108
	(b)	84, 101, 108
	(c)	84, 101, 108
	(9)	84, 102
	r 8	82, 84, 87, 96, 100, 108, 101, 150, 151, 316
	(1)(a)	84
	(2)	109
	(a)	84
	r 9	46, 47, 104, 124, 316
	(c)	124
	(d)	124
	(e)	124
	rr 9–11	124
	r 10	46, 86, 87, 102, 104, 124, 125, 126, 316–317
	(1)	102
	(2)(a)	103

2010 Scottish Arbitration Rules (*cont*)
  r 10(2)(a)(i) 102
     (ii) 102
     (iii) 102
    (c) 102
    (d) 102
   (4) 102, 124
  rr 10–14 96
  r 11 .... 46, 47, 124, 317
   (1) 103
  rr 11–14 103
  r 12 .... 19, 53, 85, 86, 103, 104, 124, 125, 126, 317
   (a) 85, 125, 151
   (b) 85, 125, 151
   (c) 85, 125, 151
   (d) 85, 125, 151
   (e) 85, 109, 125, 151
  rr 12–16 .... 82, 124, 150
  r 13 .... 53, 85, 103, 125, 151, 318
   (a) 85
   (b) 85
   (c) 85
  r 14 .... 85, 125, 126, 151, 318
   (1)(a)–(b) 125
    (b)(i)–(ii) 85
   (2) 85, 125
   (3) 85, 125
  r 15 .... 85, 104, 124, 126, 127, 318
   (1) 104, 152
    (a) 86, 126
    (b) 126
    (c) 86, 126
    (d) 86, 126
    (e) 86, 126
   (2) 86, 126
   (3) 126
  r 16 .... 85, 104, 152, 319
   (1)(a) 126
    (b) 127
    (c) 94, 127
   (2) 127
  r 17 .... 46, 47, 104, 124, 319
   (1)(a) 104, 127
    (b) 127
   (2) 104

2010	Scottish Arbitration Rules (*cont*)	
	r 17(2)–(3)	127
	r 18	46, 47, 124, 319
	Pt 2	17, 47, 70, 319–321
	r 19	86, 90, 127, 128, 319–320
	(a)	86, 127
	(b)	86, 127
	(c)	86, 127
	rr 19–21	82, 150, 152
	rr 19–23	127
	r 20	320
	(1)	128
	(2)	128
	(a)	86
	(b)	86
	(3)	250
	(a)	86, 128
	(b)	86, 128
	(4)	128
	(a)	86
	(b)	86
	r 21	128, 129, 253, 320
	(1)	86
	(2)	87, 128
	(3)	86, 128
	r 22	47, 87, 129, 253, 320
	r 23	82, 87, 129, 150, 152, 321
	(2)(a)	129
	(b)(i)–(iii)	129
	Pt 3	17, 47, 48, 70, 152, 321–322
	r 24	82, 87, 96, 109, 150, 152, 321
	(1)(a)	87, 109, 152
	(b)	87, 109, 152
	(c)	109, 152, 229
	(i)–(ii)	87
	(2)	87, 109
	r 25	82, 87, 109, 150, 152, 321
	r 26	19, 20, 34, 47, 48, 96, 131, 321–322
	(1)	19, 255
	(a)	19
	(b)	19
	(c)	255
	(i)	19
	(ii)	19
	(iii)	20

2010 Scottish Arbitration Rules (cont)
    r 26(1)(d) 255
        (e) 20, 255
        (f) 20, 255
        (g) 20
      (2) 20
      (3) 20
      (4) 19
    r 27 .... 34, 47, 48, 131, 322
      (1) 131
      (2) 131
  Pt 4 .... 17, 48, 49, 70, 225, 322–326
    r 28 .... 48, 49, 225, 322–323
      (1) 225
      (2) 225
        (a) 225
        (b) 226
        (c) 226
        (d) 226
        (e) 225
        (f) 226
        (g) 226
        (h) 225
    rr 28–39 70
    r 29 .... 48, 49, 148, 228, 323
    r 30 .... 49, 228, 229, 323–324
      (1) 228, 229
      (2)(a) 229
        (b)(i) 229
          (ii) 229
    r 31 .... 49, 228, 324
      (1) 229
      (2) 229
    r 32 .... 49, 229, 324
      (1) 229
      (2) 229
    r 33 .... 49, 229, 324
      (2) 229
    r 34 .... 49, 230, 324
      (1) 86, 104, 126
      (2)(a) 230
        (b) 230
    r 35 .... 49, 232, 233, 324–325
      (a)(i) 233
        (ii) 233

2010	Scottish Arbitration Rules (*cont*)	
	r 35(b)	233
	r 36	49, 233, 325
	r 37	49, 50, 233, 234, 325
	(1)	250
	(2)	234
	r 38	49, 234, 325–326
	(a)(i)	50
	(ii)	50
	r 39	49, 234, 326
	(1)(a)	50
	(b)(i)–(iii)	50
	(2)(a)–(d)	235
	r 40	49, 50, 64, 236, 326
	(1)	64, 237
	(2)	64, 237
	Pt 5	17, 50, 239, 241, 326–328
	r 41	50, 87, 239, 240, 326
	r 42	82, 87, 150, 239, 240, 327
	(2)(a)	152, 240
	(b)(i)	87, 152
	(i)–(iii)	240
	(ii)	87, 152
	(iii)	87, 152
	(3)	240
	(4)	240
	r 43	12, 50, 87, 241, 327
	(a)–(b)	241
	r 44	50, 82, 87, 150, 151, 152, 241, 327
	(1)(a)	172
	(2)(a)	87, 241
	(b)	87, 241
	(4)	88
	(5)	88
	r 45	82, 88, 151, 241, 327–328
	(1)(a)	88, 152
	(a)–(b)	241
	(b)	88, 152
	(2)	88, 242
	(3)	88, 242
	(4)	88, 242
	r 46	50, 242, 243, 328
	(1)(a)	50, 242
	(b)	50, 242
	(c)	50, 242

2010 Scottish Arbitration Rules (cont)
- r 46(1)(d) 50, 242
  - (e) 50, 242
  - (f) 50, 242
  - (g) 50, 242
  - (2)(b)(i) 243
    - (ii) 243
  - (3) 243
  - (4)(a) 243
    - (b)(i) 243
    - (ii) 243
  - (5)(a) 243
    - (b) 243
- Pt 6 .... 18, 51, 245, 329–333
- r 47 .... 47, 51, 171, 188, 218, 245, 329
  - (1)(a) 172
    - (a)–(b) 51
    - (b) 178
  - (1)–(2) 245
  - (2) 172, 246
  - (3) 171, 246
    - (b) 51
- r 48 .... 82, 88, 150, 151, 329
  - (1) 88, 152, 246
  - (2) 88, 152, 246
- r 49 .... 51, 329
  - (a) 51
  - (a)–(c) 246
  - (b) 51
  - (c) 51
- r 50 .... 82, 88, 150, 151, 152, 247, 330
  - (1)(a) 88
    - (a)–(b) 247
    - (b) 88
    - (c) 247
  - (2)(a) 88, 247
    - (b) 247
    - (c) 88
  - (3) 89, 247
  - (4) 89
- r 51 .... 51, 247, 330
  - (1) 51, 247
  - (2)(a) 247
    - (b) 247
    - (c)–(d) 247

2010	Scottish Arbitration Rules (*cont*)	
	r 51(3)	247
	r 52	51, 247, 331
	r 53	51, 248, 331
	r 54	82, 88, 89, 150, 151, 152, 331
	(1)	89
	(2)	89, 248
	(3)	89
	r 55	51, 331
	(a)	248
	(b)	248
	r 56	82, 88, 89, 90, 151, 249, 331
	(1)	89, 153, 284, 249
	(2)(a)	250
	(b)	89, 250
	(c)	89, 250
	(3)	89, 250
	(4)	89
	r 57	51, 332
	(1)	250
	(2)	250
	(3)	250
	(4)	250
	r 58	51, 93, 282, 249, 252, 332–333
	(1)	249
	(2)	249
	(3)	249
	(4)(a)	249
	(b)	249
	(5)	249
	(6)	249
	(7)(a)	249
	(b)	249
	(8)	249
	Pt 7	18, 51, 281, 333–336
	r 59	51, 52, 96, 281, 283, 333
	(a)	281
	(b)	281
	(c)	281
	(d)(i)–(ii)	281
	rr 59–66	131
	r 60	52, 82, 90, 96, 132, 151, 153, 281, 282, 283, 284, 333–334
	(1)	90, 282
	(a)	282

2010 Scottish Arbitration Rules (cont)
　　r 60(1)(a)(i) 90, 282
　　　　　(i)–(ii) 132
　　　　　(ii) 90, 282
　　　　(b) 132, 282
　　　　　(i) 282
　　　　　(i)–(iv) 90, 132
　　　　　(ii) 282
　　　　　(iii) 283
　　　　　(iv) 283
　　　(1)–(2) 132
　　　(2) 281
　　　　(a) 90
　　　　(b) 90
　　　(3) 90, 132
　　　　(a) 283
　　　　(b) 132, 283
　　　(4)(a) 90, 283
　　　　(b) 90, 283
　　　(5) 90, 283
　　　(6)(a) 283
　　　　(b) 283
　　r 61 .... 51, 52, 132, 283, 334–335
　　　(1) 96
　　　　(a) 283
　　　　(b) 284
　　　　(c) 284
　　　(2) 132
　　　　(a) 284
　　　　(b) 284
　　　(3)(a) 284
　　　　(b) 284
　　r 62 .... 51, 52, 283, 284, 335
　　　(1) 132, 284
　　　(2) 284
　　　(3)(a) 284
　　　　(b) 284
　　　(4)(a) 284
　　　　(b) 284
　　r 63 .... 82, 90, 132, 151, 153, 285, 335
　　r 64 .... 51, 52, 335–336
　　　(1)(a) 133, 285
　　　　(b) 133, 285
　　　(2) 133
　　　　(a) 285

2010	Scottish Arbitration Rules (*cont*)	
	r 64(2)(b)	285
	r 65	52, 92, 129, 283, 336
	(1)	285
	(2)	285
	r 66	52, 284, 336
	Pt 8	18, 52, 251, 252, 253, 336–342
	r 67	83, 86, 90, 91, 93, 151, 153, 253, 336–337
	(1)	90, 251
	(2)	251
	(a)	91
	(b)	91
	(c)	91
	(3)	91, 251
	(4)	251
	(5)	251
	(a)	91
	(b)	91
	(6)	91
	(7)	91
	r 68	53, 83, 90, 91, 93, 96, 109, 151, 153, 337–338
	(1)	91, 252
	(2)(a)	109, 252
	(i)–(iii)	91
	(b)	91
	(b)–(k)	252
	(c)	91
	(d)	91
	(e)	91
	(f)(i)	91
	(ii)	91
	(g)	92
	(h)	92
	(i)	92
	(j)	92
	(k)	92
	(7)–(8)	92
	r 69	52, 92, 93, 240, 339
	(1)	52, 252
	r 70	92, 93, 150, 153, 339–340
	(2)(a)	92
	(b)	92
	(3)(a)	92
	(b)	92
	(c)(i)	92

2010 Scottish Arbitration Rules (cont)
- r 70(3)(c)(ii) 92
- (4)(a) 92
- (b) 93
- (6) 93
- (7) 93
- (8) 93
  - (a) 93
  - (b) 93
  - (c) 93
- (12) 93
- rr 70–72 .... 83, 90, 151
- r 71 .... 12, 153, 340–342
  - (2) 91, 93, 251
  - (4) 91, 251
    - (a) 93
    - (b) 93
    - (c) 93
  - (6) 93
  - (7) 93
  - (8)(a) 93
    - (b) 93
  - (9) 94
  - (10)(a) 93
    - (b) 93
  - (12)(a) 93
    - (b) 93
- r 72 .... 153, 342
  - (1) 94
- Pt 9 .... 18, 52, 342–347
- r 73 .... 96, 153, 342–343
  - (1) 94, 134
  - (2)(a) 94, 134
    - (b) 94, 134
  - (3) 94, 134
- rr 73–75 .... 83, 133, 151
- rr 73–77 94
- r 74 .... 153, 343
  - (1) 94, 134
    - (a) 94
  - (2) 134
- r 75 .... 84, 95, 134, 153, 343
- r 76 .... 83, 95, 151, 343–344
  - (1) 95
    - (a) 153

2010 Scottish Arbitration Rules (*cont*)
  r 76(1)(a)–(f) 95
   (b) 153
   (c) 153
   (d) 153
   (e) 153
   (f) 153
   (2)(a) 95
    (b)(i) 95
     (ii) 95
     (iii) 95
    (c) 95
   (3)(a) 95
    (b) 95
   (4) 95
  rr 76–79 96
  r 77 .... 83, 109, 111, 151, 154, 344
   (a)–(c) 95
  r 78 .... 52, 53, 109, 344
   (1)(a)–(b) 110
   (2) 53
    (a)–(b) 110
  r 79 .... 83, 94, 96, 124, 133, 151, 154, 345
  r 80 .... 12, 52, 53, 133, 345
   (1) 133
   (2) 133
  r 81 .... 53, 109, 345
  r 82 .... 83, 94, 96, 151, 154, 345
  r 83 .... 53, 247, 345–346
  r 84 .... 53, 346–347
  Sch 2 14

Singapore

2002 International Arbitration Act (Cap 143A, rev ed)
  s 22 34
  s 23 34
2007 Singapore International Arbitration Centre (SIAC) Rules
  Art 34 36

Spain

2003 Arbitration Act (Law 60/2003)
  Art 24 34

Sweden

| 1999 | Arbitration Act | 34 |
| | Art 182(1) | 72 |

Switzerland

1911	Code of Procedure of the Canton of Vaud
	Art 516	161
1987	Private International Law Act	34, 187
	Chap 12	130
	Art 176	82
	(1)	159
	(2)	159
	Art 178(3)	43
	Art 186	130
	Art 187(1)	187
	(2)	221
	Art 190	275
	(2)	266, 274
	Art 192	266, 276
	(1)	274, 275
2004	Swiss Rules of International Arbitration	36
	Art 15(5)	36
	Art 27	36
	Art 43	36
	Art 44	36
	(2)	36

United Kingdom

1906	Marine Insurance Act (6 Edw 7 c 41)	182
1950	Arbitration Act (14 Geo 6 c 27)	14, 116
	Pt II	2
	s 12(6)	166
	s 13(3)	132
	s 27	56, 57
1966	Arbitration (International Investment Disputes) Act (c 41)	2
1975	Arbitration Act (c 3)	2, 14, 255
1990	Contracts (Applicable Law) Act (c 36)	178
1996	Unfair Arbitration Agreements (Specified Amount) Order (SI 1996/3211)	12
1999	Unfair Terms in Consumer Contracts Regulations (SI 1999/2083)	12–13, 41

United States of America

| 1890 | Sherman Anti-Trust Act (15 USC) | 143 |
| 1925 | Federal Arbitration Act | 54 |

1933	Securities Act	54
	Art 12(2)	54
1938	Federal Rules of Civil Procedure	
	r 60(b)	121
1952	Uniform Code of Commerce (UCC)	
	s 1–105(1)	174
1971	Restatement (Second) Conflict of Laws	178
	s 187	174, 178
	(2)(b)	178
	s 188	178
	s 218	184
2000	Federal Arbitration Act (9 USC)	30, 120
	§ 1	121
	§§ 1–16	30
	§ 9	280
	§§ 9–11	276, 280
	§ 10	276, 277, 279, 280
	(a)(2)	118, 123
	§ 11	276, 277, 280
	American Arbitration Association International Arbitration Rules (ICDR Rules)	35, 71, 72, 149, 172
	Art 5	72
	Art 6	72
	Art 8	124
	Art 13	72
	Art 18	72
	Art 28	72, 221
	(1)	172, 183
2009	American Arbitration Association Commercial Arbitration Rules	122
	r 18	121
	r 19	123

Venezuela

1998	Law on Commercial Arbitration	
	Art 42	34

International provisions

1923	Geneva Protocol on Arbitration Clauses	2
	para 1	40
1927	Geneva Convention on the Execution of Foreign Arbitral Awards	2
	Art 1	40

1945	Statute of the International Court of Justice	
	Art 38	189
	Art 59	189
1957	EC Treaty	
	Art 81 (ex Art 85)	63
	(ex Art 85(1))	63
1958	New York Convention on the Recognition and Enforcement of Foreign Arbitral Awards	2, 13, 15, 16, 17, 76, 162, 163, 245, 255, 257, 262, 266, 276
	Art I	13, 260, 262
	Art II	263
	(1)	40, 41
	(2)	41
	Art III	256, 263
	Art IV	13, 256
	Art V	13, 76, 262, 269, 271
	(1)(a)	40, 76, 257
	(b)	176, 258
	(c)	258
	(d)	76, 170, 176, 258
	(e)	76, 81, 259, 260, 262, 263, 265, 266, 267, 270
	(2)	77
	(a)	60, 76, 77
	(b)	76, 77, 79
	Art VII	260, 264, 266, 267, 268, 269, 270, 271, 272
	Art XI	256
1961	European Convention on International Commercial Arbitration	
	Art VII	183
	(1)	211, 212
	(2)	220
1965	Convention on the Settlement of Investment Disputes between States and Nationals of Other States (ICSID Convention or Washington Convention)	2, 201
	Art 42	183
	(3)	220
1975	ICC Arbitration Rules	163
1976	Arbitration Rules of the United Nations Commission on International Trade Law (UNCITRAL Arbitration Rules)	16, 29, 35, 37, 69, 70, 71, 112, 149, 172, 233, 275, 290
	Art 1(2)	261
	Art 4	229
	Art 5	71
	Art 12	112

1976	Arbitration Rules of the United Nations Commission on International Trade Law (UNCITRAL Arbitration Rules) (*cont*)	
	Art 15	226
	Art 16	71, 228
	(1)	228
	(2)	228
	(3)	228, 233
	(4)	228
	Art 17	71
	Art 25(6)	226
	Art 27	230
	(1)	230
	(2)	230
	(3)	230
	(4)	230
	Art 33	183
	(1)	71, 172, 212
	(2)	221
	(3)	212
1980	Rome Convention on the Law Applicable to Contractual Obligations	179, 183
	Art 1(2)(d)	178, 183
	Art 3	173, 177, 178, 179, 183
	(1)	179
	(3)	177, 179
	Art 4	173, 179
	(1)	183
	Art 5(2)	179
	Art 6(1)	179
	Art 7	176, 177
	(1)	177
	(2)	177, 179
	Art 16	176, 177, 179
	United Nations Convention on Contracts for the International Sale of Goods (Vienna Convention)	183, 202
1983	Iran–US Claims Tribunal Rules	
	Art 33(1)	212
	(2)	221
1985	UNCITRAL Model Law on International Commercial Arbitration (as amended 2006)	2, 3, 7, 14, 15, 16, 28, 30, 32, 42, 69, 70, 71, 113, 127, 130, 149, 230, 235, 243, 253
	Art 1	11
	(3)	2
	(a)	2

1985	UNCITRAL Model Law on International Commercial Arbitration (as amended 2006) (Art 1) (*cont*)	
	Art 1(3)(b)	2
	(c)	2
	Art 6	253
	Art 7(1)	40
	(2)–(6)	42
	(5)	59
	(6)	59
	Art 9	168
	Art 10(1)	71
	Art 11(2)	71
	(2)–(5)	253
	Art 12	111, 124
	(1)	112
	(2)	113
	Art 13	124
	Art 16	43, 130
	(1)	130
	Art 17	235
	(1)	235
	(2)	236
	Art 17A	236
	Art 17B	236
	Art 17E	236
	Art 18	109
	Art 19(1)	71, 226
	(2)	226
	Art 20	228
	(1)	71, 228
	(2)	228
	Art 21	71
	Art 22(1)	71
	Art 24	71
	Art 25(1)	234
	(c)	234
	Art 26(1)	230
	(2)	230
	Art 28(2)	212
	(4)	212
	Art 36(1)(b)(i)	60
1992	Permanent Court of Arbitration Rules of Arbitration and Conciliation for Settlement of International Disputes between Two Parties of Which Only One is a State	220
	Art 30	220

1998 Rules of Conciliation and Arbitration of the International Chamber of Commerce (ICC Rules).............. 35, 36, 55, 70, 71, 72, 149, 159, 163, 172, 175, 213, 261, 286
    Art 1 286
    Art 2.7 118
    Art 4(6) 66
    Art 6 36
        (4) 43
    Art 7(2) 113
    Art 8 71
        (5) 168
    Art 11 .... 124, 163
    Art 13(4) 213
    Art 14 71
    Art 16 166
    Art 15.1 159
    Art 17 212
        (1) 72, 172, 183, 212
        (2) 212
        (3) 221
    Art 19(3) 221
    Art 20(7) 36
    Art 28(6) 275
    Art 30(1) 286
        (2) 286
        (3) 287
        (4) 287
    Art 31(1) 287
        (2) 287
        (3) 287
    Appendix 1 36
London Court of International Arbitration (LCIA) Rules 70, 72, 149, 172, 289, 290
    Art 7 72
    Art 10 124
    Art 13(1)(a) 72
    Art 14 72
    Art 15 72
    Art 16 72
    Art 17 72
    Art 21 72
    Art 22 72
        22.3 172
    Art 23(1) 43
    Art 24.1 291

1998	London Court of International Arbitration (LCIA) Rules (*cont*)	
	Art 25	72
	Art 26	72
	Art 28.1	289
	Art 28.2	290
	Art 28.4	290
	Art 30	36, 72
	Principles of European Contract Law	202
2002	World Intellectual Property Organization (WIPO) Arbitration Rules	37
	Arts 24–29	124
	Art 73	37
	Art 74	37
	Art 75	37
2004	IBA Guidelines on Conflicts of Interest in International Commercial Arbitration	110, 111
	UNIDROIT Principles of International Commercial Law	202
2007	ICC Uniform Customs and Practice for Documentary Credits (UCP 600)	202
2010	IBA Rules on the taking of Evidence in International Arbitration	226, 227, 231
	Art 2	227
	2.1	227
	Art 3	227
	3.1	227
	3.3	227
	3.4–3.8	227
	3.5	227
	3.5–3.8	231
	3.6	227
	3.10	227
	Art 6	231
	6.1	231
	6.2	231
	6.3	231
	6.4	231–232
	6.5	232
	6.6	232
	6.7	232
	6.8	232
	Art 7	227
	Art 9	228
	9.1	228
	9.2	227, 231
	International Chamber of Commerce (ICC) INCOTERMS	202

CHAPTER 1

LEGAL DEVELOPMENT IN SCOTLAND

GENERAL

Before the enactment of the Arbitration (Scotland) Act 2010, arbitration laws in Scotland were criticised for being scattered among various elements of common law, cases and statutes dating as far back as 1695. With the aim of putting Scotland on the map of international arbitration and persuading international businessmen to choose Scotland as the place of their arbitration in order to generate revenue, the Scottish Government promulgated the Arbitration (Scotland) Act 2010 which is designed to offer a "one-stop shop" providing a single track of arbitration law corresponding with the modern trends in arbitration, covering both domestic and international arbitration.

PRE-ARBITRATION (SCOTLAND) ACT 2010

A combination of common law and piecemeal statutory provisions

Before the enactment of the Arbitration (Scotland) Act 2010, an arbitration held within Scotland or subject to the Scottish arbitration laws was subject to a dual track of arbitration law. Leaving aside international commercial arbitration, the law of arbitration in Scotland was based almost entirely on the common law, with piecemeal statutory provisions dealing with specific points. These statutory provisions included:

- the 25th Act of the Articles of Regulation 1695, which lays down grounds on which the validity of awards may be challenged;
- the Arbitration (Scotland) Act 1894, which regulates the naming of arbitrators and the court's power to appoint arbitrators;
- the Administration of Justice (Scotland) Act 1972, which stipulates the stated case procedure;
- the Arbitration Act 1996, ss 89–91 and Schs 3 and 4.

For international commercial arbitration, the laws that had governed international commercial arbitration in Scotland were as follows:

- Pt II of the Arbitration Act 1950, which gives effect to the 1927 Geneva Convention on the Execution of Foreign Arbitral Awards and the 1923 Protocol on Arbitration Clauses;
- the Arbitration (International Investment Disputes) Act 1966, which gives effect to the 1965 Washington Convention on the Settlement of Investment Disputes between States and the Nationals of Other States;
- the Arbitration Act 1975, which gives effect to the 1958 New York Convention on the Recognition and Enforcement of Foreign Arbitral Awards (the "New York Convention"); and
- the Law Reform (Miscellaneous Provisions) (Scotland) Act 1990, which applies the UNCITRAL Model Law on International Commercial Arbitration 1985 (the "UNCITRAL Model Law") to international commercial arbitrations in Scotland.

Through s 66 of and Sch 7 to the Law Reform (Miscellaneous Provisions) (Scotland) Act 1990, the UNCITRAL Model Law governed any arbitration categorised as international. Accordingly, Art 1(3) of the UNCITRAL Model Law stipulates that an arbitration is international, even if the disputes are between two Scottish parties, if:

"a. the parties to an arbitration agreement have, at the time of the conclusion of that agreement, their places of business in different States; or
b. one of the following places is situated outside the State in which the parties have their places of business:
  (i) the place of arbitration if determined in, or pursuant to, the arbitration agreement;
  (ii) any place where a substantial part of the obligations of the commercial relationship is to be performed or the place with which the subject-matter of the dispute is most closely connected; or
c. the parties have expressly agreed that the subject-matter of the arbitration agreement relates to more than one country."

THE SCOTTISH ARBITRATION CODE 1999 [1]

As mentioned at the beginning of this book, Scottish arbitration law was frequently criticised as being "riddled with anomalies and uncertainties"[2] and "found in a myriad of different places – from obscure statutes to inaccessible case law or, more often than not, not expressed at all".[3]

---

[1] Excerpts from Lord Dervaird, J Campbell, S Walker and H Dundas, "Arbitration in Scotland – a new era dawns", 2006 SLT 125 at p 133.
[2] *Ibid* at p 125.
[3] S P Walker, "The Renaissance of Scottish International Arbitration", Conference paper for Edinburgh Centre for Commercial law Conference, 29 November 2000, at p 3.

These legal drawbacks on the arbitration laws in Scotland have deterred businessmen from choosing Scotland as the place of arbitration for resolving their disputes.

To remedy this situation, the Scottish Council for International Arbitration (SCIA) and the Chartered Institute of Arbitrators (Scottish Branch) (CIArb(SB)) produced the Scottish Arbitration Code in 1999. It was stated:

> "This Code sought to set out a clear general framework for arbitration and the rules under which arbitrations in Scotland might be conducted. Although it has been widely welcomed and has been recommended by major institutions for use in arbitration, the major weakness of this Code is that it is no more than a voluntary code, requiring all parties to agree to its adoption. In addition, it cannot deal adequately with many matters which can be effectively managed only by statute. It is fair to say that the code was regarded by its framers as a stopgap pending the introduction of legislation."
>
> "A committee drawn from SIAC and CIArb(SB) has continued work on an Arbitration Bill, relying heavily on the work of the previous committee, and also having regard to legislative changes in many other – countries, in particular, experience in England with the Arbitration Act 1996. It has consulted widely on its proposals. The intended result is a new Bill which seeks to put virtually the whole of arbitration law in Scotland into a single statute. The aim is that in future anyone in Scotland, or anyone seeking to do business in Scotland, will be able to find, in one place, the principles governing the law of arbitration in Scotland, in language which can be readily understood. In certain respects, such as the powers of arbitral tribunals to award interest and damages, the Bill will produce much-needed reforms, when enacted. In other respects it provides in statutory terms what was at the time part of the common law, remote from users and not easily available without research."

THE ARBITRATION (SCOTLAND) BILLS 2002 AND 2009

With the aims of re-launching arbitration as the dispute resolution process of choice in Scottish commercial life, putting Scots law at the forefront of modern arbitration laws and bringing almost all Scots arbitration law, both domestic and international, into a single and user-friendly form, the Arbitration (Scotland) Bill first appeared in 2002. The 2002 Bill adopted the practice of the UNCITRAL Model Law and shares many similarities with the (English) Arbitration Act 1996.[4] However, the Bill was shelved until the Scottish National Party showed its support for the new arbitration law later in 2008, in order to create a supportive business environment by providing a coherent statutory framework which would bring international businessmen to arbitrate in Scotland. It stated:

---

[4] Lord Dervaird *et al*, n 1 above, at p 125.

"The Arbitration Bill will modernise arbitration law in Scotland – something which has been under consideration for at least 20 years. By ensuring that Scotland has codified arbitration rules in statute, the arbitration procedure will become more accessible and user friendly – benefiting individuals and businesses in Scotland who wish to settle disputes outwith the court system."[5]

This statement is echoed by Jim Mathers MSP, the Minister for Enterprise of the Scottish Parliament, who stated:

"Arbitration is also flexible, so that the process can be adapted to suit the dispute. The location, timing and other arrangements can be planned to suit the parties' needs. They are not therefore tied to rigid court procedures and timetables.

...

Members might be interested to know that there is considerable interest in the bill among academics and students of arbitration. That bodes well for both the use of arbitration in Scotland in future and the necessary supply of well-qualified arbitrators and arbitration specialists.

...

Let us hope ... the use of arbitration at home increases markedly as a result of the reforms and modernisation that the bill has introduced. We hope that, as a result, more international arbitration work will be attracted to Scotland and we will see a renaissance of Scottish arbitration."[6]

THE ARBITRATION (SCOTLAND) ACT 2010

Objectives

According to its Policy Memorandum, "[i]t is hoped that the Bill – once enacted – will encourage the use of arbitration domestically and will attract international arbitration business to Scotland".[7] Four objectives are set out in the Arbitration (Scotland) Act 2010. They are:

- clarify and consolidate Scottish arbitration law, filling in gaps where these exist;
- provide a statutory framework for arbitrations which will operate in the absence of agreement to the contrary;
- ensure fairness and impartiality in the process; and
- minimise expense and ensure that the process is efficient.[8]

---

[5] A Salmond, First Minister, "Moving Scotland Forward: Programme for Scotland", legislative statement, Scottish Parliament, 3 September, 2008. (Accessed at http://www.snp.org/node/14215 (3 June 2010).)
[6] Scottish Parliament, Official Report, 18 November 2009, cols 21269–21270, http://www.scottish.parliament.uk/business/officialReports/meetingsParliament/or-09/sor1118-02.htm.
[7] Policy Memorandum, 29 January 2009, at para 28.
[8] Ibid, at para 26.

Clarify and consolidate Scottish arbitration law, filling in gaps where these exist

To achieve the objective of providing a clear system and "one-stop shop" for arbitration law, the Act replaces most of the piecemeal statutory provisions and codifies the vast majority of the general Scots law of arbitration into a single statute to provide international businessmen and their legal counsel with easy access to the principles and rules governing the law of arbitration in Scotland in language which can be readily understood.[9]

Provide a statutory framework for arbitrations which will operate in the absence of agreement to the contrary

As Gavin Brown MSP pointed out in the Parliament session:

> "The codification of arbitration is a useful exercise, as it helps to present a more modern and dynamic offering of Scottish arbitration law. There is also a good economic case for the bill. It will increase slightly the number of domestic consumer and commercial arbitrations, and there is potential for a greater number of international arbitrations to come to Scotland. ... [W]e hope that the number of international arbitrations will increase, without putting bold figures on that hope."[10]

A very interesting aspect of the Arbitration (Scotland) Act 2010 is the combination of 37 sections governing the main principles applied in arbitration and a set of 84 rules termed "Scottish Arbitration Rules" regulating arbitration procedures. The 37 sections lay down the founding principles to be followed by the courts and arbitrators: the rule of separability; the rules related to arbitration agreement; the status of the Scottish Arbitration Rules; the rule of suspension of court proceedings involving a valid arbitration agreement; the rules on recognition or enforcement of arbitral awards; statutory arbitration; and other supplementary provisions. The incorporation of the Scottish Arbitration Rules into Sch 1 is designed to provide flexibility in amending the rules in order to keep up with international trends without the need to go through the Scottish Parliament.

Ensure fairness and impartiality in the process

The Bill therefore places a duty on the arbitrator(s) to conduct an arbitration in a fair and impartial way without unnecessary delay and without incurring unnecessary expense. Similar duties are placed on the parties

---

[9] Policy Memorandum, 29 January 2009, at para 27.
[10] Scottish Parliament, Official Report, 18 November 2009, cols 212729–21273, http://www.scottish.parliament.uk/business/officialReports/meetingsParliament/or-09/sor1118-02.htm.

to the dispute and the Bill seeks to limit the opportunities for seeking to delay the process by making unnecessary or spurious applications to a court. Arbitrators and parties are therefore required to drive the arbitral process forward without unnecessary delay.[11]

Minimise expense and ensure that the process is efficient

To ensure that arbitration in Scotland would be a cost- and time-efficient method of alternative dispute resolution, the draftsmen set out to restrict the parties' ability to submit their disputes or ancillary disputes arising during the arbitration proceedings to the court. Various ways to provide for greater efficiency of arbitration in Scotland are identified. They are:

- an up-to-date, modern arbitration law which reflects the best of modern arbitral practice will increase the attraction of using arbitration as a method of dispute resolution for parties to disputes in preference to going to court, with all of the cost, stress and possible delay that that entails;
- if use of arbitration increases in the resolution of commercial and consumer disputes, this will reduce the pressure of business on the courts;
- the arbitral appointments referee procedure for appointing the arbitrator(s) where no procedure is agreed by the parties, or where that procedure fails, rather than parties routinely having to go to court;
- an arbitrator may decide to rule on a dispute on the basis of documents only rather than holding expensive hearings;
- the provision of a set of rules on a default basis (though some are mandatory) means that even if the parties have agreed nothing beyond a bare agreement to use arbitration as their method of dispute resolution, then those rules guide the arbitrator and the parties through the process. The arbitration can begin immediately, with no protracted exchange of submissions as to which rules are to be followed;
- the rules are not too prescriptive: the arbitrator is obliged to adopt procedures which are appropriate to the circumstances of the case, bearing in mind his duty to conduct the arbitration without unnecessary delay. It is hoped that arbitrators will take a more dynamic, proactive role in procedural matters;
- a rule which permits arbitrators to rule on their own jurisdiction (i.e. to decide what they have been engaged to arbitrate on). In the past this may have required a decision by a court which would involve more time and expense and could be used as a delaying tactic by a reluctant party.
- in the past, clerks (usually solicitors) were often employed by non-lawyer arbitrators in Scotland to organise the arbitration, keep track of papers and advise on the law. Sometimes clerks were paid a higher hourly rate than the arbitrator. The use of clerks has declined in recent years and it is hoped

---

[11] Policy Memorandum, 29 January 2009, at para 2.

that the rules in the Bill will reduce the need to employ clerks yet further (though provision is still made to cover the possibility);
- strictly limited availability of recourse to the courts.[12]

To summarise, the Act is promulgated to clarify, consolidate and extend the Scottish arbitration law, and to provide a statutory framework for arbitration. It is intended to ensure fairness and impartiality in the arbitration process. For businesses, it will minimise expense and ensure that the process is efficient and fair. The Act repeals the UNCITRAL Model Law and replaces the dual arbitration regimes that used to be applied in Scotland with a single codified set of rules, which in principle will apply to domestic, cross-border and international arbitrations.

---

[12] Policy Memorandum, 29 January 2009, at para 37.

CHAPTER 2

FEATURES OF THE ARBITRATION (SCOTLAND) ACT 2010

FOUNDING PRINCIPLES: s 1

The Policy Memorandum on the Arbitration (Scotland) Act 2010 clearly recognises the main features of arbitration as "[a]rbitration is ... a private means of dispute resolution",[1] as well as:

> "[t]he essence of arbitration is that it is a procedure whereby parties agree to submit a dispute between them to a third party, who often has special expertise or knowledge, and who will act as a private tribunal to produce a final and binding determination of the dispute. By agreeing to go to arbitration, the parties voluntarily deny themselves recourse to the courts or to another method of alternative dispute resolution".[2]

This approach is clearly adopted in s 1 of the 2010 Act which provides that the founding principles of the Act are:

> "(a) that the object of arbitration is to resolve disputes fairly, impartially and without unnecessary delay or expense,
> (b) that parties should be free to agree how to resolve disputes subject only to such safeguards as are necessary in the public interest,
> (c) that the court should not intervene in an arbitration except as provided by this Act.
> Anyone construing this Act must have regard to the founding principles when doing so."

Section 1 is a mirror provision of s 1 of the (English) Arbitration Act 1996. The draftsmen expected that the Scottish courts and arbitrators will refer to these three general principles when they are called on to intervene or to interpret the legislation. They also pointed out that, by setting similar principles in Scotland, the Scottish courts may be able

---

[1] Policy Memorandum, 29 January 2009, at para 4.
[2] *Ibid*, para 2.

to make use of the case law that has been built up under the 1996 Act.[3] During the enactment process, the draftsmen were asked to decide whether the three principles should be ranked in order of priority or importance. Not surprisingly, they decided not to take such an approach and stated: "Given the level of generality at which the principles apply, however, it is not considered that a hierarchy of principles would assist the courts."[4]

Among these three founding principles, s 1(a) sets out that the objective of arbitration is to ensure that fairness and impartiality are to be applied during the arbitration proceedings. Both parties and arbitrators are also charged with general duties to carry out the resolution properly, without unnecessary delay or incurring unnecessary expense.

The internationally followed principle of party autonomy is also laid down in s 1(b) of the Act. Similar to the practice in most jurisdictions, this freedom offered to the parties is subject to the so-called "public interest safeguards" the notions of public policy and mandatory rules which will be discussed in detail in Chapter 5.

The final founding principle of "limited court intervention" is provided in s 1(c) of the Act. This requires the courts to refrain from exercising intervention in the arbitration proceedings except in the circumstances expressly stipulated in the Act. It was made clear in the Explanatory Notes that the Scottish courts should intervene only where necessary to "support" the arbitration process, such as on the appointment of arbitrator, ordering the attendance of witnesses or in the recognition or enforcement of awards.[5]

SCOPE OF APPLICATION: ss 2–3

Types of arbitration

Section 2 of the Arbitration (Scotland) Act 2010 provides definitions of various terms used in the Act and the Scottish Arbitration Rules. Those related to the scope of application are the definitions of "arbitration" and "dispute". According to s 2(1) of the Act, "arbitration" includes domestic arbitration,[6] international arbitration,[7] and arbitration between parties residing or carrying on business anywhere in the United Kingdom.[8] This is an effort to modernise the Scottish arbitration laws by providing a single track of the arbitration law offering easy and "one-stop shop" access for international businessmen and their legal counsel.

---

[3] Policy Memorandum, 29 January 2009, at para 62.
[4] *Ibid*, para 63.
[5] Revised Explanatory Notes 2009, para 20.
[6] Arbitration (Sc) Act 2010, s 2(1)(a).
[7] *Ibid*, s 2(1)(c).
[8] *Ibid*, s 2(1)(b).

Types of dispute

Instead of following Art 1 of the UNCITRAL Model Law, which provides a long list of possible commercial transactions falling within its scope of application, the draftsmen of the Arbitration (Scotland) Act 2010 made it clear that it was not their intention to prescribe the types of dispute which are allowed to be submitted to arbitration under the Act. This is because the issue of arbitrability (whether disputes are arbitrable) is substantially linked to the notion of public policy, which evolves constantly; consequently, it would be difficult, if not impossible, to provide a list of unarbitrable disputes which would cover the needs of current and future society. It was also highlighted that the best approach taken by the Act is to provide an inclusive definition[9] and ensure that arbitration laws "remain in line with general contract law on this issue".[10] This attitude can be seen clearly in the definition of "dispute" in s 2(1), which provides that "'dispute' includes (a) any refusal to accept a claim, and (b) any other difference (whether contractual or not)".

SEAT OF ARBITRATION: s 3

The seat of arbitration is generally defined as the country or the place in which the arbitration is based. The determination of the seat of arbitration has a strong influence over the arbitration process, as the arbitration laws of the seat will ultimately govern the arbitration held within its territory. This is the approach adopted in Scotland. The draftsmen opined that provisions must be made for the determination of the seat of arbitration in order to avoid disputes developing over the law applicable to the procedures to be adopted and, moreover, to ensure that arbitration can be carried out effectively.[11] Section 3 provides that an arbitration will be regarded as being seated in Scotland if Scotland is designated as the juridical seat of the arbitration by the parties, or by any other party to whom the parties give power to so designate, or where the parties fail to designate or so authorise a third party, by the tribunal, or, in the absence of any such designation, the court determines that Scotland is to be the juridical seat of the arbitration. Once the juridical seat of arbitration is deemed to be in Scotland, the arbitration is subject to the Arbitration (Scotland) Act 2010 and the mandatory rules listed in the Scottish Arbitration Rules will apply. Nevertheless, it is worth noting that the choice of Scotland as the juridical seat of arbitration does not affect the choice and the application of the substantive law to be used to decide the dispute.[12] In other words,

---

[9] Revised Explanatory Notes 2009, para 21.
[10] Policy Memorandum, 29 January 2009, para 64.
[11] *Ibid*, para 67.
[12] Arbitration (Sc) Act 2010, s 3(2).

the Arbitration (Scotland) Act 2010 will apply to an arbitration which is seated in Scotland, however, the parties can choose a foreign substantive law to determine the rights and obligations of the parties.

STATUTORY ARBITRATION: ss 16–17

According to s 16 of the Arbitration (Scotland) Act 2010, a statutory arbitration is an arbitration pursuant to an enactment which provides for a dispute to be submitted to arbitration. The purpose of s 16 is to allow the interactions between the Act and other Acts or statutory instruments which provide particular arbitration procedures for particular statutory purposes. The Act allows the parties to those arbitrations to apply the relevant provisions contained in the Act and the Scottish Arbitration Rules if other Acts fail to stipulate the procedures to be followed. This can be seen in s 16 which reads: "References in the Scottish Arbitration Rules (or in any other provision of this Act) to an arbitration agreement are, in the case of a statutory arbitration, references to the enactment which provides for a dispute to be resolved by arbitration." However, in the case of inconsistency between the Act and the provisions in other legislation, the other legislation will prevail.[13] It is also stipulated that every statutory arbitration is to be seated in Scotland. The purpose of this provision is to "prevent parties to a statutory arbitration from agreeing to seat the arbitration outwith Scotland".[14] However, it is also pointed out that this provision is subject to conflicts of law rules in order to accommodate the interaction with other jurisdictions of the UK.[15]

It is worth noting that not all provisions in the Act will apply to statutory arbitration. Among them, s 16(5), r 43 (extension of time limits), r 71 (power to declare provisions of arbitration void) and r 80 (death of party) do not apply to statutory arbitration. On the issue of consolidation of arbitration proceedings, unless the arbitrations or hearings are to be conducted under the same legislation, parties to a statutory arbitration may not agree to consolidate the arbitration with another arbitration,[16] hold concurrent hearings,[17] or authorise the tribunal to order such consolation or the holding of concurrent hearings.[18]

Regarding consumer arbitrations, it should be borne in mind that ss 89–91 of the (English) Arbitration Act 1996, the Unfair Arbitration Agreements (Specified Amount) Order 1996[19] and the Unfair Terms in

---

[13] Arbitration (Sc) Act 2010, s 16(3).
[14] Ibid, s 16(4).
[15] Revised Explanatory Notes 2009, para 62.
[16] Arbitration (Sc) Act 2010, s 16(6)(a).
[17] Ibid, s 16(6)(b).
[18] Ibid, s 16(6)(c).
[19] SI 1996/3211.

Consumer Contracts Regulations 1999[20] apply to consumer arbitrations in Scotland in order to protect individuals who inadvertently agree to unfair low-value consumer arbitration clauses.[21]

NEW YORK CONVENTION AWARDS: ss 18–22

As the United Kingdom is one of the signatory countries of the New York Convention, it is necessary to enact domestic provisions to implement the Convention. This is achieved by the enactment of ss 18–22 of the Arbitration (Scotland) Act 2010. Following the territorial principle of Art I of the New York Convention, similar to s 100 of the (English) Arbitration Act 1996, s 18 of the 2010 Act sets out to define the term "convention award". Accordingly, a "convention award" is one made in pursuance of a written arbitration agreement in the territory of a signatory state, other than the United Kingdom, which is a party to the New York Convention.[22] If an award falls into the category of the New York Convention awards, the parties can rely on the award as a defence or set-off in any legal proceedings in the Scottish courts.

The binding force of an award is provided in s 19(1) of the Arbitration (Scotland) Act 2010. It stipulates that New York Convention awards are recognised as binding on the parties between whom they are made.[23] Furthermore, such an award is enforceable in the same manner as a judgment or order of the court to the same effect, as s 19(2) provides: "The court may order that a Convention award may be enforced as if it were an extract registered decree bearing a warrant for execution granted by the court."

The grounds listed in Art V of the New York Convention are stipulated in s 20 of the Arbitration (Scotland) Act 2010.[24] Detailed discussion on the grounds and relevant development are contained in Chapter 12.

The relevant provisions require evidence to be produced when the winning party seeks recognition or enforcement of a New York Convention award under Art IV of the Convention: this is implemented in s 21(1) of the Arbitration (Scotland) Act 2010.[25] According to s 21(1), the winning party to an award seeking recognition or enforcement of a Convention award must produce the duly authenticated original award and the original arbitration agreement (or a duly certified copy of it). If the original award or arbitration agreement is not submitted then a duly certified copy of the relevant document must be submitted to the Scottish courts. In the event that the document is in foreign language, then a

---

[20] SI 1999/2083.
[21] Revised Explanatory Notes 2009, para 16.
[22] Arbitration (Sc) Act 2010, s 18(1).
[23] Similar provision can be seen in s 101 of the (English) Arbitration Act 1996.
[24] Similar provision can be seen in s 103 of the (English) Arbitration Act 1996.
[25] Similar provision can be seen in s 102 of the (English) Arbitration Act 1996.

translation which is certified by an official or sworn translator or by a diplomatic or consular agent must be submitted.[26]

REPEAL: ss 26 and 29

To achieve the aim of modernising the Scottish arbitration law to provide a single-track and "one-stop shop" Act, s 29 of and Sch 2 to the Arbitration (Scotland) Act 2010 repeals various relevant arbitration laws, namely: the Arbitration (Scotland) Act 1894; the Arbitration Act 1950; the Arbitration Act 1975; s 3 of the Administration of Justice (Scotland) Act 1972; and ss 17 and 66 of and Sch 7 to the Law Reform (Miscellaneous Provisions) (Scotland) Act 1990.

Among them the most controversial issue is the repeal of s 66 of and Sch 7 to the Law Reform (Miscellaneous Provisions) (Scotland) Act 1990 which was enacted to adopt in Scotland the UNCITRAL Model Law on International Commercial Arbitration. The decision to repeal the UNCITRAL Model Law is based on two grounds: the failure to attract international arbitration to Scotland under the UNCITRAL Model Law regime and the policy towards removal of the dual arbitration regimes.[27] Regarding the lack of success in attracting international arbitration, though it was said that the adoption of the UNCITRAL Model Law "may yet be one of the most important developments which have ever occurred in the Scottish law of arbitration",[28] only 10–15 reported international arbitration cases have taken place in Scotland between 1990 and 2009.[29] Even if international arbitrations chose Scotland as the place of arbitration, the general feedback on the Scottish arbitration laws is the difficult access because of its piecemeal legislation. Taking these grounds into consideration, the draftsmen decided to reconsider the impact the dual arbitration regimes had on the lack of development of commercial arbitration in Scotland. After consultation with the stakeholders, changes were prompted by the opinions that the UNCITRAL Model Law "does not provide a comprehensive arbitration regime. It is thus much better to look to the example of states such as England which used the Model Law as the basis for the creation of a comprehensive, modern arbitration statute",[30] as well as "[i]f Scotland is going to attract international arbitrations … being able to boast an effective, comprehensive, modern arbitration statute is going

---

[26] Arbitration (Sc) Act 2010, s 21(2).
[27] Policy Memorandum, 29 January 2009, para 47.
[28] F Davidson, *Arbitration* (2000), p 5.
[29] H R Dundas, "The Arbitration (Scotland) Act 2010: Converting vision into reality" (2010) 76 *Arbitration* 1 at 5. The figure of 10–15 is debateable as more unreported arbitration cases are said to have been held in Scotland
[30] Policy Memorandum, 29 January 2009, para 50.

to be more of an incentive than being one of a large number of states across the globe which has adopted the Model Law".[31] Consequently, the draftsmen decided to remove the dual arbitration regimes, and the separate treatment in Scotland of international commercial arbitrations under the UNCITRAL Model law is replaced by a single code informed by the UNCITRAL Model Law principles.[32]

While this change raised some eyebrows,[33] eight reasons were highlighted for such a change. The Policy Memorandum states:

- "The Model Law is incomplete and contains many crucial gaps (for example, no powers are given to the arbitrator to award damages, expenses or interest). It does not therefore provide a comprehensive arbitration regime and has to be supplemented by domestic law. The Bill, which (like the UK Arbitration Act 1996) is based on Model Law principles, will, however, provide a comprehensive framework for arbitration in Scotland.
- The Model Law has not attracted any significant amount of international arbitration business for Scotland since 1990.
- Non-Model Law venues such as London, Paris, Stockholm, Geneva/Zurich and New York are thriving.
- Model Law jurisdictions such as Germany, Australia, New Zealand, Norway and Denmark are not successful and therefore the Model Law alone cannot be considered to be a panacea for attracting international arbitration business.
- There are Model Law jurisdictions which are successful, such as Singapore, Hong Kong and Vienna, but we believe that these are successful for other reasons, not simply because they have the Model Law. Hong Kong benefits from business from the People's Republic of China, where Hong Kong awards can be enforced under the New York Convention of 1958. Vienna is the venue of choice for central and eastern Europe, including Russia. Vienna is also seen as neutral (also the case with Geneva/Zurich): as noted, it has been suggested Scotland might also be seen as a neutral venue by, for example, a foreign party in dispute with an English company.
- Even if the Model Law is repealed, it will still be possible for parties to adopt the Model Law for their arbitration if they so wish (apart from the procedural rules which will be mandatory under Scots law).
- If the Model Law is not repealed, this will perpetuate the position where there are two arbitration laws in Scotland, one for domestic arbitration and one for international commercial arbitrations. It may lead to discrimination claims in EC law, in relation to other Member States – analogous case law in the Court of Appeal in England and Wales suggests at least some

---

[31] Policy Memorandum, 29 January 2009, para 50.
[32] *Ibid*, para 47.
[33] Concerned about the potential barrier that might be caused by the repeal, the Scottish Council for International Arbitration (SCIA) and the Law Society of Scotland have argued that the Model Law should be retained. The Chartered Institute of Arbitrators and the judges in the Commercial Court of the Court of Session advocated repeal.

elements of a discriminatory regime may breach EC law, depending on any justification advanced for discriminating between the regimes.
- The model of the 1996 Act may be more familiar to other parties in the UK who may consider using Scotland as the seat of their arbitration."[34]

Although the UNCITRAL Model Law was repealed, three specific measures are introduced in order fully to reflect its status and address concerns raised by the stakeholders who opposed to the change. The draftsmen first pointed out that the international principles adopted in the UNCITRAL Model Law are included in the Act because the Act has drawn from the UNCITRAL Model Law, the (English) Arbitration Act 1996 and the Arbitration Bill 2002. As a result, the Act is broadly consistent with the UNCITRAL Model Law.[35] Secondly, s 9(4)(a)(ii) of the Act expressly recognises that the UNCITRAL Model Law, UNCITRAL Arbitration Rules and other institution rules can be opted into by the parties' agreement and replace the default rules contained in the Scottish Arbitration Rules. Thirdly, to keep up to date with international arbitral practice and reflect fully the amendment made to the UNCITRAL Model Law, the UNCITRAL Arbitration Rules and the New York Convention, after consulting with the relevant stakeholders,[36] Ministers are given the power to order modification of the Scottish Arbitration Rules, any other provisions of this Act, or any enactment which provides for disputes to be resolved by arbitration in the manner as they consider appropriate.[37]

STRUCTURE OF THE ARBITRATION (SCOTLAND) ACT 2010

The Act contains 37 sections outlining the general principles applied in the Scottish arbitration in the main part of the Act and 84 rules in Sch 1 providing detailed arbitration procedure rules to be followed. The general principles of arbitration stipulated in the 37 sections contained in the main part of the Act include:

- s 1 outlines the founding principles to be followed by the courts and arbitral tribunals in dealing with arbitration cases, such as party autonomy, limited court interventions and fair, impartial and efficient method of dispute resolution;
- s 3 places strong emphasis on the link between arbitration and the place of arbitration;
- s 4 recognises the validity of an arbitration agreement;
- s 5 provides the statutory legislation for the principle of separability of arbitration agreement to ensure that the arbitration agreement does not

---

[34] Policy Memorandum, 29 January 2009, para 48.
[35] Revised Explanatory Notes 2009, para 8.
[36] Arbitration (Sc) Act 2010, s 26(2).
[37] *Ibid*, s 26(1).

become void following the voidness or invalidity of the main contract between the parties;
- ss 7–9 establish the detailed arbitration rules to be followed by an arbitration seated in Scotland. Among these three provisions, s 7 expressly provides that the Scottish Arbitration Rules set out in Sch 1 to the Act are to govern every arbitration seated in Scotland. The Scottish Arbitration Rules contains both mandatory rules and default rules. Thirty-six mandatory rules are listed in s 8. The parties' rights to disapply or modify the default rules in the Scottish Arbitration Rules are provided in s 9;
- s 10 requires the courts to suspend legal proceedings concerning any disputes covered by a valid arbitration agreement between the parties;
- s 11 stipulates the final binding force of an arbitral award;
- ss 12–15 outline the supporting role played by the Scottish courts in the matters of recognition and enforcement of arbitral awards, no review of the substance of awards, attendance in arbitral proceedings and anonymity in legal proceedings;
- ss 16–17 provide a statutory framework for statutory arbitration;
- ss 18–22 stipulate the procedures to be followed in seeking the recognition and enforcement of New York Convention awards;
- s 24 provides the legal definition of arbitral appointments referee who plays an important role in the appointment of arbitrators;
- s 25 lists the circumstances allowing a judge to act as an arbitrator or an umpire;
- s 26 offers Ministers the powers to modify the Scottish Arbitration Rules, the provisions of the Act and any enactment which provides for disputes to be resolve by arbitration;
- s 29 contains repeals of the previous piecemeal arbitration laws.

An interesting aspect of the Act's design is that the main part of the Act provides only the general principles to be followed by both courts and arbitral tribunals. The detailed procedural rules regulating arbitration seated in Scotland are provided in the Scottish Arbitration Rules, containing both mandatory and default rules. Among them:

- Pt 1 provides the procedures to be followed in matters such as commencement of arbitration and the constitution of a tribunal;
- Pt 2 confirms the principle of competence/competence which offers the tribunal the power to rule on its own jurisdiction and the procedures to be followed if the parties raise objections in the matter;
- Pt 3 imposes the duties of independence, impartiality and fairness on the tribunal as well as the duty of efficiency and confidentiality on both the tribunal and the parties;
- Pt 4 provides default rules to be applied in the arbitral proceedings;
- Pt 5 stipulates the power of the court in relation to arbitral proceedings, especially the referral of point of law, time limit and attendance of witnesses;

- Pt 6 sets out the formalities required in the making or correction of an award;
- Pt 7 provides the rules in relation to arbitration expenses;
- Pt 8 provides the procedures to be followed challenging awards;
- Pt 9 contains various miscellaneous rules in relation to arbitration proceedings, such as those on immunity of arbitrators and arbitration institutions; independence of arbitrators; the death of an arbitrator or a party; and communications.

CHAPTER 3

CONFIDENTIALITY

SCOTTISH ARBITRATION RULES, r 26

One of the advantages of arbitration is confidentiality, which allows the parties to keep their disputes away from the gaze of the outside world. The duty of confidentiality is particularly acute in the information in relation to arbitration. Confidential information is defined as any information related to the dispute, the arbitral proceedings, the award or any civil proceedings relating to the arbitration in respect of which an order has been granted under s 15 of the Arbitration (Scotland) Act 2010 which is not, and has never been, in the public domain.[1]

As a default rule, r 26 imposes on the arbitrator(s) and the parties a legal duty not to disclose any confidential information relating to the arbitration. A breach of the confidentiality duty is actionable by the party or parties to whom the duty was owed. In the case of a breach leading to substantial injustice, the arbitrator(s) involved will be subject to removal under r 12. A breach of confidentiality allows the party or parties to seek remedy in the forms of interdict or damages.[2]

However, the duty of confidentiality is subject to a few exceptions listed in r 26(1). In accordance with this provision, first, confidential information can be revealed with the parties' expressed or implied authorisation.[3] Second, confidential information can be disclosed if such disclosure is required by the tribunal or is necessary for the conduct of the arbitration proceedings.[4] Third, disclosure of confidential information can be made if it is required by an enactment or rule of law[5] for the discharge of the public functions performed by the discloser's[6] or

---

[1] Scottish Arbitration Rules, r 26(4).
[2] Revised Explanatory Notes 2009, para 142.
[3] Scottish Arbitration Rules, r 26(1)(a).
[4] Ibid, r 26(1)(b).
[5] Ibid, r 26(1)(c)(i).
[6] Ibid, r 26(1)(c)(ii).

a public body or office.[7] Citing the decision made by Lawrence Collins LJ in *Emmott v Michael Wilson & Partners Ltd*,[8] the draftsmen believe that the duty of confidentiality can be breached legally for personal lawful interests for "the establishment or protection of an arbitrating party's rights vis-à-vis a third party in order to found a cause of action against that third party or to defend a claim, or counterclaim, brought by that third party".[9] Finally, confidential information can be disclosed on the grounds of public interest,[10] the interests of public justice[11] as well as a defence of absolute privilege in a defamation action.[12]

The duty of confidentiality is imposed only upon the parties and the arbitrators. This duty does not apply to third parties, such as expert witnesses and advisers. While disclosure of confidential information by third parties is not a breach of the duty of confidentiality, the draftsmen expect that "the parties or tribunal will enter into private arrangements with third parties under which an agreement or undertaking to keep matters confidential is obtained".[13] This expectation is evidently demonstrated in r 26(2) which imposes an express duty on the tribunal and the parties to take reasonable steps to prevent unauthorised disclosure of confidential information by any third parties. Arbitrators also have a duty to inform the arbitrating parties of any proceedings that they are to be confidential.[14]

INTERNATIONAL PRACTICE

It is commonly agreed that arbitrations are private and the materials used or arising from arbitration shall remain confidential. This is because the character of confidentiality is one of the reasons that the parties have chosen arbitration as the means of resolving disputes. Taking England as an example, unlike in Scotland, where a duty of confidentiality was imposed under r 26, no statutory duty was provided in the Arbitration Act 1996. However, the duty of confidentiality is implied into the terms of arbitration agreements in the common law.

England

Dolling-Baker v Merrett[15]

Dolling-Baker v Merrett was one of the cases examining the issue of confidentiality. In this case, the plaintiff claimed against the defendants'

---

[7] Scottish Arbitration Rules, r 26(1)(c)(iii).
[8] [2008] EWCA Civ 184.
[9] *Ibid*; see also revised Explanatory Notes 2009, para 101.
[10] Scottish Arbitration Rules, r 26(1)(e).
[11] *Ibid*, r 26(1)(f).
[12] *Ibid*, r 26(1)(g).
[13] Revised Explanatory Notes 2009, para 147.
[14] Scottish Arbitration Rules, r 26(3).
[15] [1990] 1 WLR 1205.

money due under a reinsurance policy for which the first defendant was one of the insurers and the second defendant as the placing broker. On the plaintiff's application, the court ordered the first defendant to make a list of all documents relating to an arbitration where the two defendants were involved and such a list would lead automatically to inspection of the documents. Claiming confidentiality, the first defendant applied for an injunction restraining the second defendants from disclosing the documents. The application was refused. Subsequently, the first defendant appealed to the Court of Appeal. Relying on the decision in *Science Research Council v Nasse*[16] that the ultimate test is whether discovery was necessary for disposing fairly of the proceedings, Parker LJ allowed the appeal and refused the disclosure of the documents. He was convinced that the methods of interrogatories or notice to admit could sufficiently dispose of the issues in the action fairly. Then he implied the duty of confidentiality into the arbitration agreement by stating that:

> "As between parties to an arbitration, although the proceedings are consensual and may thus be regarded as wholly voluntary, their very nature is such that there must, in my judgment, be some implied obligation on both parties not to disclose or use for any other purpose any documents prepared for and used in the arbitration, or disclosed or produced in the course of the arbitration, or transcripts or notes of the evidence in the arbitration or the award, and indeed not to disclose in any other way what evidence had been given by any witness in the arbitration, save with the consent of the other party, or pursuant to an order or leave of the court. That qualification is necessary, just as it is in the case of the implied obligation of secrecy between banker and customer."[17]

Hassneh Insurance v Mew[18]

The same issue was raised in *Hassneh Insurance Co of Israel v Steuart J Mew*,[19] where an interim award and the materials leading to the award were at issue. The defendant wished to disclose both materials, while the plaintiffs agreed to disclose the award but objected to the disclosure of the whole of the reasons or the disclosure of any other documents such as pleadings or witness statements or transcripts. Mr Justice Colman pointed out that disclosure would not be ordered unless (1) the documents were relevant;[20] and (2) disclosure was necessary for disposing fairly of the cause or matter or for saving costs. He further explained the "necessary for disposing fairly of the cause or matter" test by citing the definition given by Lord Wilberforce in the *Nasse* case:

---

[16] [1980] AC 1028.
[17] *Dolling-Baker v Merrett* [1990] 1 WLR 1205 at 1213.
[18] [1993] 2 Lloyd's Rep. 243.
[19] *Ibid.*
[20] *Compagnie Financière du Pacifique v Peruvian Guano Co* (1882) 11 QBD 55.

"What does 'necessary' in this context mean? It, of course, includes the case where the party applying for an order for discovery and inspection of certain documents could not possibly succeed in the proceedings unless he obtained the order; but it is not confined to such cases. Suppose, for example, a man had a very slim chance of success without inspection of documents but a very strong chance of success with inspection, surely the proceedings could not be regarded as being fairly disposed of, were he to be denied inspection."[21]

Following the "reasonable necessity" rule, he decided that the raw materials leading to the award was subject to a duty of confidence, and stated:

"They are materials which were used to give rise to the award which defined the rights and obligations of the parties to the arbitration. Accordingly, that qualification to the duty of confidentiality based on the reasonable necessity for the protection of an arbitrating party's rights against a third party cannot be expected to apply to them. It is the final determination of rights expressed in the award which is pertinent as against third parties, not the raw materials for that determination."[22]

Ali Shipping Corp v Shipyard Trogir[23]

From the implied obligation in *Dolling-Baker* to reasonable necessity as discussed in *Hassneh Insurance*, the issue of confidentiality was made even clearer in *Ali Shipping Corp v Shipyard Trogir* where the Court of Appeal was asked to determine whether the materials from the first arbitration could be disclosed in other closely connected arbitrations between the same parties. The court upheld that the confidentiality duty applied where the parties to whom disclosure was contemplated were in the same beneficial ownership and management as the complaining party.[24] Furthermore, Lord Justice Potter highlighted five exceptions to the duty of confidentiality. They were: (1) consent of the parties; (2) order of the court; (3) leave of the court; (4) disclosure when, and to the extent to which, it is reasonably necessary for the protection of the legitimate interests of an arbitrating party, such as the establishment or protection of an arbitrating party's legal right, *vis-à-vis* a third party, in order to found a cause of action against that third party or to defend a claim (or counterclaim) brought by the third party; and (5) where the public interest requires disclosure.[25]

---

[21] [1980] AC 1028 at 1071.
[22] [1993] 2 Lloyd's Rep 243 at 250.
[23] [1998] 2 All ER 136; [1998] 1 Lloyd's Rep 643.
[24] [1998] 1 Lloyd's Rep 643 at 652–653.
[25] *Ibid* at 651.

Emmott v Michael Wilson & Partners Ltd[26]

Emmott (respondent) left Michael Wilson (appellant) after 5 years' service as a director and senior lawyer, to set up a competing business venture. The appellant claimed that that was part of a scheme by Emmott to divert the appellant's business, in breach of contract and in breach of trust. In terms of the arbitration clause contained in the employment agreement, the appellant commenced arbitration in London and court proceedings against Emmott and others in England, New South Wales, the British Virgin Islands, Jersey and Colorado. Emmott sought a court order permitting disclosure of documents from the London arbitration to prevent the appellant from providing the foreign courts with a misleading or inaccurate picture from those presented in the arbitration. The judge ordered disclosure on the basis that it was in the interests of justice so that the foreign courts would not be misled or potentially misled where the cases that were being advanced in the various proceedings were essentially raising the same or similar allegations. The appellant appealed against this decision on the ground of lack of jurisdiction and on the argument that the disclosure order constituted an unwarranted intrusion into the confidentiality of arbitrations which could only be overridden in the public interest in the context of a dispute between a party to the arbitration and a stranger.

Following *Ali Shipping Corp v Shipyard Trogir*,[27] the Court of Appeal dismissed the appeal and ruled that the trial judge had been right to order disclosure in the interests of justice since otherwise there was a possibility that the foreign court would be misled. Lord Justice Lawrence Collins explained:

> "[T]he confidentiality was subject to two possible exceptions in the present case. The first was where disclosure was reasonably necessary for the protection of the legitimate interests of an arbitrating party, including reasonably necessary for the establishment or protection of an arbitrating party's legal rights *vis-à-vis* a third party in order to found a cause of action against a third party, or to defend a claim or counterclaim brought by the third party ... The second relevant exception was the exception of public interest."[28]

And

> "[The] case law over the last 20 years has established that there is an obligation, implied by law and arising out of the nature of arbitration, ... the content of the obligation may depend on the context in which it arises

---

[26] [2008] EWCA Civ 184.
[27] [1999] 1 WLR 314.
[28] *Ibid* at paras 27–28.

and on the nature of the information or documents at issue. The limits of that obligation are still in the process of development on a case-by-case basis. On the authorities as they now stand, the principal cases in which disclosure will be permissible are these: the first is where there is consent, express or implied; second, where there is an order, or leave of the court (but that does not mean that the court has a general discretion to lift the obligation of confidentiality); third, where it is reasonably necessary for the protection of the legitimate interests of an arbitrating party; fourth, where the interests of justice require disclosure, and also (perhaps) where the public interest requires disclosure."[29]

Finally, he concluded:

"I have no doubt that the judge had jurisdiction to make the order. In essence the application was the mirror imagine of what often happens in cases of this kind, namely an application for an injunction by a party seeking to restrain disclosure. ... [B]ecause the confidentiality rule has developed as an implied term of the arbitration agreement, any dispute as to its scope would fall within the scope of the arbitration agreement. ... These matters lead me to the conclusion that the interests of justice required disclosure. The interests of justice are not confined to the interests of justice in England. The international dimension of the present case demands a broader view."[30]

Singapore

Myanmar Yaung Chi Oo Co Ltd v Win Win Nu

A similar line, but with a twist, was adopted in Singapore. In this case the Singapore High Court accepted the arguments of implied confidentiality obligations in relation to arbitral documents but decided that leave of the court would not be required if the disclosure were necessary.[31] In this case, the disclosure was decided to be unnecessary because the tribunal decided that it did not have jurisdiction over the disputes. As the court held:

"[B]etween the time of her decision and the appeal coming on before me the position changed. The arbitration tribunal has held that it had no jurisdiction to hear the matter. By that decision, the arbitration proceedings were brought to an end. Any assertion of oppression or duplicity in the actions must be confined to the two court actions in Myanmar. If the arbitration proceedings were part of the oppression they have ceased to be that, and the disclosure is no longer necessary."[32]

---

[29] [1999] 1 WLR 314 at para 107.
[30] Ibid at paras 109–111.
[31] *Myanmar Yaung Chi Oo Co Ltd v Win Win Nu* [2003] SGHC 124.
[32] Ibid at para 24.

Bermuda

Associated Electric & Gas Insurance Services Ltd v European Reinsurance Company of Zurich[33]

In this case submitted to the Privy Council, the approach taken in *Dolling-Baker* and *Ali Shipping* was questioned. By an agreement dated 31 March 1980, Associated Electric & Gas Insurance Services Ltd of Hamilton, Bermuda, a company incorporated under the laws of Bermuda ("Aegis"), entered into an automatic facultative reinsurance agreement with European Reinsurance Company of Zurich ("European Re"). The agreement included an arbitration clause containing an expressed confidentiality clause. Two separate disputes regarding the obligation of European Re to indemnify Aegis were referred to arbitration under this clause. The first award was issued on 19 January 2000. The second dispute was referred to a differently constituted panel. In the second arbitration, European Re wanted to rely upon the award in the first arbitration. Aegis contended that it was not at liberty to do so and Aegis submitted that European Re could not show any part of the first award in the second arbitration as it would breach the duty of confidentiality arising from the first arbitration. Aegis obtained an *ex parte* injunction to restrain European Re. European Re applied to discharge the injunction. Mr Justice Dennis Mitchell refused the application and continued the injunction. European Re appealed. The Court of Appeal allowed the appeal and discharged the injunction. Aegis subsequently appealed. While the Privy Council ruled that the confidentiality clause did not prevent the disclosure of the award if the disclosure was essential to enforce a party's legal rights conferred by the award, their Lordships also took the opportunity to review the approach applied in both *Dolling-Baker* and *Ali Shipping*. The opinion stated:

> "Their Lordships have reservations about the desirability or merit of adopting this approach. It runs the risk of failing to distinguish between different types of confidentiality which attach to different types of document or to documents which have been obtained in different ways and elides privacy and confidentiality. Commercial arbitrations are essentially private proceedings and unlike litigation in public courts do not place anything in the public domain. This may mean that the implied restrictions on the use of material obtained in arbitration proceedings may have a greater impact than those applying in litigation. But when it comes to the award, the same logic cannot be applied. An award may have to be referred to for accounting purposes or for the purpose of legal proceedings (as Aegis referred to it for the purposes of the present injunction proceedings) or for the purposes of enforcing the rights which the award confers (as European Re seek to do in the Rowe arbitration). Generalisations and the formulation of detailed implied terms are not appropriate. But in any event, the *Ali Shipping* case

---

[33] [2003] UKPC 11.

provides no assistance for either argument of Aegis. It is interesting to note that the reasoning in the above referred to passages of the judgment of Potter LJ seem to have been strongly influenced by the description of the duty of confidentiality a banker owes to his customer given in *Tournier v National Provincial and Union Bank of England* [1924] 1 KB 461 both in the implied term and the exceptions to the duty. The *Tournier* case was not cited or expressly referred to in *Ali Shipping*. But the use of parallel reasoning in both cases shows that the court in *Ali Shipping* was not considering what rights an award gave rise to nor any question of what is involved in the enforcement of an award."[34]

Australia

Esso Australia Resources Ltd v *The Honourable Sidney James Plowman*[35]

Similar doubts were also expressed in this Australian case concerning two agreements for the sale of natural gas from the Bass Strait fields to two public utilities, the Gas and Fuel Corporation of Victoria ("GFC") and the State Electricity Commission of Victoria ("SEC"). Disputes arose and were referred to two different arbitrations (GFC and SEC arbitrations). The claims for confidentiality arose out of the appellants' response to requests by the Minister, GFC and SEC for details of the calculations on which the appellants' claims for price increases were based. The appellants declined to give details unless GFC and SEC entered into agreements that they would not disclose the information to anyone else, including the Minister, the Executive Government and the people of Victoria. The appellants asserted that the details sought were commercially sensitive. On the other hand, the Executive Government wanted the details and claimed that, if GFC and SEC obtained them, GFC and SEC were under a statutory duty to pass them on. The issue here was whether an arbitrating party was under an obligation of confidence in relation to documents and information disclosed in, and for the purposes of, a private arbitration. Chief Justice Mason held that confidentiality should be secured by a private agreement which would impose contractual obligations to keep confidential information from the public domain.[36] He further pointed out that confidentiality was not an essential attribute of a private arbitration and the duty of confidentiality could not be implied into an arbitration agreement as *Dolling-Baker* suggested. In relation to "essential attribute", he stated:

> "Despite the view taken in *Dolling-Baker* and subsequently by Colman J in *Hassneh Insurance*, I do not consider that, in Australia, having regard to the various matters to which I have referred, we are justified in concluding that

---

[34] [2003] UKPC 11 at para 20.
[35] *Esso Australia Resources Ltd v Plowman* [1995] HCA 19; (1995) 128 ALR 391; (1995) 69 ALJR 404; (1995) 183 CLR 10 (7 April 1995)
[36] [1995] HCA 19 at para 33.

confidentiality is an essential attribute of a private arbitration imposing an obligation on each party not to disclose the proceedings or documents and information provided in and for the purposes of the arbitration."[37]

He also denied that the duty of confidentiality should be implied into an arbitration agreement. He stated that:

"The implication of a term as a matter of law is made by reference to 'the inherent nature of a contract and of the relationship thereby established', to use the words of Lord Wilberforce. As Deane J pointed out in *Hawkins v Clayton*, his Lordship focused on the nature of the contract and formulated the relevant test in terms of what is necessary or required in the circumstances on the footing that 'such obligation should be read into the contract as the nature of the contract itself implicitly requires, no more, no less.' It follows that the case for an implied term must be rejected for the very reasons I have given for rejecting the view that confidentiality is an essential characteristic of a private arbitration. In the context of such an arbitration, once it is accepted that confidentiality is not such a characteristic, there can be no basis for implication as a matter of necessity."[38]

USA

United States v Panhandle Eastern Corp[39]

In the United States, similar rejection can be seen in this case where the US Government requested that Panhandle disclose documents used in an ICC arbitration held in Switzerland. Panhandle resisted the disclosure and cited the Internal Rules of the ICC Court requiring all participants to observe confidentiality. A Federal District Court held that the confidentiality duty applied only to the members of the ICC court, rather than the arbitrating parties or the members of a tribunal. Furthermore, confidentiality did not apply to what happened during the arbitration proceedings unless arbitration procedural law expressly prohibited the disclosure of arbitration materials or a confidentiality agreement was reached between the parties, or between the parties and any third parties, taking part in the arbitration proceedings.

Sweden

Bulgarian Foreign Trade Bank v AI Trade Finance Inc[40]

The Swedish Supreme Court also denied the implied legal duty of confidentiality in arbitration in this case where it[41] held that there

---

[37] *Esso Australia Resources Ltd v Plowman* [1995] HCA 19 at para 35.
[38] Ibid at paras 36–37.
[39] *United States v Panhandle Eastern Corp* (D Del 1988) 118 FRE 346.
[40] 27 October 2000, Supreme Court of Sweden. See the discussion in O Oakley-White, "Confidentiality Revisited: Is international arbitration losing one of its major benefits" (2003) 6(1) Int ALR 29 at 32.
[41] 27 October 2000, Supreme Court of Sweden.

is no implied legal duty of confidentiality in arbitration unless an agreement securing the confidentiality of arbitration materials indicated so.

ILA confidentiality in international commercial arbitration report 2010

The issue of confidentiality also prompted the International Law Association to produce a report in its 74th conference at The Hague, in August 2010. This report conducted a survey of the sources of confidentiality and covered the UNCITRAL Model Law, 30 national jurisdictions and 22 international commercial arbitration institutions. The report groups the survey jurisdictions into three categories, namely: those imposing no statutory confidentiality obligation; limited statutory confidentiality obligations; and those imposing a strict statutory confidentiality obligation.

The first group of jurisdictions which impose no statutory confidentiality on either the parties or arbitrators includes Australia, England, the United States, Belgium, China, Canada, Costa Rica, Denmark, Finland, Iran, Ireland, Italy, Japan, Norway, Sweden and Switzerland. For institutions, the Iran Chamber of Commerce makes no provision on this issue. In the case of England, the report specifically points out that the confidentiality duties are implied through case law in England, even though the (English) Arbitration Act 1996 imposes no statutory obligation on this issue. In the case of Denmark, no confidentiality duties are imposed upon the arbitrating parties, but the duties are imposed on the arbitrators through their general duties. Apart from the national jurisdictions, the report also stated that confidentiality is not addressed in the UNCITRAL Model Law because of the complexity of this issue.

Austria, Ecuador, France, Hong Kong, Singapore and Venezuela belong to the group of jurisdictions imposing a limited obligation of confidentiality. In the case of Austria, there are statutory provisions governing the issue of confidentiality. However, a statutory confidentiality obligation is imposed on the court proceedings when they deal with arbitration matters.[42] The report indicates that while no statutory obligation can be found in the French Code of Civil Procedure Book IV, 1981, the French case law seems to suggest a limited duty of confidentiality exists. In the report, *Aïta v Ojjeh*[43] was used as an example illustrating that duty of confidentiality may be imposed by the French court; furthermore, in breach of such duty, the award can be set aside and damages can be ordered. However, in the same breath, the report emphasises that the case is an exceptional case of manifest abuse since

---

[42] Austrian Code of Civil Procedure, Art 616(2).
[43] Rev arb (1986) 583.

the French courts obviously lacked jurisdiction in that case on the ground that the award had been rendered in London. The report stated that the principle of confidentiality in arbitration was upheld in more general terms, citing the private and confidential nature of arbitration by the Tribunal de Commerce of Paris.[44] However, the report pointed that an obligation of confidentiality cannot be taken for granted.[45] In the case *NAFIMCO v Foster Wheeler*, the Paris Court of Appeal rejected a claim for damages for violation of confidentiality, the court pointed out that the claimant had failed to "explain the existence and reasons of a principle of confidentiality in French international arbitration law, irrespective of the nature of the arbitration and, in the event, the waiver of the principle by the parties in the light of the applicable rules".[46]

In the case of Hong Kong, it is highlighted that s 2 of the Hong Kong Arbitration Ordinance 1997 allows the court to hold court proceedings relation to arbitration in private but no other specific provision can be found on the issue of confidentiality. However, the report suggests that, following the English common law, the duty of confidentiality seems to be implied into the arbitration agreement through case law.

Regarding the arbitration institutions, the UNCITRAL Arbitration Rules, the International Arbitration Court of the Chamber of Commerce and Industry of the Russian Federation (ICAC), the International Chamber of Commerce (ICC), the Japan Commercial Arbitration Association (JCAA) and the Stockholm Chamber of Commerce (SCC) require limited duties of confidentiality.

The last group examined the practice of the jurisdictions which impose a strict duty of confidentiality. It includes the Dominican Republic, Dubai, the Netherlands, New Zealand, Nicaragua, Peru, Scotland and Spain. With the exceptions of the Iran Chamber of Commerce, ICAC, ICC, JCAA and SCC, all other surveyed institutions have provisions imposing the duties of confidentiality.

The following table, presented in the Annex to the report, provides an easy overview of this issue.[47]

---

[44] Tribunal de Commerce de Paris, 22 February 1999, *Bleustein et autres v Société True North et société FCB International*, Rev arb 2003, p 373. Discussed in F De Ly, L di Brozolo and M Friedman and the members of the committee, *Confidentiality in international commercial arbitration*, reported by International Commercial Arbitration Committee, International Law Association, The Hague Conference (August 2010) at p 9. Available at http://www.ila-hq.org/en/committees/index.cfm/cid/19

[45] Paris Court of Appeal, 22 January 2004, *NAFIMCO v Foster Wheeler*, Rev arb (2004), p 647.

[46] *Ibid*, reported in F De Ly, L di Brozolo and M Friedman and the members of the committee, *Confidentiality in international commercial arbitration*, reported by International Commercial Arbitration Committee, International Law Association, The Hague Conference (August 2010) at p 10.

[47] *Ibid*, Annex I.

COUNTRY	CONFIDENTIALITY OBLIGATION	
	Statute	*Case law*
UNCITRAL Model Law	No – UNCITRAL Model Law 1985 makes no provision for confidentiality	
England	No – (English) Arbitration Act 1996 makes no provision for confidentiality	Yes – implied duty of confidentiality, with certain exceptions
United States	No – United States Federal Arbitration Act, 9 USC, §§ 1–16 (2000) makes no provision for confidentiality	No – no inherent duty of confidentiality unless the parties contract for it
Australia	The Australian International Arbitration Act as amended in 2010 includes in s 23 detailed provisions on confidentiality, subject to exceptions, which the parties can choose to apply to their arbitration on an "opt-in" basis	No – *Esso Australia* case provides that there is no implied duty of confidentiality
Austria	Limited – explicit statutory provision, in Art 616(2) of the Austrian Code of Civil Procedure following the introduction of the Austrian Arbitration Act 2006, relating to the confidentiality of court proceedings dealing with arbitration matters. There are no other statutory provisions regarding confidentiality	
Belgium	No – provision of the Belgian Judicial Code makes no provision for confidentiality	Yes – case law seems to suggest that such a duty exists
Canada	No – no express statutory provision for confidentiality. Each province has adopted the UNCITRAL Model Law, which does not contain a provision for confidentiality	Yes – recent recognition that confidentiality is a well-accepted benefit and a critical advantage of commercial arbitration and parties have reasonable legitimate expectations of confidentiality in arbitration
China	No – China's Arbitration Act 1994 does not regulate the matter. Article 40 simply prohibits arbitration from being held in public unless the	

CONFIDENTIALITY

COUNTRY	CONFIDENTIALITY OBLIGATION	
	Statute	*Case law*
China (*cont.*)	parties otherwise agree. However, it seems to be accepted under Chinese law, that arbitration commissions, arbitrators, parties and participants in arbitral proceedings have a duty of confidentiality	
Costa Rica	No – Costa Rica's Arbitration Law (No 7727 of 1997) does not regulate the matter. It simply states at Art 60 that arbitral awards shall be made public, except when the parties have agreed to the contrary. The arbitral tribunal's deliberations are secret, by virtue of Art 15 of the Code of Ethics of the International Center for Conciliation and Arbitration of Costa Rica	
Denmark	No – no statutory provision in relation to confidentiality in the Danish Arbitration Act 2005	No for parties/Yes for arbitrators – prevailing view is that there is no general duty of confidentiality on the parties but that the arbitrators are subject to a general duty of confidentiality. Further, it is generally agreed that arbitral hearings are private
Dominican Republic	Yes – although limited in scope – Art 22 of the Dominican Republic Commercial Arbitration Law (No 489-08 of 2008) provides for an express duty of confidentiality by the parties, arbitrators and arbitral institutions with respect to the information to which they are made privy in the course of the arbitral proceedings	
Dubai International Financial Centre	Yes – Law No 1 of 2008 provides for all information relating to the arbitration to be confidential, except by order of the DIFC court	
Ecuador	Limited – the Ecuador Law on Arbitration and Mediation (No 000. RO/145 of 1997) contains a provision at Art 34 relating to the possibility of the parties agreeing to keep the	

COUNTRY	CONFIDENTIALITY OBLIGATION	
	Statute	*Case law*
Ecuador (*cont.*)	arbitral proceedings confidentiality, but that is all	
Finland	No – no statutory provision in relation to confidentiality in the Finnish Arbitration Act 1992	Although there do not appear to be any binding cases on this point, there are certain acknowledged principles when it comes to confidentiality
France	Limited – the French Code of Civil Procedure, Book IV, 1981 at Art 1469, includes a statutory provision for the secrecy of arbitrators deliberations, but nothing else	Yes – case law seems to suggest such a duty exists, although it is limited in scope
Hong Kong	Limited – the current Hong Kong Ordinance 1997 contains in Section 2 a statutory provision relating to the ability to hold court proceedings relating to arbitration in private. Other than that there are no further provisions for a general duty of confidentiality. Clause 18 of Hong Kong's Law Reform Commission's consultation paper contains a recommendation for a provision similar to the one contained in New Zealand's 1996 legislation, prohibiting disclosure of information relating to arbitral proceedings	Yes – case law (following English common law) seems to suggest an obligation of confidentiality is implied into the arbitration agreement
Iran	No – the 1997 International Commercial Arbitration Act (based on the 1985 UNCITRAL Model Law) is completely silent on the confidentiality of arbitration	
Ireland	No – statutory provision for confidentiality under either the 1954 or the 2010 Irish Arbitration Act. Constitutional requirement for all court proceedings to be in public	No court decisions on confidentiality, although certain general assumptions in relation to confidentiality exist
Italy	No – the Italian provisions on arbitration (Arts 806ff of the Code of Civil Procedure) contain no express provision on confidentiality, although it may be argued that it is an implied term resulting from commercial usage	

CONFIDENTIALITY

COUNTRY	CONFIDENTIALITY OBLIGATION	
	Statute	*Case law*
Italy (*cont.*)	or custom. Arbitral awards filed in the context of enforcement proceedings are considered public documents available to anyone who requests a copy (Art 744 Code of Civil Procedure). The "privacy code" (Legislative Decree of 30 June 2003, Art 52, para 6) entitles parties having a "legitimate interest" to request that the arbitrators omit the names and other data through which the party could be identified in case of publication of the award	
Japan	No – there is no express provision in the Japanese Arbitration Law No 138 of 2003. Court proceedings arising from arbitration are treated as "non-contentious proceedings" closed to the public	
Netherlands	Yes in the future – a draft proposal dating from 2005 proposes to revise the Dutch arbitration law to provide for confidentiality	
New Zealand	Yes – there is an explicit and comprehensive confidentiality regime in the New Zealand Arbitration Act 1996 at Art 14, as a result of the Arbitration Amendment Act 2007	
Nicaragua	Yes – under the Nicaragua Arbitration and Mediation Law (Law 540) while there is no specific provision regulating issues of confidentiality, privacy and confidentiality are expressly stated under Art 3 to be governing principles of its Arbitration Law	
Norway	No – express provision at Chapter 1, Section 5 of the General Provisions ruling out confidentiality	
Peru	Yes – the Peruvian Legislative Decree No 1071 of 2008 contains at Art 51 an express, comprehensive and broad provision providing for a duty of confidentiality	

COUNTRY	CONFIDENTIALITY OBLIGATION	
	Statute	*Case law*
Scotland	Yes – confidentiality obligations are contained in rr 26 and 27 of Sch 1 to the Scottish Arbitration Act 2010	
Singapore	Limited – Section 22 of the Singapore International Arbitration Act (Cap 143A, 2002 rev ed) ("IAA") allows a party to apply to court for proceedings under the IAA to be heard otherwise than in open court. Section 23 IAA (applicable if a party obtained an order under Section 22) restricts the reporting of proceedings heard otherwise than in open court	Yes – case law (following English common law) recognises that an obligation of confidentiality is implied into the arbitration agreement
Spain	Yes – although limited in scope – under Art 24 of the Spanish Arbitration Act (Law 60/2003) parties, arbitrators and arbitral institutions have a duty to keep confidential information made known to them during the course of the arbitral proceedings. Further, the arbitral tribunal's deliberations are confidential	
Sweden	No – no duty of confidentiality in the Swedish Arbitration Act 1999	No – current case law states that there is no duty of confidentiality imposed on the parties
Switzerland	No – Swiss Federal Private International Law Act 1987 is silent as to the issue of confidentiality	No – there have been no known Swiss court cases confirming an implied duty of confidentiality of the parties
Venezuela	Limited – the Venezuelan Law on Commercial Arbitration 1998 imposes at Art 42 an obligation on the arbitrators to keep all matters relating to the arbitration confidential, but nothing other than that	

SUMMARY OF ARBITRATION RULES

Rules	Confidentiality obligation
UNCITRAL Arbitration Rules	Limited – these address the privacy of the hearings and the confidentiality of the award, but not confidentiality more generally
American Arbitration Association International Arbitration Rules (ICDR Rules)	No – there is no provision
Australian Centre for International Commercial Arbitration (ACICA)	Yes – Art 18 provides for the arbitration to be private and confidential
Belgian Centre for Mediation and Arbitration (CEPANI)	Yes – Appendix 2, point 9 of the CEPANI Rules provides that the arbitrator, mediator or third person shall obey the rules of strict confidentiality. Further point to provide for awards only to be published anonymously and with explicit approval of the parties. Article 17.5 provides for privacy of the hearings, save with the approval of the Tribunal and the parties
Milan Chamber of Arbitration	Yes – there are provisions at Arts 43(1) and 44(2) of the 2004 Rules
China International Economic and Trade Arbitration Commission	Yes – there are provisions at Arts 43(1) and 44(2) of the 2004 Rules
Dubai International Arbitration Centre (DIAC)	Yes – provision at Art 41(1) of the 2007 Rules
German Institution of Arbitration (DIS)	Yes – provision at Art 43(1) of the 1998 Rules
Hong Kong International Arbitration Centre (HKIAC)	Yes – extensive confidentiality regime at Art 39(1) of the 2008 Rules, which deals with the confidentiality of matters and documents in the arbitral proceedings, the deliberations of the arbitral tribunal and the confidentiality of the award
Iran Chamber of Commerce	No – the 2007 Rules, otherwise inspired by the ICC Rules, raise the issue but clearly limit it to the privacy of the proceedings (Art 43, para E)
International Arbitration Court of the Chamber of Commerce and Industry of the Russian Federation (ICAC)	Limited – Art 25 provides that arbitrators, reporters, experts appointed by the arbitral tribunal, the ICAC and its staff refrain from disclosing information about disputes which

SUMMARY OF ARBITRATION RULES

Rules	Confidentiality obligation
ICAC (cont.)	may impair the legitimate interests of the parties
International Chamber of Commerce (ICC)	Limited – the rules provide for the arbitral tribunal to take measures to protect trade secrets and confidential information (Art 20(7)); for the work of the court to be kept confidential by everyone who participates in that work in whatever capacity (Art 6, Appendix 1) and for parties not involved in the arbitration not to be admitted to hearings save with the approval of the arbitral tribunal and the parties
Japan Commercial Arbitration Association (JCAA)	Limited – provision at r 40(2) of the 2008 Rules in relation to the arbitrators, the officers and staff of the association
Kuala Lumpur Regional Centre for Arbitration (KLRCA)	Yes – provision at r 9 of the 1998 Rules
London Court of International Arbitration (LCIA)	Yes – specific duties in Art 30 of the 1998 Rules to keep the award, disclosed materials and the deliberations of the Arbitral Tribunal confidential
Netherlands Arbitration Institute (NAI)	Yes – subject to timely objection (less than 28 days) NAI is entitled to publish award in anonymous form (Art 55(2))
Singapore International Arbitration Centre (SIAC)	Yes – Art 34 of the 2007 Rules
Stockholm Chamber of Commerce (SCC)	Limited – arbitrators and the institution have to maintain the confidentiality of the award
Swiss Rules of International Arbitration (Swiss Rules)	Yes – obligation to keep the award, submitted materials and the deliberations of the arbitral tribunal confidential under Arts 43 and 44. Applies also to tribunal-appointed experts (Art 27), the secretary of the tribunal (Art 15(5)) and the Chambers. No mention of witnesses or party-appointed experts. Further, under Art 44(2) a party cannot seek to make a member of the Chambers, an arbitrator, a tribunal appointed expert or the secretary of the arbitral tribunal a witness in any legal or other proceedings arising out of the arbitration

SUMMARY OF ARBITRATION RULES	
Rules	*Confidentiality obligation*
Tehran Regional Arbitration Centre (TRAC)	Yes – both the 2005 TRAC Rules (otherwise based on the UNCITRAL Rules) and the internal regulations provide for confidentiality of the arbitral proceedings and the dispute. Article 4 of the Rules contained an express and comprehensive duty of confidentiality on the arbitrators, parties, counsel, experts, secretaries and institution. Article 4 of the regulations contains an express and comprehensive duty of confidentiality on the Director, members of the Secretariat and Arbitration Board
International Arbitral Centre of the Austrian Federal Economic Chamber (Vienna Rules)	Yes – Arts 3(6), 5(3), 7(4) and 20(4) of the 2006 Rules expressly provide that the arbitral proceedings shall take place in private, and that the arbitral institution and the arbitrators shall keep all relevant matters confidential. However, no provision for confidential with respect to the parties
World Intellectual Property Organization (WIPO)	Yes – the 2002 Rules contain very detailed provisions on confidentiality at Arts 73, 74 and 75

CHAPTER 4

ARBITRATION AGREEMENT

GENERAL

Contractualists explore the nature of arbitration from a contractual viewpoint. Although contractualists admit the fact that arbitration proceedings and arbitration agreements can be influenced by the relevant national laws, they argue that arbitration has a contractual character that originates in the parties' arbitration agreement. Accordingly, an arbitration agreement between the parties is regarded as a contract which expressly states the parties' wish to have their disputes resolved by means of international commercial arbitration. This kind of contract is voluntarily reached between the parties, allowing them to determine the time and place of arbitration, select the arbitrators to hear their case and choose the laws governing both procedural and substantive matters.

The proponents of the contractual theory believe that the settlement of the dispute in arbitration should not be influenced by the power of any states. The concept of *pacta sunt servanda*[1] should prevail and it binds the parties to perform the arbitration agreement made between them without the pressure from the state. As is illustrated by Kellor:

> "Arbitration is wholly voluntary in character. The contract of which the arbitration clause is a part is a voluntary agreement. No law requires the parties to make such a contract, nor does it give one party power to impose it on another. When such an arbitration agreement is made part of the principal contract, the parties voluntarily forgo established rights in favour of what they deem to be the greater advantages of arbitration."[2]

---

[1] The term *"pacta sunt servanda"* represents the idea that agreements should be observed.
[2] F Kellor, *Arbitration in Action*, quoted by P Stone in "A Paradox in the Theory of Commercial Arbitration" (1966) 21 Arb J 156 at 156 and J Lew, *Applicable laws in international commercial arbitration* (1978), p 55.

The importance of an arbitration agreement can be seen in various international documents. For instance, the issue of recognition and enforcement of international arbitration agreement is recognised in para 1 of the Geneva Protocol 1923, Art 1 of the Geneva Convention 1927, Arts II(1) and V(1)(a) of the New York Convention, and Art 7(1) of the UNCITRAL Model Law 1985 (amended 2006).

THE ARBITRATION (SCOTLAND) ACT 2010

Modelled on s 1 of the (English) Arbitration Act 1996, s 1 of the Arbitration (Scotland) Act 2010 sets out three founding principles which provide guidance on the Scottish approach on how arbitration is conducted as a whole. Arbitrators or judges must take the following three principles into consideration when they interpret the provision of the Act:

> "(a) that the object of arbitration is to resolve disputes fairly, impartially and without unnecessary delay or expense,
> (b) that parties should be free to agree how to resolve disputes subject only to such safeguards as are necessary in the public interest,
> (c) that the court should not intervene in an arbitration except as provided by this Act".

Within these three principles, (b) and (c) have direct impact on the parties' arbitration agreement. Establishing party autonomy, principle (b) allows the parties the freedom to decide themselves on procedures concerning how to resolve disputes. This freedom is only subject to the mandatory rules listed in the Act and public policy. Principle (c) establishes that the courts shall restrain from exercising interventions on arbitration process, especially the issues that have been agreed in the parties' agreements.

Arbitration agreements – s 4

Definition

There are two types of arbitration agreement. The first type, termed the "arbitration clause", is inserted into the main contract or contained in the relevant documents dealing with potential future disputes. The second type is called the "submission clause", which is an agreement between the parties to submit the existing disputes to arbitration. A broad definition of an arbitration agreement is defined in s 4 of the Act: "[a]n 'arbitration agreement' is an agreement to submit a present or future dispute to arbitration (including any agreement which provides for arbitration in accordance with arbitration provisions contained in a separate document)". While pointing out in its consultation paper that the arbitration agreement between the parties is fundamental to arbitration, s 4 makes clear that the agreement can either be in a past agreement between the parties or in a submission to the arbitrator when the dispute arises.[3] This also includes a statutory arbitration.

Format of arbitration agreement

There is no specific format required for a valid arbitration agreement. Although it is acknowledged that most arbitration agreements are in writing, either existing in an independent clause or forming part of a larger contract, following the Scottish practice, the Act does not exclude the oral agreement expressing parties' wishes to submit their disputes to arbitration. In other words, both written and oral agreements are recognised in Scotland in order to benefit all arbitration from the Act. As stated in the Policy Memorandum:

> "At present Scots law generally recognises both oral and written agreements to refer to arbitration. The policy of the Bill is that arbitration agreements should continue to be recognised whether they are concluded orally or in writing so that all arbitrations in Scotland benefit from the provisions in the Bill (although the general law may require some arbitration agreements to be in writing). If oral agreements were not recognised, they would continue to be subject to the present unsatisfactory common law and would not benefit from the provisions in the Bill."[4]

This is different from the approach taken by the English 1996 Act that arbitration agreement must be in writing and an oral arbitration agreement is allowed by reference to terms or recorded in writing.[5]

In the case of consumer contracts, the Unfair Terms in Consumer Contracts Regulations 1999 and ss 89–91 of the English 1996 Arbitration Act, applicable to Scotland, apply to cases where unsuspecting parties inadvertently signed up to arbitration agreement.[6]

The written requirements can be observed in various international instruments. For instance, Art II(1) of the New York Convention provided that the Contracting States shall recognise an arbitration agreement in writing. In order to ascertain the parties' intention to subject themselves to the jurisdiction of arbitration, Art II(2) explains that "[t]he term 'agreement in writing' shall include an arbitral clause in a contract or an arbitration agreement, signed by the parties or contained in an exchange of letters or telegrams". It is worth noting that signature is not regarded as essential in practice.

The definition of exchange of communication is now extended to cover faxes and e-mails. Such a widening in scope to accommodate

---

[3] Consultation on Arbitration (Scotland) Bill (2008), para 10.
[4] Policy Memorandum, 29 January 2009, paras 70–71.
[5] (English) Arbitration Act 1996, s 5.
[6] Consultation on Arbitration (Scotland) Bill (2008), para 13.

the development of new technology can be seen in Art 7(2)–(6) of the UNCITRAL Model Law 1985 and 2006, which provides:

> "(2) The arbitration agreement shall be in writing.
> (3) An arbitration agreement is in writing if its content is recorded in any form, whether or not the arbitration agreement or contract has been concluded orally, by conduct, or by other means.
> (4) The requirement that an arbitration agreement be in writing is met by an electronic communication if the information contained therein is accessible so as to be useable for subsequent reference; 'electronic communication' means any communication that the parties make by means of data messages; 'data message' means information generated, sent, received or stored by electronic, magnetic, optical or similar means, including, but not limited to, electronic data interchange (EDI), electronic mail, telegram, telex or telecopy.
> (5) Furthermore, an arbitration agreement is in writing if it is contained in an exchange of statements of claim and defence in which the existence of an agreement is alleged by one party and not denied by the other.
> (6) The reference in a contract to any document containing an arbitration clause constitutes an arbitration agreement in writing, provided that the reference is such as to make that clause part of the contract".[7]

However, the UNCITRAL Model Law 2006 adds a second option which provides a more general guideline on this issue to allow different jurisdictions to adopt a wider definition of an arbitration agreement. Option 2 of Art 7 reads: "'Arbitration agreement' is an agreement by the parties to submit to arbitration all or certain disputes which have arisen or which may arise between them in respect of a defined legal relationship, whether contractual or not." This less rigid approach is adopted in s 4 of the Arbitration (Scotland) Act 2010.

Separability of arbitration agreement (autonomy of arbitration agreement)

The parties' intention to use arbitration as a dispute resolution mechanism may be manifested in an arbitration agreement which is an independent dispute resolution contract or in an arbitration clause which forms part of the main contract between the parties. During the dispute resolution process, the validity of the main agreement may be called into question. Consequently, from the viewpoint of dispute resolution, it is important to clarify to what extent the validity of the arbitration clause can be separated from the validity of the main contract.

---

[7] UNCITRAL Model Law on International Commercial Arbitration (as adopted by the United Nations Commission on International Trade Law on 21 June 1985, and as amended by the United Nations Commission on International Trade Law on 7 July 2006).

Considering that arbitration agreements are mainly used to set out how a dispute from the main contract is to be resolved, as well as to interpret defective or ambiguous contractual terms, it is recognised that such an agreement has a different character from other clauses contained in the contract. Similar to s 7 of the (English) Arbitration Act 1996, s 5 of the Arbitration (Scotland) Act 2010 requires that an arbitration agreement which forms, or was intended to form, part of an agreement is to be treated as a distinct agreement.[8] This is called the doctrine of separability of arbitration agreement or autonomy of arbitration agreement. According to this doctrine, in a case where the main contract is void, voidable or otherwise unenforceable, the arbitration agreement still stands.[9] Furthermore, an arbitral tribunal is empowered to decide on whether a contract that contains an arbitration agreement may be arbitrated in accordance with the arbitration agreement.[10] Most jurisdictions have the similar provisions.

Scotland apart, the issue of separability is also stipulated in international instruments, institutional rules and national arbitration laws. For instance, provisions similar to s 5 of the Arbitration (Scotland) Act 2010 are provided in Art 16 of the UNCITRAL Model Law; Art 23(1) of the LCIA Rules; Art 6(4) of the ICC Rules; Art 178(3) of the Swiss Private International Law Act 1987; s 7 of the (English) Arbitration Act 1996; s 1029(2) of the German Arbitration Act 1998; Art 1697(2) of the Sixth Part of the Belgian Judicial Code 1998; and Art 1903 of the Dutch Arbitration Act 1986. They state that an arbitration clause forming or being intended to form part of another agreement shall be treated as independent from the main contract, and the non-existence, invalidity or ineffectiveness of the main contract shall not entail *ipso jure* the non-existence, invalidity or ineffectiveness of the arbitration clause.

Law governing arbitration agreement – s 6

Under the doctrine of party autonomy, parties are free to agree on the law governing the arbitration agreement. In general, an arbitration clause forming part of the main contract is usually governed by the same substantive law governing the main contract, unless the parties specified otherwise. For an independent arbitration agreement, it is subject to the law chosen by the parties. This can be the same substantive law of the main contract or a different law. However, not all arbitration agreements

---

[8] Arbitration (Sc) Act 2010, s 5(1). This provision negatives the effect of earlier case law (*Sanderson* v *Armour* 1909 SC 146 (117)). There may, however, be situations in which the agreement relates to matters which are illegal or such that they cannot be the subject of a valid arbitration agreement as it would be contrary to public policy to permit them to be arbitrated (eg *Soleimany* v *Soleimany* 1999 QB 785).
[9] Arbitration (Sc) Act 2010, s 5(2).
[10] *Ibid*, s 5(3).

or arbitration clauses contain the choice of law. If an arbitration is seated in Scotland and the parties failed to agree on, or specify, the law governing the arbitration agreement, the issues arising from an arbitration agreement are interpreted in accordance with Scots law.[11]

Suspension of legal proceedings – s 9

In practice, two approaches are adopted by the courts once a valid arbitration agreement is found between the parties. One is that a valid arbitration agreement dismisses the legal proceedings completely. The other approach is that the legal proceedings act as a standby to arbitration until the arbitration is aborted. Convinced that a total preclusion of access to the courts may discourage some parties from using arbitration, Scotland has adopted the latter approach in both the previous arbitration laws and the Arbitration (Scotland) Act 2010. This can be seen in the policy behind promulgation of the Act that places emphasis on the reviving role of the courts when arbitration fails. It was pointed out that:

> "The traditional approach of the Scottish courts is that a valid and binding arbitration agreement suspends the jurisdiction of the courts and commits the parties to arbitrate the dispute. This does not oust the jurisdiction of the court entirely, however. Should the arbitration prove abortive, the full jurisdiction of the court will revive to the effect of enabling it to hear and determine the action upon its merits. The party who is seeking to enforce the arbitration agreement should apply to the court – at the earliest opportunity after the action is raised – asking that the action should be sisted (i.e. suspended) pending the determination of the dispute by arbitration. The court must of course satisfy itself that the subject of dispute is covered by the arbitration agreement."[12]

This policy is shown in s 10 of the Act which stipulates that, on an application by a party to legal proceedings, the courts must sist the proceedings on any matter if a valid arbitration agreement[13] provides that a dispute on the matter is to be resolved by arbitration.[14] This application must be raised by a party to the arbitration agreement or a third party claiming through or under such party.[15] The applicant must give the other parties to the legal proceedings the notice of the application.[16] However, the applicant must not have taken any step in the legal proceedings to

---

[11] Arbitration (Sc) Act 2010, s 6. Similar provisions can be seen in ss 5–8 of the (English) Arbitration Act 1996.
[12] Policy Memorandum, 29 January 2009, para 89.
[13] Arbitration (Sc) Act 2010, s 10(1)(e).
[14] Ibid, s 10(1)(a). Similar provision can be seen in s 9 of the (English) Arbitration Act 1996.
[15] Arbitration (Sc) Act 2010, s 10(1)(b).
[16] Ibid, s 10(1)(c).

answer any substantive claim against the applicant[17] or have behaved in such a manner as to express their wishes to have the dispute resolved by the legal proceedings rather than by arbitration.[18]

To ensure that justice can successfully be carried out, any proceedings which the court refuses to sist will not be affected by any provision in an arbitration agreement which intends to prevent the legal proceedings.[19] However, statutory arbitration falls outside the scope of this exception to the rule of suspension of legal proceedings. The rule of suspension of legal proceedings contained in s 10 applies regardless of whether the arbitration concerned is to be seated in Scotland or in a foreign jurisdiction but subject to the Arbitration (Scotland) Act 2010.[20]

Contents of arbitration agreement

The design of the Scottish Arbitration Rules – s 7

An interesting design of the Arbitration (Scotland) Act 2010 is to set out the general principles and framework of arbitration in the Act while the Scottish Arbitration Rules, laid out in Sch 1 to the Act, constitute a single and self-standing code. It is designed to provide general laws of arbitration to govern all arbitration seated in Scotland, or seated elsewhere but subject to the Arbitration (Scotland) Act 2010. Both the main body of the Act and the Scottish Arbitration Rules form the primary legislation of Scotland. This design was welcomed by some of the consultees during the consultation stage since the Rules can be "read as a relatively self-standing 'code' which could be used as a guide by practitioners and users and also compared easily with the rules of arbitral institutions. It was pointed out that arbitrators would not have to search for the rules in the middle of the 'legalese' of the main body of the legislation".[21]

Being subject to the Arbitration (Scotland) Act 2010, the Scottish Arbitration Rules are intended to be the implied terms of every arbitration agreement unless the parties explicitly or impliedly disapply or modify the rules. This is to help the parties to proceed with arbitration without delay in the case where there is not further agreement beyond the arbitration agreement.[22]

The provisions of the Act and the Rules are expressly categorised into "mandatory rules" or "default rules". As discussed further in Chapter 5, mandatory rules are the rules which cannot be contracted out of by the parties' agreement. Rules signified as default rules can be disapplied or

---

[17] Arbitration (Sc) Act 2010, s 10(1)(d)(i).
[18] *Ibid*, s 10(1)(d)(ii).
[19] *Ibid*, s 10(2).
[20] *Ibid*, s 10(3).
[21] Policy Memorandum, 29 January 2009, para 79.
[22] Consultation on Arbitration (Sc) Bill (2008), para 16.

modified by the parties' agreement. The majority of the Scottish Arbitration Rules are default rules which give the parties freedom to modify or disapply the relevant rules in their agreements.[23] The agreements can be expressed in the form of an arbitration agreement[24] or by any other means at any time before or after the arbitration begins.[25] The default rules can also be impliedly disapplied or modified if the parties choose a law other than Scots law as the applicable law to regulate the relevant default rules[26] or if the relevant default rules are inconsistent with the arbitration agreement,[27] any arbitration rules or other arbitration documents which the parties agree are to govern the arbitration,[28] or anything done with the agreement of the parties.[29]

Default rules can be modified or disapplied by the parties' agreement

Among 84 rules in the Scottish Arbitration Rules, 48 of them are default rules (detailed as follows):

Part 1 – Commencement and constitution of tribunal etc
- r 1   Commencement of arbitration
- r 2   Appointment of tribunal
- r 5   Number of arbitrators
- r 6   Method of appointment
- r 9   Arbitrator's tenure
- r 10 Challenge to appointment of arbitrator
- r 11 Removal of arbitrator by parties
- r 17 Reconstitution of tribunal
- r 18 Arbitrators nominated in arbitration agreements

According to Pt 1 of the Rules, the parties are given a great deal of freedom to disapply or modify the rules dealing with the commencement and constitution of a tribunal. For instance, instead of following the Scottish Arbitration Rules to have the date of commencement on the date when a notice was served by one party to the other regarding the submission of the dispute to arbitration,[30] parties can agree that arbitration shall start on a specific date if the dispute had already arisen or start on the appointment of arbitrators. The parties can also reach different agreements from the

---

[23] Arbitration (Sc) Act 2010, s 9(2).
[24] *Ibid*, s 9(3)(a).
[25] *Ibid*, s 9(3)(b).
[26] *Ibid*, s 9(4)(b).
[27] *Ibid*, s 9(4)(a)(i).
[28] *Ibid*, s 9(4)(a)(ii).
[29] *Ibid*, s 9(4)(a)(iii).
[30] Scottish Arbitration Rules, r 1. Relevant provision can be seen in s 14 of the (English) Arbitration Act 1996.

default rules of the Scottish Arbitration Rules on the appointment of the tribunal, the appointing referees,[31] the number of arbitrators to be appointed to form the tribunal,[32] the methods of appointment,[33] the grounds for the termination of an arbitrator's tenure,[34] the right to challenge the appointment of arbitrators on the grounds of lack of impartiality, independence, fairness and qualification,[35] the removal of an arbitrator by the parties jointly or by any third party authorised to do so,[36] the methods of reconstitution of tribunal[37] and the ceasing of effect on the agreed appointment of an arbitrator[38] after the termination of an arbitrator's tenure.

Part 2 – Jurisdiction of tribunal
r 22   Referral of point of jurisdiction

Most provisions contained in Pt 2 of the Scottish Arbitration Rules are designed as mandatory to deter any delaying tactics from either party, the intention being to ensure the smooth and efficient operation of arbitration. The only default rule is r 22 concerning the issue of referral of point of jurisdiction. This rule offers the parties the freedom to exclude the opportunity to ask the court to determine a point of jurisdiction.

Part 3 – General duties
r 26   Confidentiality
r 27   Tribunal deliberations

In Pt 3, while both parties and arbitrators are charged with mandatory duties to avoid unnecessary delay and expenses during arbitration proceedings, rr 26 and 27 allow the parties to rule out the duty of confidentiality and to modify the method of deliberations.

Scots law on confidentiality was said to be underdeveloped and unclear on whether such a duty was implied into arbitration before the

---

[31] Scottish Arbitration Rules, r 2. Similar provision can be seen in s 16(1) of the (English) Arbitration Act 1996.
[32] Scottish Arbitration Rules, r 5. Similar provision can be seen in s 15(2)–(3) of the (English) Arbitration Act 1996.
[33] Scottish Arbitration Rules, r 6. Similar provision can be seen in s 16(3)–(4) of the (English) Arbitration Act 1996.
[34] Scottish Arbitration Rules, r 9.
[35] *Ibid*, r 10. Relevant provision can be seen in s 24(1) of the (English) Arbitration Act 1996.
[36] Scottish Arbitration Rules, r 11. Similar provision can be seen in s 23 of the (English) Arbitration Act 1996.
[37] Scottish Arbitration Rules, r 17. Similar provision can be seen in s 27 of the (English) Arbitration Act 1996.
[38] Scottish Arbitration Rules, r 18.

introduction of the Act.[39] In the consultation stage, the Bill proposed that the identity of the parties to an appeal to the court must not be disclosed on the basis that confidentiality is the second most important factor influencing the parties' choice of arbitration.[40] The result of the consultation shows that a narrow majority of the consultees preferred to leave this matter to the parties' agreement, whereas the Chartered Institute of Arbitrators was of the opinion that the confidentiality rule should be included in the Bill. Taking into consideration the different opinions and the potential impacts an unexpected duty of confidentiality may have on the parties, r 26 clarified the Scots law on this issue by introducing the duty of confidentiality into the law but providing that such duty can be contracted out by the parties' agreement if they do not wish to have their arbitration subject to the rule of confidentiality. Considering the English decision in *Emmott* v *Michael Wilson & Partners*,[41] it was also pointed out that in the absence of the parties' agreement on the rule of confidentiality before the appointment of the tribunal, the tribunal will be obliged to advise the parties that law requires the arbitration to remain confidential unless they decide otherwise.

Another issue arising from the rule of confidentiality is whether third parties are bound by it. As arbitration only binds the arbitrating parties, consequently, any breach by third parties is not actionable under r 26. However, it was suggested that such a loophole can be addressed by private agreements between third parties and the parties or the tribunal to ensure the confidentiality of arbitration.[42]

Another default rule in Pt 3 is r 27, which allows the parties to require the tribunal to share and disclose its deliberations with them.

Part 4 – Arbitral proceedings

The strength of arbitration lies in the principle of party autonomy, which allows the parties freedom to design how their arbitration shall be carried out. In order to make Scotland more appealing to international businessmen as *the* place of arbitration, party autonomy is adapted in Pt 4 of the Scottish Arbitration Rules. All the rules in Pt 4 are default rules, enabling the parties to disapply or modify them if they deem it necessary. They are as listed below:

    r 28   Procedure and evidence
    r 29   Place of arbitration

---

[39] Policy Memorandum, 29 January 2009, para 152.
[40] *Ibid*, para 150. Also see Consultation on Arbitration (Scotland) Bill (2008), para 153 and question 23.
[41] *Emmott* v *Michael Wilson & Partners Ltd* [2009] EWHC 1 (Comm). This case confirmed that the rule of confidentiality is implied into an arbitration agreement by common law.
[42] Revised Explanatory Notes, para 147.

r 30 Tribunal decisions
r 31 Tribunal directions
r 32 Power to appoint clerk, agents or employees etc
r 33 Party representatives
r 34 Experts
r 35 Powers relating to property
r 36 Oaths or affirmations
r 37 Failure to submit claim or defence timeously
r 38 Failure to attend hearing or provide evidence
r 39 Failure to comply with tribunal direction or arbitration agreement
r 40 Consolidation of proceedings

All these rules are enacted to ensure the speedy operation of arbitration in case the parties failed to agree on the detailed rules governing arbitration proceedings. Accordingly, these default rules allow the parties to determine the procedure to be followed in arbitration and the admissibility, relevance, materiality and weight of any evidence,[43] and the place where arbitration is to be held.[44] The parties also have the power to exclude or modify the majority rule applied in the tribunal's decisions,[45] the tribunal power to give parties direction where it is appropriate for the purposes of conducting the arbitration,[46] and the tribunal's power to appoint clerks, agents, employees or other persons as it thinks fit to assist the tribunal in conducting the arbitration.[47]

The parties are also given freedom to change the rules regarding representation during the arbitration proceedings.[48] The tribunal's default power in obtaining an expert opinion on any matter arising in arbitration,[49] directing a party to allow inspection, preservation of any property, documents or evidence related to the arbitration,[50] and directing a party or witness to take an oath or affirmation[51] can all be modified by the parties' agreement. The parties are allowed to reach different agreements from the default rules in Pt 4 of the Scottish Arbitration Rules

---

[43] Scottish Arbitration Rules, r 28. Similar provision can be seen in s 34 of the (English) Arbitration Act 1996.
[44] Scottish Arbitration Rules, r 29.
[45] *Ibid*, r 30.
[46] *Ibid*, r 31.
[47] *Ibid*, r 32.
[48] *Ibid*, r 33. Similar provision can be seen in s 36 of the (English) Arbitration Act 1996.
[49] Scottish Arbitration Rules, r 34. Similar provision can be seen in s 37 of the (English) Arbitration Act 1996.
[50] Scottish Arbitration Rules, r 35. Similar provision can be seen in s 38(4) of the (English) Arbitration Act 1996.
[51] Scottish Arbitration Rules, r 36.

regarding the timing to submit claims or defence[52] as well as the rules allowing the tribunal to proceed with the arbitration if a party fails to attend a hearing[53] or produce documents requested by the tribunal,[54] or fails to comply with any directions[55] made or obligations[56] imposed by the tribunal. Finally, the parties can also exclude the possibility of the consolidation of different arbitrations.[57]

Part 5 – Powers of court in relation to arbitral proceedings
r 41   Referral of point of law
r 43   Variation of time limits set by parties
r 46   Court's other powers in relation to arbitration

Apart from the power to disapply or modify the procedural rules governing the arbitration, to a certain extent the parties can also reach an agreement to rule out the power of the court in relation to arbitral proceedings. Rule 41 allows the parties to rule out the jurisdiction of the Outer House to rule on any point of Scots law arising in the arbitration. This provision is intended to eliminate the possibility of delaying tactics applied by either party. The parties can also exclude the court's powers in varying any time limit relating to the arbitration which was agreed between the parties,[58] as well as the power to appoint a person to safeguard the interests of any party lacking capacity[59], to order the sale of any property in dispute in the arbitration,[60] to make an order securing any amount in dispute in the arbitration,[61] to make an order under s 1 of the Administration of Justice (Scotland) Act 1972,[62] to grant warrant for arrestment or inhibition,[63] to grant interdict (or interim interdict),[64] or to grant any other interim or permanent order.[65]

---

[52] Scottish Arbitration Rules, r 37. Similar provision can be seen in s 41(3) of the (English) Arbitration Act 1996.
[53] Scottish Arbitration Rules, r 38(a)(i). Similar provision can be seen in s 41(4) of the (English) Arbitration Act 1996.
[54] Scottish Arbitration Rules, r 38(a)(ii).
[55] *Ibid*, r 39(1)(a). Similar provision can be seen in s 41(5)–(7) of the (English) Arbitration Act 1996.
[56] Scottish Arbitration Rules, r 39(1)(b)(i)–(iii).
[57] *Ibid*, r 40. Similar provision can be seen in s 35 of the (English) Arbitration Act 1996.
[58] Scottish Arbitration Rules, r 44.
[59] *Ibid*, r 46(1)(a). Similar provision can be seen in s 44 of the (English) Arbitration Act 1996.
[60] Scottish Arbitration Rules, r 46(1)(b).
[61] *Ibid*, r 46(1)(c).
[62] *Ibid*, r 46(1)(d).
[63] *Ibid*, r 46(1)(e).
[64] *Ibid*, r 46(1)(f).
[65] *Ibid*, r 46(1)(g).

Part 6 – Awards

r 47   Rules applicable to the substance of the dispute
r 49   Other remedies available to tribunal
r 51   Form of award
r 52   Award treated as made in Scotland
r 53   Provisional awards
r 55   Draft awards
r 57   Arbitration to end on last award or early settlement
r 58   Correcting an award

Apart from the rules governing the arbitration proceedings, the parties are empowered to exclude the application of the majority default rules on the awards. The parties can use an agreement to exclude the application of the default rule used to determine the rules or law applied to the substantive issues of the dispute,[66] or the application of trade usage in arbitration.[67] The tribunal's default powers in making declaratory awards,[68] making provisional awards,[69] correcting awards,[70] ordering specific performance, prohibiting specific performance,[71] rectifying or reducing any deed or other document can also be contracted out by the parties' agreement.[72] Party autonomy also enables the parties using agreements to agree on the matters such as the formality of an award,[73] whether an award shall bear the arbitrators' signatures,[74] whether a draft award shall be delivered to the parties before making the final award,[75] and the time when arbitration ends.[76]

Part 7 – Arbitration expenses

r 59   Arbitration expenses
r 61   Recoverable arbitration expenses
r 62   Liability for recoverable arbitration expenses
r 64   Security for expenses

---

[66] Scottish Arbitration Rules, r 47(1)(a)–(b). Similar provision can be seen in s 46(1) of the (English) Arbitration Act 1996.
[67] Scottish Arbitration Rules, r 47(3)(b).
[68] *Ibid*, r 49(a). Similar provision can be seen in s 48(5) of the (English) Arbitration Act 1996.
[69] Scottish Arbitration Rules, r 53.
[70] *Ibid*, r 58. Similar provision can be seen in s 57 of the (English) Arbitration Act 1996.
[71] Scottish Arbitration Rules, r 49(b). Similar provision can be seen in s 48(5) of the (English) Arbitration Act 1996.
[72] Scottish Arbitration Rules, r 49(c).
[73] *Ibid*, r 51. Relevant provision can be seen in s 52 of the (English) Arbitration Act 1996.
[74] Scottish Arbitration Rules, r 51(1).
[75] *Ibid*, r 55.
[76] *Ibid*, r 57. Similar provision can be seen in s 51 of the (English) Arbitration Act 1996.

r 65   Limitation of recoverable arbitration expenses
r 66   Awards on recoverable arbitration expenses

While a legal obligation is imposed upon the parties to be severally liable for the arbitrators' fees and expenses,[77] the parties are free to define the meaning of arbitration expenses.[78] The parties can also exclude or modify the application of the default rules on the meaning and determination of recoverable arbitration expenses,[79] the limitation of recoverable arbitration expenses[80] and the allocation of liability for recoverable arbitration expenses[81] as well as tribunal's power to order security for expenses.[82] The parties can also agree otherwise on the issue whether an expenses award shall form part of the main award.[83]

Part 8 – Challenging awards

r 69   Challenging an award: legal error

To ensure that arbitration remains a valid alternative dispute resolution mechanism for resolving international commercial disputes, it is important to have an enforceable award from the perspective of the winning parties. Consequently, it is not surprising to find out that most rules governing the challenge procedures are mandatory and cannot be modified or disapplied, thus ensuring the stability of the arbitration mechanism. The only rule which can be modified or disapplied by the parties' agreement is r 69 governing the legal error appeal. According to this rule, the parties can exclude legal error as a valid ground for challenging the award in the Outer House.[84]

Part 9 – Miscellaneous

r 78   Consideration where arbitrator judged not to be impartial and independent
r 80   Death of party

---

[77] Scottish Arbitration Rules, r 60. Similar provision can be seen in s 59 of the (English) Arbitration Act 1996.
[78] Scottish Arbitration Rules, r 59. Similar provision can be seen in s 59 of the (English) Arbitration Act 1996.
[79] Scottish Arbitration Rules, r 61. Similar provision can be seen in s 64 of the (English) Arbitration Act 1996.
[80] Scottish Arbitration Rules, r 65. Similar provision can be seen in s 65 of the (English) Arbitration Act 1996.
[81] Scottish Arbitration Rules, r 62. Similar provision can be seen in ss 61(1) and 62(2) of the (English) Arbitration Act 1996.
[82] Scottish Arbitration Rules, r 64.
[83] *Ibid*, r 66. Relevant provision can be seen in s 61(1) of the (English) Arbitration Act 1996.
[84] Scottish Arbitration Rules, r 69(1). Similar provision can be seen in s 69(1) of the (English) Arbitration Act 1996.

r 81   Unfair treatment
r 83   Formal communications
r 84   Periods of time

Rule 78 allows the parties to reach a different agreement from the default rule to exclude the court's power to make an order about the arbitrator's entitlement to fees or expenses or repaying fees or expenses already paid to the arbitrator[85] when the arbitrator is removed or dismissed by the Outer House for lack of impartiality, independence or failure in complying with his duty,[86] or the award is returned for reconsideration or set aside for either of those grounds listed in r 68.

The parties can reach an agreement about how and whether an arbitration agreement will survive following the death of a party and the consequential enforcement of the award against the executor or other representative of that party.[87] The parties can disapply or modify the default rule on the assumption of unfair treatment suffered by the parties jointly if a tribunal treats any party unfairly.[88] They can also change the default rules about how formal communications shall be carried out between the tribunal and the parties or between the parties themselves.[89] Finally, the parties have freedom to change the way periods of time are to be calculated or whether Saturdays, Sundays or public holidays shall be included in the calculation for the purpose of arbitration.

INTERNATIONAL PERSPECTIVE

Historical hostility

Historically, the previous hostility towards an agreement ousting the jurisdiction of courts can be observed in various jurisdictions. Taking the US courts as an example, the courts, both federal and state, have declined to enforce a clause which had the effect of ousting the jurisdiction of the court.[90] Such a hostile attitude was strongly shown in the leading case,

---

[85] Scottish Arbitration Rules, r 78(2). Similar provision can be seen in s 24(4) of the (English) Arbitration Act 1996.
[86] Scottish Arbitration Rules, rr 12 and 13. Relevant provisions can be seen in s 24 of the (English) Arbitration Act 1996.
[87] Scottish Arbitration Rules, r 80.
[88] Ibid, r 81. Relevant provisions can be seen in ss 24(1)(a) and 33(1)(a) of the (English) Arbitration Act 1996.
[89] Scottish Arbitration Rules, r 83. Relevant provision can be seen in s 76 of the (English) Arbitration Act 1996.
[90] See *Nute v Hamilton Mutual Ins Co*, 72 Mass (6 Gray) 174 (1856), *Nashua River Paper Co v Hammermill Paper Co*, 223 Mass 8, 111 NE 678 (1916) and *Benson v Eastern Bldg & Loan Assn*, 174 NY 83, 66 NE 627 (1903).

Wilko v Swan,[91] which ruled that arbitrators were bound to follow the law, even though the arbitration agreement did not specifically so provide. In this case, the plaintiff, a purchaser of securities, sued the seller to recover damages under Art 12(2) of the Securities Act of 1933 for false representations made in concluding the sale. An arbitration agreement was contained in the contract. Nonetheless, the court decided that an agreement to arbitrate could not preclude a buyer of a security from seeking a judicial remedy under the Securities Act of 1933. Again, the court observed:

> "Arbitrators may not disregard the law. Specially they are, as Chief Judge Swan pointed out, 'bound to decide in accordance with the provisions of section 12(2)', ... It is suggested, however, that there is no effective way of assuring obedience by the arbitrators to the governing law. But since their failure to observe this law 'would constitute grounds for vacating the award pursuant to section 10 of the Federal Arbitration Act', ... Appropriate means for judicial scrutiny must be implied, in the form of some record or opinion, however informal, whereby such compliance will appear or want of it will upset the award."[92]

Therefore, following this rule, it could be possible for the courts to vacate awards for a type of excess of authority on the basis of manifest disregard of the law.

From hostility to friendliness
USA

However, the centuries of judicial hostility towards arbitration were reversed by the enactment of the Federal Arbitration Act 1925. The freedom of selection of forum and choice of governing law by the parties to an international contract was confirmed in the case of *M/S Bremen v Zapata Off-Shore Co*[93] in 1972, where the earlier judicial resistance to being denied of jurisdiction in international commercial disputes was reversed. Also, the forum selection clause was recognised as valid and enforceable, the court saying:

> "For at least two decades we have witnessed an expression of overseas commercial activities by business enterprises based in the United States. The barrier of distance that once tended to confine a business concern to a modest territory no longer does so. ... The expansion of American business and industry will hardly be encouraged if, notwithstanding solemn contracts, we insist on a parochial concept that all disputes must be resolved under our laws and in our court."[94]

---

[91] 346 US 427 (1953), 98 L Ed 168, 74 S Ct 182.
[92] 346 US 427 at 440.
[93] US 1, 32 L Ed 2d 513, 92 S Ct 1907.
[94] 32 L Ed 2d 513 at 519–520.

Moreover, this new approach was described as "substantially that followed in other common-law countries including England. ... It accords with ancient concepts of freedom of contract and reflects an appreciation of the expanding horizons of American contractors who seek business in all parts of the world".[95]

Once arbitration is accepted as a viable alternative dispute resolution mechanism, the principle of party autonomy is consequently accepted in international arbitration laws or instruments and a valid arbitration agreement is regarded as the foundation of international commercial arbitration. However, an important issue arising from the topic of arbitration agreement is the scope of interpretations of the agreements by different national courts. This issue is especially acute when different national courts give out different interpretations, some more relaxed and some more strict, on the same issues where there are ambiguities arising from the parties' arbitration agreement. For instance, would "English law-arbitration, if any, London according to ICC Rules" be held as a valid arbitration agreement?[96]

Scotland

Prior to the Arbitration (Scotland) Act 2010, there seems to have been a lack of supportive interpretation for ambiguous arbitration agreements, as seen in *Gifford William Bruce v Keith Robert William Kordula*.[97] This case involved a dispute between the pursuer and his former partners concerning the measure of the pursuer's financial entitlement on his retirement from the partnership of the solicitor firm. The pursuer raised the court action, but the defenders applied to the court to have the action sisted pending arbitration on the subject matter of the action. The defenders relied on cl 17 of the partnership agreement which stated:

> "If any dispute, difference or question shall arise out of these presents or as to the meaning, intent or construction hereof (or in respect of the accounts of the partnership, the retiral of any partner from the partnership, dissolution of the partnership, or any valuation herein provided for, otherwise in relation to the partnership), whether arising during the existence of the partnership or after its termination, the same shall be referred to an Arbiter to be chosen by both the partners or, failing agreement, to be nominated by the Dean of the Faculty of Arbiters on the application of any party, and his decree arbital (*sic*), interim or final, shall be final and binding ..."

---

[95] 32 L Ed 2d 513 at 520. Also see *National Equipment Rental Ltd v Szukhent*, 375 US 311, 11 L Ed 2d 354, 84 S Ct 411 (1964).
[96] Such an agreement is held as valid in *Arab African Energy Corp Ltd v Olieprodukten Nederland BV* [1983] 2 Lloyd's Rep 419.
[97] (2001) APP L R 05/15.

The pursuer submitted that cl 17 was void from uncertainty on the grounds that the expression "chosen by both the partners" was meaningless in the context of the five partners involved in this case. He also claimed that there was no effective mechanism for nomination of an arbiter by a third party as there was no such body as "the Faculty of Arbiters" or "any office of Dean".

Lord Hamilton stated that cl 17 as a whole was void from uncertainty. He pointed out that the court can only be empowered to make a nomination of arbiters if both parts of s 2 of the 1894 Act are satisfied (ie the existence of a valid arbitration agreement to refer and the default provision for the court to nominate the arbiter). However, this was not the situation in this particular case. He was of the opinion that there was no agreement to refer and, consequently, the purported default provision was ineffectual. While acknowledging that a mere reference to arbitration would exclude the jurisdiction of the court, he pointed out that doubts have been expressed in the *Stair Memorial Encyclopaedia*[98] as to enforceability in such a situation. He concluded that:

> "[T]he earlier part of section 2 proceeds on the hypothesis that there is an agreement to refer (to a single arbiter), which agreement is not capable of being carried through by reason of one of the parties to it refusing to concur in the nomination of such arbiter. It does not empower the court to appoint an arbiter when there has been no agreement at all to refer to such arbiter. Nor, in my view, does it empower the court to make an appointment where a purported agreement does not expressly or by necessary implication identify who are the persons to make the nomination."

Now, in light of s 1, and s 10(1)(e) of the Arbitration (Scotland) Act 2010 which requires the court to sist the court proceedings if nothing has caused the court to be satisfied that the arbitration agreement concerned is void, inoperative or incapable of being performed, it is clear that the draftsmen have reached a consensus that a supportive attitude is needed for the arbitration, in particular, the interpretation of arbitration agreements.

England – wider interpretation of arbitration agreements

The first issue is related to whether an arbitration agreement can be used to submit future disputes to arbitration. Taking England as an example, the judge in *Pittalis v Sherefettin*[99] was asked to decide on the extension of time under s 27 of the Arbitration Act 1950 as well as whether a future dispute could be referred to arbitration when the lease stipulated that the parties should within 3 months of notification refer the question

---

[98] *Stair Memorial Encyclopaedia*, Vol 2, para 427.
[99] [1986] QB 868, [1986] 2 All ER 227.

of the revised rent to arbitration. The Court of Appeal decided that, despite the rent review clause conferring the right to initiate arbitration proceedings upon one party only, rather than bilaterally, the phrase "agreement to refer future disputes to arbitration" in the clause fell into the scope of s 27 of the Arbitration Act 1950. Therefore, the appellant could insist on arbitration.[100] This was also confirmed in s 6(1) of the (English) Arbitration Act 1996.

On the issue of the definition of a dispute, the question whether "differences" is included in the meaning of disputes was raised in *Cruden Construction Ltd v Commission for the New Towns*[101] where the term "difference" used in cl 35(1) of the JCT Standard Form of Building Contract was raised by the defendant. Judge Gilliland QC decided that "disputes" include "differences" and stated that "[t]he words 'dispute or difference' are ordinary English words and unless some binding rule of construction has been established in relation to the construction of those words in cl 35 of the JCT contract I am of the opinion that the words should be given their ordinary every day meaning".[102]

Section 6(1) of the (English) Arbitration Act 1996 allows the submission of a non-contractual dispute to arbitration as long as it is closely linked to the contractual disputes covered by the arbitration agreement. This attitude can be observed in an earlier case, *Aggeliki Charis Compania Maritima SA v Pagnan SpA (The Angelic Grace)*,[103] where the Court of Appeal, by citing *Empresa Exportadora de Azucar v Industria Azucarera Nacional SA (The Playa Larga and Marble Islands)*,[104] confirmed that "it was accepted that an arbitration clause could cover a claim in tort if there was a sufficiently close connection between the contractual and tortious claim".

The answer to the question whether the parties' intention to submit disputes to arbitration is evidenced by a reference in an agreement which can be interpreted as a valid arbitration agreement depends on whether the language used is clearly written and this reference has to be part of the agreement.[105] This can be seen in a series of cases involving bills of lading issued under charter parties. For instance, in *Siboti K/S v BP France SA*,[106] Justice Gross pointed out the importance of precise reference to the parties' intention to be subject to arbitration. He stated:

---

[100] See *Tote Bookmakers Ltd v Development & Property Holding Co Ltd* [1985] Ch 261.
[101] [1995] 2 Lloyd's Rep 387.
[102] *Ibid* at 393. *Tradax International SA v Cerrahogullari TAS (The M Eregli)* [1981] 2 Lloyd's Rep 169. Also see the discussion on the decision made by Lord Justice Templeman in *Ellerine Brothers (Pty) Ltd v Klinger* [1982] 1 WLR 1375.
[103] [1995] 1 Lloyd's Rep 87.
[104] [1983] CLY 411, [1983] 2 Lloyd's Rep 171.
[105] (English) Arbitration Act 1996, s 6(2).
[106] [2003] EWHC 1278 (Comm), [2003] 2 Lloyd's Rep 364.

"As already discussed a bill of lading has the status of a negotiable commercial instrument. If the word 'terms' lacks the necessary width, there can be no good reason for the rights of holders to hinge on the addition of the word 'whatsoever'. No authority on the word 'whatsoever' compels such a conclusion; instead, the interests of certainty support the conclusion that a general formula involving no wider wording than 'terms' will not suffice for present purposes."[107]

It was also decided that the court will grant a stay under the Arbitration Act 1996 if there was sufficient evidence that an arbitration clause may have been incorporated into the contract.[108] This was pointed out in the *obiter dictum* in *Aughton Ltd v MF Services Ltd*[109] that the self-contained contract is to be incorporated in this case, but "[i]t must be expressly referred to in the document which is relied on as the incorporating writing. It is not incorporated by mere reference to the terms of the conditions of contract to which the arbitration clause constitutes a collateral contract". This was followed by Judge Jack in *Trygg Hansa Insurance Co Ltd v Equitas Ltd*[110] concerning whether an arbitration clause in the primary insurance contract is incorporated in the reinsurance contract. It was held that, in accordance with s 6(2) of the (English) Arbitration Act 1996, general words of incorporation were not effective to incorporate an arbitration clause. Later, in *General Trading Company (Holdings) Ltd v Richmond Corporation Ltd*, the court held that a reference to "the outline provided in the email" in the terms of the sale and purchase agreement was apt to incorporate the email into the sale and purchase agreement.[111]

Recently, the House of Lords has demonstrated reluctance in interfering with an arbitration clause in *Fiona Trust & Holding Corp v Privalov*.[112] Lord Hoffmann confirmed that the arbitration clause between the parties covered the disputes submitted to the tribunal and stated that:

> "[i]n my opinion the construction of an arbitration clause should start from the assumption that the parties, as rational businessmen, are likely to have intended any dispute arising out of the relationship into which they have entered or purported to enter to be decided by the same tribunal. The clause should be construed in accordance with this presumption unless the language makes it clear that certain questions were intended to be

---

[107] [2003] 2 Lloyd's Rep at 374. See *Thomas (T W) & Co Ltd v Portsea Shipping Co Ltd* [1912] AC 1 (HL); *The Merak* [1964] 2 Lloyd's Rep 527 (CA); *The Annefield* [1971] 1 Lloyd's Rep 1; *The Miramar* [1984] 2 Lloyd's Rep 129, [1984] AC 676 (HL).
[108] *Modern Building (Wales) Ltd v Limmer & Trinidad Co Ltd* [1975] 1 WLR 1281, [1975] 2 Lloyd's Rep 318.
[109] (1991) 57 BLR 1 per Sir John Megaw at 6.
[110] [1998] 2 Lloyd's Rep 439.
[111] [2008] EWHC 1479 (Comm), [2008] 2 Lloyd's Rep 475.
[112] [2007] UKHL 40, [2008] 1 Lloyd's Rep 254.

excluded from the arbitrator's jurisdiction. As Longmore LJ remarked, at paragraph 17, 'if any businessman did want to exclude disputes about the validity of a contract, it would be comparatively easy to say so'."[113]

These wider interpretations of an arbitration agreement can also be seen in the amended Art 7(5) of the UNCITRAL Model Law 2006 which provides: "Furthermore, an arbitration agreement is in writing if it is contained in an exchange of statements of claim and defence in which the existence of an agreement is alleged by one party and not denied by the other." And, Art 7(6) discusses the issue of reference to a document and stipulates that "[t]he reference in a contract to any document containing an arbitration clause constitutes an arbitration agreement in writing, provided that the reference is such as to make that clause part of the contract".

Separability of arbitration agreement

The contract incorporating the arbitration clause is called the main contract or the underlying contract which involves the transactions agreed between the parties. The arbitration agreement is an agreement containing parties' wishes to subject any disputes arising from the underlying contract to arbitration. It is now widely accepted that an arbitration clause and the contract which incorporates it are two different contracts. The principle of separability stipulated in s 7 of the (English) Arbitration Act 1996 means that:

> "Invalidity or rescission of the main contract does not necessarily entail the invalidity or rescission of the arbitration agreement. The arbitration agreement must be treated as a 'distinct agreement' and can be void or voidable only on grounds which relate directly to the arbitration agreement. Of course there may be cases in which the ground upon which the main agreement is invalid is identical with the ground upon which the arbitration agreement is invalid."[114]

The principle of separability can be seen as early as *Heyman v Darwins Ltd*.[115] A dispute arose between the parties, the appellants commencing an action against the respondents on the basis that the respondents had "repudiated and/or evinced an intention not to perform" the contract. The respondents denied repudiation and applied for a stay of court proceedings as there was an arbitration clause in the contract which provided that "if any dispute shall arise between the parties hereto in respect of this agreement or any of the provisions herein contained or anything arising hereout the same shall be referred for arbitration in

---

[113] [2008] 2 Lloyd's Rep 254 at 257 (para 13).
[114] *Fiona Trust & Holding Corp v Privalov* [2007] UKHL 40, [2008] 1 Lloyd's Rep 254 at 257 (para 17).
[115] [1942] AC 356.

accordance with the provisions of the Arbitration Act, 1889". The court accepted that repudiation or a total breach of contract may relieve the injured party of the duty of further fulfilling the obligations which he had by the contract undertaken to the repudiating party; additionally, any further performance of the obligations undertaken by each party in favour of the other may cease. However, the contract still existed, and the court pointed out that: "It survives for the purpose of measuring the claims arising out of the breach, and the arbitration clause survives for determining the mode of their settlement. The purposes of the contract have failed, but the arbitration clause is not one of the purposes of the contract."[116] As a result, the respondents were entitled to insist on having damages assessed by arbitration notwithstanding the other party's repudiation.

A similar discussion on the principle of separability can also been seen in *Harbour Assurance Co (UK) Ltd v Kansa General International Insurance Co Ltd*[117] where the defendant argued for the principle of separability and that it should be within the arbitrator's jurisdiction to determine a dispute over the initial validity of the contract. The Court of Appeal allowed the appeal and held that the illegality pleaded had not affected the validity of the arbitration clause, even though the underlying contract was void due to illegality. In fact the arbitration clause, as a matter of construction, was wide enough to cover the issue and did not have to be void at the same time as the underlying contract. Consequently, a stay of action was granted and the issue of initial illegality was left to arbitrators to decide.

Issue of arbitrability

The other issue related to an arbitration agreement is the issue of arbitrability. The issue of arbitrability is to look into which types of dispute can be referred to arbitration and subject to its jurisdiction. The issue of arbitrability can directly influence the enforceability of an award. Article V(2)(a) of the New York Convention provided that: "Recognition and enforcement of an arbitral award may also be refused if the competent authority in the country where recognition and enforcement is sought finds that the subject matter of the difference is not capable of settlement by arbitration under the law of that country."[118]

In theory, any rights the parties are free to dispose of can be submitted to international commercial arbitration. In practice, this statement is subject to the exception of public policy which enables the courts to exercise an exclusive jurisdiction on matters such as patents, trademarks,

---

[116] [1942] AC 356 at 374.
[117] [1993] QB 701, [1993] 3 WLR 42, [1993] 3 All ER 897, [1993] 1 Lloyd's Rep 455.
[118] Similar provision can also be seen in Art 36(1)(b)(i) of the UNCITRAL Model Law.

copyrights, competition law issues,[119] securities transactions, insolvency, natural resources, bribery, corruption and fraud.

Scotland

Regarding the issue of arbitrability, s 30 of the Arbitration (Scotland) Act 2010 provides:

> "'Nothing in this Act makes any dispute capable of being arbitrated if, because of its subject-matter, it would not otherwise be capable of being arbitrated.' It is clear from this provision that the Act does not make any dispute arbitrable where the subject-matter of the dispute would not otherwise be capable of arbitration under Scots Law. The example the lawmaker gave includes matters which affect public rights or the status of parties in law."[120]

France

Similar provisions are also contained in the French Civil Code. Article 2059 sets out the principle and provides that "[a]ll persons may agree to arbitration in relation to rights which they are free to dispose of". However, this principle is subject to Art 2060, which excludes the disputes related to public policy. It reads:

> "It is not permissible to submit to arbitration matters of civil status and capacity of individuals, or relating to divorce or judicial separation of spouses or disputes concerning public communities and public establishments and more generally all matters which concern public policy."[121]

Germany

The tenth book of the German Code of Civil Procedure allows any disputes involving economic interest to be submitted to arbitration, with the exception of statutory prohibitions and disputes arising from residential accommodation lease. Section 1030 stipulates:

> "(1) Any claim involving an economic interest ('*vermögensrechtlicher Anspruch*') can be the subject of an arbitration agreement. An arbitration agreement concerning claims not involving an economic interest shall have legal effect to the extent that the parties are entitled to conclude a settlement on the issue in dispute.
> (2) An arbitration agreement relating to disputes on the existence of a lease of residential accommodation within Germany shall be null and void.

---

[119] However, competition law issues appear to arbitrable following the decision in *Eco Swiss China Time Ltd v Benetton International NV* [1999] ECR 1–03055.
[120] Revised Explanatory Notes (2009), para 87.
[121] Nevertheless, in accordance with Art 2060(2), certain categories of public establishments of an industrial and commercial character may be authorised by decree to submit to arbitration.

This does not apply to residential accommodation as specified in s 549 subs. 1 to 3 of the Civil Code.

(3) Statutory provisions outside this Book by virtue of which certain disputes may not be submitted to arbitration, or may be submitted to arbitration only under certain conditions, remain unaffected."

USA

Disputes arising from competition law are now receiving more favourable treatment in both the US Supreme Court and the European Commission. The well-known *Mitsubishi* case[122] opened the floodgates for antitrust disputes to be resolved by arbitration by overruling the *American Safety* doctrine which determined that the American Congress had no intention to allow antitrust disputes to be submitted to arbitration due to the fact that a potentially huge number of people can be affected by the violation of such kind of dispute.[123] Justice Blackmun asserted that national courts will need to "shake off the old judicial hostility to arbitration" if they want to take a central place in the international legal order.[124] He stated:

> "There is no reason to assume at the outset of the dispute that international arbitration will not provide an adequate mechanism. To be sure, the international arbitral tribunal owes no prior allegiance to the legal norms of particular states; hence, it has no direct obligation to vindicate their statutory dictates. The tribunal, however, is bound to effectuate the intentions of the parties. Where the parties have agreed that the arbitral body is to decide a defined set of claims which includes, as in these cases, those arising from the application of American antitrust law, the tribunal therefore should be bound to decide that dispute in accord with the national law giving rise to the claim. And so long as the prospective litigant effectively may vindicate its statutory cause of action in the arbitral forum, the statute will continue to serve both its remedial and deterrent function."[125]

Consequently, he permitted the antitrust disputes arising from this case to be submitted to arbitration in Japan and pointed out that the US Supreme Court had already, in the case of *Scherk* v *Alberto-Culver Co*, upheld that, on the basis of "concerns of international comity, respect for the capacities of foreign and transnational tribunals, and sensitivity to the need of the international commercial system for predictability in the resolution of disputes require that we enforce the parties' agreement, even assuming that a contrary result would be forthcoming in a domestic context".[126]

---

[122] *Mitsubishi Motors Corps* v *Soler Chrysler Plymouth Inc*, 473 US 614, 105 S Ct 3346 (1985).
[123] *American Safety Equipment Corp* v *J P Maguire & Co*, 391 F 2d 821 (2nd Cir 1968).
[124] Above, n 122. Also, *Kulukundis Shipping Co* v *Amtorg Trading Corp*, 126 F 2d 978 at 985 (CA2 1942).
[125] Above, n 122 at 636–637.
[126] *Ibid*, referring to *Scherk* at US 506 (1974).

EU

In the EU, the European Court Justice has not confirmed the arbitrability of competition law disputes. However, commentators drew a conclusion from an ICC award and the case *Eco Swiss China Time Ltd v Benetton International NV*[127] that it is no longer in dispute that competition issues are arbitrable.[128]

In ICC arbitral award no 8626 (1999), considering the possibility of enforcement of awards in Germany and the extra-territoriality jurisdiction the EC may exercise over the parties through trading between the Member States of the EU, the tribunal determined that the EC competition law must be applied to the disputed agreement when the parties raised a possible breach of Art 85 EC (now Art 81).

To maintain uniformity of the interpretations of EC law, the ECJ, in *Eco Swiss China Time Ltd v Benetton International NV*,[129] ruled that "where domestic rules of procedure require a national court to grant an application for annulment of an arbitration award where such an application is founded on failure to observe national rules of public policy, it must also grant such an application where it is founded on failure to comply with the prohibition laid down in Art 85(1) of the Treaty".[130]

Moreover,

> "It should be recalled that, as explained in paragraph 34 above, arbitrators, unlike national courts and tribunals, are not in a position to request this Court to give a preliminary ruling on questions of interpretation of Community law. However, it is manifestly in the interest of the Community legal order that, in order to forestall differences of interpretation, every Community provision should be given a uniform interpretation irrespective of the circumstances in which it is to be applied (Case C-88/91 *Federconsorzi* [1992] ECR I-4035, paragraph 7). It follows that in the circumstances of the present case, unlike Van Schijndel and Van Veen, Community law requires that questions concerning the interpretation of the prohibition laid down in Art 85(1) of the Treaty should be open to examination by national courts when asked to determine the validity of an arbitration award and that it should be possible for those questions to be referred, if necessary, to the Court of Justice for a preliminary ruling."[131]

Issue of multi-party arbitration

A valid arbitration agreement can only have effects on the contracting parties submitting their dispute to arbitration. In international commercial

---

[127] [1999] ECR I-03055.
[128] C Bellsham-Revell and T Roberts, "*Arbitrating disputes involving competition law*" OLSWANG News article. Accessed at http://www.competitionlaw.cn/upload// temp_08031718108986.pdf on 2 February 2010.
[129] Above, n 127.
[130] *Ibid* at para 37.
[131] *Ibid* at para 40.

arbitration, especially construction disputes, it is common to have more than two parties involved in the same dispute. To make arbitration an efficient method of dispute resolution and avoid conflicting decisions on the same issues, sometimes it makes sense to bring the different parties to the same arbitration to resolve the disputes once and for all. However, unlike national courts empowering judges to order the relevant parties to the same issues to take part in the same court proceedings, arbitrators do not have such a power unless the parties involved are willing to be part of a multi-party arbitration.

Scotland

The issue of multi-party arbitration is dealt with in r 40 of the Scottish Arbitration Rules. Rule 40 expresses that the parties have the freedom to exclude the possibility of multi-party arbitration or disapply the default r 40 in relation to this issue. If the parties fail to agree otherwise, r 40 allows the parties to agree to consolidate the arbitration with another arbitration or hold concurrent hearings.[132] The tribunal may not make orders to consolidate arbitrations or hold concurrent hearings on its own initiative.[133]

England

Similar provision can also be seen in s 35 of the (English) Arbitration Act 1996, which provides:

> "The parties are free to agree –
> (a) that the arbitral proceedings shall be consolidated with other arbitral proceedings, or
> (b) that concurrent hearings shall be held,
> on such terms as may be agreed.
> (2) Unless the parties agree to confer such power on the tribunal, the tribunal has no power to order consolidation of proceedings or concurrent hearings."

Both r 40 of the Scottish Arbitration Rules and s 35 of the (English) Arbitration Act 1996 confirmed the common law position. The requirement of parties' consent on multi-parties arbitration is essential at common law as "[t]he inconvenience of multiple arbitrations, though it exists, can be exaggerated".[134] In *Oxford Shipping Co Ltd* v *Nippon Yusen Kaisha*,[135] a case involving disputes arising from the interrelationship of the standard war risk policy and special cover under the New York

---

[132] Scottish Arbitration Rules, r 40(1).
[133] Ibid, r 40(2).
[134] *World Pride Shipping Ltd* v *Daiichi Chuo Kisen Kaisha* (*The Golden Anne*) [1984] 2 Lloyd's Rep 489 per Mr Justice Lloyd at 497.
[135] [1984] 2 Lloyd's Rep 373.

Produce Exchange form, Leggat J expressed his opinion on this issue by stating:

> "[A]rbitrators in the position of these arbitrators enjoy no power to order concurrent hearings, or anything of that nature, without the consent of the parties. The concept of private arbitrations derives simply from the fact that the parties have agreed to submit to arbitration particular disputes arising between them and only between them. It is implicit in this that strangers shall be excluded from the hearing and conduct of the arbitration and that neither the tribunal nor any of the parties can insist that the dispute shall be heard or determined concurrently with or even in consonance with another dispute, however convenient that course may be to the party seeking it and however closely associated with each other the disputes in question may be. The only powers which an arbitrator enjoys relate to the reference in which he has been appointed. They cannot be extended merely because a similar dispute exists which is capable of being and is referred separately to arbitration under a difference agreement."[136]

Netherlands

The Netherlands Arbitration Act 1986 also provides resolutions to the issue of multi-parties arbitration. In the case of a third party who has an interest in the outcome of the arbitral proceedings, Art 1045(1) stipulates that an arbitral tribunal may permit such third party to join the proceedings, or to intervene therein at the written request of the third party. However, the arbitral tribunal shall send a copy of the request to the parties without delay. In the case of consolidation of arbitrations or holding concurrent hearings, providing that arbitral proceedings have been commenced before an arbitral tribunal in the Netherlands concerning a subject matter which is connected with the subject matter of arbitral proceedings commenced before another arbitral tribunal in the Netherlands, at the request of any of the parties, the President of the District Court in Amsterdam has the power to order a consolidation of the proceedings, unless the parties have expressed agreement to exclude such powers.[137]

Hong Kong

Chapter 341(6B) of the Hong Kong Arbitration Ordinance also allows the consolidation of arbitration proceedings. It provides:

> "Where in relation to two or more arbitration proceedings it appears to the Court –
> (a) that some common question of law or fact arises in both or all of them, or

---

[136] [1984] 2 Lloyd's Rep 373 *at* 379.
[137] Netherlands Code of Civil Procedure (Book four: arbitration enacted in 1986 and amended in 2004), Art 1046(1).

(b) that the rights to relief claimed therein are in respect of or arise out of the same transaction or series of transactions, or
(c) that for some other reason it is desirable to make an order under this section,

the Court may order those arbitration proceedings to be consolidated on such terms as it thinks just or may order them to be heard at the same time, or one immediately after another, or may order any of them to be stayed until after the determination of any other of them."

Australia

Similar provisions can also be seen in s 24(1) of the Australian International Arbitration Act 1989. Once the application for consolidation is received, if all the related proceedings are being heard by the same tribunal, the tribunal may make such order under this section as it thinks fit in relation to those proceedings and, if such an order is made, the proceedings shall be dealt with in accordance with the order.[138] In the case where the arbitrations are being heard by two or more arbitral tribunals, the tribunal that received the application shall communicate the substance of the application to the other tribunals concerned;[139] and the tribunals shall, as soon as practicable, deliberate jointly on the application.[140]

ICC arbitration

Multi-parties arbitration is also allowed in the ICC arbitrations. According to Art 4(6) of the ICC Arbitration Rules 1998, when a party submits a request in connection with a legal relationship in respect of which arbitration proceedings between the same parties are already pending under the Rules, provided that the terms of reference have not been signed or approved by the court, the court may, at the request of a party, decide to include the claims contained in the request in the pending proceedings. However, once the terms of reference have been signed or approved by the court, claims may only be included in the pending proceedings subject to the arbitral tribunal's approval based on the nature of such new claims or counterclaims, the stage of the arbitration and other relevant circumstances.[141]

---

[138] Australian International Arbitration Act 1989, s 24(4).
[139] Ibid, s 24(5)(a).
[140] Ibid, s 24(5)(b).
[141] ICC Arbitration Rules 1998, Art 4(6).

CHAPTER 5

PARTY AUTONOMY AND ITS RESTRICTIONS

GENERAL

The characteristics of flexibility and speed which influence disputing parties to choose international commercial arbitration as the means to resolve their disputes are credited to the adoption of the principle of party autonomy. The principle of party autonomy is manifested in the parties' freedom in designing the arbitration procedures to suit their needs. For instance, they can agree the number of arbitrators to be chosen to decide the disputes, the format and length of the procedures shall take, the place of arbitration, the language of arbitration, the laws applicable to the arbitration agreement or the main contract, ... and so on. However, it shall be borne in mind that party autonomy is not unlimited. It can be restricted by mandatory rules and public policy, which are used to make sure that arbitration is carried out according to a minimum level of standard. The first part of this chapter will provide a theoretical basis for the principle of party autonomy. Second, the discussion will be focused on how such a principle is adopted in practice, both internationally and nationally. Then it will be followed by an examination of the exceptions to the principle of party autonomy: namely mandatory rules and public policy.

THEORETICAL BASIS OF PARTY AUTONOMY

The focus of the principle of party autonomy is firmly placed on the parties' powers/rights to determine how their arbitration procedures shall be carried out. This idea is rooted in freedom of contract originated from the philosophy of *laissez-faire*: that is, the doctrine invoking unrestricted freedom in commerce flourished and similarly indicated that the law should interfere with people as little as possible.[1] As Cohen observes:[2]

---

[1] P S Atiyah, *An Introduction to the Law of Contract* (3rd edn, 1989), p 7.
[2] M Cohen, "The Basis of Contract" (1993) 46 HarvLR 553.

"Contractualism in the law, that is, the view that in an ideally desirable system of law all obligation would arise only out of the will of the individual contracting freely, rests not only on the will theory of contract but also on the political doctrine that all restraint is evil and that the government is best which governs least."[3]

Following this idea, considering the nature of contracts, the will of the parties is regarded as the most significant concept in the classical contract theory. Rights and obligations can arise only from the fact of an agreement or an exchange of promises or wills between the parties. By the middle of the 19th century, the classical contract theory had taken root in English law through the acceptance that an obligation was created by a communication of wills.[4]

As discussed in Chapter 4, among different theories outlining the nature of arbitration, the contractual theory is the best positioned to provide the foundation for the principle of party autonomy. The contractual theory explores the nature of arbitration from a contractual viewpoint. According to the proponents of the contractual theory,[5] arbitration is based on the agreement between the parties. They deny that any strong links exist between the arbitration proceedings and the law of the place in which the arbitration takes place. They maintain that parties have the freedom to decide the relevant issues concerning the arbitration procedures and this freedom should generally not be interfered with by the powers of any states.

It was argued that, with the exceptions of arbitrability and public policy which are reserved for the *lex fori*, the *lex fori* has very little influence over the procedures and outcome of the arbitration. Moreover, it has been concluded that "national arbitration laws are only to supplement and fill lacunae in the parties' agreement as to the arbitration proceedings and to provide a code capable of regulating the conduct of an arbitration".[6]

---

[3] Cohen above at n 2 at 558.
[4] P S Atiyah, *The Rise and Fall of Freedom of Contract* (1979), p 407.
[5] Such as Merlin, Foelix, Balladore-Pallieri, Bernard and Klein in France and Kellor, Domke and Kitagawa outside France. See Frances Kellor, *Arbitration in Action*, quoted by P Stone in "A Paradox in the Theory of Commercial Arbitration" (1996) 21 ArbJ 156; M Domke, *Commercial Arbitration* (1965), p 31, who stated that "the express intent of both parties to enter into the arbitration agreement is essential existence"; T Kitagawa, "Contractual Autonomy in International Commercial Arbitration" in P Sanders (ed), *Liber Amicorum for Martin Domke* (1957) at p 138, who believes that "the binding force of the arbitration agreement comes from '*pacta sunt servanda*' as well as other ordinary contracts without any state authorisation".
[6] Klein, *Considerations*, p 182, discussed in J Lew, *The Applicable Laws in International Commercial Arbitration* (1978), p 56.

THE ARBITRATION (SCOTLAND) ACT 2010

The principle of party autonomy is firmly rooted in s 1 of the Arbitration (Scotland) Act 2010 which stipulates that "parties should be free to agree how to resolve disputes subject only to such safeguards as are necessary in the public interest". Section 9 of the Act offers the parties the freedom to modify or disapply the default rules contained in the Scottish Arbitration Rules. It stipulates that the non-mandatory rules which are identified in the Scottish Arbitration Rules in Sch 1 by a "D" at the end of the rule heading are termed the "default rules".[7] In general, s 9 is a reflection of the belief that the parties and the arbitrators can adopt procedures which are most appropriate to deal with the circumstances of the particular case. Consequently, arbitration under the Act can provide flexible procedures allowing the parties to make arrangements to suit their particular needs.[8] In the policy memorandum, it was pointed out that the design of default rules has the advantage of allowing the parties the opportunity to submit their disputes to arbitration with a bare arbitration agreement without spending time agreeing on a joint submission to arbitrator setting out how the arbitration is to proceed. This can speed up the dispute resolution process, especially in cases where the parties are already in dispute.[9]

However, these default rules can be expressly modified or disapplied by the parties by the means of the arbitration agreement[10] or by any other means at any time before or after the arbitration begins.[11] Alternatively, the default rules can be implied to be modified or disapplied by the parties to the extent that the rule is inconsistent with or disapplied by the arbitration agreement,[12] any arbitration rule or rules or other document which the parties agree are to govern the arbitration,[13] or anything done with the agreement of the parties.[14] Furthermore, parties can also be treated as having agreed to modify or disapply a default rule if they choose a law other than Scots law as the applicable law in respect of the rule's subject matter.[15] However, such an inferred intention does not affect the generality of s 9(2) and (3) of the Act. To sum up, only where there is

---

[7] Arbitration (Sc) Act 2010, s 8(1). Relevant provision can be seen in s 4 of the (English) Arbitration Act 1996.
[8] Policy Memorandum, 29 January 2009, para 86.
[9] Ibid, paras 87 and 88.
[10] Arbitration (Sc) Act 2010, s 8(3)(a).
[11] Ibid, s 8(3)(b).
[12] Ibid, s 8(4)(a)(i).
[13] Ibid, s 8(4)(a)(ii): the "document" mentioned in this provision can be the UNCITRAL Model Law, the UNCITRAL Arbitration Rules or other institutional rules.
[14] Arbitration (Sc) Act 2010, s 8(4)(a)(iii).
[15] Ibid, s 8(4)(b).

no such agreement between the parties to modify or disapply the default rules, will the default rules apply.[16]

The Scottish Arbitration Rules contain 48 default rules, ranging from the commencement of arbitration to methods of formal communication. As most of the rules are discussed in Chapter 4, a brief discussion on the default rules will be provided below. Part 1 of the Scottish Arbitration Rules allows the parties to modify or disapply the rules regulating the issues of commencement of arbitration, appointment of tribunal, number of arbitrators, method of appointment, arbitrator's tenure, challenge to appointment of arbitrator, removal of arbitrator by parties and reconstitution of tribunal. While Pts 2 and 3 contain the default rules concerning the referral of point of jurisdiction, confidentiality and tribunal deliberations, Rules 28–39 in Pt 4 offer the parties the freedom to replace the default rules on the arbitral proceedings with their own chosen rules. Further default rules are related to the following issues: referral of point of law, variation of time limits set by parties, court's other powers in relation to arbitration, rules applicable to the substance of the dispute, other remedies available to tribunal, forms of awards, awards treated as made in Scotland, provisional awards, draft awards, arbitration to end on last award or early settlement, correction of an award, arbitration expenses, recoverable arbitration expenses and liability, security for costs, limitation of an award on recoverable arbitration expenses, challenge of awards on the basis of legal error, consideration where arbitrator judged not to be impartial and independent, death of party, unfair treatment, formal communications and periods of time.

PARTY AUTONOMY IN INTERNATIONAL PRACTICE

Party autonomy in international documents

The theory of the freedom of contract also has some effect on the mechanism of international commercial arbitration. Based on the idea of freedom of contract, the theory of party autonomy is invoked as the basis of international commercial arbitration. Based on such autonomy, the parties have a cardinal right to choose the proper law to govern the main contract. This theory is not only recognised in the academic studies, but also contained in the international Conventions, the institutional arbitration rules and the different national arbitration statutes. For instance, in the case of international documents, the UNCITRAL Model Law, the UNCITRAL Arbitration Rules, the ICC Rules, the LCIA Rules

---

[16] Revised explanatory notes of the Arbitration (Scotland) Bill as amended at Stage 2, para 32.

and the ICDR International Dispute Resolution Procedures, all contain provisions adopting party autonomy.

In the UNCITRAL Model Law, the concept of party autonomy is incorporated in various provisions. For instance:

> "The parties are free to determine the number of arbitrators."[17]
>
> "The parties are free to agree on a procedure of appointing the arbitrator or arbitrators, ..."[18]
>
> "Subject to the provisions of this Law, the parties are free to agree on the procedure to be followed by the arbitral tribunal in conducting the proceedings."[19]
>
> "The parties are free to agree on the place of arbitration."[20]
>
> "The parties are free to agree on the language or languages to be used in the arbitral proceedings."[21]

The parties are also empowered to agree on how the arbitral proceedings are commenced[22] and whether to hold an oral hearing to present evidence.[23]

Under the Arbitration Rules of the United Nations Commission on International Trade Law of 1976 (the "UNCITRAL Arbitration Rules"), parties are allowed to have the default rules replaced by their own agreements on the following issues: the number of arbitrators,[24] the place of arbitration[25] and the language of arbitration.[26] Article 33(1) of the Rules also allows the parties to choose the law designated by the parties as applicable to the substance of the dispute.[27]

Similar default rules can also be observed in the International Chamber of Commerce Rules of Conciliation and Arbitration of 1998 (the "ICC Rules"), where the parties can agree on the number of arbitrators to be either one or three,[28] the place of arbitration,[29] the language of the arbitration,[30] and the choice of the applicable rules of

---

[17] UNCITRAL Model Law, Art 10(1).
[18] Ibid, Art 11(2).
[19] Ibid, Art 19(1).
[20] Ibid, Art 20(1).
[21] Ibid, Art 22(1).
[22] Ibid, Art 21.
[23] Ibid, Art 24.
[24] UNCITRAL Arbitration Rules, Art 5.
[25] Ibid, Art 16.
[26] Ibid, Art 17.
[27] Ibid, Art 33(1).
[28] ICC Rules, Art 8.
[29] Ibid, Art 14.
[30] Ibid.

law.[31] The ICDR International Dispute Resolution Procedures of the American Arbitration Association ("AAA") also has similar default rules to those contained in the ICC Rules.[32]

The Rules of the London Court of International Arbitration ("LCIA")[33] offer the parties a wider scope in modifying the default rules in the following provisions: nomination of arbitrators (Art 7), conduct of the proceedings (Art 14), submission of written statements and documents (Art 15), the seat of arbitration and the place of hearings (Art 16), language of arbitration (Art 17), appointment of experts to the arbitral tribunal (Art 21), arbitrator's additional powers (Art 22), refusal of tribunal to make interim and conservatory measures (Art 25), agreement to have reasons stated in the awards (Art 26), and, unless the parties expressly agree otherwise in writing, a duty of confidentiality imposed (Art 30).

Party autonomy in national laws

In most jurisdictions, the mechanism of international commercial arbitration is undeniably designed on the basis of the contractual theory. Recognising business persons' desires to have a more flexible and informal method of dispute settlement, most courts tend to follow the contractual theory and interpret the relationship between the parties and the arbitrators as a contract. This can be seen in, for instance, Art 182(1) of the Swedish Arbitration Act, which provides: "The parties may, directly or by reference to arbitration rules, determine the arbitral procedure; they may also submit it to a procedural law of their choice."[34] Using the term "non-mandatory provisions", s 4(2) of the (English) Arbitration Act 1996 provides: "The parties may make such arrangements by agreeing to the application of institutional rules or providing any other means by which a matter may be decided." Such agreements can be made by reference to the institutional rules.[35]

Most legal systems recognise the parties' freedom to express their intention that the law of a given country shall govern the contract. This intention will direct the arbitrators to apply the chosen law to settle the

---

[31] ICC Rules, Art 17(1).
[32] Eg number of arbitrators (Art 5), procedures to be followed in appointment of arbitrators (Art 6), the place of arbitration (Art 13), the language of arbitration (Art 18) and the choice of substantive law (Art 28) of the International Arbitration Rules of the American Arbitration Association, 1 June 2009.
[33] Rules of the London Court of International Arbitration 1998, Art 13(1)(a).
[34] The leading international arbitration institutions include the ICC, LCIA, and AAA, each of which has adopted the rule that parties are free to choose the law under which to conduct the proceedings.
[35] (English) Arbitration Act 1996, s 4(3).

dispute between the parties. As Rabel states: "The practice of allowing parties to determine the law applicable to their contractual relations ... for centuries has been applied by courts throughout the world with slight dissent."[36] Once their intention is found, it is compulsory for the arbitrators to apply this choice of law in order to decide the substantive issues arising from the main contract between the parties. This freedom is based on the doctrine of party autonomy, which is originated from the idea of "freedom of contract" (it is also called the "classical contract theory" or the "will theory").

In relation to the issue of the choice of the proper law, *R v International Trustee for the Protection of Bondholders*[37] pointed out that the proper law of the contract is the law which the parties intended to apply. Moreover, the choice "will be ascertained by the intention expressed in the contract if any, which will be conclusive".[38] This autonomy is again confirmed by a leading case.[39] In the case of *Vita Food Products Inc v Unus Shipping Co Ltd*, the court upheld the parties' express choice of law and indicated: "It is now well settled that by English law the proper law of contract 'is the law' which the parties intended to apply. The intention to apply a specific national law as the proper law is objectively ascertained."[40]

Several decades later, the parties' freedom in choosing the proper law of the contract was again upheld, in the case of *Whitworth Street Estates (Manchester) Ltd v James Miller and Partners*.[41] In this case, Lord Reid set out that:

> "The general principle is not in doubt. Parties are entitled to agree what is to be the proper law of the contract, and if they do not make any such agreement then the law will determine what the proper law is. There have been from time to time suggestions that parties ought not to be so entitled, but in my view there is no doubt that they are entitled to make such an agreement, and I see no good reason why, subject it may be to some limitations, they should not be so entitled. But it must be a contractual agreement. It need not be in express words. Like any other agreement it may be inferred from reading their contract as a whole in light of relevant circumstances known to both parties when they made their contract."[42]

---

[36] Rabel, *Comparative Conflicts* (2nd edn, 1958), Vol I, p 90. Also see Lew, *The Applicable Law in International Commercial Arbitration*, p 71.
[37] [1937] AC 500.
[38] *Ibid* at 529.
[39] *Vita Food Products Inc v Unus Shipping Co Ltd* [1939] AC 277.
[40] *Ibid* at 289.
[41] [1970] AC 583.
[42] *Ibid* at 603.

RESTRICTIONS ON PARTY AUTONOMY – MANDATORY RULES AND PUBLIC POLICY

Theoretical basis of mandatory rules and public policy

The absolute freedom of contract enjoyed by the parties throughout the 18th century and part of the 19th century suffered a setback by the end of 19th century. In addition, the classical principle of *laissez-faire* was challenged because of the changes in the social and economic environments. Atiyah regarded the classical contract theory as a failure, and argued "... in the modern world, where many people see the functions of Government and Parliament as virtually limitless, it is absurd to think of society as regulated by freedom of contract subject only to limited instances of State interference".[43]

Following the economic and social changes since the 19th century, the classical contract theory no longer accords with the modern world in many respects. For instance, the classical concept of freedom of contract takes little account of social and economic pressures which might virtually force a man to enter into a contract which is obviously unfair to him. In addition, the classical concept of freedom of contract ignores the possible inequalities of the bargaining powers between the contracting parties. Literally, the classical contract theory can be supported only if the bargaining powers of both contracting parties are equal; however, this is not always the case in reality. Considering the criticisms mentioned above and the possible involvement of third parties, the issues of monopolies, restrictive agreements, consumer protection and compensation for workmen, freedom of contract is more restricted than it was previously claimed to be.

These arguments correspond with the jurisdictional theory emphasising the importance of jurisdictional elements of arbitration and providing an excellent legal basis for the mandatory rules and public policy as exceptions to the principle of party autonomy.

The jurisdictional theory invokes the significance of the supervisory powers of states, especially those of the place of arbitration. Although the jurisdictional theory does not dispute the idea that an arbitration has its origin in the parties' arbitration agreement, it maintains that the validity of arbitration agreements and arbitration procedures needs to be regulated by national laws and the validity of an arbitral award is decided by the laws of the seat and the country where the recognition or enforcement is sought. Proponents of the jurisdictional theory maintain that all arbitration procedures have to be regulated by the rules of law chosen by the parties if there are any and those rules of law in force in the place of arbitration. They also believe that arbitrators resemble judges of

---

[43] [1970] AC 693.

national courts because the arbitrators' powers are drawn from the states by means of the rules of law. As with judges, arbitrators are required to apply the rules of law of a specific state to settle the disputes submitted to them. Moreover, the awards made by the arbitrators are regarded as having the same status and effect as a judgment handed down by judges sitting in a national court. As a result, they maintain that the awards will be enforced by the court where the recognition or enforcement is sought in the same way as judgments made by the courts.

Proponents of the jurisdictional theory stress, in particular, the significance of the seat of arbitration. For instance, Dr Mann[44] emphasised the significance of the laws of relevant states to an arbitration, especially the law of the place where the arbitration takes place, that is, the *lex loci arbitri*. The premise of Dr Mann's argument is that every sovereign state is entitled to approve or disapprove the activities carried out within its territory.[45] Following this premise, consequently every arbitration is subject to the law where it takes place. Moreover, an arbitrator is required to carry out the arbitration proceedings in accordance with the will of the parties to the extent that the *lex loci arbitri* allows. Any acts of arbitrators that contradict the mandatory rules and public policy of the place of arbitration are regarded as judicially unjustified.[46] In other words, the various issues arising from international commercial arbitration, such as the validity of the arbitration agreement, the arbitral procedures, the arbitrator's power, the scope of submission and the enforceability of arbitral awards, have to be decided within the mandatory rules and public policy of the *lex loci arbitri*. Failure to do so may result in the awards being set aside by the court of the place of arbitration; furthermore, recognition or enforcement of the awards may be refused by the courts of the enforcing states.

Dr Mann asserted that, in accordance with a strict interpretation, every arbitration is a national one and it should be governed by the municipal laws of the country where it is held. The so-called "international" arbitration is, in fact, a fallacy,[47] since no arbitration can exist in a legal vacuum. Dr Mann strongly criticised the delocalisation theory and the autonomous theory,[48] which maintained that international commercial arbitration should be free from the restraints of the *lex loci arbitri*. He argued: "In the legal sense no international commercial arbitration exists. Just as, notwithstanding its notoriously misleading name, every

---

[44] F Mann, "*Lex Facit Arbitrum*", reprinted in (1983) 2(3) Arbitration Int 245; also see M Mustill, "Transnational Arbitration in English Law" (1984) 37 CurrLPr 133 at 142.
[45] *Ibid*.
[46] F Mann, "State Contracts and International Arbitration" (1967) 42 BritYrbkIntlL 10 at 14–16.
[47] Above, n 44; Mann at 244.
[48] This will be discussed in a later section of this chapter.

system of private international law is a system of national law, every arbitration is a national arbitration, that is to say, subject to a specific system of national law."[49]

In Dr Mann's opinion, any arbitration procedures, the composition of arbitral tribunals and the structure of arbitration procedures have to be subject to a national law of a specific country. Within the framework of international commercial arbitration, only the *lex loci arbitri* can provide such a complete and effective control over the arbitration procedures to decide the relevant issues arising from an arbitration. Finally, he concluded that "it would be intolerable if the country of the seat could not override whatever arrangements the parties may have made. The local sovereign does not yield to them except as a result of freedom granted by himself".[50]

Regarding the relationship between arbitration and the national courts where the arbitration takes place or the courts where recognition or enforcement of the arbitral award is sought, the jurisdictional theory provides a strong basis for the national courts exercising supervisory powers over the arbitration.[51] Such supervisory powers are also confirmed in the New York Convention. For instance, in accordance with Art V, in the absence of the express choice of law, the validity of arbitration agreements,[52] arbitral awards,[53] the composition of the arbitral authority and the arbitral procedures[54] have to be decided in accordance with the law of the country where the arbitration takes place. Also, the supervisory powers over the validity of arbitral awards can be exercised by the courts where recognition or enforcement is sought, if the subject matter of the difference is not arbitrable under the law,[55] or the enforcement of such an award would be against its public policy.[56]

In relation to the supervisory powers of the national courts where the arbitration takes place, the jurisdiction over the arbitration, which might have no connection with this country, is based on three theoretical arguments: the arbitrator's right to make binding adjudications is derived from a delegation by the state of its exclusive powers in this field; every act is subject to the law in force where it occurred; and the application of the *lex loci arbitri* and the use of its courts are sometimes more efficient than any other system.[57]

---

[49] Above, n 44, Mann at 245.
[50] *Ibid* at 246.
[51] With the exception of Belgium.
[52] New York Convention, Art V(1)(a).
[53] *Ibid*, Art V(1)(e).
[54] *Ibid*, Art V(1)(d).
[55] *Ibid*, Art V(2)(a).
[56] *Ibid*, Art V(2)(b).
[57] A Samuel, *Jurisdictional Problems in International Commercial Arbitration: A Study of Belgian, Dutch, English, French, Swedish, Swiss, US, and West German Law* (1989), p 63.

In addition, under the jurisdictional theory, the courts in the country where recognition or enforcement is sought also have a supervisory power over the issue of arbitrability at the stage of recognition or enforcement. Accordingly, under Art V(2) the courts have the discretion to refuse to recognise or enforce an arbitral award if it finds that "[t]he subject matter of the difference is not capable of settlement by arbitration under the law of that country"[58] or "recognition or enforcement of the award would be contrary to the public policy of that country".[59] The same approach has also been adopted by the United States Supreme Court, which confirmed the federal policy favouring arbitration in the *Mitsubishi* case.[60] The *Mitsubishi* case involved an antitrust dispute which was prohibited from being resolved by means of arbitration in a domestic case. The United States Supreme Court enforced the parties' arbitration agreement involving an antitrust dispute, even assuming that a contrary result would be forthcoming in a domestic context;[61] as Justice Blackmun pointed out: "the national courts of the United States will have the opportunity at the award-enforcement stage to ensure that the legitimate interest in the enforcement of the antitrust laws has been addressed".[62] This was because "[t]he convention reserves to each signatory country the right to refuse enforcement of an award where the recognition or enforcement of the award would be contrary to the public policy of that country".[63]

Based on this argument, one may be able to say that the relationship between the courts and arbitration is of a supervisory nature in accordance with the jurisdictional theory.

Public policy

Public policy is widely accepted as one of the exceptions restricting the scope of party autonomy. As early as 1824, Burroughs J's judgment in *Richardson* v *Mellish* famously stated: "Public policy – it is an unruly horse and when once you get astride it, you never know where it will carry you. It may lead you from the sound law. It is never argued at all but when other points fail."[64] Later in 1853, the House of Lords delivered a definition on public policy in *Egerton* v *Brownlow*,[65] which stated that public policy is "that principle of law which holds that no subject can lawfully do that

---

[58] New York Convention, Art V(2)(a).
[59] Ibid, Art V(2)(b).
[60] *Mitsubishi Motors Co* v *Soler Chrysler-Plymouth, Inc*, 473 US 614 (1984), 87 L Ed 2d 444, 105 S Ct 3346.
[61] 473 US 614 (1984) at 629.
[62] Ibid at 638.
[63] Ibid at 638.
[64] *Richardson* v *Mellish* (1824) 2 Bingham 229, 130 ER 294.
[65] 10 ER 359, (1853) 4 HL Cas 1.

which has a tendency to be injurious to the public, or against the public good". In the US, the most frequently cited definition on public policy was delivered by Justice Smith in *Parsons & Whittemore*.[66] In this case, Judge Smith stated that the refusal of enforcement of a foreign arbitral award on the basis of public policy is only allowed "where enforcement would violate the forum state's most basic notions of morality and justice".[67]

The term "public policy" is said to have three possible origins, namely domestic public policy, international public policy and transnational public policy.

Domestic public policy

On the domestic level, domestic public policy is frequently overlapped with mandatory rules to safeguard the most basic concepts of morality and justice of the domestic society. Therefore, Rubino-Sammartano pointed out the similarity between domestic public policy and mandatory rules in their intention is to maintain the national significance or basic interests, the principle of fundamental rules and the concepts of fairness, justice and morality, the exclusion or restrictions of the application of a foreign law, the refusal of recognition or enforcement of a foreign judgment and an arbitral award, the reflection of the concept and fundamental principle of politics, economics, society, law, morality and religion, and, finally, the compliance of the aim of national public policy in setting the mandatory rules.[68] However, it must be borne in mind that the public policy rule is mandatory, but not every mandatory rule forms part of public policy. Using the issue of arbitrability as an example, Böckstiegel said: "It may well be that such restrictions only have to be applied by arbitrators or courts if they form part of the law applicable to the dispute, but need not be considered as being so fundamental that they are part of the public policy of the state with the effect of having to be applied even if another law is applicable to the dispute."[69]

International public policy

The second type of public policy is international public policy which represents the basic notion of justice of morality of a group of nations. This type of public policy is invoked to highlight the unsuitability of the application of domestic public policy in international commercial arbitration. As Fouchard, Gaillard and Goldman stated: "Not every breach of a mandatory rule of the host country could justify refusing recognition

---

[66] *Parsons & Whittemore Overseas Co v RAKTA*, United States Court of Appeals for the Second Circuit, 23 December 1974, 508 F 2d 969.
[67] Ibid.
[68] M Rubino-Sammartano, *International Arbitration Law* (1990), p 291.
[69] K Böckstiegel, "Public Policy as a Limit to Arbitration and its Enforcement" (2008) IBA Journal of Dispute Resolution, Special Issue 1 at 4.

or enforcement of a foreign award. Such refusal is only justified where the award contravenes principles which are considered in the host country as reflecting its fundamental convictions, or as having an absolute, universal value."[70] This is because what may be a relevant public policy in one country may not apply in other countries. Considering the importance of the public policy issue at the various stages of international commercial arbitration, jurists feel that it is necessary to bring in the concept of international public policy in arbitration.

This trend can be witnessed in changes in the interpretation of Art V(2)(b) of the New York Convention, which has seen issues raised regarding the meaning of "public policy" used in the provision. Before the concept of international public policy was adapted, it was argued that the so-called public policy in Art V(2)(b) indicated domestic public policy as been seen in various older court cases on the recognition or enforcement of arbitral awards. However, most scholars now lend their support to the conception of international public policy and submit that, although Art V(2)(b) of the New York Convention is not exactly specific on this point, it is believed that the reference in this provision to public policy is actually a reference to the international public policy of the host jurisdiction.[71]

In the US, the most frequently cited definition of public policy was delivered by Justice Smith in *Parsons & Whittemore Overseas Inc v RAKTA*.[72] In this case, Justice Smith stated that the refusal of enforcement of a foreign arbitral award on the basis of public policy is allowed only "where enforcement would violate the forum state's most basic notions of morality and justice".[73]

Judge Joseph Smith in *Parsons & Whittemore*,[74] agreed with the arguments of a narrow interpretation of public policy defence and enforcement of an award may be rejected if it violates the forum State's most basic notions of morality and justice. To support his judgment, he stated that it is not national public policy that is to be considered and:

> "To comprehend the public policy defence as a parochial device that protects national political interests would seriously weaken the utility of the Convention. This provision was not provided to place the vagaries of international politics according to the rubric of 'public policy'. Rather, a restricted public policy doctrine was considered by the drafters of the Convention and every indication shows that the United States, in agreeing to the Convention, meant to support this supranational emphasis."[75]

---

[70] P Fouchard, E Gaillard and B Goldman, *Fouchard Gaillard Goldman on International Commercial Arbitration* (1999), p 996.
[71] Ibid at 996.
[72] Above n 66 at 969.
[73] Ibid.
[74] Ibid.
[75] Ibid.

This change can also be observed in Art 1502(5) of the New French Code of Civil Procedure (NCPC), which provides that "an appeal against a decision which grants recognition or enforcement is available ... where the recognition or enforcement is contrary to international public policy".[76]

Transnational public policy

Transnational public policy is about public policy in the form of the common principles of universal justice and the general principles of morality recognised by all civilised nations and applied in the international community as a whole.[77] It is also termed as "supranational public policy", "truly international public policy", "really international public policy", "genuinely international public policy", or *"ordre public réellement international"*. This type of public policy reflects, as Lew stated, "only the fundamental standards of the international community" and it "is developed common standards of national policies, as well as fundamental concepts which have been embodied in international Conventions or other international instruments".[78]

Hunter and Silva once said that transnational public policy contains the "principles that are commonly recognised by political and legal systems around the world".[79] Lalive also defined that the transnational public policy lies in the really international public policy of the law of the nations.[80] The examples include human or drug trafficking, breach of embargoes, corruptions and customs offences. Lord Steyn, in *Kuwait Airways Corp* v *Iraqi Airways Company (Nos 4 and 5)*, stated: "In recent years, particularly as a result of French scholarship, principles of international public policy (*l'ordre public véritablement international*) have been developed in relation to subjects such as traffic in drugs, traffic in weapons, terrorism and so forth ..."[81]

However, it is worth noting that not everybody embraces the idea of transnational public policy due to its lack of definition and rigorous proof. As Reisman pointed out:

> "[P]ublic policy in domestic law is a legal concept with a verifiable judicial history. Not so in international law. When an alleged international public

---

[76] B Hanotiau and O Caprasse, "Arbitrability, Due Process, and Public Policy Under Art V of the New York Convention – Belgian and French Perspectives" (2008) 25(6) Journal of International Arbitration 730.
[77] International Law Association, Report on Sixty Ninth Conference, London (2000), p 345.
[78] J Lew (ed), *Contemporary problems in international arbitration* (1987), p 83.
[79] M Hunter and G Silva, "Transnational public policy and its application in investment arbitration" (2003) 49(3) The Journal of World Investment 367.
[80] P Lalive, "Transnational (or truly international) Public Policy", VIII International Congress on Arbitration, ICCA (1986) Congress Series No 3, pp 295–296.
[81] [2002] 2 AC 883.

policy is given the force of law by an international commercial arbitral tribunal, it is not subject to the discipline of customary international law analysis, which requires that the state practice justifying the inference that a customary rule has been produced must be shown to be wide and extensive and to be accompanied by *opinio juris*. Without this discipline, the invocation of 'transnational public policy' becomes an easy way for those claiming to have an insight into the heart and the soul of international law to effect their own preferences without having to prove that they have become customary international law."[82]

Mandatory rules

Generally speaking, in international commercial arbitration, mandatory rules are the rules of law of a country which cannot be derogated from by the parties. Such mandatory rules are promulgated to ensure that the basic domestic notion of justice is carried out during the process. As Rubino-Sammartano said, with public interest in mind, mandatory rules "compulsorily apply to all relationships which have a connection with that legal system and which prevail on any contrary conflict of laws or rules".[83] For instance, mandatory rules can be asserted in different stages of arbitration, such as the execution of a contract, taking place of arbitration and enforcement of awards. Consequently, the relevant mandatory rules of the countries which can influence the arbitration proceedings and the results of arbitration are those which are the place of execution of a contract, the place of recognition and enforcement of an award and the states that are closely related to the contract.[84]

For instance, in accordance with Art V(1)(e) of the New York Convention, the recognition or enforcement of the award may be refused when an award "has been set aside or suspended by a competent authority of the country in which, or under the law of which, that award was made".

Among national laws, Art 595(6) of the Austrian Code of Civil Procedure provides: "If the award is incompatible with the basic principles of the Austrian legal system or if it infringes mandatory provisions of the law, the application of which cannot be set aside by a choice of law of the parties even in a case where a foreign contract according to Art 35 of

---

[82] W M Reisman, "International Public Policy (so-called) and Arbitral Choice in International Commercial Arbitration", ICCA Paper for delivery in Montreal, 3 June 2006 Accessed on 6 January 2009 at http://www.law.yale.edu/documents/pdf/reisman.icca_speech_for_montreal.6.15.06.pdf.

[83] M Rubino-Sammartano, *International Arbitration Law and Practice* (2nd edn, 2001), p 505.

[84] A F M Maniruzzaman, "International Arbitrator and Mandatory Public Law Rules in the Context of State Contracts: An Overview" (1990) 7(3) Journal of International Arbitration 63.

the International Private Law Act is involved." Article 3 of the French Civil Code provides: "The laws of police and public security bind all the inhabitants of the territory."

Article 176 of the Swiss Private International Law Act 1987 stipulates:

> "1. The provisions of this chapter shall apply to any arbitration if the seat of the arbitral tribunal is in Switzerland and if, at the time when the arbitration agreement was concluded, at least, one of the parties had neither its domicile nor its habitual residence in Switzerland.
> 2. The provisions of this chapter shall not apply where the parties have in writing excluded its application and agreed to the exclusive application of the procedural provisions of cantonal law relating to arbitration."

Mandatory rules in the Arbitration (Scotland) Act 2010

Section 6 of the Arbitration (Scotland) Act 2010 makes made it clear that every arbitration seated in Scotland, but where the parties have failed to specify the governing law, is governed by the Scots law in accordance with s 7. Among the Scottish Arbitration Rules, 36 of the rules are classified as mandatory rules, identified by an "M" at the end of the rule heading. These mandatory rules cannot be modified or disapplied by an arbitration agreement, by any other agreement between the parties or by any other means if an arbitration is seated in Scotland.[85]

To stress the importance of the mandatory rules, s 8 of the Act contains a long list including the following:

- r 3   Arbitrator to be an individual
- r 4   Eligibility to act as an arbitrator
- r 7   Failure of appointment procedure
- r 8   Duty to disclose any conflict of interests
- rr 12–16   Removal or resignation of arbitrator or dismissal of tribunal
- rr 19–21 and 23   Jurisdiction of tribunal
- rr 24 and 25   General duties of tribunal and parties
- r 42   Point of law referral: procedure etc
- r 44   Time limit variation: procedure etc
- r 45   Securing attendance of witnesses and disclosure of evidence
- r 48   Power to award payment and damages
- r 50   Interest
- r 54   Part awards
- r 56   Power to withhold award if fees or expenses not paid
- r 60   Arbitrators' fees and expenses
- r 63   Ban on pre-dispute agreements about liability for arbitration expenses

---

[85] Arbitration (Sc) Act 2010, s 8.

rr 67, 68, 70–72   Challenging awards
rr 73–75   Immunity
r 76   Loss of right to object
r 77   Independence of arbitrator
r 79   Death of arbitrator
r 82   Rules applicable to umpires

These mandatory rules take precedence over any arbitration agreement or agreement between the parties which contradicts those rules. An award may be liable to challenge and the arbitrator may be subject to removal or dismissal if the arbitration proceeding is not conducted in accordance with the mandatory rules.[86] The need for such a huge list of mandatory rules is said to be for public policy and to ensure the fairness and impartiality of the arbitration process.[87] It is said:

> "The mandatory rules are provided in key areas of the process to ensure the smooth and efficient running of an arbitration and to reduce the prospect of delay. If an arbitration is not conducted in accordance with the rules which apply to it (including all mandatory rules), the arbitrator may, depending on the breach, lay himself or herself open to removal and any award may be liable to challenge."[88]

Mandatory rules on commencement and constitution of tribunal etc

Rule 3 of the Scottish Arbitration Rules stipulate that an arbitrator must be an individual. Apart from the requirement of being a natural person, r 4 makes it mandatory that an arbitrator must be over 16 years old and a legally capable adult to act as an arbitrator within the meaning of s 1(6) of the Adults with Incapacity (Scotland) Act 2000.

To ensure that arbitration proceedings are not delayed by the lack of or objection to appointment of arbitrators, r 7 sets out the mandatory rule to be followed in relation to the appointment of the tribunal.[89] To initiate the appointment procedures, both parties can refer the dispute to an arbitral appointment referee who will be in charge of the appointment matters.[90] However, the referring party must give notice of the reference to the other party.[91] Within 7 days of receiving the notice of reference, the other party may make an objection to the referring party[92] and the arbitral appointment referee.[93] If no such objection is

---

[86] Revised Explanatory Notes (2009), para 30.
[87] Policy Memorandum, 29 January 2009, para 82.
[88] Ibid, para 83.
[89] Scottish Arbitration Rules, r 7(1). Similar provision can be seen in ss 17–18 of the (English) Arbitration Act 1996.
[90] Scottish Arbitration Rules, r 7(2).
[91] Ibid, r 7(3).
[92] Ibid, r 7(4)(a).
[93] Ibid, r 7(4)(b).

made within the 7-day period[94] or the other party waives the right to object[95] before the end of the 7-day period, the arbitral appointments referee may make the necessary appointment. If a party objects to the referee making an appointment,[96] the referee fails to make an appointment within 21 days of a referral[97] or the parties agree not to use a referee,[98] any party can apply to the court to make the necessary appointment. To avoid further delay, such an appointment made by the court is final[99] and must take into account the nature and subject matter of the dispute,[100] the terms of the arbitration agreement,[101] especially any terms relating to appointment of arbitrators, and the attributes (such as suitability in relation to skills, qualifications, knowledge and experience) of the appointee.[102] Rule 7(8) provides that an appointment made by the arbitral appointments referee will have the same effect as if made with the agreement of the parties, even if the composition of the tribunal or a single arbitrator appointed by the referee differs from the arbitration agreement.[103]

To avoid any disputes relating to the arbitrator's independence and impartiality arising at a later stage, r 8 imposes upon arbitrators[104] or prospective arbitrators[105] a mandatory duty to disclose to the parties any circumstances known or becoming known to the individual which might reasonably be considered relevant when considering whether the individual is impartial or independent.[106] In the case where an individual has not yet been appointed as an arbitrator, the disclosure must be made to any arbitral appointments referee, other third party or to the courts in charge of appointment. It is clear that such arbitrator's duty of disclosure is a continuous one throughout the arbitral proceedings. The court can take a failure to do so into consideration as regards arbitrator's expenses when removing them in accordance with r 75. However, it is worth noting that the mandatory effect of the rule only requires disclosure on the arbitrator's part. Parties can choose to ignore disclosure on the issue of independence and carry on the proceedings with the appointed or to be appointed arbitrators if the parties have no concerns over the issue of impartiality. The result of such choice is that "[a] challenge

---

[94] Scottish Arbitration Rules, r 7(5)(a).
[95] Ibid, r 7(5)(b).
[96] Ibid, r 7(6)(a).
[97] Ibid, r 7(6)(b).
[98] Ibid, r 7(6)(c).
[99] Ibid, r 7(7).
[100] Ibid, r 7(8)(a).
[101] Ibid, r 7(8)(b).
[102] Ibid, r 7(8)(c).
[103] Ibid, r 7(9) and Revised Explanatory Notes (2009), para 111.
[104] Scottish Arbitration Rules, r 8(1)(a).
[105] Ibid, r 8(1)(b).
[106] Ibid, r 8(2)(a).

to that arbitrator, or an award would only be successful if substantial injustice is shown to have resulted in lack of impartiality, independence or fairness, which may be unlikely in the event of disclosure where the parties have agreed to proceed".[107]

Rules 12, 13 and 14 make provision for the removal and dismissal of the arbitrator or tribunal by the court. Rule 12 provides that the Outer House may remove an individual arbitrator if satisfied on the application by any party that (a) the arbitrator is not impartial and independent,[108] (b) the arbitrator has not treated the parties fairly,[109] (c) the arbitrator is incapable of acting as an arbitrator in the arbitration (or that there are justifiable doubts about the arbitrator's ability to so act),[110] (d) the arbitrator does not have the qualification which the parties agreed before the appointment that the arbitrator must have,[111] (e) substantial injustice has been or will be caused to that party because the arbitrator has failed to conduct the arbitration in accordance with the arbitration agreement, the applicable Scottish Arbitration Rules or any other agreement by the parties relating to conduct of the arbitration.[112] In relation to the arbitral tribunal, the Outer House has the mandatory power to dismiss the entire tribunal if the tribunal has failed to conduct the arbitration in accordance with the parties' agreement,[113] the Scottish Arbitration Rules (such as conducting proceedings without unnecessary delay)[114] or agreed procedure,[115] and substantial injustice has been caused due to such a failure. Though the Outer House's power in removing or dismissing arbitrators is final,[116] such powers can be exercised only if the arbitrator or tribunal has been notified of the application for removal or dismissal and given the opportunity to make representations and any other available recourse to the tribunal has been exhausted.[117] To avoid the tactic of delaying or frustrating arbitration, r 14(3) allows the arbitration to continue while the objection is heard by the Outer House.[118]

Rules 15 and 16 set out to replace the common law restrictions on resignation by an arbitrator and provide the mandatory rules governing arbitrator's resignation and the consequential liability. According to r 15, an arbitrator is allowed to resign if they wish to do so. Such resignation

---

[107] Revised Explanatory Notes (2009), para 114.
[108] Scottish Arbitration Rules, r 12(a). Similar provision can be seen in s 24 of the (English) Arbitration Act 1996.
[109] Scottish Arbitration Rules, r 12(b).
[110] Ibid, r 12(c).
[111] Ibid, r 12(d).
[112] Ibid, r 12(e).
[113] Ibid, r 13(a).
[114] Ibid, r 13(b).
[115] Ibid, r 13(c).
[116] Ibid, r 14(2).
[117] Ibid, r 14(1)(b)(i)–(ii).
[118] Revised Explanatory Notes (2009), para 122.

can be carried out if the parties consent to it,[119] if the arbitrator's appointment is challenged under r 10 or r 12,[120] if the parties disapply or modify r 34(1) relating to expert opinions after the appointment of arbitrators,[121] or if the Outer House has authorised the resignation when it is satisfied that such resignation is reasonable.[122]

Mandatory rules on jurisdiction of tribunal

Adapting the international accepted principle of competence-competence, r 19 offers the arbitrator a mandatory power to rule on his own jurisdiction, such as the issues of validity of arbitration agreement,[123] the constitution of the tribunal[124] and the scope of submission.[125] Any objection to the tribunal's jurisdiction must be made as soon as is reasonably practicable after the matter is first raised in the arbitration,[126] or such later time as the tribunal allows.[127] If the objection is upheld by the tribunal, the tribunal must end the proceedings[128] and set aside any partial or provisional awards made.[129] If a final award has been made, the party shall appeal under r 67. Once the objection is raised, the parties can agree whether the tribunal shall rule on this issue first[130] or delay such a ruling.[131] If the parties opt for delaying the ruling, any appeal will have to be made as a jurisdictional appeal against an award under r 67 rather than as appeal against the decision on the objection to jurisdiction.[132] Once the tribunal makes a decision on the jurisdictional objection, the parties have the mandatory rights of 14 days to appeal against the decision to the Outer House[133] for the final decision[134] on this matter. While the appeal is pending, the tribunal can carry on

---

[119] Scottish Arbitration Rules, r 15(1)(a). Similar provision can be seen in s 25(1) of the (English) Arbitration Act 1996.
[120] Scottish Arbitration Rules, r 15(1)(c).
[121] Ibid, r 15(1)(d).
[122] Ibid, r 15(1)(e) and (2). Similar provision can be seen in s 25(4) of the (English) Arbitration Act 1996.
[123] Scottish Arbitration Rules, r 19(a). Similar provision can be seen in s 30 of the (English) Arbitration Act 1996.
[124] Scottish Arbitration Rules, r 19(b).
[125] Ibid, r 19(c).
[126] Ibid, r 20(2)(a).
[127] Ibid, r 20(2)(b). Similar provision can be seen in s 31 of the (English) Arbitration Act 1996.
[128] Scottish Arbitration Rules, r 20(3)(a).
[129] Ibid, r 20(3)(b).
[130] Ibid, r 20(4)(a).
[131] Ibid, r 20(4)(b).
[132] Revised Explanatory Notes, para 131.
[133] Scottish Arbitration Rules, r 21(1). Relevant provision can be seen in s 30(2) of the (English) Arbitration Act 1996.
[134] Scottish Arbitration Rules, r 21(3).

with the arbitration proceedings.[135] The parties are at liberty to contract out of r 22 relating to the referral of point of jurisdiction to the Outer House. If the parties decide to opt out of r 22, r 23 will not apply. On the other hand, if the parties failed to do so, the parties have to follow the mandatory procedures provided in r 23 on parties' application for a referral of point of jurisdiction when they apply to the Outer House to determine this issue.[136]

Mandatory rules on general duties

Corresponding with rr 8 and 10, r 24 imposes mandatory duties on an arbitrator to be impartial, independent[137] and fair.[138] Arbitrators are also required to conduct the arbitration without unnecessary delay and without incurring unnecessary expense.[139] Similar mandatory duties are also imposed on the parties under r 25.

Mandatory rules on powers of court in relation to arbitral proceedings

Similar to r 23, rr 42 and 44 were added to the Act in the final stage to be presented to the Parliament. Rule 42 only applies to the referral of point of law if the parties decide not to exclude the default rule in r 41. According to r 42, on an application by any party, the Outer House may decide any point of Scots law arising in the arbitration. However, such an application is valid only if the parties consent to have such an application made or if the arbitrators agree to the application on the grounds that there will be substantial saving in expenses,[140] the application was made without delay[141] and there are good reasons for such application.[142]

Rule 43 is a default rule which allows the court on the application of the tribunal or any party to vary time limits agreed by the parties. If the parties decide not to exclude r 43, r 44 makes it mandatory that the court will make such variation only if the court is satisfied that no arbitral process for varying the time limit is available,[143] and someone would suffer a substantial injustice if no variation was made.[144]

---

[135] Scottish Arbitration Rules, r 21(2).
[136] Ibid, r 24(2).
[137] Ibid, r 24(1)(a). Similar provision can be seen in s 33 of the (English) Arbitration Act 1996.
[138] Scottish Arbitration Rules, r 24(1)(b).
[139] Ibid, r 24(1)(c)(i)–(ii).
[140] Ibid, r 42(2)(b)(i). Similar provision can be seen in s 45(2) of the (English) Arbitration Act 1996.
[141] Scottish Arbitration Rules, r 42(2)(b)(ii).
[142] Ibid, r 42(2)(b)(iii).
[143] Ibid, r 44(2)(a).
[144] Ibid, r 44(2)(b).

Similar to the issue of jurisdictional referrals and point of law referrals, the court's decision on time limit variation is final.[145] The tribunal may continue with the arbitration pending the determination of the application.[146]

In relation to the court's power to order attendance of witnesses and disclosure of evidence, under r 45, the court, upon an application by the tribunal or any party, has the same power in arbitration proceedings as it would have in ordinary civil proceedings to order the attendance of a witness or the taking of evidence[147] or to order the disclosure of documents or other material evidence.[148] However, if a person is entitled to refuse to give evidence or disclose information in civil proceedings, then the courts may not make such an order.[149] Any decision made by the court is final[150] and the arbitration proceedings can continue pending the determination of the application.[151]

Mandatory rules on awards – rr 48, 50, 54 and 56

Rule 48 is a mandatory rule which gives the tribunal the power to award payment and damages in the form of a sum of money.[152] The tribunal's decision to award payment and damages has to be specified in the currency agreed by the parties. In the absence of the agreement the tribunal will determine the currency it deems appropriate.[153] Although the tribunal is empowered to award payment and damages, it is no way an obligation imposed on the tribunal to award damages.[154]

The tribunal is also empowered to award interest under r 50, which is mandatory in nature. Similar to the power to award damages, the tribunal is not obliged to do so. The tribunal's power to award interest to be paid covers both the pre-arbitration[155] and post-arbitration[156] periods. The interest rate[157] and the periods[158] for which interest is to

---

[145] Scottish Arbitration Rules, r 44(5).
[146] *Ibid*, r 44(4).
[147] *Ibid*, r 45(1)(a). Similar provision can be seen in s 43 of the (English) Arbitration Act 1996.
[148] Scottish Arbitration Rules, r 45(1)(b).
[149] *Ibid*, r 45(2).
[150] *Ibid*, r 45(4).
[151] *Ibid*, r 45(3).
[152] *Ibid*, r 48(1). Similar provision can be seen in s 48(4) of the (English) Arbitration Act 1996.
[153] Scottish Arbitration Rules, r 48(2).
[154] Revised Explanatory Notes (2009), para 183.
[155] Scottish Arbitration Rules, r 50(1)(a). Similar provision can be seen in s 50 of the (English) Arbitration Act 1996.
[156] *Ibid*, r 50(1)(b).
[157] *Ibid*, r 50(2)(a).
[158] *Ibid*, r 50(2)(c).

be paid will have to be specified in the award ordering payment of interest. An award may make different provision in respect of different amounts.[159] Rule 50(4) provides the manner of calculating interest. In principle, the tribunal has to follow the parties' agreement on the method of calculation. In the absence of agreement, the tribunal will decide the appropriate method. Subject to the parties' agreement, compound interest may be awarded.[160]

Rule 54 offers the tribunal the mandatory power to make more than one award on different aspects of the matters to be determined[161] as well as partial awards dealing with some of the matters which the tribunal is required to decide.[162] However, the tribunal must specify the matters to which the partial award is related to.[163]

Rule 56 offers the tribunal the mandatory power to withhold the award if any fees and expenses due to the tribunal are not paid in full.[164] However, the parties are allowed to apply to the court to order the delivery of the award if the applicant makes payment into the court of an amount equal to the fees and expenses demanded by the tribunal. Such an order is final[165] and can be made only if the applicant has exhausted any available arbitral process of appeal or review of the amount of the fees and expenses demanded.[166] If the applicant party decides to pay the fees and expenses in full first in order to obtain the award, he may have to demand payment of the other party's share separately from the other party or parties to the arbitration.[167] Once the amount is paid into the court, the court will decide how the fees and expenses properly payable are to be determined to pay the tribunal and these are met from the fund in court.[168] Any balance will be refunded to the applicant.[169] It is said that this provision is designed to provide assistance to a party who considers the fees to be excessive and wants them reviewed, but not a party who considers the tribunal's fees are excessive where the other party has already paid the tribunal's fees.[170]

---

[159] Scottish Arbitration Rules, r 50(3).
[160] Revised Explanatory Notes (2009), para 185.
[161] Scottish Arbitration Rules, r 54(1). Similar provision can be seen in s 47 of the (English) Arbitration Act 1996.
[162] Scottish Arbitration Rules, r 54(2).
[163] *Ibid*, r 54(3).
[164] *Ibid*, r 56(1). Similar provision can be seen in s 56 of the (English) Arbitration Act 1996.
[165] Scottish Arbitration Rules, r 56(4).
[166] *Ibid*, r 56(3).
[167] Revised Explanatory Notes (2009), para 194.
[168] Scottish Arbitration Rules, r 56(2)(b).
[169] *Ibid*, r 56(2)(c).
[170] Revised Explanatory Notes (2009), para 194.

Mandatory rules on arbitration expenses – rr 60 and 63

Corresponding with r 56, r 60 makes it mandatory for the parties to be severally liable for the fees to the arbitrators[171] or any arbitral appointments referee,[172] or any other third party to whom the parties give powers in relation to the arbitration.[173] The fees and expenses due to arbitrators can be the fees and expenses incurred for conducting the arbitration,[174] the expenses incurred personally by the arbitrators when conducting the arbitration,[175] and the expenses incurred by the tribunal when conducting the arbitration, such as the fees and expenses of any clerk, agent, employee or other person appointed by the tribunal to assist it in conducting the arbitration, the fees and expenses of any experts from whom the tribunal obtains an opinion, any expenses in respect of meeting and hearing facilities, and any expenses incurred in determining recoverable arbitration expenses.[176] Rule 60(3) provides a right for any party, arbitrator, arbitral appointments referee or other third party to apply for the fees and expenses to be fixed by the Auditor of Court of Session who will consider a reasonable commercial rate of charge[177] and reasonable amount of expenses.[178] The Auditor of the Court may order the repayment of any fees or expenses already paid if he deems them excessive.[179]

Designed to protect the weaker party in an unequal bargaining position, r 63 stipulates that a party can be liable to pay the whole or any part of the expenses of arbitration only if the agreement on expenses is made after the dispute in question arises.[180] However, this mandatory rule does not apply to the deposit paid to an institution.[181]

Mandatory rules on challenging awards – rr 67, 68 and 70–72

While r 19 gives the arbitrator a mandatory power to rule on the issue of jurisdiction, r 67 offers the party a mandatory right to apply to the court to challenge the arbitrator's decision on his own jurisdiction. This is termed "a jurisdictional appeal" in r 67(1). Once the party appeals against the arbitrator's decision on jurisdiction to the Outer House,

---

[171] Scottish Arbitration Rules, r 60(1). Similar provision can be seen in s 59 of the (English) Arbitration Act 1996.
[172] Scottish Arbitration Rules, r 60(2)(a).
[173] Ibid, r 60(2)(b).
[174] Ibid, r 60(1)(a)(i).
[175] Ibid, r 60(1)(a)(ii).
[176] Ibid, r 60(1)(b)(i)–(iv).
[177] Ibid, r 60(4)(a).
[178] Ibid, r 60(4)(b).
[179] Ibid, r 60(5).
[180] Revised Explanatory Notes (2009), para 214.
[181] Ibid, para 215.

the court has a legal duty to decide whether to confirm the award,[182] vary the award (or part of it),[183] or set aside the award (or part of it).[184] If the Outer House is satisfied that the proposed appeal would raise an important point of principle or practice[185] or there is another compelling reason for the Inner House to consider the appeal,[186] the court can give the party leave to appeal. Once the leave is given, an appeal may be made to the Inner House against the Outer House's decision on a jurisdictional appeal.[187] Both the Outer House's decision on whether to grant such leave[188] and the Inner House's decision on such an appeal[189] is final. However, it has been pointed out that any appeal under r 67 is subject to the limits on review in r 71(2) and (4), which will be discussed below.[190]

Rule 68 is about "serious irregularity appeal". This provision allows the parties a mandatory right to challenge the arbitral awards if any serious irregularity can be proven.[191] The serious irregularity includes irregularity which has caused or will cause substantial injustice to the appellant, such as:

(a) the tribunal failing to conduct the arbitration in accordance with the arbitration agreement or the Scottish Arbitration Rules, or any other agreement by the parties relating to conduct of the arbitration,[192]

(b) the tribunal acting outwith its powers (other than by exceeding its jurisdiction),[193]

(c) the tribunal failing to deal with all the issues that were put to it,[194]

(d) any arbitral appointments referee or other third party to whom the parties give powers in relation to the arbitration acting outwith powers,[195]

(e) uncertainty or ambiguity as to the award's effect,[196]

(f) the award being contrary to public policy, or obtained by fraud or in a way which is contrary to public policy,[197]

---

[182] Scottish Arbitration Rules, r 67(2)(a). Similar provision can be seen in s 67 of the (English) Arbitration Act 1996.
[183] Scottish Arbitration Rules, r 67(2)(b).
[184] *Ibid*, r 67(2)(c).
[185] *Ibid*, r 67(5)(a).
[186] *Ibid*, r 67(5)(b).
[187] *Ibid*, r 67(3).
[188] *Ibid*, r 67(6).
[189] *Ibid*, r 67(7).
[190] Revised Explanatory Notes (2009), para 220.
[191] Scottish Arbitration Rules, r 68(1). Similar provision can be seen in s 68 of the (English) Arbitration Act 1996.
[192] Scottish Arbitration Rules, r 68(2)(a)(i)–(iii).
[193] *Ibid*, r 68(2)(b).
[194] *Ibid*, r 68(2)(c).
[195] *Ibid*, r 68(2)(d).
[196] *Ibid*, r 68(2)(e).
[197] *Ibid*, r 68(2)(f)(i) and (ii).

(g) an arbitrator having not been impartial and independent,[198]
(h) an arbitrator having not treated the parties fairly,[199]
(i) an arbitrator having been incapable of acting as an arbitrator in the arbitration (or there being justifiable doubts about an arbitrator's ability to so act),[200]
(j) an arbitrator not having a qualification which the parties agreed (before the arbitrator's appointment) that the arbitrator must have,[201] or
(k) any other irregularity in the conduct of the arbitration or in the award which is admitted by the tribunal, or any arbitral appointments referee or other third party to whom the parties give powers in relation to the arbitration.[202]

As in r 65, the decision made by the court is final.[203] This limited list of irregularities is designed to guard against vexatious or frivolous appeals brought by parties whose intention is to delay the arbitration proceedings.

Another ground allowing the parties to challenge the award is legal error appeal stipulated in r 69. Rule 69 is designed to be a default rule and parties are free to exclude the challenge against the award on the ground of the tribunal's error on a point of Scots law. However, if the parties decide to apply or include r 69 in their agreement, then r 70 becomes a mandatory rule regulating the procedures involving a legal error appeal. According to the provision, the appeal can be made with the leave of the Outer House.[204] Alternatively, the parties can agree to appeal against the award (such an agreement usually exists in the arbitration clause) in order to bypass the hurdle to apply for leave to appeal on the grounds of legal error.[205] Leave can be given only if the Outer House is satisfied that the legal error substantially affects a party's rights[206] and the tribunal was already asked to decide on this point,[207] and the tribunal's decision on the point was obviously wrong[208] or is open to serious doubt.[209] The applicant party must identify the point of law at issue[210] and state the

---

[198] Scottish Arbitration Rules, r 68(2)(g).
[199] *Ibid*, r 68(2)(h).
[200] *Ibid*, r 68(2)(i).
[201] *Ibid*, r 68(2)(j).
[202] *Ibid*, r 68(2)(k).
[203] *Ibid*, r 68(7)–(8).
[204] *Ibid*, r 70(2)(b). Similar provision can be seen in s 69(2), (4), (7) and (8) of the (English) Arbitration Act 1996.
[205] Scottish Arbitration Rules, r 70(2)(a).
[206] *Ibid*, r 70(3)(a).
[207] *Ibid*, r 70(3)(b).
[208] *Ibid*, r 70(3)(c)(i).
[209] *Ibid*, r 70(3)(c)(ii).
[210] *Ibid*, r 70(4)(a).

reason for such an application for leave.[211] To avoid delay, any leave to appeal against legal error expires 7 days after it is granted.[212] The Outer House has the final decision on whether to grant such leave.[213] If the leave is granted, the Outer House may decide to confirm the award,[214] order the tribunal to reconsider the award[215] or set aside the award[216] if the appellant party brings the appeal before the leave expires. An appeal may be made to the Inner House against the Outer House's decision on a legal error appeal made under r 70(8)[217] but the Inner House's decision on such an appeal is final.[218]

In the case of jurisdictional appeals under r 67, serious irregularity appeals under r 68 or legal error appeals under rr 69 and 70, it is mandatory for the appellant to prove to the courts that he has exhausted any available arbitral process of appeal or review, which includes any recourse available under r 58.[219] The appellant party must bring an appeal within 28 days after the award being appealed against is made,[220] after the tribunal decides whether to correct the award if it is subject to a correction process under r 58,[221] or after the appellant was notified of the result of an arbitral process of appeal or review.[222] Once the appellant decides to make an appeal, he has a mandatory legal duty to give notice of appeal to the other party and the tribunal.[223] As with most arbitration laws, the tribunal may continue with the arbitration proceedings while the appeal is pending.[224] During the appeal the court may order an appellant to provide security for the expenses of the appeal,[225] or order any amount due under an award being appealed to be paid in court or secured[226] and dismiss the appeal,[227] order the tribunal to state its reasons[228] or order additional expenses arising from the order.[229] One

---

[211] Scottish Arbitration Rules, r 70(4)(b).
[212] *Ibid*, r 70(7).
[213] *Ibid*, r 70(6).
[214] *Ibid*, r 70(8)(a).
[215] *Ibid*, r 70(8)(b).
[216] *Ibid*, r 70(8)(c).
[217] *Ibid*, r 70(8).
[218] *Ibid*, r 70(12).
[219] *Ibid*, r 71(2). Similar provision can be seen in s 70 of the (English) Arbitration Act 1996.
[220] Scottish Arbitration Rules, r 71(4)(a).
[221] *Ibid*, r 71(4)(b).
[222] *Ibid*, r 71(4)(c).
[223] *Ibid*, r 71(6).
[224] *Ibid*, r 71(7).
[225] *Ibid*, r 71(10)(a).
[226] *Ibid*, r 71(12)(a).
[227] *Ibid*, r 71(10)(b) and (12)(b).
[228] *Ibid*, r 71(8)(a).
[229] *Ibid*, r 71(8)(b).

very interesting mandatory provision is r 71(9), which offers the courts mandatory power to order that provision in an arbitration agreement which prevents the bringing of legal proceedings in relation to the subject matter of the award (or that part of it) is void if the courts decide to uphold the appeal by setting aside the award (or part of it).[230]

Rule 72(1) provides the courts, during the serious irregularity or legal error appeals, a mandatory power to order the tribunal to reconsider its decision and make a new award within 3 months or any period directed by the courts after the decision or the appeal against the decision is made by the court. Also, the Scottish Arbitration Rules still apply to the new award as they apply in relation to the appealed award.[231]

Mandatory rule on miscellaneous provisions – rr 73–77, 79 and 82

The Scottish Arbitration Rules expressly offer mandatory protection for the arbitrators, appointing arbitral institutions, experts, witnesses and legal representatives. To ensure that the arbitrators are not compromised by a lack of immunity, arbitrators and their clerks, agents, employees or anybody assisting the tribunal to perform its tasks enjoy immunity from actions for damages and are not liable for anything done or omitted in their performance or purported performance of their functions.[232] However, such "almost" absolute immunity is subject to the exceptions of bad faith and resignation. In other words, no immunity will be offered if the act or omission is shown to have been in bad faith.[233] Liability can still be upheld if it arises from their resignation.[234] However, the latter exception is subject to the Outer House's decision on the tribunal's entitlement under r 16(1)(c).

For the arbitral appointment referees, their agents and employees, subject to the bad faith exception,[235] they are neither liable for anything done or omitted in the performance, or purported performance, of that function, nor liable for the acts or omissions of the arbitrators appointed or the tribunal of which such an arbitrator forms part. This immunity is also extended to any omission or acts of the clerk, agent, or employee of that tribunal.[236]

---

[230] Scottish Arbitration Rules, r 71(9).
[231] *Ibid*, r 72(2). Relevant provisions can be seen in ss 69(7)(c) and 68(3)(a) of the (English) Arbitration Act 1996.
[232] Scottish Arbitration Rules, r 73(1) and (3). Similar provision can be seen in s 29 of the (English) Arbitration Act 1996.
[233] Scottish Arbitration Rules, r 73(2)(a).
[234] *Ibid*, r 73(2)(b).
[235] *Ibid*, r 74(1)(a). Similar provision can be seen in s 74 of the (English) Arbitration Act 1996.
[236] Scottish Arbitration Rules, r 74(1).

Believing that experts, witnesses and the parties' legal representatives are placed in a vulnerable position in private arbitration proceedings; r 75 extends immunity to anybody participating in an arbitration as an expert, witness or legal representative for any acts or omissions done during the arbitration proceedings. This is similar to the protection offered in civil proceedings.

Rule 76 sets out the grounds which may compromise arbitrators or the arbitration proceedings and the consequential rights the parties have under such grounds. A party must raise a timeous objection if he is aware of: the ineligibility of the arbitrators; lack of impartiality, independence and jurisdiction of arbitrators; unfair treatment; failure to carry out the proceedings according to the arbitration agreement, the relevant Scottish Arbitration Rules, or any other agreements between the parties; and serious irregularities.[237] As a result of failing to do so and of further participation in the arbitration proceedings, a party may not be allowed to raise the objection later before the arbitral tribunal or the court.[238] The requirement of "timeous" is defined as "as soon as reasonably practicable after the circumstances giving rise to the ground for objection first arose".[239] A later date for objection may be allowed if it is stipulated in the arbitration agreement,[240] the Scottish Rules,[241] consented to by the other party,[242] or allowed by the tribunal where it considers that circumstances justify a later objection.[243] Nevertheless, the timeous requirement does not apply if the party did not know of the ground for objection[244] and could not have discovered that ground with reasonable diligence.[245] Finally, a party cannot raise a timely objection on matter which it is not allowed to object to.[246]

It is also mandatory for the arbitrators to maintain their independence. If the arbitrator's relationship with any party, the arbitrator's financial or other commercial interests or anything else gives rise to justifiable doubts as to the arbitrator's impartiality, an arbitrator will be regarded as lacking independence.[247]

---

[237] Scottish Arbitration Rules, r 76(1)(a)–(f). Similar provision can be seen in s 73 of the (English) Arbitration Act 1996.
[238] Scottish Arbitration Rules, r 76(1).
[239] Ibid, r 76(2)(a).
[240] Ibid, r 76(2)(b)(i).
[241] Ibid, r 76(2)(b)(ii).
[242] Ibid, r 76(2)(b)(iii).
[243] Ibid, r 76(2)(c).
[244] Ibid, r 76(3)(a).
[245] Ibid, r 76(3)(b).
[246] Ibid, r 76(4).
[247] Ibid, r 77(a)–(c). Relevant provisions can be seen in ss 24(1)(a) and 33(1) of the (English) Arbitration Act 1996.

Rule 79 is mandatory and stipulates that an arbitrator's authority is personal and ceases on his death.[248] The final mandatory provision contained in the Scottish Arbitration Rules is r 82, which is designed to clarify the application of certain specific Scottish Arbitration Rules to umpires.[249]

---

[248] Scottish Arbitration Rules, r 7. Similar provision can be seen in s 26 of the (English) Arbitration Act 1996.

[249] Rules 4, 8, 10–14, 24, 26, 59, 60, 61(1), 68, 73 and 76–79 remain mandatory in disputes decided by the umpires.

CHAPTER 6

COMMENCEMENT OF ARBITRATION PROCEEDINGS AND CONSTITUTION OF TRIBUNAL

GENERAL

To resolve disputes between the parties, it is essential to provide for how the aggrieved party should initiate the arbitration proceedings, as well as how an arbitral tribunal should be appointed. Without a clear indication on the timing for the commencement, the parties may easily argue that the arbitration proceedings have not started: consequently, this will have a knock-on effect on the relevant issues of prescription and limitation later on. It is also necessary to have a system in place to appoint the arbitral tribunal either by the parties or by default rules. Part I of the Scottish Arbitration Rules contain both mandatory and default rules governing the commencement of arbitration; the composition of the arbitral tribunal; the procedures to be followed in the failure of appointment of the tribunal; the arbitrator's duty to declare any conflict of interest which may affect the parties' opinions on the relevant appointment; and the procedures to follow in the event of removal of the arbitrator by the parties and by the court; the resignation of arbitrators; the liability of an arbitrator when his tenure ends; and the reconstitution of the arbitral tribunal after the removal, resignation or death of arbitrators.

COMMENCEMENT OF ARBITRATION – r 1

The draftsmen of the Arbitration (Scotland) Act 2010 deliberately provided a simple means of commencing arbitration.[1] According to r 1, arbitration begins on the service of notice by one of the parties submitting the dispute to arbitration or by a third party through or under a party to the arbitration agreement: for instance, a third party will gain the right to initiate arbitration through assignment or changes in a

---

[1] Policy Memorandum, 29 January 2009, at para 122.

group of companies.² This straightforward provision takes the consultees' opinion into account and is designed to remove any potential issues which may arise from the original proposal of "an intention to submit a dispute to arbitration" in the consultation paper. Since r 1 is a default rule, parties' agreement to modify or disapply r 1 will apply if they agree that other alternatives should be used as the commencement of arbitration in the arbitration agreement, such as a specific date. Similar wording can be seen in Art 21 of the UNCITRAL Model Law[3] and in Art 3(1) and (2) of the UNCITRAL Arbitration Rules 1985[4] which provides:

> "1. The party initiating recourse to arbitration shall give to the other party a notice of arbitration. 2. Arbitral proceedings shall be deemed to commence on the date on which the notice of arbitration is received by the respondent."

For arbitrations conducted under the ICC Arbitration Rules,[5] the Vienna Rules[6] and the LCIA Arbitration Rules,[7] arbitration is deemed to be commenced on the date which the request for arbitration sent by claimant is received by the Secretariat.

The (English) Arbitration Act 1996 has more detailed discussion on the issue of commencement of arbitration. While upholding the parties' right to mutually agree how arbitral proceedings are to be regarded as commenced,[8] failing such agreement, the timing of commencement depends whether the arbitrator is named or designated in the arbitration agreement, and whether the appointment is to be made by the parties or by a third party. If the arbitrator is named or designed in the arbitration agreement, arbitral proceedings are commenced in respect of a matter when one party serves on the other party, or parties, a notice in writing requiring him, or them, to submit that matter to the person so named or designated.[9] If the arbitrator, or arbitrators, is or are to be appointed by the parties, arbitral proceedings are commenced in respect of a matter when one party serves on the other party, or parties, notice in writing requiring him, or them, to appoint an arbitrator or to agree

---

[2] Revised Explanatory Notes 2009, para 101.
[3] UNCITRAL Model Law 1985 (2006 amendment).
[4] General Assembly Resolution 31/98.
[5] International Chamber of Commerce, Rules of Arbitration 1998 (ICC Arbitration Rules), Art 4(2).
[6] Rules of Arbitration and Conciliation of the International Arbitral Centre of the Austrian Federal Economic Chamber (Vienna Rules) 2006, Art 9(1).
[7] Arbitration Rules of the London Court of International Arbitration 1998 ("LCIA Arbitration Rules"), Arts 1.1 and 1.2. The administrative body to receive the request is called "the Registrar".
[8] (English) Arbitration Act 1996, s 14(1).
[9] *Ibid*, s 14(3).

to the appointment of an arbitrator in respect of that matter.[10] In the event that the arbitrator, or arbitrators, is or are to be appointed by a person other than a party to the proceedings, arbitral proceedings are commenced in respect of a matter when one party gives notice in writing to that person requesting him to make the appointment in respect of that matter.[11]

APPOINTMENT OF TRIBUNAL – r 2

Appointment

Under the Scottish Arbitration Rules, the parties may agree among themselves as to who the arbitrator should be, and such an agreement will prevail. However, if the parties fail to agree on or to provide the details of the appointment, rr 2, 6 and 7 are designed to fill in such gaps and take arbitration forward. This design is important to the dispute resolution process: as the draftsmen pointed out, this provision is enacted so as to remedy the vacuum[12] left in ss 2 and 3 of the Arbitration (Scotland) Act 1894 and the common law. Furthermore, it is "essential that a system is in place to facilitate the swift appointment of a single arbitrator or an arbitral tribunal composed of several members to allow the arbitration to proceed quickly and efficiently".[13]

According to r 2, an arbitration agreement need not specify the names of the arbitrators or the details of the appointment. However, if the parties decide to provide such details in the agreement then it must specify who is to form the tribunal; require the parties to appoint the tribunal; permit another person to appoint the tribunal; and provide for the tribunal to be appointed in any other way.[14] In the event that such information is not provided, r 2 (a default rule) will fill in the gaps by providing that, where a sole arbitrator is to be appointed, the parties must appoint an eligible individual jointly within 28 days of either party requesting the other to do so.[15] If there is to be a tribunal consisting of two or more arbitrators, each party must appoint an eligible individual as an arbitrator within 28 days of either party requesting the other to do so.[16] The two arbitrators appointed by the parties shall appoint eligible individuals as the remaining arbitrators.[17]

---

[10] (English) Arbitration Act 1996, s 14(4).
[11] *Ibid*, s 14(5).
[12] It failed to provide a procedure to be followed in the cases where both parties failed or could not perform the appointment of arbitrators.
[13] Policy Memorandum, 29 January 2009, para 124.
[14] Scottish Arbitration Rules, r 2(a)–(d).
[15] *Ibid*, r 6(a).
[16] *Ibid*, r 6(b)(i).
[17] *Ibid*, r 6(b)(ii).

The imposition of a shorter time limit for making appointment is generally in line with international practice. For instance, both the UNCITRAL Model Law[18] and the Arbitration Rules[19] impose a 30-day time limit upon the parties as well as a 60-day time limit upon the appointing authority in appointing arbitrators in the case of the UNCITRAL Arbitration Rules.[20] In the case of institutional arbitration, the 30-day time limit is set for some institutions[21] or the parties[22] to appoint the arbitrator.

Apart from time limits, some jurisdictions impose written requirements in this matter, For instance, s 16 of the (English) Arbitration Act 1996 provides:

"(3) If the tribunal is to consist of a sole arbitrator, the parties shall jointly appoint the arbitrator not later than 28 days after service of a request in writing by either party to do so.
(4) If the tribunal is to consist of two arbitrators, each party shall appoint one arbitrator not later than 14 days after service of a request in writing by either party to do so.
(5) If the tribunal is to consist of three arbitrators—
  (a) each party shall appoint one arbitrator not later than 14 days after service of a request in writing by either party to do so, and
  (b) the two so appointed shall forthwith appoint a third arbitrator as the chairman of the tribunal.
(6) If the tribunal is to consist of two arbitrators and an umpire—
  (a) each party shall appoint one arbitrator not later than 14 days after service of a request in writing by either party to do so, and
  (b) the two so appointed may appoint an umpire at any time after they themselves are appointed and shall do so before any substantive hearing or forthwith if they cannot agree on a matter relating to the arbitration."

Eligibility, number of arbitrators and duty of disclosure – rr 3, 4, 5 and 8

It is mandatory that an arbitrator is a natural person[23] who is over the age of 16[24] and is not declared as having lack of legal capacity[25] within the meaning of s 1(6) of the Adults with Incapacity (Scotland) Act 2000.

Regarding the number of arbitrators, the default position under r 5 of the Scottish Arbitration Rules is that the tribunal is to consist of a

---

[18] Art 11(3)(a).
[19] Art 6(2).
[20] Art 7(2).
[21] LCIA Arbitration Rules, Art 5(4).
[22] Vienna Arbitration Rules, Art 14(3) and (4).
[23] Scottish Arbitration Rules, r 3.
[24] *Ibid*, r 4(a).
[25] *Ibid*, r 4(b).

sole arbitrator unless the parties agree otherwise. A similar provision also appears in s 15(3) of the (English) Arbitration Act 1996.

Once an arbitrator is appointed or an individual is approached by the parties regarding the appointment, such an individual must declare any conflict of interest known to him which might reasonably be considered relevant when considering the issue of independence or impartiality.[26] The debates concerning this issue are examined in detail in Chapter 7.

Failure of appointment procedure – r 7

In cases where the agreed appointment procedures have broken down in relation to the appointment procedures agreed between the parties or r 6, it is mandatory for the parties to follow r 7 in order to complete the process.[27] According to r 7, unless the parties otherwise agree, such a deadlock shall be referred to an arbitral appointment referee[28] who is authorised by the Ministers to carry out such a task.[29] The arbitral appointments referee must consider the nature and subject-matter of the dispute;[30] the terms of the arbitration agreement;[31] and the skills, qualifications, knowledge and experience of the individuals to be appointed[32] when making an appointment.[33] The design of an arbitral appointment referee is to ensure the minimum of applications to the court in such matters and to avoid unnecessary expense and delay incurred in resorting to the court for an appointment. However, to ensure the smooth operation of arbitration, the court retains a supervisory and assisting role when the procedure breaks down.[34]

Under Scots law, it is a legal requirement for the referring party to send a notice of the reference to the other party,[35] to allow the other party an opportunity to object to the reference within 7 days of notice of reference.[36] The other party must send a notice to both the referring

---

[26] Scottish Arbitration Rules, r 8.
[27] Ibid, r 7(1)(a) and (b).
[28] Ibid, r 7(2).
[29] Arbitration (Sc) Act 2010, s 24(1). According to s 24(2), Ministers must, when making such an order, have regard to the desirability of ensuring that arbitral appointments referees (a) have experience relevant to making arbitral appointments and (b) are able to provide training, and to operate disciplinary procedures, designed to ensure that arbitrators conduct themselves appropriately.
[30] Scottish Arbitration Rules, r 7(8)(a).
[31] Ibid, r 7(8)(b).
[32] Ibid, r 7(8)(c).
[33] Such considerations can also be seen in s 19 of the (English) Arbitration Act 1996; Art 5.5 of the LCIA Arbitration Rules Art 11(5) of the UNCITRAL Model Law; and Art 6(4) of the UNCITRAL Arbitration Rules.
[34] Policy Memorandum, 29 January 2009, para 126.
[35] Scottish Arbitration Rules, r 7(3).
[36] Ibid, r 7(4).

party[37] and the arbitral appointments referee if he decides to exercise his right to object to the reference.[38] Provided that no such objection is made with the 7-day period or the other party waives the right to object, the arbitral appointment referee may make the necessary appointment.[39]

Where a party objects to the arbitral appointments referee making an appointment;[40] an arbitral appointments referee fails to make an appointment within 21 days of the matter being referred;[41] or the parties agree not to refer the matter to an arbitral appointment referee,[42] upon an application made by any party, the court may make the necessary appointment.[43] Any appointment made by the arbitral appointments referee or the court under r 7 will have the same effect as if made with the agreement of the parties, even if the composition of the tribunal appointed differs from the arbitration agreement.[44]

Challenge to the appointment of an arbitrator – r 10

From time to time, one party may object to the arbitrator appointed, on the grounds of lack of impartiality, independence,[45] fairness[46] or qualification[47] required to carry out the task as an arbitrator. Under these circumstances, r 10 allows the objecting party to exercise his rights to challenge before the tribunal the appointment of such an arbitrator.[48] However, the notice of objection must be sent to the other party[49] and the objection must be made within 14 days of the objecting party becoming aware of those facts,[50] and the grounds must be stated in the objection made to the tribunal.[51] If the tribunal fails to rule on the objection within 14 days from the date the objection was made, the appointment is revoked.[52]

Similar provision can be seen in s 24(1) of the (English) Arbitration Act 1996, and Art 12 of the Model Law, as well as in a few institutional rules. For instance, the UNCITRAL Arbitration Rules allow the challenge to be

---

[37] Scottish Arbitration Rules, r 7(4)(a).
[38] *Ibid*, r 7(4)(b).
[39] *Ibid*, r 7(5).
[40] *Ibid*, r 7(6)(a).
[41] *Ibid*, r 7(6)(b).
[42] *Ibid*, r 7(6)(c).
[43] The court must take r 7(8) into consideration when make the appointments.
[44] Scottish Arbitration Rules, r 7(9).
[45] *Ibid*, r 10(2)(a)(i).
[46] *Ibid*, r 10(2)(a)(ii).
[47] *Ibid*, r 10(2)(a)(iii).
[48] *Ibid*, r 10(1).
[49] *Ibid*, r 10(2)(d).
[50] *Ibid*, r 10(2)(a)(i).
[51] *Ibid*, r 10(2)(c).
[52] *Ibid*, r 10(4).

made only on the grounds of lack of impartiality and independence,[53] while the Vienna Rules allow the challenge to be made not only on the grounds of lack of impartiality or independence, but also where it is shown to be in conflict with the parties' agreement.[54] The LCIA holds a similar position.[55] For ICC arbitration, the party is required to submit to the Secretariat a challenge in writing for an alleged lack of independence or otherwise.[56]

REMOVAL OF ARBITRATOR – rr 11–14

An arbitrator may be removed by the parties acting jointly or by any third party to whom the parties give power to remove an arbitrator.[57] Alternatively, an arbitrator can also be removed[58] or dismissed[59] by the Outer House if any ground listed in r 10(2)(a) can be established by the parties or substantial injustice has been or will be caused due to the arbitrator's failure to conduct the arbitration according to the arbitration agreement, the Scottish Arbitration Rules and any agreement between the parties. Similar but more detailed power to revoke the arbitrator's authority can be found in ss 23(3) and 24 of the (English) Arbitration Act 1996.

For institutional arbitration, Art 10.1 of the LCIA Arbitration Rules provides:

"If either (a) any arbitrator gives written notice of his desire to resign as arbitrator to the LCIA Court, to be copied to the parties and the other arbitrators (if any) or (b) any arbitrator dies, falls seriously ill, refuses, or becomes unable or unfit to act, either upon challenge by a party or at the request of the remaining arbitrators, the LCIA Court may revoke that arbitrator's appointment and appoint another arbitrator."

And Art 17(2) of the Vienna Rules reads:

"Any party may request the termination of the mandate of an arbitrator if the latter's incapacitation is not merely temporary, if he otherwise fails to perform his duties or unduly delays the proceedings. The request must be submitted to the Secretariat. The Board shall decide upon the request after hearing the arbitrator in question. If it is clear that incapacitation is not merely temporary, the Board may terminate the arbitrator's mandate even without a request from a party."

---

[53] UNCITRAL Arbitration Rules, Art 10.
[54] Vienna Rules, Art 16(1).
[55] LCIA Arbitration Rules, Art 10.2 and 10.3.
[56] ICC Arbitration Rules, Art 11(1).
[57] Scottish Arbitration Rules, r 11(1).
[58] *Ibid*, r 12.
[59] *Ibid*, r 13.

RESIGNATION OF ARBITRATOR – r 15

Before the Act came into effect, at common law, "an arbitrator who accepts office has no inherent right to withdraw, retire or resign except where there is good cause, the validity of which the court may be asked to judge".[60] Following the example of s 25(1) of the (English) Arbitration Act 1996, r 15 lists the grounds entitling an arbitrator to hand in resignation. They are:

> "(a) the parties consent to the resignation,
> (b) the arbitrator has a contractual right to resign in the circumstances,
> (c) the arbitrator's appointment is challenged under rule 10 or 12,
> (d) the parties disapply or modify rule 34(1) (expert opinions) after the arbitrator is appointed, or
> (e) the Outer House has authorised the resignation".[61]

TENURE OF ARBITRATOR – rr 9 and 16

An arbitrator's tenure ends if:

> (a) the arbitrator becomes ineligible to act as an arbitrator;
> (b) the tribunal revokes the arbitrator's appointment;
> (c) the arbitrator is removed by the parties, a third party or the Outer House;
> (d) the Outer House dismisses the tribunal of which the arbitrator forms part; or
> (e) the arbitrator resigns or dies.[62]

Once an arbitrator's tenure ends, the Outer House may make an order to determine the arbitrator's liability, entitlement to the fees and expenses or the repaying of the fees or expenses if they have already been paid to the arbitrator.[63]

RECONSTITUTION OF TRIBUNAL – r 17

When an arbitrator's tenure ends, the tribunal must be reconstituted in order to proceed with the arbitration proceedings in accordance with the same procedures followed in the original appointment.[64] The reconstituted arbitral tribunal has the power to decide the extent to which previous proceedings should stand.[65]

---

[60] Policy Memorandum, 29 January 2009, para 129.
[61] Scottish Arbitration Rules, r 15(1).
[62] Ibid, r 9.
[63] Ibid, r 16.
[64] Ibid, r 17(1)(a).
[65] Ibid, r 17(2).

CHAPTER 7

ARBITRATORS

GENERAL

Apart from demonstrating their intention to subject themselves to the jurisdiction of arbitration, the first step the parties have to take in order to resolve the dispute between them is to appoint an arbitrator or a number of arbitrators to compose an arbitral tribunal. Before the coming into force of the Arbitration (Scotland) Act 2010, the term "arbiter" was commonly used in Scots law. An arbiter is defined as a person appointed by the parties to determine the disputes only in accordance with the law. However, a study into the practice of international commercial arbitration indicates that the term "arbitrator" is widely used and international arbitrators not only apply the law but also apply general equitable considerations to determine the disputes between the parties. Consequently, in order to keep up with modern international arbitration practice, the term "arbitrator" is used throughout the Act. According to s 2(1) of the Arbitration (Scotland) Act 2010, "arbitrator" is defined as a sole arbitrator or a member of a tribunal, while "tribunal" means a sole arbitrator or panel of arbitrators. As an arbitrator is essential in deciding the disputes between the parties, the Arbitration (Scotland) Act 2010 provides detailed provisions governing the appointment of arbitrators, jurisdiction of arbitrators, duties of arbitrators, powers of arbitrators and immunity of arbitrators, as well as the issues of the arbitrator's expenses and fees. All these issues will be discussed in turn in this chapter.

APPOINTMENT OF ARBITRATORS
    ss 24–25 of the Arbitration (Scotland) Act 2010
    rr 2–18 of the Scottish Arbitration Rules
    ss 15–21 of the (English) Arbitration Act 1996

According to the Act, arbitrators can be appointed by the parties or, in the absence of a valid appointment between the parties, by an arbitral appointments referee. Following international arbitration practice, parties are offered the freedom to choose the suitable candidates to act as arbitrators. Rule 2 of the Scottish Arbitration Rules provides that it is not necessary for the parties to appoint or provide for appointment of the tribunal in the arbitration agreement. However, if the parties wish to make an appointment in the arbitration agreement, the arbitration agreement must contain details regarding who is to form the tribunal,[1] who is to appoint the tribunal (either the parties or any third person or institution),[2] or the method of appointment of the tribunal.[3] Rule 2 of the Scottish Arbitration Rules is a default rule. Therefore, the parties' agreed alternative provisions about the appointment of a tribunal will prevail. If no such agreement can be found, or if there are some gaps existing in the agreed appointment procedures, rr 2–18 will provide mandatory or default rules to allow for the appointment of a tribunal in order to proceed with arbitration.

By virtue of s 2(1) of the Arbitration (Scotland) Act 2010, "arbitrators" means a sole arbitrator, or a member of a tribunal. As a definition, this is scarcely helpful, and it is worth noticing that it does not refer to the word "arbiter", which is used in certain statutes as the title to be used in respect of the person carrying out the task of arbitrating (eg the agricultural holdings legislation). By s 36(6), "Any reference to an arbiter in an arbitration agreement made before commencement is to be treated as being a reference to an arbitrator". It is curious that no provision is similarly made as to the use of "arbiter" in statutory provisions.

Method of appointment

The Act is not prescriptive about who should be eligible to be appointed as an arbitrator. The eligibility of an arbitrator will be wholly within the parties' discretion. An arbitrator can be appointed by the parties, the appointed arbitrators or any third party who is given the authority to make such an appointment. The so-called third party can be an appointment referee or any arbitration institution. The term "arbitral appointment referee" is defined in s 24 of the Arbitration (Scotland) Act 2010 as the persons or types of person authorised by the minister's order to undertake such an appointment. An arbitrator may be chosen from any field as diverse as farming, construction, forestry, trade, commodities, engineering, and the legal or accounting professions. The default rules on the method of appointment of arbitrators provided in the Scottish Arbitration Rules are, in the case of a sole arbitrator, the parties must jointly appoint the arbitrator within 28 days of either party

---

[1] Scottish Arbitration Rules, r 2(a). Similar provision can be seen in s 16(1) of the (English) Arbitration Act 1996.
[2] *Ibid*, r 2(b)–(c).
[3] *Ibid*, r 2(d).

requesting the other party to make the appointment.[4] If the parties agree to have multiple arbitrators, each party must appoint an eligible individual as an arbitrator within 28 days of receiving the request from the other party,[5] and, where more arbitrators are to be appointed, the arbitrators appointed by the parties must appoint eligible individuals as the remaining arbitrators.[6]

Mandatory rules on appointment procedures – rr 3, 4 and 7

Despite the parties being given a great extent of freedom to appoint arbitrators, it is mandatory to appoint a natural person[7] who is over the age of 16[8] and has legal capacity[9] to act as an arbitrator under the Arbitration (Scotland) Act 2010.

By r 3 of the Scottish Arbitration Rules only an individual may act as an arbitrator. This is a change from the common law position where it was competent to appoint a legal person, eg a firm as arbiter. In some other legal systems it is possible for a judicial person to be an arbitrator. For instance, Art 871 of the Greek Code of Civil Procedure VII provides "One or several persons as well as a court in its entirety may be appointed as arbitrators". In particular in several jurisdictions a firm of accountants may be appointed as arbitrator. The Scottish Arbitration Rule is mandatory and thus cannot be varied or dis-applied by the parties. Further, by r 4 an individual is ineligible to act as an arbitrator if under 16 or an incapable adult under the Adults with Incapacity (Scotland) Act 2000.

According to r 5 of the Scottish Arbitration Rules, where there is no agreement as to the number of arbitrators, the tribunal is to consist of a sole arbitrator. The English statutory provisions, s 15(3) of the Arbitration Act 1996, is to the same effect.

If, for any reason, a tribunal is not or cannot be appointed according to the procedures set out in the arbitration agreement or the default method of appointment within 28 days provided in r 6, r 7 provides mandatory appointment procedures to resolve the deadlock caused by the failure of appointment of arbitrators.[10] Recognising that appointment of arbitrators is the first essential step towards resolving disputes and the difficulties in appointing arbitrators in multi-parties arbitrations, the draftsmen's intention of ensuring that a party's delaying tactics do not

---

[4] Scottish Arbitration Rules, r 6(a). Similar provision can be seen in s 16(3)–(4) of the (English) Arbitration Act 1996.
[5] Scottish Arbitration Rules, r 6(b)(i).
[6] *Ibid*, r 6(b)(ii).
[7] *Ibid*, r 3.
[8] *Ibid*, r 4(a).
[9] *Ibid*, r 4(b).
[10] *Ibid*, r 7(1). Similar provisions can be seen in ss 17–18 of the (English) Arbitration Act 1996.

stall the arbitration proceedings is evident from the modification of this particular provision from: having been a default rule in the second stage of the Bill, a mandatory nature was imposed in the final Act.[11]

Providing that the referring party gives notice of reference to the other party,[12] either party may seek assistance from an arbitral appointment referee when the agreed appointment procedures have failed.[13] Once the notice is given, the other parties have the right to express their objections to the reference to the referring party and the arbitral appointment referee within 7 days of notice of reference.[14] Failing to make such an objection or exercising a waiver to this right within this period, the arbitral appointment referee can make appointment of arbitrators in order to carry on with the arbitration procedures.[15] On the application by any party, the court may make necessary appointment if the right of objection is exercised by the other parties,[16] the arbitral appointment referee fails to make necessary appointment with 21 days,[17] or the parties agree not to refer the matter to the arbitral appointment referee.[18] The appointment made by the court is subject to no appeal.[19] To make an appointment, either the arbitral appointment referee or the court must consider the nature and subject matter of the dispute,[20] the terms of the arbitration agreement[21] and the skills, qualifications, knowledge and experience[22] of the individual to be appointed.

This provision may be contrasted with the English provision, s 17 of the Arbitration Act 1996, whereby if a party fails to act to appoint an arbitrator then the other party may give notice that his already appointed arbitrator shall be sole arbitrator, and if within 7 days the other party has not made the required appointment, that already appointed arbitrator may act as sole arbitrator.

ARBITRATOR'S DUTIES

Duty to disclose any conflict of interest – r 8

An individual who is an arbitrator or has been enquired about his willingness to act as an arbitrator must disclose to the parties any

---

[11] Revised Explanatory Notes, para 107.
[12] Scottish Arbitration Rules, r 7(3).
[13] *Ibid*, r 7(2).
[14] *Ibid*, r 7(4).
[15] *Ibid*, r 7(5).
[16] *Ibid*, r 7(6)(a).
[17] *Ibid*, r 7(6)(b).
[18] *Ibid*, r 7(6)(c).
[19] *Ibid*, r 7(7).
[20] *Ibid*, r 7(8)(a).
[21] *Ibid*, r 7(8)(b).
[22] *Ibid*, r 7(8)(c).

circumstances known to the individual, which might reasonably be considered as conflict of interest to the arbitral appointment referee, other third party or court empowered to make appointments.[23]

Duty of impartiality and independence, efficiency and fair treatment – rr 24, 77, 78 and 81

Apart from disclosing any reasonably suspected conflict of interests, the tribunal is also required by law to act impartially and independently,[24] conduct the arbitration procedures without necessary delay or incurring unnecessary expense,[25] and treat the parties fairly by giving each party a reasonable opportunity to present a case and to deal with the other party's case.[26] The obligation to treat the parties fairly is fundamental. The principle is embodied in Art 18 of the UNCITRAL Model Law which requires that each party is given a full opportunity to present its case. It does not follow that there must necessarily be, for example, an identical allocation of time to each for the presentation of its case although that may be appropriate in particular circumstances. The important issue is that each is given the same treatment. If the tribunal does not act fairly this may amount to a serious irregularity giving rise to a right to appeal, but that only if the test of substantial injustice is met. The obligation to conduct the arbitration without unnecessary delay is not a specified ground for challenge to an award under r 68, although it might fall under r 68(2)(a), in respect that the tribunal had failed to conduct the arbitration in accordance with the arbitration agreement or these Rules. Equally, in accordance with r 12(e), it may give rise to an application by a party to the Outer House to remove the arbitrator on the ground of his failure to conduct the arbitration provided substantial injustice has been or will be caused.

Independence of arbitrator from the parties usually indicates that there is a personal or financial tie between them. To avoid any ambiguity arising from the issue of independence, r 77 provides a mandatory list of circumstances in which an arbitrator is not independent if any of those circumstances may give the parties justifiable doubts as to the arbitrator's impartiality: the arbitrator's relationship with any party, the arbitrator's financial or other commercial interests, or any other possible links between them. The approach in Scots law can best be considered as whether there is suspicion of bias through the eyes of the reasonable man who was

---

[23] Scottish Arbitration Rules, r 8(2).
[24] *Ibid*, r 24(1)(a). Similar provision can be seen in s 33 of the (English) Arbitration Act 1996.
[25] Scottish Arbitration Rules, r 24(1)(c). Similar mandatory duty is imposed upon the parties under r 25.
[26] Scottish Arbitration Rules, r 24(1)(b) and (2).

aware of the circumstances.[27] If an arbitrator is removed by the Outer House on the grounds of lack of independence and impartiality,[28] the court has the power to consider whether to make an order regarding the arbitrator's entitlement to fees or expenses and repaying fees or expenses already paid to the arbitrator.[29] However, such power can be modified or disapplied by the parties' agreement.

The duty to remain independent and impartial is also stressed in the influential IBA Guidelines on Conflicts of Interest in International Commercial Arbitration 2004. The Guidelines were prompted by the increasing use of challenging arbitrators as a tactic to delay arbitrations or to deny the opposing party the arbitrator of its choice, due to the interlocking corporate relationships and larger international law firms. The IBA Working Group put together the Guidelines reflecting the current international practice to provide clarity, consistency and uniformity in the standards of impartiality and independence.

To balance, on the one hand, the parties' right to a fair hearing and to disclosure of situations that may reasonably call into question an arbitrator's impartiality or independence, and the parties' right to select arbitrators of their choosing on the other, the Guidelines put different relationships between the parties and arbitrators into four lists: non-waivable Red list, waivable Red list, Orange list and Green list. The non-waivable red list includes situations deriving from the overriding principle that no person can act as an arbitrator in his own case. The waivable Red list encompasses situations that are serious but not as severe, but the arbitrators involved shall be required to disclose the relationship to the parties and obtain an express agreement from them. The Orange list contains a non-exhaustive enumeration of specific situations which in the eyes of the parties may give rise to justifiable doubts as to the arbitrator's impartiality or independence. Under these circumstances, the arbitrator has a duty to disclose such situations. With no timely objection made by the parties, the parties are deemed to have accepted the arbitrator. The Green list includes a non-exhaustive list of situations where no appearance of, and no actual conflict of, interest exists from the relevant objective point of view. The arbitrator has no duty to disclose situations falling within the Green list.

Difference between independence and impartiality

In relation to the issues of independence and impartiality, two observations have to be raised. The first one is the use of "and" linking independence and impartiality in the Act and the Rules. In commercial practice, it is

---

[27] *Bradford v McLeod* 1986 SLT 244; *Millar v Dickson* 2001 SLT 988.
[28] Scottish Arbitration Rules, r 78(1)(a)–(b).
[29] *Ibid*, r 78(2)(a)–(b). Similar provision can be seen in s 24(4) of the (English) Arbitration Act 1996.

widely accepted that independence and impartiality are two different concepts. Independence is a concept more to do with personal or financial ties between the parties and the arbitrators, such as identity, family relations, civil partner or spouse of the parties, legal representatives, and shareholders, board member, employee and executives of the enterprise involved in the disputes submitted to the arbitration. These scenarios are objective to determine but can cast doubt on whether the award made by the tribunal or the particular arbitrator involved is influenced by such relationship. On the other hand, impartiality is more subjective and difficult to prove. Impartiality is about the state of mind of the arbitrator involved. For example, ethical grounds, bias, racism, sexism, ageism or simply the dislike of one party may influence the arbitrator's decision-making process.

The language of the Act and Rules uses "independence *and* impartiality" which may imply that independence and impartiality are considered to be the same thing. This is especially obvious in the wording in r 77, which states: "For the purposes of these rules, an arbitrator is not *independent* in relation to an arbitration if – (a) the arbitrator's relationship with any party, (b) the arbitrator's financial or other commercial interests, or (c) anything else, gives rise to justifiable doubts as to the arbitrator's *impartiality*."

Examining the policy memorandum and the explanatory notes of the Act, no emphasis was made about the difference between impartiality and independence. Consequently, it is questionable whether the draftsmen of the Act mistakenly believe that the lack of independence will definitely lead to impartiality or vice versa.

This issue is even more apparent when the wording is compared with the relevant international instruments. For instance, in relation to the grounds for challenging the arbitrators, the language in Art 12 of the UNCITRAL Model Law uses the word "or" to distinguish the difference between independence and impartiality. It reads:

> "(1) When a person is approached in connection with his possible appointment as an arbitrator, he shall disclose any circumstances likely to give rise to justifiable doubts as to his impartiality *or* independence. ...
> (2) An arbitrator may be challenged only if circumstances exist that give rise to justifiable doubts as to his impartiality *or* independence, or if he does not possess qualifications agreed to by the parties. ..."[30]

Similar emphasis can also be seen in the IBA Guidelines on Conflicts of Interest in International Arbitration 2004 which represent the most comprehensive work to date defining the framework by which the impartiality of arbitration in the international arena can be most effectively assured. Within the Guidelines, the word "and" is used to

---

[30] UNCITRAL Model Law, Art 12.

stress the arbitrators' duty to be impartial and independent during the arbitration procedures. In other words, arbitrators are imposed with the duties of independence, impartiality *and* disclosure. None of the duties can be derogated. For example, in one of its paragraphs, it reads: "[T]he Working Group believes that the broad standard of 'any doubts as to an ability to be impartial and independent' should lead to the arbitrator declining the appointment."[31]

However, in the various paragraphs discussing the disqualification of arbitrators, the word "or" can be observed: "(b) if facts or circumstances exist, or have arisen since the appointment, that, from a reasonable third person's point of view having knowledge of the relevant facts, give rise to justifiable doubts as to the arbitrator's impartiality or independence, unless the parties have accepted the arbitrator in accordance with the requirements set out in General Standard (4)".[32] In short, arbitrators must disclose or can be disqualified on either lack of independence *or* lack of impartiality.

Justifiable doubts

Second, the issue arising from the words "justifiable doubts" used to determine the arbitrator's impartiality in international practice deserves some discussion. While a more subjective test is used in the duty of disclosure, an objective test of "justifiable doubts" is used in most of the international instruments and national arbitration laws to determine the issue of impartiality or independence. The major arbitral institutions, such as the International Chamber of Commerce (ICC), the London Court of International Arbitration (LCIA), the American Arbitration Association (AAA) and the Stockholm Chamber of Commerce (SCC), all have similar provisions regulating the procedures to be followed in the event of a challenge.[33] For instance, Art 12(1) of the UNCITRAL Model Law provides: "(1) When a person is approached in connection with his possible appointment as an arbitrator, he shall disclose any circumstances likely to give rise to justifiable doubts as to his impartiality or independence."

Moreover, the IBA Guidelines suggest:

> "(b) In order for standards to be applied as consistently as possible, the Working Group believes that the test for disqualification should be an objective one. The Working Group uses the wording 'impartiality or independence' derived from the broadly adopted Art 12 of the UNCITRAL Model Law, and the use of an appearance test, based on

---

[31] *IBA Guidelines on Conflict of Interests in International Arbitration* (2004), p 8.
[32] Ibid at pp 7–8.
[33] In the case of *ad hoc* arbitration under the UNCITRAL Arbitration Rules, the appointing institution, under Art 12, makes the decision when a challenge is contested.

justifiable doubts as to the impartiality or independence of the arbitrator, as provided in Art 12(2) of the UNCITRAL Model Law, to be applied objectively (a 'reasonable third person test').
(c) Doubts are justifiable if a reasonable and informed third party would reach the conclusion that there was a likelihood that the arbitrator may be influenced by factors other than the merits of the case as presented by the parties in reaching his or her decision.
(d) Justifiable doubts necessarily exist as to the arbitrator's impartiality or independence if there is an identity between a party and the arbitrator, if the arbitrator is a legal representative of a legal entity that is a party in the arbitration, or if the arbitrator has a significant financial or personal interest in the matter at stake."[34]

Is the "justifiable doubts" test compromised?

However, such an objective test bows to the pressure of "the perspectives of the parties". As extensively discussed in the Guidelines:

> "General Standard 2(b) above sets out an objective test for disqualification of an arbitrator. However, because of varying considerations with respect to disclosure, the proper standard for disclosure may be different. A purely objective test for disclosure exists in the majority of the jurisdictions analyzed and in the UNCITRAL Model Law. Nevertheless, the Working Group recognizes that the parties have an interest in being fully informed about any circumstances that may be relevant in their view. Because of the strongly held views of many arbitration institutions (as reflected in their rules and as stated to the Working Group) that the disclosure test should reflect the perspectives of the parties, the Working Group in principle accepted, after much debate, a subjective approach for disclosure. The Working Group has adapted the language of Art 7(2) of the ICC Rules for this standard. However, the Working Group believes that this principle should not be applied without limitations."[35]

Court cases – England and USA[36]

England – The real bias standard

Cases on the disqualification of arbitrators often come to the national courts because an arbitral institution has refused to grant a challenge made by one of the parties. The compromise noted in the Guidelines can also be seen in various court cases.

Locabail (UK) Ltd v Bayfield Properties Ltd[37]   During proceedings in the High Court involving equitable interests in properties, one of the

---

[34] Above, n 31, at p 8.
[35] Ibid, p 10.
[36] For a detailed examination on this issue, see H Yu and L Shore, "Independence, impartiality and immunity of arbitrators" (2003) 52 ICLQ 935.
[37] [2000] QB 451, [2000] 2 WLR 870.

defendants raised an issue of conflict of interest by showing a press cutting from which the judge learned that his (ie the judge's) solicitor's firm was acting for clients in litigation against the defendant's former husband. The judge immediately disclosed that connection, stating that he knew no more of that litigation than had appeared from the cutting. The defendant lost the case and applied to the court to disqualify the judge. The court first pointed out the dangers of defining or listing the factors which may or may not give rise to a real danger of bias. It said:

> "Everything will depend on the facts, which may include the nature of the issue to be decided. We cannot, however, conceive of circumstances in which an objection could be soundly based on the religion, ethnic or national origin, gender, age, class, means or sexual orientation of the judge. Nor, at any rate ordinarily, could an objection be soundly based on the judge's social or educational or service, or employment background or history, nor that of any member of the judge's family, or previous political associations; or membership of social or sporting or charitable bodies; or Masonic associations; or previous judicial decisions, or extra curricular utterances; or previous receipts of instructions to act for or against any party, solicitor or advocate engaged in a case before him; or membership of the same Inn, circuit, local Law Society or chambers."[38]

In reaching its decision in believing the deputy judge's statement about his knowledge and finding that there was no real danger that the judge was biased, the court stated that: "In our view, once the hypothesis that the judge 'did not know of the connection' is accepted, the answer, ..., becomes obvious. How can there be any real danger of bias, or any real apprehension or likelihood of bias, if the judge does not know of the facts that, in argument, are relied on as giving rise to the conflict of interest?"[39]

Laker Airways Inc FLS Aerospace Ltd and Burnton FLS Aerospace Ltd v Laker Airways Inc[40] Involving an arbitration, this case provides another example of the policy need to see the issue of independence from the eyes of the parties, but under the control of the state in determining how far the parties can see. In *Laker Airways*, Laker Airways objected to the appointment to the tribunal of a barrister from the same chambers as the barrister arguing the case for the opposing party.[41] Mr Justice Rix's

---

[38] [2007] QB 451 at 480.
[39] *Ibid* at 487.
[40] *Laker Airways Inc v FLS Aerospace Ltd* [1999] 2 Lloyd's Rep 45.
[41] This case has already prompted extensive commentary, and the present writers do not propose to discuss further the judgment of Mr Justice (now Lord Justice) Rix. See A H Merjian, "Caveat arbiter" (2000) 17 Journal of International Arbitration 31; J Kendall, "Barristers, independence and disclosure revisited" (2000) 16 Arbitration

decision to apply the "real danger of bias" test by following the same line of the arguments given by Saville J in *Pilkington plc v PPG Industries Inc*[42] was supported by his reasoning that:

> "The fact that members of chambers share expenses does not mean that they have a financial interest in the outcome of each other's cases. Counsels do not share fees or profits. Nor, which is a different point again, does the fee of either counsel or of course arbitrator depend on the outcome of the proceedings. ... A conflict of interest properly so called only arises as an impediment when the same person (or which is in law regarded as the same person) undertakes conflicting duties to different clients and puts himself in a position where he has a conflict between his duty to his client and his own self-interest. ... Barristers are self-employed. ... Barristers are prohibited by the rules of their profession from entering partnerships accepting employment precisely in order to maintain the position where they can appear against or in front of one another."[43]

The court concluded that, in order to challenge the arbitrator on the ground of lack of impartiality, "the applicant must show that the organisation of chambers gives rise to justifiable doubts about an arbitrator's impartiality because of the danger of accidental or improper dissemination of confidential information or because of the danger that the arbitrator will not observe the rule against holding conversations with only one party outside the presence of all parties to the arbitration".[44]

It was pointed out that Mr Justice Rix's reliance on certain US court decisions and assumptions about the operation of barristers' chambers makes the *Laker Airways* judgment not well founded.[45] The criticism was centred on the balance between the practice of barristers and the parties' confidence in the integrity of arbitration. It pointed out that:

> "If the challenged arbitrator had recused himself, given that the confidence of one of the parties in his impartiality was undermined by its view that, whatever English traditions might be, an arbitrator and counsel from the same chambers is a confusing relationship to outsiders, there would have been virtually no delay to the arbitral proceedings and no dearth of

---

International 343; and the debate in K V S K Nathan, "Barristers in Chambers in England – Paragons of Virtue or Just Being Boys?" (1999) 14(12) Mealey's International Arbitration Report 23 and A Malek and D Quest, "Reality of barrister arbitrators – A response to Dr K V S K Nathan" (2000) 15(1) Mealey's International Arbitration Report 22.

[42] Unreported, 1 November 1989. See *PPG Industries Inc v Pilkington plc, Libbey-Owens-Ford Co*, 825 F Supp 1465; 1993 US Dist LEXIS 9524; 1993–2 Trade Cas (CCH) P70, 368; and *PPG Industries, Inc v Pilkington, plc, et al*, 1994 US App (9th Cir) LEXIS 14427.

[43] [1999] 2 Lloyd's Rep 45 at 52.

[44] *Ibid* at 53.

[45] See the criticisms raised in Yu and Shore, above, n 35.

potential arbitrators to choose from. What was at stake in *Laker* had little to do with finding a balance between the expeditious progress of arbitral proceedings and maintaining the parties' confidence in the integrity of such proceedings. Rather, what truly was at stake was whether the English Bar would be able to stave off another blow at its exceptional status in the English legal system. Hence the remarkable involvement of the Bar Council, which in an *amicus* submission to the court argued that if membership in the same chambers created a conflict of interest, 'then the public interest would be harmed since public access to a pool of barristers, particularly in specialist fields, would be considerably reduced'.[46] "Specialists" in general commercial contract matters are simply not an endangered species. Whether English barristers are an endangered species is another matter, and is doubtful, and in any event their preservation is not dependent on their appointment to international arbitral tribunals."[47]

AT&T Corp v *Saudi Cable Co*[48]   A lawyer and arbitrator was appointed as the tribunal chairman in an ICC arbitration. The tribunal issued two partial awards before AT&T became aware that the chairman was a non-executive director of a competitor company of AT&T. The competitor company, Nortel, also had been a disappointed bidder for the contract out of which the arbitration arose. It was not disputed that it was through a secretarial omission that this link between the chairman and Nortel had not been mentioned in his CV. At the appointment, the arbitrator carried on declaring that he was independent of the parties and had nothing to disclose. AT&T lodged a challenge with the ICC based on the chairman's alleged lack of independence. The ICC rejected the challenge and final award was issued by the tribunal. Since London was the seat of the arbitration, AT&T commenced legal proceedings pursuant to England's 1950 Arbitration Act to revoke the chairman's appointment and set aside the awards.

The trial judge determined that the chairman had considered himself independent of the parties and "it had never occurred to him that his non-executive directorship of Nortel could call into question his independence in the eyes of either of the parties".[49] AT&T contended that had it known of the non-executive directorship it would not have consented to the chairman's appointment. The trial judge nonetheless dismissed AT&T's application, applying the "real danger of bias" test laid down by the House of Lords for judicial disqualification. On appeal, AT&T argued, *inter alia*, that the "real danger" test should not be applied to arbitrators. AT&T instead advanced a "reasonable apprehension or suspicion of bias" test.

---

[46] Above, n 43, at 48.
[47] Above, n 36, at 943.
[48] [2000] 2 All ER 625 (Comm).
[49] *Ibid* at 631. Excerpts from Yu and Shore, above, n 35, at 935.

This test, AT&T contended, was also closer to the "justifiable doubts" test in the (English) Arbitration Act 1996.[50]

The Court of Appeal held that "there is no principle on which it would be right in general to distinguish international arbitrations" from cases in court. Assuming, for the sake of argument, that "reasonable suspicion" actually provided a lower threshold than "real danger", Lord Woolf ruled as follows:

> "It would be surprising if a lower threshold for disqualification applied to arbitration than applied to a court of law. The courts are responsible for the provision of public justice. If there are two standards, I would expect a lower threshold to apply to courts of law than applies to a private tribunal whose "judges" are selected by the parties. After all, there is an overriding public interest in the integrity of the administration of justice in the courts."[51]

In reaching his conclusion that there was no real danger of bias in the particular case, Lord Woolf commented, *inter alia*, that the chairman was an "extremely experienced lawyer and arbitrator who, like a judge, is both accustomed and who can be relied on to disregard irrelevant considerations".[52]

Lord Woolf's decision was supported by Lord Justice Potter who stated:

> "It seems to me that, whatever the test should be, and it is clearly laid down in *Gough* in terms of the "real danger" test, it is desirable that it should apply universally in cases before the English Court, ... It may well be that adoption of the reasonable suspicion test would afford more comfort to those concerned to preserve the sanctity of Lord Hewart's dictum. However, as it seems to me, the real danger test is intended to be a working test designed to give effect to that dictum, while having regard to substance as well as appearance."

Agreeing with Lord Goff in *R v Gough*:[53]

> "It is not in dispute that reasonable apprehension of bias is a test in which reasonableness is judged by the standards of the reasonable objective observer. That is, in reality, the Court itself, embodying the standards of the informed observer viewing the matter at the relevant time, which is of course the time when the matter comes before the Court. That last qualification is important because, in judging whether there is bias or

---

[50] (English) Arbitration Act 1996, s 24(1)(a). It provides that a party may apply to the court to remove an arbitrator on the grounds "that circumstances exist that give rise to justifiable doubts as to his impartiality".
[51] *AT&T*, above, n 48, at 638.
[52] *Ibid* at 639.
[53] [1993] AC 646.

apparent bias, the Court approaches the matter on the basis of an observer informed as to the facts upon which, and the context in which the allegation of bias is made."[54]

On the other hand, while agreeing to the dismissal of the application to remove the arbitrator concerned, Lord Justice May was much more sympathetic to AT&T's challenge to the chairman. He pointed out:

> "It did seem to me that there was a reasonably persuasive general case that his non-executive directorship "might be of such a nature as to call into question [his] independence *in the eyes of [one] of the parties*'. If AT&T had known of this directorship at the outset, an objection by them to his acting as arbitrator would, in my view, probably have been regarded as reasonable and would have been sustained."[55]

Yet, in light of all the facts and the unanimous awards already issued by the tribunal, Lord Justice May viewed the chairman's non-disclosure as an insufficient basis for the court to exercise its discretion in AT&T's favour.

Lord Woolf and Lord Justice Potter's decision was seen by some as "a troubling perspective". It was said: "But one cannot rely on an arbitrator to disregard a conflict of interest. If experience could negate bias, then the application of any test would have to take experience levels into account. That is not justifiable under any analysis. Lord Woolf's deference to the tribunal chairman extended far beyond what was reasonable."[56]

USA – the "reasonable person would have to conclude partiality" standard

Commonwealth Coatings[57] The Supreme Court assessed a challenge to the arbitral chairman under § 10(2) of the US Arbitration Act, which provides for vacation of an award where, *inter alia*, "there was evident partiality or corruption in the arbitrators, or either of them". The chairman conducted an engineering consulting business in which one of his regular customers was the prime contractor that was a party to the arbitration. The arbitration went forward without the arbitrator disclosing these details and without the challenging party (the petitioner) knowing of them until after the award was issued. The losing party appealed against the award on the ground of lack of impartiality.

In the Supreme Court, Mr Justice Black held that the subcontractor was entitled to have the award set aside despite the fact that the supposedly neutral member of arbitration panel appointed in dispute was not alleged

---

[54] *AT&T*, above, n 48, at 637.
[55] *Ibid* at 646. The phrase "eyes of the parties" is from Art 2.7 of the ICC Rules 1998.
[56] Yu and Shore, above, n 36, at 941.
[57] *Commonwealth Coatings Corp* v *Continental Casualty Co*, 393 US 145 (1968).

to have been guilty of fraud or bias in deciding the case: neither he nor the prime contractor had intimated to the subcontractor the close financial relations that had existed between the prime contractor and the arbitrator for a period of years. On the basis of the non-disclosure, Justice Black reversed the appellate court and vacated the arbitral award. Justice Black stated:

> "It is true that arbitrators cannot sever all their ties with the business world, since they are not expected to get all their income from their work deciding cases, but we should, if anything, be even more scrupulous to safeguard the impartiality of arbitrators than judges, since the former have completely free rein to decide the law as well as the facts and are not subject to appellate review."[58]

He further announced the efficacy of "the simple requirement that arbitrators disclose to the parties any dealings that might create an impression of possible bias".[59] He supported this disclosure requirement with provisions from the rules then in force of the American Arbitration Association and from the Canon of Judicial Ethics,[60] and concluded that "any tribunal permitted by law to try cases and controversies not only must be unbiased but must also avoid even the appearance of bias".[61]

However, Justice Black was able to form a majority only by virtue of a concurring opinion by Justice White, joined by Justice Marshall. Consequently, "courts have given this concurrence particular weight".[62] Justices White and Marshall were concerned about losing "the best informed and most capable arbitrators; accordingly, arbitrators are not automatically disqualified by a business relationship with the parties before them if both parties are informed of the relationship in advance, or if they are unaware of the facts but the relationship is trivial".[63] An arbitrator "cannot be expected to provide the parties with a complete and unexpurgated business biography".[64] Thus, the concurring justices limited the Court's holding and stated that "where the arbitrator has a substantial interest in a firm which has done more than a trivial

---

[58] *Commonwealth Coatings*, above, n 57, at 148–149.
[59] *Ibid* at 149.
[60] Rule 18 provided for the arbitrator "to disclose any circumstances likely to create a presumption of bias or which he believes might disqualify him as an impartial Arbitrator". The 33rd Canon provided that in pending or prospective litigation before him a judge should be "careful to avoid such action as may reasonably tend to awaken the suspicion that his social or business relations or friendships, constitute an element in influencing his judicial conduct".
[61] Above, n 57, at 149.
[62] *ANR Coal Co v Cogentrix of North Carolina, Inc*, 173 F 3d 493 (4th Cir 1999) at 499.
[63] *Commonwealth Coatings*, above, n 57, at 150–152.
[64] *Ibid*.

business with a party, that fact must be disclosed".[65] This limitation drained Justice Black's opinion of much of its clear guidance and good sense.

Cook Industries[66]   Decided by the Second Circuit Court in 1971, *Cook* is an example of such further limitation. The challenge involved the contention that the employer of one of the arbitrators had substantial business dealings with one of the parties to the arbitration. The panel majority noted that the arbitrator's employer also did business with the challenging party and employees of the challenging party knew of the arbitrator's employer's dealings with the other party. The majority stated that, taking the *Commonwealth Coatings* principle of disclosure of "any dealings that might create an impression of possible bias" into account, it was appropriate to define the arbitrator's obligation to be disclosure of dealings of which "the parties cannot reasonably be expected to be aware, i.e., dealings 'not in the ordinary course of ... business'."[67] On this basis, the majority rejected the disqualification application.

In dissent, Judge Oakes pointed to conflicting and ambiguous affidavit testimony on the issue of the extent of the business dealings between the arbitrator's employer and one of the parties. Moreover, the applicable Grain Arbitration Rules of the New York Produce Exchange required a written waiver from all parties in the event that an arbitrator had any financial or personal interest in the result of the arbitration, and no such waiver had been obtained. Citing Justice Black's position that the courts should be even more scrupulous to safeguard the impartiality of arbitrators than judges, Judge Oakes could not accept the conclusion that a party waived disqualification because it knew that the arbitrator was employed by a company that did business with the other party. The majority's view, he believed, did not do justice to the arbitral rules, to the US Arbitration Act, to *Commonwealth Coatings*, or to the parties in the case. In his opinion, the parties could not know in advance whether to waive unless there is full disclosure. He stated: "How are they to know whether there are transactions 'out of the ordinary course of business' unless pending transactions are disclosed?"[68] He accepted that the burden of proof should rest on the party claiming partiality, but commented that the court still had the obligation to ascertain the facts. Above all, he did not want the doctrine of waiver to be turned into a carte blanche for the non-disclosure decried in *Commonwealth Coatings*.[69]

---

[65] *Commonwealth Coatings*, above, n 57, at 150–152.
[66] *Cook Industries, Inc v C Itoh & Co (America) Inc*, 449 F 2d 106, 107–8 (2nd Cir 1971), cert denied, 405 US 921, 92 S Ct 957, 30 L Ed 2d 792 (1972).
[67] 449 F 2d 106 at 108.
[68] Ibid at 109.
[69] Ibid.

Merit Ins Co v Leatherby Ins Co[70] Judge Oakes's concern over preserving the core of Justice Black's *Commonwealth Coatings* opinion became very much a minority view. This case involves an appeal from an order setting aside an award under r 60(b) of the Federal Rules of Civil Procedure. Based on the alleged discovery that the arbitral chairman had earlier worked under Merit's president and principal stockholder (Mr Stern) when they were at another company, the court was asked to determine whether the failure of one of the arbitrators to disclose a prior business relationship with a principal of one of the parties to the arbitration justified the district court in using its powers[71] to set aside the award. The District Court granted Leatherby's motion and set aside the award. Merit then appealed. The Seventh Circuit reversed the District Court and reinstated its earlier ruling confirming the arbitral award.[72] The influential Judge Posner, in ruling on a non-disclosure issue in *Merit Ins Co v Leatherby Ins Co*,[73] made pronouncements about impartiality that are striking for their departure from Justice Black's view, and for providing no practical guidance on disqualification standards.

Judge Posner accepted that r 18 of the AAA's Commercial Arbitration Rules, which governed the arbitration, as well as the AAA–ABA's Code of Ethics for Arbitrators in Commercial Disputes (Canon IIA) required disclosure of relationships that are likely to affect impartiality or reasonably create an appearance of bias, and the chairman failed to disclose his relationship with Stern. But Judge Posner noted that the broad language of r 18 and Canon IIA did not require disclosure of *every* former social or financial relationship with a party or its principals. Here he made his first pronouncement:

> "The ethical obligations of arbitrators can be understood only by reference to the fundamental differences between adjudication by arbitrators and adjudication by judges and jurors. No one is forced to arbitrate a commercial dispute unless he has consented by contract to arbitrate. The voluntary nature of commercial arbitration is an important safeguard for the parties that is missing in the case of the courts. Courts are coercive, not voluntary, agencies, and the American people's traditional fear of government oppression has resulted in a judicial system in which impartiality is prized above expertise. Thus, people who arbitrate do so because they prefer a tribunal knowledgeable about the subject matter of their dispute to a generalist court with its austere impartiality but limited knowledge of subject matter. ... There is a tradeoff between impartiality and expertise."[74]

---

[70] 714 F 2d 673 (7th Cir 1983), cert denied, 464 US 1009 (1983).
[71] The power under r 60(b) and the United States Arbitration Act (9 USC), § 1.
[72] 714 F 2d 673 at 676–677.
[73] *Ibid*.
[74] *Ibid* at 679.

Accordingly, the test for disqualification should be as follows: "[I]t is whether, having due regard for the different expectations regarding impartiality that parties bring to arbitration than to litigation, the relationship between Clifford [the chairman] and Stern was so intimate – personally, socially, professionally, or financially – as to cast serious doubt on Clifford's impartiality."[75]

Not surprisingly, Leatherby failed this new serious doubt test as the relationship with Stern was a long time ago, and "[t]ime cools emotions, whether of gratitude or resentment".[76] Time might well seem to have that effect from the upper echelons of appellate discourse. But, the question remains whether a party involved in a $10.6 million case such as this might prefer a stronger need of impartiality rather than a questionable maxim.

Morelite Constr Corp v New York City District Council Carpenters Benefit Fund[77] This is another case following the serious doubt test. Judge Kaufman, like Judge Posner, dismissed Justice Black's *Commonwealth Coatings* opinion as *obiter dicta*, and viewed his task as "attempting to delineate standards of impartiality on a relatively clean slate". Upon that slate, the court relied, *inter alia*, on *Merit Ins Co v Leatherby Ins Co* and held as follows:

> "Mindful of the trade-off between expertise and impartiality, and cognizant of the voluntary nature of submitting to arbitration, we read s 10(b) [of the United States Arbitration Act] as requiring a showing of something more than the mere 'appearance of bias' to vacate an arbitration award. To do otherwise would be to render this efficient means of dispute resolution ineffective in many commercial settings."[78]

ANR Coal Co[79] Following the *Morelite* case, *ANR Coal Co* is a case where the parties' arbitration was governed by the AAA Commercial Arbitration Rules. ANR objected to a name on the neutral arbitrator (chairman) list provided by AAA on the grounds that the individual's law firm had represented a company (Carolina Power) that had a contractual relationship with the opposing party (Cogentrix) in the arbitration. The AAA declined to remove the name, stating that the individual had never personally represented Carolina Power, though his firm had done so, and his firm had only represented the company in a particular type of matter. The chairman himself, after his appointment by AAA, also disclosed that through a temporary law firm merger he briefly practised

---

[75] 714 F 2d 673 at 680.
[76] Ibid.
[77] 748 F 2d 79 (2nd Cir 1984).
[78] Ibid at 83–84.
[79] ANR Coal Co v Cogentrix of North Carolina, Inc, 173 F 3d 493 (4th Cir 1999).

with the counsel for the other party in the arbitration. ANR did not renew its objection, but stated in court that it did not renew because a failed challenge would potentially have offended the arbitrator. ANR lost the arbitration. It contended that it learned, post-award, that, contrary to the earlier disclosures, the relationship between the chairman and the firm was more extensive with Carolina Power and that during the time of the temporary merger his firm had represented Cogentrix. ANR applied to set aside the award, which the lower court did.[80]

On appeal, the Fourth Circuit observed that AAA r 19 (a neutral arbitrator "shall disclose to the AAA any circumstance likely to affect impartiality") requires only disclosure of an interest or relationship likely to affect impartiality, as well as ANR's misguided reliance on Justice Black's opinion in *Commonwealth Coatings*. The Fourth Circuit cited Judge Posner's opinion in *Merit Ins* as supporting its holding, and in particular quoted with approval his view that parties choose arbitration because they prefer expertise to impartiality. The court further held that ANR could not carry its heavy burden to meet the onerous standard under 9 USC, § 10(a)(2) "of objectively demonstrating such a degree of partiality that a reasonable person could assume that the arbitrator had improper motives".[81]

It appears that the US courts were unwilling to adopt an "actual bias" standard, since bias could often be almost impossible to prove and the federal courts – which by statute had responsibility for enforcement of "private" remedies – could not lend their imprimatur to an award grounded in bias. Accordingly, as "actual bias" was too high and "appearance of bias" too low, the court defined the test as follows: "evident partiality" would be found "where a reasonable person would have to conclude that the arbitrator was partial to one party in the arbitration. In assessing a given relationship, courts must remain cognizant of peculiar commercial practices and factual variances".[82] If such partiality is found, for example, in a relationship between the arbitrator and one of the parties, the merits of the award itself need not be examined.[83] Moreover, the US courts' continuing reluctance to set aside awards even though an arbitrator failed to disclose a relationship or dealing that might create an impression of possible bias further suggests that the American and English standards are in practice similar.

---

[80] 173 F 3d 493 at 496.
[81] *Ibid* at 500. The Fourth Circuit set out a four-factor test for the determination of whether a claimant has demonstrated "evident partiality": (i) the extent or character of the arbitrator's personal interest, pecuniary or otherwise; (ii) the "directness" of the relationship between the arbitrator and the allegedly favoured party; (iii) the connection of that relationship to the arbitration; and (iv) the proximity in time between the relationship and the arbitral proceedings.
[82] *Morelite*, 748 F 2d 79 (2nd Cir 1984) at 84.
[83] *Ibid* at 85.

COMPOSITION OF ARBITRAL TRIBUNAL

Default rules on composition of arbitral tribunal – rr 9–11, 17 and 18

Subject to the parties' agreement, the Arbitration (Scotland) Act 2010 sets out a few default provisions governing the issues of arbitrator's tenure, challenge to appointment of arbitrator, removal of arbitrators by parties, reconstitution of tribunal and the ceasement of effects on the specified arbitrator.

A few circumstances listed in r 9 can bring arbitration to an end before the intended completion of arbitration proceedings providing that no agreement has otherwise been reached between the parties. Rule 9 provides that an arbitrator's tenure ends if the arbitrator becomes ineligible to act as an arbitrator[84] because of being underage or lack of legal capacity.[85] If an arbitrator's powers are revoked by the tribunal under r 10 or an arbitrator is removed[86] by the parties jointly, a third party or the Outer House on the grounds of lack of independence, impartiality, due process, qualification or justice, his tenure will also be brought to an end.[87] An arbitrator's tenure also ends on the resignation[88] or the death[89] of the arbitrator[90] or if the Outer House dismisses the tribunal of which the arbitrator forms part.[91]

According to r 10(4), if the tribunal fails to make a decision within 14 days of objection being made, the appointment is revoked. These provisions are not mandatory and may thus be varied or removed altogether. It should be observed that in cases where an arbitration is being held under institutional rules, such as those of the ICC or LCIA, those bodies will have a power to remove member of the arbitral tribunal rather than the Tribunal itself having such power, eg Art 11 of the ICC Rules; Art 8 of the AAA International Arbitral Rules; Art 10 of the LCIA Arbitration Rules; Arts 24–29 of the WIPO Arbitration Rules. See also Arts 12 and 13 of the UNCITRAL Model Law.

Mandatory rules on removal, dismissal, resignation and liability of tribunal – rr 12–16

The Scottish Arbitration Rules contain a number of mandatory provisions concerning the removal, dismissal, and resignation of arbitrators.

---

[84] Scottish Arbitration Rules, r 9.
[85] Ibid, r 4.
[86] Ibid, r 9(c).
[87] Ibid, rr 11 and 12. Similar provisions can be seen in ss 23–24 of the (English) Arbitration Act 1996.
[88] Scottish Arbitration Rules, r 15. Similar provision can be seen in s 25(1) of the (English) Arbitration Act 1996.
[89] Scottish Arbitration Rules, r 79. Similar provision can be seen in s 26(1) of the (English) Arbitration Act 1996.
[90] Scottish Arbitration Rules, r 9(e).
[91] Ibid, r 9(d).

Removal of arbitrator

On the application by any party, the court has the power to remove an arbitrator who has failed in his duty to be impartial and independent[92] as well to treat the parties fairly.[93] If there is any evidence or doubt about an arbitrator's eligibility, capacity, ability or qualification to act as an arbitrator, the court is empowered to remove the particular arbitrators concerned.[94] Regarding qualification specified by the parties, the arbitrator must possess the necessary qualifications required by the parties before his appointment.[95] Rule 12(e) requires the application of the "substantial injustice" test to determine whether an arbitrator should be removed because his failure to conduct the arbitration proceedings according to the arbitration agreement, the Scottish Arbitration Rules, or any other agreement by the parties relating to conduct of the arbitration has caused or will cause substantial injustice to the party concerned.[96]

The court's power in removing arbitrators is limited by the conditions listed in r 14. Accordingly, for the court to exercise its power to remove the arbitrator under r 12, the court must be satisfied that the arbitrator or the tribunal concerned has been given a notice about the application for the removal and given the opportunity to make representation, and that the parties have exhausted any possible recources available to them under r 10 to challenge the arbitrators or a third party empowered to remove the arbitrator.[97] The court decision on this issue is subject to no appeal.[98] To avoid the possibility of delaying or frustrating the arbitration, r 14(3) allows the arbitral tribunal to carry on with the arbitration while the objection based on r 12 is heard.[99]

Dismissal of arbitrator

Apart from the power to remove arbitrators, the Outer House may also apply the substantive injustice test and exercise the mandatory power to dismiss the tribunal if a party can prove to the court that substantial injustice has been or will be caused to him because the tribunal has failed to conduct the arbitration in accordance with the arbitration agreement, the Scottish Arbitration Rules or any other agreement between the parties regarding how the arbitration proceedings shall be carried out.[100] The

---

[92] Scottish Arbitration Rules, r 12(a). Similar provision can be seen in s 24 of the (English) Arbitration Act 1996.
[93] Scottish Arbitration Rules, r 12(b).
[94] *Ibid*, r 12(c).
[95] *Ibid*, r 12(d).
[96] *Ibid*, r 12(e).
[97] *Ibid*, r 14(1)(a)–(b).
[98] *Ibid*, r 14(2).
[99] *Ibid*, r 14(3).
[100] *Ibid*, r 13.

same conditions imposed on the court when it exercises the power of removal of arbitrators, as discussed in the previous paragraph, also apply to the issue of dismissal of tribunal.[101]

Resignation of arbitrator

As the contractual elements are widely used to interpret the relationship between arbitrators and parties involving commercial arbitration, it is not surprising to learn that r 15 sets out various circumstances in which an arbitrator is allowed to resign from his post. An arbitrator is allowed to resign if both parties consent to his resignation[102] or if he already secured a contractual right to resign in the circumstances listed in the appointment agreement.[103] Apart from consensual agreement, an arbitrator may also resign if his appointment is challenged on the grounds of lack of impartiality, independence or fair treatment under r 10 or r 12.[104] An arbitrator is also allowed to resign if he has accepted the appointment on the basis that he would be assisted by an expert during the course of the arbitration under r 34(1) but the parties subsequently refused to pay for such an expert.[105] If the parties do not agree to the arbitrator's resignation, the Outer House may authorise a resignation if it is satisfied that there are reasonable grounds for the resignation.[106] The court's decision on this matter is final and subject to no appeal.[107]

When arbitrator's tenure ends

Two issues arise once the arbitrator's tenure ends due to the dismissal, removal or resignation of an arbitrator. One is the issue of the arbitrator's entitlement or liability, if any. The other issue concerns the reconstitution of the tribunal.

Arbitrator's entitlement or liability

On the application by any party, the Outer House has the mandatory power to order the parties to pay any outstanding fees or expenses due to the arbitrator whose tenure has ended.[108] On the other hand, if the court considers it is reasonable, it may order to the arbitrators who ended the tenure to repay the parties the fees or expenses which have already been

---

[101] Scottish Arbitration Rules, r 14.
[102] *Ibid*, r 15(1)(a). Similar provisions can be seen in s 25(1), (4) and (5) of the (English) Arbitration Act 1996.
[103] Scottish Arbitration Rules, r 15(1)(b).
[104] *Ibid*, r 15(1)(c).
[105] *Ibid*, r 15(1)(d).
[106] *Ibid*, r 15(1)(e) and (2).
[107] *Ibid*, r 15(3).
[108] *Ibid*, r 16(1)(a). Similar provision can be seen in s 25(3) of the (English) Arbitration Act 1996.

made.[109] The court may also make an order to grant an arbitrator relief from liability incurred or to impose liability due to the termination of the tenure.[110] However, the court must consider whether the arbitrator's resignation was in breach of r 15 (resignation of arbitrators) when the order is made.[111]

Reconstitution of the tribunal

Once an arbitrator's tenure ends, the tribunal must be reconstituted in accordance with the procedure agreed between the parties[112] or, in the absence of any agreement, the default rules on the appointment of arbitrators under rr 6 and 7.[113] Once the tribunal is reconstituted, the tribunal has the power, subject to the parties' objection or appeal, to determine the extent to which previous arbitration proceedings should stand.[114]

JURISDICTION OF TRIBUNAL – rr 19–23

Once appointed, the critical question underlying any arbitral tribunal is the nature and extent of its jurisdiction. To ensure that the arbitrator's jurisdiction is not used as a delaying tactic by the parties or to avoid an award being set aside after the award is made or at the stage of recognition or enforcement of arbitral awards, it is essential for an arbitrator to determine the extent and scope of his mandate. This power offered to the arbitrators to rule on his own jurisdiction is the widely accepted principle of "competence-competence" in international practice. Before the UNCITRAL Model Law era and the introduction of the new Act, the principle was criticised as unwarrantable in principle as it is inexpedient in practice.[115] Nevertheless, this principle is now adopted in r 19 of the Scottish Arbitration Rules which clearly stipulates that an arbitrator has the mandatory power to determine his own jurisdiction. The issues which can be decided by the arbitrators regarding their jurisdiction range from the validity of the arbitration agreement[116] to the constitution of the arbitral tribunal[117] and the scope of submission.[118] As r 19 provides:

---

[109] Scottish Arbitration Rules, r 16(1)(b).
[110] *Ibid*, r 16(1)(c).
[111] *Ibid*, r 16(2).
[112] *Ibid*, r 17(1)(a). Similar provision can be seen in s 27 of the (English) Arbitration Act 1996.
[113] Scottish Arbitration Rules, r 17(1)(b).
[114] *Ibid*, r 17(2)–(3).
[115] *Caledonian Rly Co v Greenock & Wemyss Bay Rly Co* (1872) 10 M 892.
[116] Scottish Arbitration Rules, r 19(a). Similar provision can be seen in s 30 of the (English) Arbitration Act 1996.
[117] Scottish Arbitration Rules, r 19(b).
[118] *Ibid*, r 19(c).

"The tribunal may rule on –
(a) whether there is a valid arbitration agreement (or, in the case of a statutory arbitration, whether the enactment providing for arbitration applies to the dispute),
(b) whether the tribunal is properly constituted, and
(c) what matters have been submitted to arbitration in accordance with the arbitration agreement."

However, the tribunal's decision to rule on its own jurisdiction can be objected to by the parties if they believe that the tribunal does not have or has exceeded its jurisdiction in relation to the matters submitted to it.[119] Any party may object to the jurisdiction of the tribunal either in whole or as to part of the matters before it, but must do so as soon as is reasonably practicable after the relevant matters have been raised. To maintain the stability of arbitration, it is mandatory for the objecting party to raise the objection before, or as soon as is reasonably practicable after the matter is first raised in the arbitration, or such later time if the tribunal considers the circumstances justify such a delay. However, in either case, an objection must be made before the final award is handed down by the tribunal.[120] If a tribunal finds that it does not have jurisdiction over the disputes submitted, it must uphold the objection and end the arbitration as far as it relates to a matter over which it does not have jurisdiction.[121] In the case where the tribunal has already made a provisional or partial award on a matter over which it does not have jurisdiction, it must set aside the relevant awards.[122]

Regarding the timing of making such a ruling, in accordance with r 20(4), subject to the parties' agreement on the course the tribunal shall take, the tribunal has the following options: ruling on an objection to its jurisdiction in an award independent from the merits of the dispute, or delaying the ruling on an objection until it makes its award on the merits of the dispute. In the former option, the objecting party can make an application to the Outer House on a question of arbitrator's jurisdiction with 14 days after the tribunal's decision is reached.[123] While the appeal is pending in the court under r 21, the tribunal can continue the arbitration proceedings until the court reaches a final decision[124] on the issue of jurisdiction.[125] One point which needs to be borne in mind is that, if the

---

[119] Scottish Arbitration Rules, r 20(1).
[120] Ibid, r 20(2). Similar provision can be seen in s 31 of the (English) Arbitration Act 1996.
[121] Scottish Arbitration Rules, r 20(3)(a).
[122] Ibid, r 20(3)(b).
[123] Ibid, r 21. Relevant provisions can be seen in ss 30(2) and 32(4) of the (English) Arbitration Act 1996.
[124] Scottish Arbitration Rules, r 21(3).
[125] Ibid, r 21(2).

tribunal decides to delay the ruling, any appeal against the decision will have to be made as a jurisdictional appeal against an award under r 65,[126] rather than following the proceedings for an appeal against the decision on the objection to jurisdiction under r 21.

Recognising the fact that, in arbitration, "there may be some difficult issues of jurisdiction where the tribunal's ruling is almost certain to be challenged",[127] subject to the parties' agreement otherwise, r 22 allows the parties to seek assistance from the Outer House to determine a point of jurisdiction. However, such right is restricted by r 23, a mandatory rule, that it can be exercised only if all parties agree that an application can be made,[128] or the tribunal has consented to it and the court is satisfied that the court ruling on this matter will produce a substantial saving in expenses and the application was made swiftly by the parties, and the court must be convinced by the reasons why such an issue should be decided by the court rather than the arbitral tribunal.[129]

International practice

The principle of competence-competence allowing the tribunal to rule on its own jurisdiction over the parties and the disputes is termed as "positive" effect[130] on the arbitral tribunal by Delvolvé, Rouche and Pointon because the principle acknowledges the tribunal's mandate to adjudicate the disputes referred to it. The confirmation of jurisdiction is viewed as another positive effect of the arbitration agreement as it fulfils the purposes of arbitration being a speedy method of dispute resolution.

England

The principle of competence-competence is provided in s 30 of the (English) Arbitration Act 1996 which states that, unless otherwise agreed by the parties, the arbitral tribunal may rule on its own substantive jurisdiction as to the validity of an arbitration agreement, the composition of the arbitral tribunal and the scope of the submission. As Devlin J ruled in *Christopher Brown Ltd v Genossenschaft Oesterreichischer Waldbesitzer*:[131]

> "It is not the law that arbitrators if their jurisdiction is challenged are bound immediately to refuse to act until their jurisdiction has been determined by [the court]. Nor is it the law that they are bound to go on without investigating the merits of the challenge and determine the matter in

---

[126] Revised Explanatory Notes (2009), para 131.
[127] *Ibid*, para 133.
[128] Scottish Arbitration Rules, r 23(2)(a). Similar provision can be seen in s 32(2) of the (English) Arbitration Act 1996.
[129] Scottish Arbitration Rules, r 23(2)(b)(i)–(iii).
[130] J Delvolvé, J Rouche and G Pointon, *French arbitration law and practice* (2003), p 93.
[131] [1954] 1 QB 8.

dispute.... They are entitled to inquire into the merits of the issue whether they have jurisdiction or not."[132]

France, Switzerland and Belgium

Taking French law as an example, Art 1466 of the New Code of Civil Procedure (NCPC) provides that, in domestic arbitration, "[i]f one of the parties contests, before the arbitral tribunal, the basis or scope of its jurisdiction, then it shall itself rule on the validity of, or limits to, the authority which has been conferred on it". Similar provision in Art 1495 NCPC also applies to international arbitration provided that the arbitration is subject to French procedural law. The tribunal's mandate to rule on its own jurisdiction is also recognised in Art 186 of the Swiss Private International Law Act which provides: "1. The arbitral tribunal shall decide on its own jurisdiction. 2. Any objection to its jurisdiction must be raised prior to any defence on the merits. 3. The arbitral tribunal shall, as a rule, decide on its jurisdiction by a preliminary award."[133] Similar attitude can also be observed in Art 1697(1) of the Belgian Judicial Code, which provides that "[t]he arbitral tribunal may decide on its own jurisdiction, and for this purpose may examine the validity of the arbitration agreement".[134]

Hong Kong

As Hong Kong adopted the UNCITRAL Model Law, the issue concerning arbitrator's jurisdiction is governed by Art 16 of the UNCITRAL Model Law. Article 16(1) provides:

> "The arbitral tribunal may rule on its own jurisdiction, including any objections with respect to the existence or validity of the arbitration agreement. For that purpose, an arbitration clause which forms part of a contract shall be treated as an agreement independent of the other terms of the contract. A decision by the arbitral tribunal that the contract is null and void shall not entail *ipso jure* the invalidity of the arbitration clause."

Adopting the UNCITRAL Model Law, the principle of competence-competence is well received in both international and domestic arbitration as stipulated in UNCITRAL Model Law, Art 16, and s 13B of and Sch 5 to the Hong Kong Arbitration Ordinance 1997 respectively. Section 13B of the Ordinance stipulates: "Article 16 of the UNCITRAL Model Law applies to an arbitral tribunal that is conducting arbitration proceedings under a domestic arbitration agreement in the same way as it applies to

---

[132] [1954] 1 QB 8 at 12–13.
[133] Swiss Private International Law Act – Chapter 12: International Arbitration, 18 December 1987.
[134] Belgian Judicial Code, Sixth Part: Arbitration (Adopted 4 July 1972, amended 27 March 1985 and 19 May 1998).

an arbitral tribunal that is conducting arbitration proceedings under an international arbitration agreement."[135]

ISSUE OF CONFIDENTIALITY – r 26

See detailed discussion in Chapter 3.

DELIBERATION OF TRIBUNAL'S DECISIONS – r 27

The tribunal's deliberation does not have to be disclosed to the parties.[136] However, if an arbitrator failed to take part in any of the tribunal's deliberations, the tribunal must inform that fact and the extent of the failure to the parties.[137]

ARBITRATOR'S FEES AND EXPENSES – rr 59–66

The relationship between the parties and the arbitrators is regarded as a contractual one in most jurisdictions. For instance, in England, the judges in *Cereals SA v Tradax Export SA*[138] held that a contractual relationship existed between the parties and the arbitrators. Moreover, the court stated that the arbitrators became parties to the arbitration agreement as soon as they accepted the appointment. The court observed: "It is the arbitration contract that the arbitrators become parties to by accepting appointments under it. All parties to the arbitration are, as a matter of contract (subject always to the various statutory provisions), bound by the terms of the arbitration contract."[139] Because of this contractual relationship, it was decided that arbitrators were entitled to reasonable remuneration in *K/S Norjarl A/S v Hyundai Heavy Industries Co Ltd*.[140] The court decided that the arbitrators were entitled to reasonable remuneration. This entitlement was based on a trilateral contract between the two parties and the arbitrators.[141] The implied terms of this kind of trilateral contract require arbitrators to

---

[135] Chapter 341, Hong Kong Arbitration Ordinance 1997.
[136] Scottish Arbitration Rules, r 27(1).
[137] *Ibid*, r 27(2).
[138] [1986] 2 Lloyd's Rep 301.
[139] An injunction was granted in this case where a breach of the arbitration agreement had been committed by the arbitrators who were regarded as one of the parties to the arbitration agreement.
[140] *K/S Norjarl A/S v Hyundai Heavy Industries Co Ltd* [1991] 1 Lloyd's Rep 524 (CA).
[141] *Ibid* at p 537. The court said: "So far as the parties are concerned, their obligations under the trilateral contract include the liability to pay remuneration for the service of the arbitrators ... The contractual obligation on Hyundai and Norjarl to pay such remuneration could not be altered without the consent of both." Also, at 531: "Once the arbitrator has accepted an appointment, no term can be implied that entitled him to a commitment fee, and the arbitration agreement cannot be varied in that way without the consent of all parties."

"conduct the arbitration with due diligence and at a reasonable fee",[142] by using all reasonable means in entering on, and proceeding with, the reference.[143]

In Scotland, by carrying out the tasks of resolving the parties' dispute, arbitrators are entitled to fees and expenses incurred personally or as a member of the tribunal for the purpose of conducting the arbitration. It is up to the parties to reach an agreement between them and the arbitrator(s) or the arbitral appointment referees on the amount of fees and expenses payable.[144] Failing to reach any agreement, the amounts are to be determined by the Auditor of the Court of Session.[145] Once the amounts are agreed, r 60, a mandatory rule, makes the parties severally liable to the fees of the arbitrators, the arbitral appointments referee or any other third party to whom the parties give powers in relation to the arbitration.[146] The words "severally liable" allow the arbitrators to recover the full amount of the fees and expenses from either party.

Accordingly, the parties have to pay the arbitrators (a) the arbitrators' fees and expenses,[147] and (b) expenses incurred by the tribunal when conducting the arbitration.[148] The expenses include the fees and expenses of any clerk, agent, employee or other person appointed by the tribunal to assist it in conducting the arbitration, the fees and expenses of any expert from whom the tribunal obtains an opinion, any expenses in respect of meeting and hearing facilities, and any expenses incurred in determining recoverable arbitration expenses.[149]

Rule 61 also offers the tribunal the powers to determine the amounts or to arrange for an auditor to determine the amounts which are recoverable.[150] The tribunal can also make an award allocating the parties' liability between themselves for the recoverable arbitration expenses or any part of those expenses.[151] Any agreement between the parties allocating the parties' liability for any or all of the arbitration expenses has no effect if it is entered into before the dispute being arbitrated has arisen.[152]

---

[142] [1991] 1 Lloyd's Rep 524 at 532.
[143] Arbitration Act 1950, s 13(3).
[144] Scottish Arbitration Rules, r 60(3). Similar provision can be seen in s 59 of the (English) Arbitration Act 1996.
[145] Scottish Arbitration Rules, r 60(3)(b).
[146] Ibid, r 60(1)–(2).
[147] Ibid, r 60(1)(a)(i)–(ii).
[148] Ibid, r 60(1)(b).
[149] Ibid, r 60(1)(b)(i)–(iv).
[150] Ibid, r 61(2). Similar provision can be seen in s 64(1)–(2) of the (English) Arbitration Act 1996.
[151] Scottish Arbitration Rules, r 62(1). Similar provisions can be seen in ss 61(1) and 62(2) of the (English) Arbitration Act 1996.
[152] Scottish Arbitration Rules, r 63. Similar provision can be seen in s 60 of the (English) Arbitration Act 1996.

Subject to the parties' agreement otherwise, the tribunal may order the claimant or counter-claimant to provide security for the recoverable arbitration expenses or part of the amounts to safeguard the arbitrator's rights to remuneration.[153] If a party fails to comply with the order, the tribunal has the power to make an award dismissing any claims made by that party.[154] However, residence, place of incorporation or management outside of the United Kingdom shall not be the only grounds to be relied upon by the tribunal in making such security orders.[155]

DEATH OF ARBITRATOR AND PARTY – rr 79 and 80

The death of an arbitrator will discharge his contractual obligations owed to the parties to act as an arbitrator because his authority is personal and such authority ceases on his death.[156] As arbitrators provide services based on personal knowledge, skills and experience, it makes sense to bring his contractual obligations to an end in the event of death. It is worthwhile noting that an arbitrator's liability may not be discharged after his death if the parties can prove that the arbitrator has acted in bad faith during the arbitration proceedings.

Nevertheless, in contrast with r 79, the death of a party does not discharge the arbitration agreement. A valid arbitration agreement allows the other party to enforce the agreement against the executor or other representative of that party.[157] And, this rule does not affect the operation of any law by virtue of which a substantive right or obligation is extinguished by death.[158]

IMMUNITY – rr 73–75

In the Policy Memorandum, the draftsmen state their belief that it is essential to offer arbitrators and umpires immunity from liability for damages when performing their judicial functions to resolve disputes between parties. The memorandum states:

> "If arbitrators are not given such immunity, those with needed expertise may not be persuaded to act. This would mean the loss of one of the main advantages of arbitration – that it provides experts to judge specific

---

[153] Scottish Arbitration Rules, r 64(1)(a).
[154] *Ibid*, r 64(1)(b).
[155] *Ibid*, r 64(2).
[156] *Ibid*, r 79. Similar provision can be seen in s 26(1) of the (English) Arbitration Act 1996.
[157] Scottish Arbitration Rules, r 80(1).
[158] *Ibid*, r 80(2).

forms of dispute. It can be said that arbitrators, when carrying out their functions as such, act in a judicial capacity, and in this respect, therefore, should effectively be treated as judges. Lack of immunity is also likely to deter major international arbitrators from working in Scotland: other jurisdictions which do provide such immunity would be chosen instead."[159]

Consequently, r 73(1) provides that arbitrators are not liable for anything done or omitted in the performance or purported performance of the tribunal's functions. However, their immunity is subject to the exceptions of bad faith[160] or liability arising from an arbitrator's resignation.[161]

Considering the necessity to offer similar protection to other individuals involved in arbitration, immunity is also extended to any clerk, agent, employee or other person assisting the tribunal to perform its functions,[162] arbitral appointment referees, other third party empowered to make nomination of arbitrators,[163] agents or employees of arbitral appointment referees or other third party empowered to make nomination of arbitrators.[164]

Experts, witnesses and legal representatives participating in arbitration also enjoy a similar level of immunity because they should be placed in no more vulnerable a position in a private judicial proceeding than if they are taking part in civil court proceedings, in order to encourage them to be involved in an arbitration.[165]

The issue of immunity has a long history of debates centred on the contradictions between the contractual appointment of arbitrators and the judicial nature of immunity. The immunity of arbitrators is now predicated upon the generally accepted proposition that they enjoy quasi-judicial status. It has its basis in the fact that the functions performed by the arbitrators, who are chosen by the parties, can be compared to the acts performed by judges. It has further been submitted that the absence of immunity for arbitrators could compromise their integrity in such a way that they would be inclined to make an award in favour of a party who is more likely to sue.[166] With immunity, arbitrators can do their work without constantly looking over their shoulders in the fear of being forced to defend themselves in the courts.

---

[159] Policy Memorandum (29 January 2009), paras 205–206.
[160] Scottish Arbitration Rules, r 73(2)(a). Similar provision can be seen in s 29 of the (English) Arbitration Act 1996.
[161] Scottish Arbitration Rules, r 73(2)(b).
[162] Ibid, r 73(3).
[163] Ibid, r 74(1). Similar provision can be seen in s 74 of the (English) Arbitration Act 1996.
[164] Scottish Arbitration Rules, r 74(2).
[165] Ibid, r 75 and Policy Memorandum (29 January 2009), para 213.
[166] A Redfern and M Hunter, *The Law and Practice of International Commercial Arbitration* (5th edn, 2009), p 312.

England – "Absolute immunity with the exception of bad faith" standard

Arbitrator's immunity is confirmed in s 29 of the (English) Arbitration Act 1996 which provides that an arbitrator or his employee or agent is not liable for anything done or omitted in the discharge or purported discharge of his functions as arbitrator unless the act or omission is shown to have been in bad faith. In common law, the principle of judicial immunity in England is long established. Lord Tenterden CJ observed:

> "[E]ver since the year 1613, if not before, it has been accepted in our law that no action is maintainable against a judge for anything said or done by him in the exercise of a jurisdiction which belongs to him. The words that he speaks are protected by an absolute privilege. The orders that he gives, and the sentences which he imposes, cannot be made the subject of civil proceedings against him. No matter that the judge was under some gross error or ignorance, or was actuated by envy, hatred and malice, and all uncharitableness, he is not liable to an action. The remedy of the party aggrieved is to appeal to a court of appeal or to apply for habeas corpus, or a writ of error or certiorari, or take some such step to reverse his ruling. Of course, if the judge has accepted bribes or been in the least degree corrupt, or has perverted the course of justice, he can be punished in the criminal courts. That apart, however, a judge is not liable to an action for damages. The reason is not because the judge has any privilege to make mistake or to do wrong. It is so that he should be able to do his duty with complete independence and free from fear."[167]

This decision was followed in *Sirros v Moore*,[168] where the judge refused to grant bail and the plaintiff was taken away in custody in a deportation case. However, on the following day the Divisional Court granted the plaintiff leave to move for a writ of habeas corpus and he was released on bail. Nine days later, a writ of habeas corpus was issued on the ground that the judge had been *functus officio* when he ordered the plaintiff to be detained. As a result, the plaintiff issued a writ claiming damages for assault and false imprisonment against the defendants, the circuit judge and the police officers who had acted on the judge's orders in detaining the plaintiff.

The Court of Appeal supported judge's immunity and stated that the judge had been acting within his jurisdiction when he directed that the plaintiff be detained in custody, and accordingly, although he had adopted an erroneous course of procedure, he was immune from personal liability to the plaintiff in respect of that act. As Lord Denning MR stated:

---

[167] Lord Tenterden CJ in *Garnett v Ferrand* (1827) 6 B & C 611 at 625–626, [1824–34] All ER 244 at 246.
[168] [1975] QB 118, [1974] 3 All ER 776, [1974] 3 WLR 459, 139 JP 2.

"Every judge of the courts of this land – from the highest to the lowest – should be protected to the same degree, and liable to the same degree. If the reason underlying this immunity is to ensure 'that they may be free in thought and independent in judgment', it applies to every judge, whatever his rank. Each should be protected from liability to damages when he is acting judicially. Each should be able to do his work in complete independence and free from fear. He should not have to turn the pages of his books with trembling fingers, asking himself: 'If I do this, shall I be liable in damages?' So long as he does his work in the honest belief that it is within his jurisdiction, then he is not liable to an action. He may be mistaken in fact. He may be ignorant in law. What he does may be outside his jurisdiction – in fact or in law – but so long as he honestly believes it to be within his jurisdiction, he should not be liable."[169]

Sutcliffe v *Thackrah*[170]

On the ground of public policy, "neither party, witness, counsel, jury, nor judge, can be put to answer civilly or criminally for words spoken in office".[171] Arbitrator's immunity was upheld in the decisions made by the House of Lords in *Sutcliffe* v *Thackrah*[172] and *Arenson* v *Casson Beckman Rutley & Co.*[173] *Sutcliffe* was concerned with the liability of architects who were appointed by the plaintiff as architects and quantity surveyors in connection with a building contract on an RIBA form. The defendants issued interim certificates in favour of the contractor which the plaintiff duly honoured. However, due to the defendants' negligence, the amount certified was too great. When the plaintiff could not recover the excess from the contractor, who had become insolvent, he decided to sue the defendants. The defendants were held liable at the first instance. However this decision was reversed by the Court of Appeal, which held that the defendants were entitled to immunity as quasi-arbitrators. When the case reached the House of Lords, the judges denied the defendants any judicial immunity protection on the ground that a valuer could not be classed as a quasi-arbitrator, unless he exercised a judicial function.

While deciding the case, the House of Lords established the need for such immunity by saying:

"I think that the immunity of arbitrators from liability for negligence must be based on the belief – probably well founded – that without such immunity arbitrators would be harassed by actions which would have very little chance of success. And it may also have been thought that an arbitrator might be influenced by the thought that he was more likely to be

---

[169] [1975] QB 118, [1974] 3 All ER 776, [1974] 3 WLR 459, 139 JP 2.
[170] [1974] AC 727.
[171] Lopes LJ in *Royal Aquarium and Summer and Winter Garden Society* v *Parkinson* [1892] 1 QB 431 at 451, [1891–4] All ER 429 at 436.
[172] Above, n 170.
[173] [1977] AC 405.

sued if his decision went one way than if it went the other way, or that in some way the immunity put him in a more independent position to reach the decision which he thought right."[174]

Moreover,

"It is well settled that judges, barristers, solicitors, jurors and witnesses enjoy an absolute immunity from any form of civil action being brought against them in respect of anything they say or do in court during the course of a trial. This is not because the law regards any of these with special tenderness but because the law recognises that, on balance of convenience, public policy demands that they shall all have such an immunity. It is of great public importance that they shall all perform their respective functions free from fear that disgruntled and possibly impecunious persons who have lost their cause or been convicted may subsequently harass them with litigation."[175]

Finally, "[s]ince arbitrators are in much the same position as judges, in that they carry out more or less the same functions, the law has for generations recognised that public policy requires that they too shall be accorded the immunity to which I have referred".[176]

Arenson v *Casson Beckman Rutley & Co*[177]

The same issue regarding the arbitrator's immunity was reviewed again in *Arenson* v *Casson Beckman Rutley & Co.*[178] In this case, by a written agreement, the plaintiff agreed to sell shares back to his uncle at a "fair value" on termination of his employment. The expression "fair value" was defined in the agreement as being the value determined by the company's auditors "whose valuation acting as experts and not as arbitrators shall be final and binding on all parties". After selling the shares back to his uncle, the company's share value increased dramatically due to the floatation. The plaintiff brought an action for negligence against the defendants. Following *Sutcliffe*'s decision, the House of Lords confirmed the arbitrator's immunity within his judicial function, which is determined by whether the person is required to adjudicate upon an existing formulated dispute or receive evidence and arguments from the parties as well as the terms of appointment.[179]

Lord Kilbrandon in particular could see no reason why arbitrators should be immune from liability. His doubts were shared by Lord Fraser who questioned:

---

[174] *Sutcliffe*, above, n 170, at 757.
[175] *Ibid*.
[176] *Ibid* at 758.
[177] [1977] AC 405.
[178] *Ibid*.
[179] *Ibid*, per Lord Simon and Lord Wheatley at 423 and 428.

"What was the essential difference between the typical valuer, the auditor in the present case, and an arbitrator at common law or under the Arbitration Acts? It was conceded that an arbitrator is immune from suit, aside from fraud, but why? ... I have come to be of opinion that it is a necessary conclusion to be drawn from *Sutcliffe* v *Thackrah* and from the instant decision that an arbitrator at common law or under the Acts is indeed a person selected by the parties for his expertise, whether technical or intellectual, that he pledges skills in the exercise thereof, and that *if he is negligent in that exercise he will be liable in damages.*

...

Since I can find no satisfactory distinction between the liability for negligence of persons in the position of the respondents and that of arbitrators, had I not been of the opinion that arbitrators at Common Law or under the Acts have no immunity, I would have been unable to agree that the appeal should be allowed."[180] (Emphasis added)

Palacath Ltd v *Flanaga*[181]

After *Sutcliffe* and *Arenson*, the issue of immunity was again reviewed in *Palacath Ltd* v *Flanaga*. The plaintiff brought an action against the defendant (surveyor) alleging negligence in determining the rent under a rent review clause in a lease. According to the terms of appointment, the surveyor had been appointed to determine the rent and he "will act as an expert and not as an arbitrator ... will consider any statement of reasons or valuation or report submitted to him ... but will not be in any way limited or fettered thereby [and] will be entitled to rely on his own judgement and opinion". The plaintiff contended that the defendant was under a contractual duty, or alternatively a duty of care, to the plaintiff and the tenant to use the skill and diligence which would reasonably be expected from a competent surveyor in determining the amount of the yearly rent, whereas the defendant argued that he was acting as arbitrator or quasi-arbitrator, therefore, he was entitled to immunity.

The issue to be determined was whether the surveyor had been appointed as an arbitrator or quasi-arbitrator and was therefore immune from suit. Mars-Jones J believed that a person would only be an arbitrator or quasi-arbitrator if there was a submission to him either of a specific dispute or of present points of difference or of defined differences. In this case, as the defendant was appointed as an expert, there was no basis for conferring immunity on the defendant as the parties to the lease had not intended the surveyor to act as an arbitrator or quasi-arbitrator and they had not intended to set up a judicial or quasi-judicial machinery for the resolution of disputes.

---

[180] [1977] AC 405 at 419.
[181] [1985] 2 All ER 161, 274 EG 143, [1985] 1 EGLR 86.

(English) Arbitration Act 1996

While the majority of their Lordships in *Sutcliffe* and *Arenson* were in favour of granting immunity to arbitrators, the doubts expressed by Lords Kilbrandon and Fraser have planted a time bomb on this issue. This situation is not surprising as very little rationale behind such immunity has ever been given. While it was said that, in England, the rationale behind arbitrator's immunity was drawn from the principle of similar functions performed by both arbitrators and judges, serious debates were carried out in the House of Lords during the preparation of what would become s 29 of the Arbitration Act 1996. Considering the possibility of an arbitrator failing to take a step necessary for the proper and expeditious conduct of the arbitral proceedings, Lord Brightman proposed an amendment to cl 29, providing that an arbitrator is to be liable if he fails to avoid unnecessary delay or expense. It read: "for any costs of the arbitration thrown away if by reason of his own default or the default of his employee or agent he fails to take a step necessary for the proper and expeditious conduct of the arbitral proceedings".

Lord Denning, Lord Mustill, Lord Roskill, and Lord Donaldson of Lymington disagreed with Lord Brightman's proposal. Lord Donaldson of Lymington used his own experience as an arbitrator as an example to express his concerns about imposing liability on arbitrators and said that he should really resent it very much if he was at the mercy of one of the disputants at a later stage and being accused of wasting time and money because he believed that he should not be in default in failing to take that step. In his opinion, it should be the parties who take the necessary steps to avoid costs and delays. He also expressed displeasure about the call for arbitrators to take out professional indemnity by saying: "If we are to have a straight liability here as an exception to the general exemption contained in the clause, arbitrators will be forced to take out insurance. As a very occasional arbitrator, if I had to start taking out insurance, for my part I would cease to arbitrate at all."

On the other hand, in Lord Brightman's camp, Lord Hacking pointed out that, in principle, arbitration should be conducted in a proper and expeditious way; and if the fault was with the arbitrator, he saw no reason why the arbitrator should not pick up the financial penalty. Furthermore, he said: "The noble and learned Lord, Lord Donaldson, whom we do not wish to discourage from presiding over arbitrations, is worried about insurance. All I have to say to the noble and learned Lord and to other noble Lords is that all the rest of us who are in the marketplace offering professional services must have insurance, and I do not see any reason why arbitrators should not contemplate that as well."

This uncertainty was eventually removed by s 29(1) of the (English) Arbitration Act 1996 (the Act), which states: "An arbitrator is not liable for anything done or omitted in the discharge or purported discharge of his functions as arbitrator unless the act or omission is known to have been in bad faith." The 1996 Report on the Arbitration Bill, which was prepared by the Department Advisory Committee (DAC) on Arbitration Law and led by Lord Saville, stated that "Although the general view seems to be that arbitrators have some immunity under the present law, this is not entirely free from doubt". The Committee carried on holding the view that arbitrators should have a degree of immunity because:

> "The reasons for providing immunity are the same as those that apply to Judges in our Courts. Arbitration and litigation share this in common, that both provide a means of dispute resolution which depends upon a binding decision by an impartial third party. It is generally considered that an immunity is necessary to enable that third party properly to perform an impartial decision making function. Furthermore, we feel strongly that unless a degree of immunity is afforded, the finality of the arbitral process could well be undermined. The prospect of a losing party attempting to re-arbitrate the issues on the basis that a competent arbitrator would have decided them [the matters] in favour of that party is one that we would view with dismay. The Bill provides in our view adequate safeguards to deal with cases where the arbitral process has gone wrong."[182]

Section 29 of the Act was intended by the DAC to confer absolute immunity including claims in tort and contract subject only to bad faith. So far this provision has claimed success in practice in that, as yet, none has made a valid claim against arbitrators.

Looking at s 29 in detail, in the DAC Report, both paragraph 133 (stressing the mandatory nature of this provision) and paragraph 136 (concluding that the court should be given power to remove or modify the immunity as it sees fit) clearly the origins and nature of such immunity of arbitrators derive from the state and not from the parties' agreement. This corresponds with what Lord Kilbrandon said in *Arenson*:

> "The State – I use the word for convenience – sets up a judicial system, which includes not only the Courts of Justice but also the numerous tribunals, statutory arbitrators, commissioners and so on, who give decisions, whether final or not, on matters in which the State has given them competence. ... You do not test a claim to immunity by asking whether the claimant is bound to act judicially; such a question, as Lord Reid pointed out in *Sutcliffe* v *Thackrah*, leads to arguing in a circle. Immunity is judged by the origin and character of the appointment, not by the duties which the appointee has to perform, or his methods of performing them."[183]

---

[182] DAC Report at 296.
[183] [1977] AC 405 at 420.

USA – "Absolute immunity" standard

In the United States, judicial immunity has always been offered to arbitrators.[184] The common law doctrine of judicial immunity was first recognised in the case of *Bradley v Fisher*[185] on the ground that: "If civil actions could be maintained in such cases against the judges, because the losing party should see fit to allege in his complaint that the acts of the judge were done with partiality or maliciously or corruptly, the protection essential to judicial independence would be entirely swept away."[186] The same immunity is also extended to arbitrators whose jobs have traditionally been construed to be quasi-judicial in nature,[187] since the United States courts have been convinced that arbitrators usually do not have any interest in the outcome of the awards. Arbitrators are simply appointed to perform a functionally judicial job; therefore, they are protected from civil suits under the doctrine of arbitral immunity.[188]

In *Bradley v Fisher*, Joseph H Bradley, an attorney-at-law, brought an action against George Fisher, who was one of the justices in the Supreme Court of the District of Columbia. He claimed that the defendant wilfully, maliciously, oppressively and tyrannically deprived his right to practise as an attorney in that court. In his judgment, Mr Justice Field pointed out that the order challenged by the plaintiff was made by the defendant in the lawful exercise and performance of his authority and duty as the presiding justice. In other words, it was a judicial act, done by the defendant as the presiding justice of a court of general criminal jurisdiction.[189] After confirming it was a judicial act done within the justice's jurisdiction, the Court set out to explain the need for absolute immunity to protect judges from lawsuits claiming that their decisions had been tainted by improper motives. The Court began by noting that the principle of immunity for acts done by judges "in the exercise of their judicial functions" had always been recognised through the influence of English jurisprudence. Citing Mr Justice Compton in the case of *Fray v Blackburn*:[190]

> "It is a principle of our law that no action will lie against a judge of one of the superior courts for a judicial act, though it be alleged to have been

---

[184] *Corey v New York Stock Exchange*, 691 F 2d 1205. The court said (at 1211): "Extension of arbitral immunity to encompass boards which sponsor arbitration is a natural and necessary product of the policies underlying arbitral immunity; otherwise the immunity extended to arbitrators is illusionary. It would be of little value to the whole arbitral procedure to merely shift the liability to the sponsoring association."
[185] US (13 Wall) 335, 20 L Ed 646 (1872).
[186] *Ibid* at 649–650.
[187] *Gahn v International Union Ladies' Garment Workers' Union*, 311 F 2d 113 (3rd Cir 1962) at 114–115.
[188] *Hoosac Tunnel, Dock and Elevator Co v O'Brien*, 137 Mass 424 (1984) at 426.
[189] 80 US (13 Wall) 335, 20 L Ed 646 (1872) at 347.
[190] 3 Best & Smith, 576. See also *Bradley v Fisher*, 80 US (13 Wall) 335 at 349, 20 L Ed 646 (1872).

done maliciously and corruptly; therefore the proposed allegation would not make the declaration good. The public are deeply interested in this rule, which indeed exists for their benefit, and was established in order to secure the independence of the judges, and prevent them being harassed by vexatious actions."

The rationale of such immunity offered to the judges is based on the fact that judges were often called to decide "[controversies] involving not merely great pecuniary interests, but the liberty and character of the parties, and consequently exciting the deepest feelings".[191] As a result, such adjudications invariably produced at least one losing party, who would "[accept] anything but the soundness of the decision in explanation of the action of the judge".[192] If a civil action was allowed to be brought against the judge by virtue of an allegation of malice, judges would lose their independence. Without such independence, the judiciary's functions will be significantly damaged. As Mr Justice Field stated:

> "Liability to answer to every one who might feel himself aggrieved by the action of the judge, would be inconsistent with the possession of this freedom, and would destroy that independence without which no judiciary can be either respectable or useful. ... Nor can this exemption of the judges from civil liability be affected by the motives with which their judicial acts are performed. The purity of their motives cannot in this way be the subject of judicial inquiry ... and it was observed that if they were required to answer otherwise, it would tend to the scandal and subversion of all justice, and those who are the most sincere, would not be free from continual calumniations."[193]

Accordingly, judges are entitled to immunity from civil suit for malice or corruption in their action whilst exercising their judicial functions within the general scope of their jurisdiction.

Hoosac Tunnel, Dock & Elevator Co v O'Brien[194]

The judicial immunity established in *Bradley* also applies to arbitrators. As early as in 1884, in the case of *Hoosac Tunnel, Dock & Elevator Co v O'Brien*, the Supreme Court of Massachusetts dismissed the plaintiff's claim against the arbitrator for combining, confederating, and conspiring for his own lucre, benefit, and gain to injure and defraud the plaintiff in a personal injury case. Justice Morton CJ stated:

> "It is of the highest importance that judges and others engaged in the administration of justice should be independent, and should act upon their

---

[191] *Bradley v Fisher* 80 US (13 Wall) 335 at 348, 20 L Ed 646 (1872).
[192] Ibid.
[193] Ibid.
[194] 137 Mass 424 (1984) at 426.

own free and unbiased convictions, uninfluenced by any apprehension of consequences. ... An arbitrator is a quasi-judicial officer, under our laws, exercising judicial functions. There is as much reason in his case for protecting and insuring his impartiality, independence, and freedom from undue influences, as in the case of a judge or juror. The same considerations of public policy apply, and we are of opinion that the same immunity extends to him."[195]

Gahn v International Union Ladies' Garment Workers' Union[196]

Arbitrator's immunity was also upheld in *Gahn v International Union Ladies' Garment Workers' Union*, where the appellee was appointed as an arbitrator to resolve a dispute arising out of the contract between Sidele Fashions, Inc and the Joint Board of the International Ladies' Garment Workers' Union. Sidele Fashions sued on the grounds that the appellee forced and coerced them and other association members unlawfully to adhere to and maintain contract provisions which violated the Sherman Anti-Trust Act and other federal statutes, as well as inflicting heavy fines and penalties on plaintiffs and others in order to prevent them from operating freely and economically in the market place. The appeal court agreed with the District Court that "the allegations of the said paragraphs are based upon the conduct of the appellee in his capacity as arbitrator; that in so functioning he was performing quasi-judicial duties and was clothed with an immunity, analogous to judicial immunity, against actions brought by either of the parties arising out of his performance of his duties".[197]

Corbin v Washington Fire and Marine Insurance Co[198]

Corbin v Washington Fire and Marine Insurance Co presented another example of judicial immunity enjoyed by arbitrators. In this case, the arbitrator was appointed to decide a claim of liability for failure properly to protect the subrogation rights of the defendants-insurers in the settlement effected by the other insurance group in connection with an automobile accident in which both insurance groups, through their assureds, were involved. Pursuant to an arbitration agreement between the parties, this controversy between the two insurance groups was submitted to a board of arbitrators. Both parties to the arbitration submitted their statement of facts and argument in the form of letters to the board of arbitrators. In their statement, the defendants, under the signature of E C Heard, as their representative, wrote, among other things:

---

[195] 137 Mass 424 (1984) at 426.
[196] 311 F 2d 113 (3rd Cir 1962) at 114–115.
[197] *Ibid* at 115. Also see *Cooper v O'Connor*, 69 App DC 100, 99 F 2d 135 at 141 (DC Cir 1938); *Hohensee v Goon Squad*, 171 F Supp 562 at 568, 569, MDPa 1959); *Hoosac Tunnel, Dock & Elevator Co v O'Brien*, 137 Mass 424 at 426 (1884); *Craviolini v Scholer & Fuller Associated Architects*, 89 Ariz 24, 357 P2d 611 at 613 (1960).
[198] 278 F Supp 393, 1968 US Dist.

"... We particularly call your attention to paragraph four that it was stated that negotiations were made in good faith by the attorney for Sandra Simmons and settlement was made July 2, 1964, and a release and draft was furnished that date which is a falsehood. As you know, it is a legal maxim, that false in one thing false in all things. ... We had made our payment July 7, 1964, for $1118.93 and Samuel J. Corbin was attempting to push their settlement ahead to July 2, 1964, as we have letter from respondent dated February 10, 1965, admitting that settlement was not made until July 18, 1964."

The plaintiff sued in libel, asserting that the quoted language defamed the plaintiff in his character as an attorney and adjuster. The defendants claimed absolute immunity, whereas the plaintiff argued for qualified immunity, and that the immunity had been lost in the case of malice and excessive defamation. In deciding whether to grant the defendants immunity, the court first examined the judicial attitude to arbitration and stated that:

"The arbitration of controversies, it has been repeatedly stated in the decisions and evidenced in both state and federal statutes, is favoured in law. It is regarded as quasi-judicial in character and function. Arbitration, even as any judicial hearing, cannot proceed without evidence and the right of the parties to present argument; it cannot operate in a vacuum. It accordingly contemplates and normally requires the receipt of evidence, though not bound strictly in its reception to the rules of evidence."[199]

Moreover,

"A denial of immunity to one offering such evidence or argument would make it difficult, if not impossible, in many cases for the arbitrators to secure the necessary evidence on which to proceed; it would be a severe limitation on the utility of arbitration in resolving controversies and would thwart that public policy which encourages arbitration. Freedom to develop a relevant record and to present pertinent arguments, without fear of reprisal by way of threatened libel or slander actions, is a necessary prerequisite to the fair resolution of any controversy through arbitration."[200]

Disagreeing with the plaintiff's call for qualified immunity or no immunity in the case of malice, the court expressed its concerns and stated that if arbitration is to be safely utilised as an effective means of resolving controversy, the absolute immunity attaching to its proceedings must extend beyond the arbitrators themselves; it must extend to all "indispensable" proceedings, such as the receipt of evidence and argument thereon. Consequently, the court decided that an absolute immunity is essential to the maintenance of arbitration as an effective instrument for the settlement of controversies.

---

[199] 278 F Supp 393 at 397.
[200] Ibid.

Corey v New York Stock Exchange[201]

In *Corey v New York Stock Exchange*, George Corey claimed that the procedures followed in an arbitration proceeding sponsored by the NYSE and to which he was a party were wrongful and caused him injury. Corey sued both NYSE and Cavell, the NYSE's arbitration director, for the damages caused by the conduct of the arbitrators. The court decided that the NYSE, acting through its arbitrators, is immune from civil liability for the acts of the arbitrators arising out of contractually agreed upon arbitration proceedings. By placing arbitrators on the same footing as judges, the court stated:

> "The functional comparability of the arbitrator's decision-making process and judgments to those of judges and agency hearing examiners generates the same need for independent judgment, free from the threat of lawsuits. Immunity furthers this need. As with judicial and quasi-judicial immunity, arbitral immunity is essential to protect the decision-maker from undue influence and protect the decision-making process from reprisals by dissatisfied litigants."

The court also believed there is such need for immunity when arbitrators have no interest in the outcome of the dispute and should not be compelled to become parties to that dispute. As far as concerns the decision to extend immunity to the board which sponsors arbitration, the court found support in the case law, the policies behind the doctrines of judicial and quasi-judicial immunity and policies unique to contractually agreed upon arbitration proceedings. This opinion was expressed in the following terms: "Extension of arbitral immunity to encompass boards which sponsor arbitration is a natural and necessary product of the policies underlying arbitral immunity; otherwise the immunity extended to arbitrators is illusionary. It would be of little value to the whole arbitral procedure to merely shift the liability to the sponsoring association."[202]

Calzarano v Liebowitz[203]

Following the precedents, arbitrator's judicial immunity was also upheld in *Calzarano v Liebowitz*, where the plaintiff asked for $1,050,000 in damages arising out of an arbitration award rendered by Liebowitz on 5 May 1981. Citing *Gahn*[204] and *Corey v New York Stock Exchange*,[205] the court once again confirmed the arbitrator's judicial immunity and stated:

---

[201] *Corey v New York Stock Exchange*, 691 F 2d 1205.
[202] *Ibid* at 1211.
[203] 550 F Supp 1389, 1982 US Dist, 97 Lab Cas (CCH) P10, 136.
[204] *Gahn*, above, n 196.
[205] *Corey*, above, n 201.

"An arbitrator is a quasi-judicial officer, under our laws, exercising judicial functions. There is much reason in his case for protecting and insuring his impartiality, independence, and freedom from undue influences, as in the case of a judge or juror. The same considerations of public policy apply, and we are of opinion that the same immunity extends to him."[206]

---

[206] 550 F Supp 1389 at 1391.

CHAPTER 8

PROCEDURAL LAW

GENERAL

The principle of party autonomy affords the parties to arbitration the freedom to choose the arbitrators, the language, the substantive law, the procedural law ... and so on. In order to attract more cross-border arbitration business to Scotland, the policy clearly sets the tone that the choice of procedural law can be different from the choice of the substantive law. For instance, parties to arbitration may choose Swiss law to govern disputes arising from the main contract between them but to have procedural matters governed by Scottish arbitration law. This can be seen in s 3(2) of the Arbitration (Scotland) Act 2010, which stipulates: "The fact that an arbitration is seated in Scotland does not affect the substantive law to be used to decide the dispute." What it means is that the choice of arbitrating in Scotland in accordance with the Arbitration Act 2010 does not affect the parties' choice of substantive law other than Scots law to determine the substantive issues.[1]

The parties' chosen procedural law regulates all procedural matters which have to be followed by the arbitrators in order to ensure the smooth operation of arbitration. As mentioned before, the procedural matters cover the aspects of place, language, communication between parties and arbitrators, written submissions, evidence, conduct of hearings, witnesses, expert witnesses, confidentiality, etc. Parties can choose either a set of arbitration rules, or a national procedural law, or even have a set of procedural rules tailored into their needs for this particular arbitration. However, parties' freedom in the choice of procedural law is not unlimited. Their choice is qualified by the exceptions of mandatory rules and public policy. It is worth noting that, in some cases, the parties may fail to choose the procedural law to govern the arbitration. In the absence of the parties' choice, in accordance with the usual international practice, the choice of

---

[1] Explanatory Notes, 29 January 2009, para 23 (also see Revised Explanatory Notes, 13 November 2009).

procedural law is to be made by the arbitrators. No matter whether the choice of procedural law was decided by the parties or arbitrators, the issue will become rather complicated if the parties or arbitrators decide to have the seat of arbitration designated in a country other than the one whose procedural law was chosen to govern the arbitration procedures. This is not an unusual scenario in international commercial arbitration. Frequently, arbitration can be held in Country A but the proceedings are governed by the law of Country B. Under these circumstances, the issue to be examined is to what extent the choice of the place of arbitration would affect the chosen procedural law.

SEAT OF ARBITRATION

From the Policy Memorandum published in 29 January 2009, it is clear that the Arbitration (Scotland) Act 2010 adopted the seat theory, which anchors arbitration to the place of arbitration, by defining "the seat (or place) of an arbitration is the legal seat from which the law of arbitration applying to a particular case is drawn".[2] Apart from emphasising the importance of the seat of arbitration in international arbitration, it further explains that the seat of arbitration is the legal jurisdiction which is to govern the arbitration proceedings.

In accordance with s 3 of the Arbitration (Scotland) Act, the seat of arbitration can be designated by the parties, the arbitrators, third parties authorised to so designate, or the court. Accordingly, Scotland is regarded as the juridical seat of arbitration if Scotland is designated as the seat of the arbitration by the parties directly or by any third parties, such as an institution or an individual, where authorised explicitly by the parties or by the arbitral tribunal. This issue can also be determined by the arbitral tribunal in the absence of the parties' expressed choice or designation.[3] Failing designation of the seat of arbitration, according to s 3(1)(a), the seat of the arbitration may also be decided by the tribunal[4] or courts[5] in accordance with the rules of private international law. Apart from the relevant provisions on the juridical seat of arbitration, for convenience, r 29 allows the tribunal to meet and otherwise conduct the arbitration anywhere it chooses (in or outwith Scotland).

DEFAULT RULES

It is not unusual to find that parties have failed to agree on relevant procedural matters and have left the issues in a legal vacuum. Taking this

---

[2] Policy Memorandum, 29 January 2009, para 66.
[3] Arbitration (Sc) Act 2010, s 3(1)(a)(i)–(iii). Similar provision can be seen in s 3 of the (English) Arbitration Act 1996.
[4] Arbitration (Sc) Act 2010, s 3(1)(a).
[5] Explanatory Notes, para 22 and Arbitration (Sc) Act 2010, s 3(1)(b).

possibility into account, the draftsmen felt the need to enact some default rules, which are used to fill the gaps left by the lack of agreed procedural rules to avoid delay. According to the consultation paper, most consultees were in favour of the design of default rules when they were asked the question whether they agreed that the parties to an arbitration can generally vary the procedural law application from the seat of arbitration. Consequently, there are two types of rules contained in the Scottish Arbitration Rules: they are the mandatory rules[6] and the default rules.[7] Following the principle of party autonomy, the Act allows the parties to make their own arrangements on matters covered by the default rules. Section 9 of the Act is designed to correspond with one of the funding principles, listed in s 1 that parties to arbitration should be free to agree how to resolve their disputes.[8] It is hoped that such a design can provide the parties a flexible dispute resolution mechanism, allowing them to adopt the most appropriate procedures to deal with their disputes.

The default rules are marked "D" in the Scottish Arbitration Rules. Any or all the default rules can be modified or disapplied by the parties' agreement.[9] In the absence of parties' agreement on those issues, the default rules will apply. This can be seen in s 9(2) which states: "A default rule applies in relation to an arbitration seated in Scotland only in so far as the parties have not agreed to modify or disapply that rule (or any part of it) in relation to that arbitration." Where there is any inconsistent provision between the default rules and the parties' arbitration agreement, anything done with the parties' agreement, any arbitration rules or other documents, such as the UNCITRAL Model Law, the UNCITRAL Arbitration Rules or other institutional rules (ICC, LCIA, or AAA), the parties' arbitration agreement will take precedence.[10]

The Policy Memorandum pointed out that, without the design of default rules, the parties will have to spend time and resources drafting the procedural rules to be followed and applied by the arbitrators. This may prove difficult if the parties are already in dispute.[11] To eliminate such problems and possible delay in conducting arbitral proceedings, the default rules provide a "ready-made framework"[12] to offer the parties the opportunity to fall back on them.

> "The main advantage of the default rules is that, the default rules will apply and fill the gaps if the parties do not or have not made any agreement as

---

[6] Arbitration (Sc) Act 2010, s 8. Similar provision can be seen in s 8 of the (English) Arbitration Act 1996.
[7] Arbitration (Sc) Act 2010, s 9(1).
[8] Policy Memorandum, para 86.
[9] Explanatory Notes, para 32.
[10] Arbitration (Sc) Act 2010, s 9(4).
[11] Policy Memorandum, 29 January 2009, para 88.
[12] Ibid.

to how the arbitration is to proceed. The parties may in fact have made no further agreement beyond a bare agreement to arbitrate any current or future dispute. They may, for example, have made no agreement as to who the arbitrator is or how that person is chosen and appointed."[13]

MANDATORY RULES

Following the seat theory adopted in the Arbitration (Scotland) Act 2010, it is not surprising to find a long list of mandatory rules, consisting of 36 provisions and ranging from the issue of eligibility of arbitrators to the challenging of awards, designed to take precedence over any agreement between the parties which is inconsistent with the mandatory rules and render any conflicting agreed provisions unenforceable.[14] Concerns over public policy are stated to be the main reason behind such a long list. In the draftsman's own words:

> "The mandatory rules are provided in key areas of the process to ensure the smooth and efficient running of an arbitration and to reduce the prospect of delay. If an arbitration is not conducted in accordance with the rules which apply to it (including all mandatory rules), the arbitrator may, depending on the breach, lay himself or herself open to removal and any award may be liable to challenge."[15]

With an intention to preserve party autonomy in deciding arbitration procedures, according to the Policy Memorandum, there was a conscious effort to keep the number of the mandatory rules to a minimum. However, a list of 28 mandatory rules contained in the Bill was expanded to become a much longer list of 36 mandatory rules in this Act.[16] This list of 36 mandatory rules (which are marked with an "M") is comprises the following:

- r 3   Arbitrator to be an individual
- r 4   Eligibility to act as an arbitrator
- r 7   Failure of appointment procedure
- r 8   Duty to disclose any conflict of interests
- rr 12–16   Removal or resignation of arbitrator or dismissal of tribunal
- rr 19–21 and 23   Jurisdiction of tribunal
- rr 24 and 25   General duties of tribunal and parties
- r 42   Point of law referral: procedure etc

---

[13] Policy Memorandum, 29 January 2009, para 86.
[14] Ibid, para 82.
[15] Ibid, para 83.
[16] Apart from the removal of r 50, nine further mandatory rules are added onto the list. They are: rr 4, 7, 23, 42, 44, 48, 50, 54 and 70.

r 44   Time limit variation: procedure etc
r 45   Securing attendance of witnesses and disclosure of evidence
r 48   Power to award payment and damages
r 50   Interest
r 54   Part awards
r 56   Power to withhold award if fees or expenses not paid
r 60   Arbitrators' fees and expenses
r 63   Ban on pre-dispute agreements about liability for arbitration expenses
rr 67, 68, 70–72   Challenging awards
rr 73–75   Immunity
r 76   Loss of right to object
r 77   Independence of arbitrator
r 79   Death of arbitrator
r 82   Rules applicable to umpires.

According to the mandatory rules contained therein, any arbitration procedures subject to the Arbitration (Scotland) Act 2010 cannot exclude their application. For instance, an arbitrator has to be an individual[17] who is above the age of 16[18] and not an incapable adult under s 1(6) of the Adults with Incapacity (Scotland) Act 2000 (asp 4).[19] In a case where the parties have failed to appoint the arbitrators, either party may refer the matter to an arbitral appointments referee[20] or the courts.[21] Arbitrators have the legal duty to disclose any known conflict of interests which might reasonably be considered relevant to the issue whether the arbitrator is impartial and independent.[22] The Outer House has the power to remove any arbitrators who are not independent or impartial,[23] are in breach of due process,[24] are incapable of acting as arbitrators,[25] do not hold the qualifications required by the parties,[26] or have caused substantial injustice to the party.[27] The Outer House also has the power to dismiss the tribunal in a case where substantial injustice has caused or will be caused.[28] The mandatory rules also contain provisions regulating the grounds of arbitrator's

---

[17] Scottish Arbitration Rules, r 3.
[18] *Ibid*, r 4(a).
[19] *Ibid*, r 4(b).
[20] *Ibid*, r 7(2). Similar provisions can be seen in ss 17–18 of the (English) Arbitration Act 1996.
[21] Scottish Arbitration Rules, r 7(6).
[22] *Ibid*, r 8.
[23] *Ibid*, r 12(a). Similar provision can be seen in s 23 of the (English) Arbitration Act 1996.
[24] Scottish Arbitration Rules, r 12(b).
[25] *Ibid*, r 12(c).
[26] *Ibid*, r 12(d).
[27] *Ibid*, r 12(e).
[28] *Ibid*, rr 13 and 14.

resignation,[29] arbitrator's liability and entitlement after resignation,[30] and the arbitrator's power to rule on their own jurisdiction.[31]

Part 3 of the Rules also contains mandatory rules regulating the general duties of the arbitrators and parties. For instance, the Act imposed duties on arbitrators to act independently, impartially and fairly,[32] while arbitrators and the parties have a duty to conduct arbitration without delay and unnecessary costs.[33]

Apart from mandatory provisions in relation to arbitrators, in the case where the parties choose to opt-in the clause of referral of point of law, such referral can only be made without delay[34] according to the parties' agreement,[35] or with the consent of the tribunal, and the court must be satisfied that determining the question is likely to produce substantial savings in expenses[36] and be convinced that there is a good reason why the question should be determined by the court.[37]

As concerns the court's power in arbitral proceedings, time limit provision is mandatory in nature.[38] Regarding evidence, it is mandatory that the court may, on an application by the tribunal or any party, order any person to attend a hearing for the purpose of giving evidence to the tribunal,[39] or to disclose documents or other material evidence to the tribunal.[40]

In relation to awards, the tribunal may make partial awards[41] and award interest[42] and order the payment of a sum of money in specific currency,[43] including damages.[44] In the case where the parties have

---

[29] Scottish Arbitration Rules, r 15(1). Similar provision can be seen in s 25(1), (4) and (5) of the (English) Arbitration Act 1996.

[30] Scottish Arbitration Rules, r 16. Similar provisions can be seen in s 25(3) and (5) of the (English) Arbitration Act 1996.

[31] Scottish Arbitration Rules, rr 19–21 and 23.

[32] Ibid, r 24(1)(a) and (b). Similar provision can be seen in s 33 of the (English) Arbitration Act 1996.

[33] Scottish Arbitration Rules, rr 24(1)(c) and 25.

[34] Ibid, r 42(2)(b)(ii). Similar provision can be seen in s 45(2) of the (English) Arbitration Act 1996.

[35] Scottish Arbitration Rules, rr 42(2)(a) and 24.

[36] Ibid, r 42(2)(b)(i).

[37] Ibid, r 42(2)(b)(iii).

[38] Ibid, r 44.

[39] Ibid, r 45(1)(a). Similar provision can be seen in s 43 of the (English) Arbitration Act 1996.

[40] Scottish Arbitration Rules, r 45(1)(b).

[41] Ibid, r 54. Similar provision can be seen in s 47 of the (English) Arbitration Act 1996.

[42] Scottish Arbitration Rules, r 50. Similar provision can be seen in s 49 of the (English) Arbitration Act 1996.

[43] Scottish Arbitration Rules, r 48(2). Similar provision can be seen in s 48(4) of the (English) Arbitration Act 1996.

[44] Scottish Arbitration Rules, r 48(1).

failed to pay fees and expenses in full, the tribunal may refuse to deliver or send its award to the parties.[45] It is also mandatory that the parties are jointly and severally liable to pay for the arbitrator's fees and expenses.[46] Any agreement, which is entered into before the dispute being arbitrated has arisen, between the parties to allocate their liability between themselves for any or all of the arbitration expenses has no effect.[47]

Challenge of awards on the grounds of substantive jurisdiction (lack of jurisdiction)[48] or serious irregularities[49] is also made mandatory.[50] In the case where serious irregularities are the grounds for appeal, the tribunal must make a new award in respect of the matter concerned within the time limit if either the Outer House or the Inner House orders it to reconsider its award.[51]

The Act also stipulates that arbitral tribunals,[52] the appointing arbitral institutions,[53] experts, witnesses and legal representatives[54] are not liable for acts or omissions unless the act or omission is shown to have been in bad faith. It is mandatory that the party loses their right to object before the tribunal or the court if the party failed to raise a timeous objection on the grounds of eligibility,[55] independence and impartiality,[56] jurisdiction of the arbitral tribunal,[57] due process,[58] the arbitration having been conducted beyond the scope of submission or the Scottish Arbitration Rules,[59] and serious irregularities.[60] Under the Act, an arbitrator must remain independent to avoid any justifiable doubts as to the arbitrator's

---

[45] Scottish Arbitration Rules, r 56(1). Similar provision can be seen in s 56 of the (English) Arbitration Act 1996.
[46] Scottish Arbitration Rules, r 60. Similar provision can be seen in s 59 of the (English) Arbitration Act 1996.
[47] Scottish Arbitration Rules, r 63. Similar provision can be seen in s 60 of the (English) Arbitration Act 1996.
[48] Scottish Arbitration Rules, r 67. Similar provision can be seen in s 67 of the (English) Arbitration Act 1996.
[49] Scottish Arbitration Rules, r 68. Similar provision can be seen in s 68 of the (English) Arbitration Act 1996.
[50] Scottish Arbitration Rules, rr 70 and 71. Similar provisions can be seen in ss 69–70 of the (English) Arbitration Act 1996.
[51] Scottish Arbitration Rules, r 72.
[52] Ibid, r 73.
[53] Ibid, r 74. Similar provisions can be seen in ss 69(7)(c) and 68(3)(a) of the (English) Arbitration Act 1996.
[54] Scottish Arbitration Rules, r 75.
[55] Ibid, r 76(1)(a). Similar provision can be seen in s 73 of the (English) Arbitration Act 1996.
[56] Scottish Arbitration Rules, r 76(1)(b).
[57] Ibid, r 76(1)(d).
[58] Ibid, r 76(1)(c).
[59] Ibid, r 76(1)(e).
[60] Ibid, r 76(1)(f).

impartiality.[61] Apart from the mandatory rules applicable to umpires appointed by the tribunal or the appointments referee,[62] r 79 also makes it clear that an arbitrator's authority is personal and ceases on death.

DELOCALISATION THEORY

While the Arbitration (Scotland) Act 2010 expressly endorses the importance of mandatory rules, it is worthwhile to note that, in international commercial arbitration, one of the most heated debates is whether the seat of arbitration should be given such importance. This is the debate of delocalisation theory. It was claimed that neutrality is the main consideration when parties choose the place of arbitration. Additionally, the influence of the place of arbitration and the restrictions of the *lex loci arbitri* on arbitration vary from country to country. Some countries have a more relaxed attitude towards the arbitration held in their territories, whereas others may hold a more hostile attitude towards it. Some national arbitration laws impose mandatory rules on the arbitration held within their jurisdictions, whereas other jurisdictions prefer removing these rules from international commercial arbitration. The differences existing in different arbitration procedural laws result in inconsistencies in the results of arbitration and have caused the instability of international commercial arbitration. To eliminate such inconsistencies, the delocalisation theory, which invokes a detachment of arbitration procedures from the *lex loci arbitri*, has been invoked by a group of jurists since the 1960s[63] to avoid a potential set aside of award caused by the compulsory application of the *lex loci arbitri*.

What is the delocalisation theory?

The delocalisation theory is an idea seeking to detach international commercial arbitrations from controls imposed by the law of the place of arbitration (the *lex loci arbitri*).[64] Proponents of the delocalisation theory

---

[61] Scottish Arbitration Rules, r 77. Relevant provisions can be seen in ss 24(1)(a) and 33(1) of the (English) Arbitration Act 1996.
[62] Scottish Arbitration Rules, r 82.
[63] J Paulsson, "Arbitration unbound: award detached from the law of its country of origin" (1981) 30 ICLQ 358; and "Delocalisation of international commercial arbitration: when and why it matters?" (1983) 32 ICLQ 53. G Bernini, "The Enforcement of Foreign Arbitral Awards by National Judiciaries: A Trial of the New York Convention's Ambit and Workability" in *The Art of Arbitration* (Liber Amicorum for Pieter Sanders) (1982), 50 at p 58. P Lalive, "Les règles de conflict de lois appliquées au fond litige par l'arbitre international siègeant en Suisse" (1976) RevArb 155 at 159. Lalive article discussed in J Paulsson, "Arbitration unbound: award detached from the law of its country of origin" (1981) 30 ICLQ 358.
[64] Accordingly, the delocalisation theory can be applied at two stages of the arbitration procedures. One involves delocalising the arbitral procedures from the controls of the *lex fori*. The other one is delocalising arbitral awards. Delocalising the arbitral

maintain that international commercial arbitration should not be subject to legal controls which vary from country to country. Particularly, the controls may not suit the fast development and practice of international commercial arbitration. With an intention to eliminate the compulsory controls of the *lex loci arbitri*, they maintain that controls mechanism should be exercised by the country where the recognition or enforcement of arbitral awards is sought. They believe that the development of international commercial arbitration may be impeded because of the different restraints imposed on the arbitration procedures by the different national courts since arbitrators not only have to be aware of more than one national law, but also have to juggle with the different restraints imposed by different laws.[65] To eliminate these potential obstacles, in their opinion, the best way is to free the arbitration procedures from the national court's control. Thus they argue that the arbitration procedures should be "delocalised" and completely freed from the mandatory rules and public policy of the place of arbitration. In accordance with this theory, the arbitrators do not need to look over their shoulders at the different national mandatory rules and public policy imposed by the laws of the place of arbitration, the place making the contract, the place of performance, or the place of enforcement and so on. Accordingly, the arbitrators are not only allowed to disregard the *lex loci arbitri*, but may also apply any procedural law they regard as appropriate.

In their opinion, the application of the delocalisation theory can successfully avoid the uncertainty caused by the mandatory rules and public policy exceptions of the relevant laws. One of their arguments is based on the difference between arbitrators and judges sitting in national courts. Observing the different nature of a national court's judge from a private arbitrator, they claim that arbitrators are under no duty to apply the *lex loci arbitri* to the arbitration. As Paulsson said:

> "The international arbitrator is in a fundamentally different position. Whatever one might think of the contractual source of an arbitral tribunal's authority as a purely internal matter, it is difficult to consider the international arbitrator as a manifestation of the power of a State. His mission, conferred by the parties' consent, is one of a private nature, and it would be a rather artificial interpretation to deem his power to be derived, and very indirectly at that, from a tolerance of the State of the place of arbitration."[66]

---

procedures refers to removing the supervisory authority of the *lex fori* and the local courts where the arbitration is held. As far as delocalised arbitral awards is concerned, it means removing the power of the courts at the place of arbitration to make an internationally effective declaration of the award's nullity. See J Paulsson, "The extent of independence of international arbitration from the law of the *situs*" in J Lew (ed), *Contemporary Problems in International Arbitration* (1986) at p 141.

[65] W Park, "National law and commercial justice: safeguarding procedural integrity in international arbitration" (1989) 63 TulLR 647 at 667.

[66] Above n 63 at 362.

Following the suggestion that arbitrators do not have to follow the *lex loci arbitri*, it is therefore unnecessary for them to consider the mandatory rules of the *lex loci arbitri* when they deal with an international commercial dispute. As a result, they recommend that the supervisory powers should be exercised by the courts only where the recognition or enforcement is sought. Nevertheless, to avoid misunderstanding, he points out that the purpose of this theory is not to try to escape from the national court's control, but rather to promote the acceptance of delocalised arbitral awards. As he states: "To seek completely to avoid national jurisdictions would be misguided. Indeed, the international arbitral system would ultimately break down if no national jurisdiction could be called upon to recognise and enforce awards."[67] Furthermore, "the delocalised award is not thought to be independent of any legal order. Rather, the point is that a delocalised award may be accepted by the legal order of an enforcement jurisdiction although it is independent from the legal order of its country of origin".[68]

Opinions against the delocalisation theory

Not surprisingly, the delocalisation theory is not shared by some traditionalists. The scholars who are in favour of the traditional theory argue that there would be potential risks that arbitrators may abuse their power and the most fundamental due process requirement may not be safeguarded if a complete disregard of the *lex loci arbitri* was introduced. As a result of this, the justice the parties are seeking through arbitration will not be guaranteed due to the breakdown of the control mechanism exercised by the national courts.

This school of thought recognises the arbitrators' freedom in choosing the applicable law in the case where no expressed choice is made by the parties. However, the extent of this freedom is only limited to the substantive law of the contract, rather than the procedural law. Therefore, without a procedural law being specified, it would be compulsory for the arbitrators to refer to the *lex loci arbitri* to decide the appropriate procedures they should follow. In the absence of an express choice of the proper law made by the parties, the law governing the substantive disputes of the contract will be determined in accordance with the choice of law rules of the *lex loci arbitri*.

For instance, a dispute concerning defective goods was submitted to an arbitral tribunal sitting in Edinburgh. No applicable law was mentioned in the arbitration agreement. According to the traditional approach, first of all, the arbitral tribunal has to refer to the parties' agreement. In the

---

[67] Paulsson, "Delocalisation of international commercial arbitration: When and Why It Matters" (1983) 32 ICLQ 53 at 54.
[68] *Ibid* at 57.

absence of such agreement, it has to refer to the Arbitration (Scotland) Act 2010 to examine the questions of jurisdiction of the tribunal and the validity of the arbitration agreement, and so on. Second, if the submission is valid, the mandatory aspects of the arbitration procedures will be governed by the Scottish law. Third, the tribunal is required to apply the Scottish conflict of laws rules to decide the substantive law of the contract. Failing any clear indications of the choice of law, either express or implied, the one which has the most real and closest connection with the case will be chosen by the tribunal. Failing to do so will mean that the validity of the award can be in doubt and challenged in the country where the award is made, in this case Scotland, and the country where the recognition or enforcement of the award is sought.

The basis of their argument is the denial of the existence of "international" commercial arbitration. Among this group of scholars, Mann was the most enthusiastic proponent. Mann argued that every arbitration is a national one because private international law serving as the jurisprudence of arbitration is, in fact, a system of national law after all.[69] Therefore, any international commercial arbitration should be subject to a specific system of national law. As far as the specific national law is concerned, the law of the country of the seat of arbitration is considered as the most suitable one to regulate the arbitration procedures since it can provide the most complete and effective control.

Furthermore, Mann insisted that it is essential for the procedures of international commercial arbitration to be conducted on the basis of a given national law. To emphasise his point, he stated:

> "The problem of international arbitration cannot be discussed except against the background of a given *lex arbitri*; the legal systems of the world differ so considerably that no general rule can, or is intended to, be put forward. It follows that, in principle and always subject to such freedom of choice as it may allow, the *lex arbitri* governs the validity and effect of the submission; the constitution of the tribunal; the procedure; the law applicable by the arbitrators; the making, publications, interpretation, annulment and revision of the award."[70]

Delocalisation in practice

While the practicability of the delocalisation theory is still at issue, ICC awards also have made contributions towards the development of delocalisation theory in practice. Within the ICC framework, the practitioners try to create an autonomous atmosphere with the aim of

---

[69] F Mann, "*Lex Facit Arbitrum*" in P Sanders (ed), *Liber Amicorum for Martin Domke* (1967) at p 160.
[70] Mann, "State contracts and international arbitration" (1967) XLII BritYrbkIntlL 1 at 6.

making a country attractive as a location for holding international commercial arbitration by marrying the *laissez-faire* theory and the commercial motive behind the trend in modern arbitration law. The ICC does not want the results of the ICC arbitration to depend on the *situs*;[71] therefore it tries to promote the delocalisation theory by saying: "the courts of the place of arbitration should assume a role in international commercial arbitration as one designed to control the *bona fide* of the award on an international, rather than a national level and they accordingly should function":[72]

> "only as an instrument for the control of the conformity of the award to transnational minimum standards such as those embodied in the major international conventions. Unless the parties have agreed otherwise, the judge at the place of arbitration has no mission or capacity to apply his own national criteria to the award".[73]

It also criticises the idea of a compulsory application of the *lex loci arbitri* to international commercial arbitration when no express procedural choice of law is made by the parties. First, it stresses that, in practice, the place of arbitration is often chosen by the ICC, therefore the compulsory application of the *lex loci arbitri* to the arbitration procedures does not reflect the parties' minds. Second, it emphasises that the parties' legitimate expectations may not be fully reflected by applying the *lex loci arbitri* if neutrality is the main consideration of the choice. As Delaume stated:

> "Except in those situations in which compliance with mandatory rules is required, the parties are generally free to choose by way of express stipulation the law applicable to their relationship. In the overwhelming majority of cases, the law stipulated applicable is the domestic law of a specific country to which the contract bears some connection or the law of a 'third' country selected for reason of expertise (such as English law in regard to maritime matters) or of 'neutrality' (such as Swedish, Swiss or French law) ..."[74]

While making an effort to free the parties from the restraints imposed by the relevant municipal procedural laws, the ICC also supports Paulsson's arguments concerning the difference between the judges and arbitrators.[75] In an ICC arbitration case the arbitrator said: "The rules determining the applicable law vary from one country to the next. State judges derive them

---

[71] W Craig, W Park, and J Paulsson, *International Chamber of Commerce Arbitration* (2nd edn, 1990), p 11.
[72] *Ibid* at pp 11–12.
[73] Above, n 66.
[74] Passage from Delaume, *Transnational Arbitration*, Part II, Chap VII, p 2, also quoted in Craig, Park and Paulsson, *ICC Arbitration*, at p 123.
[75] Above, n 70, at 6.

from their own national legislation, the *lex fori*. But an arbitral tribunal has no *lex fori* in the strictest sense of the word, particularly when the arbitration case is of an international nature."[76]

The ICC encourages its arbitrators to conduct an arbitration in conformity with the ICC Rules which are consistent with the delocalisation theory. As Art 15.1 of the ICC Rules,[77] which grants the arbitrators more powers in conducting the arbitration procedures, stipulates:

> "The proceedings before the Arbitral Tribunal shall be governed by these Rules, and, where these Rules are silent, by any rules which the parties or, failing them, the Arbitral Tribunal may settle on, and whether or not reference is thereby made to the rules of procedures of a national law to be applied to the arbitration."

In accordance with this provision, the ICC arbitration procedural rules take priority over other national procedural laws. In the absence of the relevant procedural rules in the ICC Rules, other chosen national procedural laws will be used to fill such a gap.

Switzerland and Belgium

To some extent the delocalisation theory has received support in limited jurisdictions, such as France, Switzerland and Belgium. In the case of Switzerland, although Art 176(1) of the Federal Statute of Private International Law 1987 (PILA) specifies that Chapter 12 of the PIL applies to all arbitration "if the seat of the arbitral tribunal is in Switzerland and if, at the time of the conclusion of the arbitration agreement, at least one of the parties had neither its domicile nor its habitual residence in Switzerland", the parties are allowed to reach a written agreement to exclude the effects the Federal Statute may have on their arbitration which so happens to take place in Switzerland.[78]

Belgium is famous for its first plunge to move into the direction of delocalisation in its Judicial Code in 1985. With an intention to attract arbitration to Belgium, Art 1717 of the Judicial Code amended in 1985 stipulates that the Belgian court would only entertain an action to set aside an award if one of the parties is a Belgian national (either physical or legal person). It provided that "the Belgian Court can take cognizance of an application to set aside only if at least one of the parties to the dispute decided in the arbitral award is either a physical person having Belgian nationality or residing in Belgium, or a legal person formed in Belgium or having a branch (*une succursale*) or some seat of operation (*un siège quelconque d'opération*) there".[79] After 13 years, it became apparent that

---

[76] ICC case no 1689; W Craig, "International ambition and national restraints in ICC arbitration" (1985) 1(1) Arbitration Int 49 at 65.
[77] ICC Rules of Arbitration 1998.
[78] Swiss PILA 1987, Art 176(2).
[79] Judicial Code (amended in 1985), Art 1717(4).

such a bold move failed to make Belgium into an arbitration paradise as it had hoped, but scared off parties who would have considered Brussels as the place of arbitration before the change. Consequently, Art 1717 was amended again in 1998 and the delocalisation theory element contained within was given a conditional application that requires parties' express agreement, as it stipulates that:

> "The parties may, by an express statement in the arbitration agreement or by a subsequent agreement, exclude any application for the set aside of the arbitral award, where none of the parties is either an individual of Belgian nationality or an individual residing in Belgium, or a legal person having its head office or a branch office in Belgium."[80]

France

French courts have always had a very friendly attitude towards international commercial arbitration conducted within their territory. A number of French jurists regard an international contract as a contract detaching from the national laws, both substantive and procedural aspects.[81] Following this idea, it is widely supported by French scholars that the parties have the rights and freedom to design or facilitate the arbitral procedures in accordance with their own wishes and expectations. Influenced by this idea, and combined with the intention to make France a more attractive venue for international commercial arbitration, the delocalisation theory, which involves detaching the arbitral procedures from the *lex loci arbitri*, has became an attractive notion among the French jurists.

Believing that lifting the restraints of the *lex loci arbitri* would promote the development of international commercial arbitration, France decided to incorporate the notion of the delocalisation theory[82] into its legal system. As a result, French courts have given international commercial arbitration a special status by limiting their judicial powers. The French courts try to interfere with the arbitration procedures as little as possible and set limited grounds for reviewing international arbitral awards.

The most significant change is the enactment of the Decree of 12 May 1981 (the "1981 Decree") which is incorporated into the New Code of Civil Procedure 1981. With the intention of making France the most attractive venue for international commercial arbitration, the 1981 Decree tries to

---

[80] Article 1717(4) of the Belgian Judicial Code, Sixth Part: Arbitration (Adopted 4 July 1972, amended 27 March 1985 and 19 May 1998).

[81] See P Fouchard, *L'arbitrage Commercial International* (1965); discussed in P Sanders, "Trends in the Field of International Commercial Arbitration" (1975) 145 II Rec dec Cours 20.

[82] W Craig, W Park and J Paulsson, "French codification of a legal framework for international commercial arbitration: the decree of May 12, 1981" (1981) 13 Law & PolIntB 728.

create an environment friendly to international commercial arbitration conducted in France.[83] This Decree represents the absoluteness of the French *laissez-faire* approach applied to international commercial arbitration, and reveals a reluctance to exercise its judicial control over the integrity of arbitral proceedings conducted in France. The spirit of the new Decree was shown in the famous cases decided by the Court of Appeal of Paris in the 1980s. They are: the *SEEE* arbitration, *General National Maritime Transport Company v Götaverken Arendal AB*[84] and the *Norsolor* case.[85]

SEEE *arbitration*

The *SEEE* arbitration[86] is a famous example where a French court (enforcing court) granted enforcement of an award which was refused a hearing by the court of the place of arbitration due to the failure to comply with the mandatory rules. It concerned a dispute arising from a railway construction project in the former Yugoslavia between Yugoslavia and a French company, later replaced by SEEE. The SEEE claimed that it did not receive full payment due to the devaluation of the French franc. An arbitral tribunal composed of two arbitrators acted as *amiables compositeurs* and rendered an award in favour of the SEEE in Lausanne in 1956 and ordered Yugoslavia to pay SEEE 62 million French francs.

Yugoslavia tried to set aside this award in the cantonal Court of Appeal in Vaud by claiming the arbitral tribunal was composed of an even number of arbitrators which violated the Vaud cantonal law. Nonetheless, the Swiss court refused to hear the case on the grounds that it was without jurisdiction because the parties had not intended to subject themselves to the law of Canton of Vaud. Furthermore, the arbitral award was returned to the party having filed it (the SEEE) since it did not constitute an arbitral decision as understood by Art 516 of the Code of Procedure of Vaud. SEEE's further appeal to the Swiss Federal tribunal was also rejected. Later, in 1975, SEEE's attempts to enforce the award in Holland also ended in failure on the grounds that the judgment delivered by the Vaud Cantonal Tribunal had the same effect as an annulment.

---

[83] T Carbonneau, "The elaboration of a French court of international commercial arbitration : A study in liberal judicial creativity" (1981) 55 TulLRev 1 at 15–16.

[84] Decision of 21 Feb 1980, Court of Appeal, Paris, 107 (1980) JDI 660, [1980] RevArb 524, reprinted in (1981) 20 ILM 883.

[85] *AKSA* v *Norsolor*, judgment of 9 December 1980, Cour d'appel, Paris (1980), published in [1981] RevArb 306. An English translation published in (1981) 20 ILM 883 at 888. Report of the Supreme Court of Vienna, 18 Nov 1982 was reprinted in [1984] IX YBCA 159.

[86] *Société Européene d'Etudes et d'Entreprise (SEEE)* v *Yugoslavia* (1959) JDI 1074; a detailed discussion is contained in Paulsson, "The extent of independence of international arbitration from the law of the *situs*" in Lew (ed), *Contemporary Problems in International Arbitration* at pp 142–146.

Despite the fact that the award was detached from its country of origin in 1977, SEEE made another attempt to enforce this award in the Court of Appeal in Rouen which became successful. The court accepted the award despite its absence of connection with the place of the arbitration. The Court of Appeal in Rouen held:

"– [t]hat the Swiss decisions did not have the effect of setting the award aside, nor eliminating its legal existence; and that they only set forth that the award escapes the judicial sovereign of Vaud;

– that the law of the place of arbitration does not always and necessarily govern the arbitral proceedings;

– that the 'procedural law' that governs the arbitration may equally be another national law or the agreement of the parties;

– that in this case the arbitration clause excludes the application of national laws of procedure since it defines its own procedure;

– that the arbitration clause provides that the arbitrators are exempt from any formality, that they may decide as *amiable compositeur*, and that their decisions, or as the case may be those of the umpire, are final and binding on both parties."[87]

Finally, the award was enforced in France by the application of the New York Convention. This case is regarded as a victory for the delocalisation theory since it illustrated that a foreign award might be enforced even though this award was detached from its country of origin.[88]

Götaverken *case*

In General National Maritime Transport Company v Götaverken Arendal AB, the French Court of Appeal held that the court lacked jurisdiction to hear the challenge because the award was not French, despite the fact that the arbitration took place in Paris. The dispute which arose in relation to a set of substantially identical contracts whereby Götaverken undertook to construct three tankers for Libyan Maritime Co. However, Libyan Maritime Co refused to take delivery of the vessels after having previously paid three-quarters of the total purchase price after the performance. The dispute was submitted to ICC in Paris for arbitration according to the contracts. The arbitral tribunal made an award by a majority decision[89]

---

[87] Translation cited from Paulsson, "The extent of independence of international arbitration from the law of the *situs*" in Lew (ed), *Contemporary Problems in International Commercial Arbitration* at p 145.

[88] Despite the decision of the Court of Appeal in Rouen, the recognition of the award was rejected by the Dutch Supreme Court on other grounds in 1975 at a later stage. The Dutch Supreme Court regarded the Swiss refusal to hear the case as equivalent to setting aside the award.

[89] The Libyan arbitrator refused to sign the award.

dated 5 April 1978, which rejected Libyan Maritime Co's defence and made an award in favour of Götaverken. Libyan Maritime Co tried to bring an action to set aside the award in the Court of Appeal in Paris. Meanwhile, in Sweden, the winning party tried to attach the vessels and sought recognition of the award.

Götaverken raised the issues whether the French courts had jurisdiction to control international arbitral proceedings on the sole grounds that France had happened to provide geographically neutral grounds for the arbitration, as well as that there was no need for the arbitral proceedings to be attached to any national legal system. It argued that under the New York Convention, the law of the place of arbitration only has control over the proceedings in the absence of a specific choice made by the parties. In the opinion of the Court of Appeal in Paris, the agreement was presented by reference to the ICC Rules. In accordance with these Rules, Art 11 authorises the detachment of arbitral proceedings from the local law.

The Court of Appeal in Paris refused to exercise jurisdiction over Libyan Maritime Co's actions against the arbitral award rendered in Paris. It confirmed that the parties had the freedom to choose any law they wished to govern the procedural issues arising from the arbitration on the ground that the ICC Arbitration Rules 1975 were selected. Considering the facts of this case, neither of the parties nor their transaction had a connection with France, neither they nor the arbitrators had chosen to declare French law to apply to the proceedings, and finally, as the ICC Rules no longer mandated the application of the law of the seat of arbitration in the absence of a choice by the parties, the Court of Appeal concluded that French law was not applicable to the arbitration and it did not have jurisdiction to hear the challenge since the case was not subject to the French legal order nor was the award French in nationality.[90] Furthermore, the Court confirmed that the parties to international commercial arbitration are free to select the legal order to which they wish to govern the proceedings, and this freedom extends to the exclusion of any national system of law.

---

[90] As far as the action brought in Sweden is concerned, one of Libyan Maritime Co's main defences against the actions was that the award was not binding anywhere and it was pending a challenge brought before the courts in the country where it was rendered, that is, France. However, the Swedish Supreme Court declared the award immediately enforceable irrespective of the existence of an action in France to set it aside. The Swedish courts deemed the award to have been "binding" – in the sense of the New York Convention – as of the moment it was rendered. This was because in accepting to arbitrate under ICC Rules, the parties had waived the right to appeal. It is significant to note that the Swedish courts did not inquire whether the award was binding under French law, but as a function of the parties' contractual stipulation, it was recognised and given effect by the Swedish legal system. The English translation was published in (1981) 21 Virginia JIntlL 244.

Norsolor *case*

Ten months later, a similar issue was submitted to the Court of Appeal in Paris. In the case of *ASKA* v *Norsolor*[91] the successful party was a French company (Norsolor). ASKA, a Turkish textile company, sought a judicial review on an ICC award which denied its claim for restitution of part of the purchase price of materials ordered by Norsolor. Similar to the *Götaverken* case, the contract between the parties included an arbitration clause which conferred jurisdiction on the ICC without specifying any procedural law to be applied to the arbitration procedures. Following the decision made in the *Götaverken* case, and regardless of the fact that France was the place of arbitration and the defendant was a French company, the Court of Appeal held that the case concerned a non-French award which was subject to the remedies available for foreign awards and dismissed the case on the ground of lack of jurisdiction.

These two decisions made by the Court of Appeal in Paris deliver a clear message concerning the acceptance of the phenomenon of the delocalisation theory by French courts. In addition, the Court of Appeal also denied the suggestion that the national courts of the place of arbitration should have an overwhelming authority to rule on the validity of the proceedings since, as stressed by the Court of Appeal of Paris, sometimes the place of arbitration was chosen only in the interest of geographical neutrality and that should not be considered an implicit expression of the parties' intention to subject themselves to the procedural law of France. This idea is reflected in Paulsson's article, as he emphasises:

> "The message seems clear: one is authorised to conclude that the binding force of an international award may be derived from the contractual commitment to arbitrate in and of itself, that is to say without a specific national legal system serving as its foundation. In this sense, an arbitral award may indeed 'drift', but of course it is ultimately subject to the post facto control of the execution jurisdiction(s)."[92]

Eventually, the influence of these two cases can be observed in the 1981 Decree, which has the intention of freeing the arbitral procedures from the restraints of the *lex loci arbitri*.

England

Contrasted with the French legal system, English courts have given the *lex loci arbitri* greater significance. Traditionally, if no choice of law is expressed by the parties, the English courts have tended to take it for granted that the arbitrators are bound to apply the English procedural law to the arbitration which is held in England. Even in the case where

---

[91] *AKSA* v *Norsolor*, above n 85, at 888.
[92] Above, n 63, at 368.

the parties express their choice of the applicable laws, the mandatory rules and public policy of English law still override the choice of law. The courts believe that the principles applied to arbitration should be the same as those applied to the court proceedings which are governed by the *lex loci arbitri*. This approach has been adopted at least since Lord Brougham's judgment in *Don* v *Lippmann*[93] as early as 1837.

More recently, Lord Mustill was the most notable proponent who fought for this traditional approach. He stated that, as far as the arbitral procedures of international commercial arbitration are concerned, it cannot "exist without an internal procedural law".[94] This unfavourable attitude towards the theory of delocalisation was observed by some foreign commentators. For instance, in a comparison study between English and Swedish arbitration, Dr G Wetter reported this trend of resistance and stated:

> "London is the locale of the greatest number of international arbitrations in the world, yet the vast majority of these are viewed by the arbitrators, counsel and the parties as wholly domestic in character in the sense that the proceedings are indistinguishable from those which take place between two English parties."[95]

Whitworth Street Estates (Manchester) Ltd v James Miller

This traditional approach is upheld by a series of cases and the case of *Whitworth Street Estates (Manchester) Ltd* v *James Miller*,[96] is one of them. Although the House of Lords held that the law governing the arbitral procedures can be different from the one applied to the substantive dispute, the arbitral procedures still had to follow the rules of the *lex loci arbitri*. Therefore, in this case the arbitral procedures should be governed by the law of the place of arbitration, that is Scotland, even though the substantive disputes arising from the contract were governed by English law.

International Tank and Pipe SAK v Kuwait Aviation Fuelling Co KSC

The same approach was also adopted by Lord Denning MR in the case of *International Tank and Pipe SAK* v *Kuwait Aviation Fuelling Co KSC*,[97] where

---

[93] Cl & Fin 1, 7 Eng Rep 303 (1837).
[94] M Mustill, "Transnational arbitration in English law" (1984) 37 CurrLPr 133 at 142.
[95] G Wetter, "Choice of law in international arbitration proceedings in Sweden" (1986) 2 Arbitration Int 294 at 298. It was discussed in a comparison between the English and Swedish arbitrations. As far as the Swedish arbitrations are concerned, he said: "In Sweden, to the contrary, arbitrations in which at least one party is non-Swedish are treated as being multi-dimensional, in recognition of the particular requirements and problems inherent in transnational disputes."
[96] [1970] AC 583 (HL).
[97] [1975] 1 QB 224.

the dispute arose from a civil engineering contract between the parties. He explained:

> "The contract itself is to be construed by English law ... But the arbitration is to be governed by the law of Kuwait or some other country. I say this because the arbitration is governed by the rules of the International Chamber of Commerce. ... And the rules of the International Chamber of Commerce say in Art 16 that the arbitration is governed by the rules:
>
>> 'of the law of procedure chosen by the parties or, failing such choice, those of the law of the country in which the arbitrator holds the proceedings'.
>
> Thus, the parties may choose that the arbitration procedure is to be governed by the law of some country other than England. If they do not so choose, the procedure will be governed by the law where the arbitrator sits. That may be in Kuwait."[98]

Bank Mellat v Helliniki Techniki SA

The hostile attitude towards the delocalisation theory was also shown in the case of *Bank Mellat* v *Helliniki Techniki SA*.[99] Supporting the supervisory and controlling role of national courts,[100] Kerr J said:

> "The fundamental principle in this connection is that under our rules of private international law, in the absence of any contractual provision to the contrary, the procedural (or curial) law governing arbitrations is that of the forum of the arbitration, whether this be England, Scotland or some foreign country, since this is the system of law with which the agreement to arbitrate in the particular forum will have its closest connections. ... Despite suggestions to the contrary by some learned writers under other systems, our jurisprudence does not recognise the concept of arbitral procedures floating in the transnational firmament, unconnected with any municipal system of law."[101]

President of India v La Pintada Compania Navigation SA

In the case of *President of India* v *La Pintada Compania Navigation SA*,[102] the House of Lords regarded the parties' submission to arbitration held in England as an indication that their arbitration procedures should be governed by English law. As the court opined: "They impliedly agree that the arbitration is to be considered in accordance in all respects with the

---

[98] [1975] 1 QB 224 at 232.
[99] [1984] QB 291.
[100] *Ibid* at 301; however, such a supervisory role discussed by Kerr J in relation to s 12(6) of the Arbitration Act has been significantly curtailed by the Arbitration Acts 1979 and 1996.
[101] Above, n 99, at 301. Also see Mann, "Lex Facit Arbitrum" in Sanders (ed), *Liber Amicorum for Martin Domke* at p 167.
[102] [1985] 1 AC 104.

law of England, unless, which seldom occurs, the agreement of reference provides otherwise."[103]

Naviera Amazonica Peruana SA v Compania International de Seguros del Peru

The need to subject arbitration to the procedural law of the place of arbitration was stressed in *Naviera Amazonica Peruana SA v Compania International de Seguros del Peru*.[104] The court stressed: "English law does not recognise the concept of a 'delocalised' arbitration or of 'arbitral procedures floating in the transnational firmament, unconnected with any municipal system of law'. Accordingly, every arbitration must have a 'seat' or *locus arbitri* of forum which subjects its procedural rules to the municipal law which is there in force."

Union of India v McDonnell Douglas Corporation

The difficulties in applying the delocalisation theory was pointed out by Saville J in *Union of India v McDonnell Douglas Corporation*.[105] He said:

> "It is clear from the authorities cited above that English law does admit of at least the theoretical possibility that the parties are free to choose to hold their arbitration in one country but subject to the procedural laws of another, but again this is the undoubted fact that such an agreement is calculated to give rise to great difficulties and complexities, ... it seems to me that the jurisdiction of the English Court under the Arbitration Acts over an arbitration in this country cannot be excluded by an agreement between the parties to apply the laws of another country, or indeed by any other means unless such is sanctioned by those Acts themselves."[106]

Coppeé Lavalin v Ken-Ren

Finally, in a minority judgment in the case of *Coppeé Lavalin v Ken-Ren*,[107] in 1994, Lord Mustill rejected the delocalisation theory once again. He denied any possibility of the development of the delocalisation and harmonisation theories by saying:

> "'Transnationalism' is a theoretical ideal which posits that international arbitration, at least as regards certain types of contractual disputes conducted under the auspices of an arbitral institution arbitration, is a self-contained juridical system, by its very nature separate from national systems of law, and indeed antithetical to them. If the ideal is fully realised national courts

---

[103] [1985] 1 AC 104 at 119.
[104] Unreported, Court of Appeal, 10 November 1987. Reprinted in (1988) XIII YBCA 156–64, at 159–60.
[105] [1993] 2 Lloyd's Rep 48.
[106] *Ibid* at 50–51.
[107] [1994] 2 WLR 631 (HL).

will not feature in the law and practice of international arbitration at all and difference between national laws will become irrelevant.

...

I doubt whether in its purest sense the doctrine now commands widespread support: as witness the recognition of court-imposed interim measures in, among others, art 9 of the UNCITRAL Model Law and art 8(5) of the ICC rules. At all events it cannot be the law of England, for otherwise this House would have dismissed at the very outset the attempt in *Channel Tunnel Group Ltd v Balfour Beatty Construction Ltd*[108] to procure an interim injunction during the currency of an ICC Arbitration."[109]

This attitude continues in the more recent *C v D*,[110] where the disputes arose from an insurance contract in Bermuda form. The contract was governed by New York law and the place of arbitration was London. The claimant received a partial award in its favour and the defendant invited the tribunal to correct that award, arguing, *inter alia*, that its findings constituted a manifest disregard of New York law. The claimant was granted an anti-suit injunction preventing a challenge to the award in any US federal courts other than England. The defender appealed but was dismissed by the court.

Longmore LJ decided that, by choosing London as the seat of the arbitration, the parties must be taken to have agreed that proceedings on the award should be only those permitted by English law. Furthermore, the judicial remedies in respect of the award should be those permitted by English law and only those so permitted. He further pointed out that:

"It follows from this that a choice of seat for the arbitration must be a choice of forum for remedies seeking to attack the award ... as a matter of construction of the insurance contract with its reference to the English statutory law of arbitration, the parties incorporated the framework of the 1996 Act ... their agreement on the seat and the 'curial law' necessarily meant that any challenges to any award had to be only those permitted by that Act."[111]

Citing the decision of Colman J in *A v B*,[112] he concluded:

"an agreement as to the seat of an arbitration is analogous to an exclusive jurisdiction clause. Any claim for a remedy going to the existence or scope of the arbitrator's jurisdiction or as to the validity of an existing interim or final award is agreed to be made only in the courts of the place designated as the seat of the arbitration. That is, in my view, a correct statement of the law".[113]

---

[108] [1993] AC 384.
[109] Above, n 107, at 640.
[110] [2008] BusLR 843.
[111] *Ibid* at 851 (para 16).
[112] *A v B* [2007] 1 All ER (Comm) 591 and *A v B (No 2)* [2007] Bus LR D 59, at para 111.
[113] [2008] BusLR 843 at 852 (para 17).

CHAPTER 9

CHOICE OF THE PROPER LAW

GENERAL

The importance of the proper law

To decide the substance of the issues submitted to arbitration, arbitrators have to apply law, or rules of law, to decide the facts of the disputes and the rights and obligations of the parties involved. This chosen law is termed proper law or substantive law in different literature. A valid choice of the proper law of the contract has its own significance in ensuring a speedy resolution of the dispute. The importance of this issue can be analysed from three aspects: the advantages of international commercial arbitration; the expectations of the parties; and the validity of arbitral awards.

As most authors[1] have agreed, compared with national court proceedings, international commercial arbitration is a more flexible and speedy way to resolve international commercial disputes. To safeguard its reputation of speed and flexibility, this mechanism offers the parties quite a high level of freedom in deciding how they would like their disputes to be resolved. In general, arbitrators are usually required to apply the parties' choice of proper law to the dispute. In the cases where no proper law of the contract is expressed by the parties or the choice is invalid, the arbitrators have to spend more time choosing the proper law from an examination of a large number of factors, such as the nationalities of the parties, the subject matter of the contract, the place of performance, the place of contracting, the form of the contract, the language used and the terms of the arbitration agreement. Apart from the fact that arbitrators have to spend more time in deciding the proper law, arbitration procedures can be delayed to a great extent if the parties object to the choice made by the arbitrators and resort to court proceedings. As a result, the aim of

---

[1] Eg P Rowland, *Arbitration Law and Practice* (1988), pp 16–19.

providing a speedy service through international commercial arbitration may not be achieved under such circumstances.

Second, the parties' expectations can be another indication of the importance of the issue of the choice of the proper law. Apart from expecting to settle the disputes as soon as possible, the parties may also want to predict the outcome of the arbitration: this may be more easily achieved if the parties have made a valid choice of proper law. In particular, by so doing, the parties will have the advantage of knowing where they stand and what rights and obligations they have.

Finally, the choice of the proper law is of critical importance at the stage of recognition or enforcement of the arbitral awards. Not only can an award made by arbitrators who failed to observe or respect the parties' express choice be successfully challenged by the losing party but also most national courts may refuse to enforce such an award. As provided by Art V(1)(d) of the New York Convention, recognition and enforcement of the award may be refused if the composition of the arbitral authority or the arbitral procedure was not in accordance with the agreement of the parties. Unless contradicted by other mandatory provisions or public policy, an award made on the basis of the proper law chosen by the parties will be enforced in most national courts. However, in the case where no proper law is chosen by the parties, the losing party may challenge the arbitrator's decisions on the choice of the proper law. This may possibly result in a further delay of the recognition or enforcement of arbitral awards, or, moreover, doubts in the validity of the awards if the court believes that the arbitrator's decision on the choice of proper law cannot be justified.

DETERMINING THE PROPER LAW

After disputes are submitted to the arbitral tribunal, it is the tribunal's duty to find the proper law of the contract in order to settle the disputes. Nevertheless, during the arbitral procedures, choosing the proper law of the contract is not as easy a task as it appears to be. Traditionally, a three-step procedure has been introduced to resolve this problem. First, arbitrators have to check the choice of law clause in order to find out whether a valid choice of the proper law has been expressly set out in the contract or the arbitration agreement. If there is, in accordance with the doctrine of party autonomy, the arbitrators are obliged to apply the expressed choice of the proper law to resolve the disputes referred to them. In fact, most international commercial contracts do contain an express choice of the proper law in order to avoid the application of a law unfavourable to the party (or the parties) because it is believed that "the determination of the proper law of the contract will not involve any difficulty if the parties have been wise enough to record expressly which legal system is to apply to their agreement".[2] Nevertheless, from time to time the importance of the choice of law is underestimated or completely ignored by the parties. Consequently, no such choice is expressed in the contract or the arbitration agreement; or such choice is invalid by reference to the mandatory rules or public policy. Under these circumstances, traditionally, the arbitrators will have to follow the second step – the implied choice of law test – to find an implied proper law of the contract from the relevant circumstances of the case. Nevertheless, in some complicated cases, it is possible that arbitrators fail to find the proper law under the first and second steps. If this happens, at this stage arbitrators will have to apply the closest and most real relationship test to choose the proper law of the contract as deemed appropriate from the objective circumstances.

Such international accepted practice is adopted in r 47 of the Scottish Arbitration Rules which reads:

"(1) The tribunal must decide the dispute in accordance with –
   (a) the law chosen by the parties as applicable to the substance of the dispute, or
   (b) if no such choice is made (or where a purported choice is unlawful), the law determined by the conflict of law rules which the tribunal considers applicable.
(2) Accordingly, the tribunal must not decide the dispute on the basis of general considerations of justice, fairness or equity unless –
   (a) they form part of the law concerned, or
   (b) the parties otherwise agree.
(3) When deciding the dispute, the tribunal must have regard to –
   (a) the provisions of any contract relating to the substance of the dispute,
   (b) the normal commercial or trade usage of any undefined terms in the provisions of any such contract,
   (c) any established commercial or trade customs or practices relevant to the substance of the dispute, and
   (d) any other matter which the parties agree is relevant in the circumstances."

Rule 47 is a default rule and is subject to the parties' agreement. If an agreed choice of proper law can be established then the tribunal must apply the parties' choice of proper law to resolve the dispute. This choice can be made either expressly or by implication. If no such choice is made or the purported choice is unlawful, the arbitral tribunal will have to follow the appropriate conflict of law rules, ie implied choice of law test or the closest and most real test to determine the proper law. Rule 47(3) also requires the arbitrators to take commercial and trade usage, custom

---

[2] C Schmitthoff, *The English Conflict of Laws* (2nd edn, 1954), p 109.

or practices into consideration when deciding the disputes. However, regarding the international practice of "*ex aequo et bono*" and "*amiable compositeur*", r 47(2) provides that an arbitrator is only allowed to disregard the law and rely solely on what he or she considers to be fair and equitable if that forms part of the law concerned or is expressly authorised by the agreement between the parties. Similar provision can be seen in s 46 of the (English) Arbitration Act 1996.

Rule 47(1)(a) – the proper law expressly chosen by the parties

Rule 47(1)(a) reads: "The tribunal must decide the dispute in accordance with the law chosen by the parties as applicable to the substance of the dispute." The parties' freedom to have their disputes governed by the law they desire is based on the theory of party autonomy. The freedom provided in r 44(1)(a) is based on the well-recognised doctrine of party autonomy, which originates from the idea of "freedom of contract" (it is also called the "classical contract theory" or the "will theory"). Within certain limitations, the parties' freedom in choosing the proper law of the contract is well recognised in international commercial arbitration cases. As Rabel states: "The practice of allowing parties to determine the law applicable to their contractual relations ... for centuries has been applied by courts throughout the world with slight dissent."[3] Based on such autonomy, the parties have a cardinal right to choose the proper law to govern the main contract.

International practice

This theory is not only recognised in the academic studies, but is also contained in the international Conventions, the institutional arbitration rules and the different national arbitration laws. For instance, Art 33(1) of the UNCITRAL Arbitration Rules provides that the arbitral tribunal is required to apply "the law designated by the parties as applicable to the substance of the dispute".[4] More directly than the UNCITRAL Arbitration Rules, the ICC Rules explicitly offer the parties the freedom "to determine the law to be applied by the arbitrator to the merits of the dispute".[5] Similar provisions also appear in the LCIA Rules[6] and the AAA International Arbitration Rules which demand that "the tribunal shall apply the substantive law or laws designated by the parties as applicable to the dispute".[7]

---

[3] E Rabel, *Comparative Conflicts*, Vol I (2nd edn, 1958), p 90. Also see J Lew, *Applicable Law in International Commercial Arbitration* (1978), p 71.
[4] The UNCITRAL Arbitration Rules were adopted on 28 April 1976.
[5] Rules of Arbitration of the International Chamber of Commerce, Art 17(1).
[6] Rules of the London Court of International Arbitration 1998, Art 22.3.
[7] American Arbitration Association – International Arbitration Rules, Art 28(1) (as amended and effective 1 September 2000).

As in Scotland,[8] parties' freedom to express their intention that the law of a given country shall govern the contract is also recognised by most jurisdictions. For instance, arbitrators are required to decide the dispute according to the rules of law chosen by the parties under the French Code of Civil Procedure.[9] This intention will direct the arbitrators to apply the chosen law to settle the dispute between the parties. Taking England[10] as an example, s 46(1)(a) of the (English) Arbitration Act 1996 provides that the arbitral tribunal shall decide the dispute in accordance with the law chosen by the parties as applicable to the substance of the dispute.

Freedom of contract has been applied in the various cases concerning the issue of the choice of the proper law. For instance, the case of *R v International Trustee for the Protection of Bondholders*[11] pointed out that the proper law of the contract is the law which the parties intended to apply. Moreover, the choice "will be ascertained by the intention expressed in the contract if any, which will be conclusive".[12] This autonomy, again, is confirmed by a leading case.[13] In the case of *Vita Food Products Inc v Unus Shipping Co Ltd*, the court upheld the parties' express choice of law and opined: "It is now well settled that by English law the proper law of contract 'is the law' which the parties intended to apply. The intention to apply a specific national law as the proper law is objectively ascertained."[14]

Several decades later, the parties' freedom in choosing the proper law of the contract was again upheld, in the case of *Whitworth Street Estates (Manchester) Ltd v James Miller and Partners*.[15] In this case, Lord Reid set out that:

> "The general principle is not in doubt. Parties are entitled to agree what is to be the proper law of the contract, and if they do not make any such agreement then the law will determine what is the proper law. There have been from time to time suggestions that parties ought not to be so entitled, but in my view there is no doubt that they are entitled to make such an agreement, and I see no good reason why, subject it may be to some

---

[8] A E Anton, *Private International Law – A Treatise from the Standpoint of Scots Law* (2nd edn, 1990), p 263.
[9] French Code of Civil Procedure, Art 1496(1).
[10] L Collins (ed), *Dicey and Morris on the Conflict of Laws* (12th edn, 1993), p 1211. In England and Scotland, in relation to the choice of the proper law, the uniform rules of Arts 3 and 4 of the Rome Convention will replace the common law rules in cases where the Convention applies. Accordingly, the general conclusion of these articles is strikingly similar in effect to the position reached by the common law. Therefore, in this chapter, discussion of the choice of proper law rules will be conducted in general terms to illustrate the underlying issues: first, on the basis of the common law rules; and, second, from the viewpoint of the Rome Convention.
[11] [1937] AC 500.
[12] *Ibid* at 529.
[13] *Vita Food Products Inc v Unus Shipping Co Ltd* [1939] AC 277.
[14] *Ibid* at 289.
[15] [1970] AC 583.

limitations, they should not be so entitled. But it must be a contractual agreement. It need not be in express words. Like any other agreement it may be inferred from reading their contract as a whole in light of relevant circumstances known to both parties when they made their contract."[16]

Nevertheless, the issue was raised regarding whether it is proper to offer the parties such an absolute freedom to choose the proper law.[17] In England, a negative attitude towards total freedom was held by a group of scholars and judges. Lord Denning was a member of this school of thought. He stated that the choice made by the parties did not have an absolute effect on the arbitrators. Furthermore, in *Boissevain* v *Weil*, he stated that "parties are free to stipulate by what law the validity of the contract is to be determined. Their intention is only one of the factors to be taken into account".[18] However, this decision was later reversed by Lord Denning himself in the *Tzortzis* case, where he contended that the parties' express choice would be "conclusive" in absence of some public policy to the contrary.[19]

Is connection necessary?

The other issue raised was whether the parties have a right to choose a law which does not have any connection with the case. In some jurisdictions, such as the USA,[20] the conflict of law rules require that the proper law chosen by the parties must bear some "reasonable relationship" to their transaction. This is to prevent the parties from taking advantage of the freedom by choosing a law which does not have any connection with the case in order to evade a possible disadvantageous situation.

England

However, the above view was questioned. It was argued that such an inference reflects only part of the truth, that the reason for the parties choosing a law bearing no connection to the transaction may be that the parties, or their legal advisers, understand this legal system better than others; alternatively, the arbitrator's background may lead the parties to choose the national law which he appreciates most. More often, choosing

---

[16] [1970] AC 583 at 603.
[17] *Whitworth Street Estates (Manchester) Ltd* v *James Miller and Partners Ltd* [1970] AC 583 at 603.
[18] *Boissevain* v *Weil* [1949] 1 KB 482 at 490–491.
[19] *Tzortzis* v *Monark Line A/B* [1968] 1 WLR 406 at 411.
[20] Under s 187 of the Restatement (Second) Conflict of Laws (1971), the parties' chosen law must be applied unless, among other things, "the chosen state has no substantial relationship to the parties or the transaction and there is no other reasonable basis for the parties' choice". Section 1–105(1) of the UCC (Uniform Code of Commerce) imposes the same sort of "reasonable relation" requirement. At common law, some New York courts applied a reasonable relationship requirement fairly strictly: see *A S Rampell, Inc* v *Hyster Co*, 165 NY 2d 475 (1957).

a law having a good reputation in a certain legal field can also be another valid justification for the parties' choice. For instance, London has been famous as a centre for the maritime industry for some time; therefore, English law might be chosen as the proper law of the contract even though so many commercial transactions have nothing to do with England.[21]

Moreover, neutrality may be another reason for such a choice. In practice, it is very common for the parties to state contracts to choose a law which has no connection with the transaction, since neither party wants to have the contract governed by the national law of the other party's country. From the viewpoint of a state or a state entity, unfamiliarity with foreign laws and the dignity of the states themselves frequently deter them from having the contracts subjected to the law of the other party's country.[22] On the other hand, with the fear of potential bias or injustice in the national courts of the host country, the private party to this kind of contract not only prefers to submit the disputes to international commercial arbitration in a neutral country, but also chooses a neutral law to be the governing law of the contract.

As the English courts stated that "[c]onnection with English law is not as a matter of principle essential",[23] therefore, it does not seem to be appropriate to deny the parties' freedom to choose a law unconnected to the transaction. This statement is supported by Lord Wright,[24] and Lord Diplock in the *Amin Rasheed* case,[25] where he said:

> "It is apparent from the terms of the contract itself that the parties intended it to be interpreted by reference to a particular system of law, their intention will prevail and the latter question as to the system of law with which, in the view of the court, the transaction to which the contract relates would, but for such intention of the parties, have had the closest and most real connection, does not arise."[26]

Arbitral awards

Similar opinion is also expressed in some of the ICC awards. In one, a dispute arose from a contract for the sale of potatoes between a Mozambique purchaser and a Dutch seller.[27] In the contract the parties were required to submit the dispute to an arbitration which would be conducted in accordance with the ICC Rules. The law applicable was

---

[21] *Vita Food Products* v *Unus Shipping Company* [1939] AC 277 at 290, per Lord Wright.
[22] For instance, the Indian and Pakistan governments will not offer contracts to foreign contractors unless they agree that the substantive law of the contract is the law of India or Pakistan.
[23] *Vita Food Products* v *Unus Shipping Company* [1939] AC 277 at 290, per Lord Wright.
[24] *Ibid* at 290.
[25] *Amin Rasheed Shipping Corp; Al Watab, The* v *Kuwait Insurance Co* [1984] AC 50.
[26] *Ibid* at 61.
[27] ICC case no 5505 (1987) XIII YBCA 110 at 116.

stated to be "that known in England". The parties disputed the meaning and effect of the above quoted clause. The arbitrator[28] ruled that the proper law was English law, even though it did not have any connection with the case. He stated:

> "The parties had valid reasons to refer to the substantive law known in England. English law is neutral; its provisions are adapted to the needs of international commerce; it is fairly well accessible and known to lawyers of other countries, such as Switzerland, Mozambique and the Netherlands; ... Although somewhat unusual, the expression 'the law known in England' is not ambiguous. It is wide enough to include, as appropriate, international rules and usages recognised in England."[29]

Choosing a law bearing no connection to the main contract is especially popular with the parties to state contracts or major international contracts. Among the different laws applied in international arbitral awards, it should be stated that not only national laws having no connection with the case are chosen, but also a-national principles, such as general principles of law, the *lex mercatoria* or amiable composition, are frequently chosen as the proper law to govern the substantive issues arising from international commercial contracts.

Limitations on the parties' expressed choice of the proper law

It should be borne in mind that neither the freedom of the parties[30] nor the arbitrators' discretion in deciding the proper law is unlimited.[31] The limitations imposed on the autonomy vary from country to country. Generally speaking, in relation to the choice of proper law, party autonomy is subject to the scrutiny of public policy and the mandatory rules of the relevant laws: the law governing the arbitration agreement, the law of the arbitral *situs*[32] or of the state where recognition or enforcement are sought.[33] Almost every set of national conflict of law rule recognises that the claim of public policy can override the parties' decision on the choice of law. Some cases have been categorised as public policy exceptions which are capable of invalidating the proper law chosen by the parties, such as discrimination prohibitions,[34] usury

---

[28] Mr G Muller was the arbitrator in this case.
[29] ICC case no 5505 (1987) XIII YBCA 110 at 118.
[30] According to Lew, the freedom in choosing the law applicable to the contract is recognised in most, if not all, national systems of law, no matter whether common law, civil law or socialist legal systems: J Lew, *Applicable Law in International Commercial Arbitration*, p 75.
[31] For example, the mandatory rules and public policy of the forum under Arts 7 and 16 of the Rome Convention.
[32] New York Convention 1958, Art V(1)(d).
[33] *Ibid*, Art V(1)(b).
[34] *Muschany v United States*, 324 US 49 (1945).

restrictions,[35] fair competition protections,[36] constitutional guarantees,[37] and protections for economically inferior parties.[38]

In addition, apart from public policy being a possible ground for invalidating the parties' choice of law, the application of mandatory rules of the otherwise applicable laws can be another way to derogate from the parties' choice.[39] In other words, the arbitrators are not obliged to apply the provisions of a particular foreign law chosen by the parties as the proper law when these provisions contradict the mandatory rules or public policy of the states which have a close connection with the transaction. This is stated in Art 7(1) of the Rome Convention,[40] which provides: "When applying under this Convention the law of a country, effect may be given to the mandatory rules of the law of another country with which the situation has a close connection, if and in so far as, under the law of the latter country, those rules must be applied whatever the law applicable to the contract."[41]

As well as in international Conventions, the exceptions of public policy and mandatory rules can be seen in most national laws. For instance, the English case law pronounces that the validity of the choice of a foreign law may be affected by the public policy and the mandatory rules of the forum.[42] In a leading case, Lord Wright stated that, unless the ground of public policy had been successfully avoided, the parties' express choice of the proper law would not be effective.[43] Lord McNair upheld this idea and stated that public policy is one of the restrictions on party autonomy in relation to the choice of proper law, while he opined: "It is often said that the parties to a contract make their own law, and it is, of course, true that, subject to the rules of public policy and *ordre public*, the parties are free to agree upon such terms as they may choose."[44]

---

[35] *Whitaker v Spiegel Inc*, 623 P 2d 1147 (Wash 1981).
[36] *Davis v Jointless Fire Brick Co*, 300 F 2d 1 (9th Cir 1924); *Blalock v Perfect Subscription Co*, 458 F Supp 123 (SD Ala 1978).
[37] *Bachvhan v India Abroad Pub Inc*, 1992 WL 110403 (NY SCt, 13 April 1992), cited in G Born, *International Commercial Arbitration in the United States – Commentary & Materials* (1994), p 138.
[38] *New York Life Ins Co v Cravens*, 178 US 389 (1900).
[39] Rome Convention, Art 3(3).
[40] Ibid, Arts 3 and 7.
[41] Despite the non-application of Art 7(1) of the Convention, it is suggested that the English court could still apply this rule, either as a mandatory rule of the forum under Art 7(2) or as a rule of English public policy by virtue of Art 16. See the commentary on Art 7(1) in the *Current Law Statutes of the Contract (Applicable Law) Act 1990*, pp 36–40.
[42] Collins, *Dicey and Morris on the Conflict of Laws*, pp 1239–1248.
[43] *Vita Food Products Inc v Unus Shipping Co Ltd* [1939] AC 277.
[44] A D McNair, "The General Principles of Laws Recognised by Civilised Nations" (1957) 33 BritYrbkIntlL 1 at 278.

A similar provision can also be seen in both the United States statutes[45] and court decisions. As the Restatement (Second) of Conflict of Laws (hereinafter "the Restatement") illustrates:

> "The law of the state chosen by the parties to govern their contractual rights and duties will be applied, even if the particular issue is one which the parties could not have resolved by an explicit provision in their agreement directed to that issue, unless ... the application of the law of the chosen state would be contrary to a fundamental policy of a state which has a materially greater interest than the chosen state in the determination of the particular issue and which, under the rule of section 188, would be the state of the applicable law in the absence of an effective choice-of-law by the parties."[46]

The "implied choice of law" test

In the absence of an expressed choice of law, the arbitrators have the same duty as those of the judges in a national court to choose a proper law for the parties. Failing to find the parties' express choice, the arbitrators have to decide the proper law of the contract by inferring it from the terms and nature of the contract and the general circumstances of the case. This power is expressed in r 47(1)(b) of the Scottish Arbitration Rules, which sets out a solution if the parties have failed to express their choice of proper law. It provides that "if no such choice is made (or where a purported choice is unlawful), the law [is] determined by the conflict of law rules which the tribunal considers applicable". In accordance with this provision, there are two possible scenarios whereby the arbitrators will be required to choose the proper law for the parties. One is that the parties made a choice but such a choice is deemed to be unlawful for various reasons. The other one is that the parties simply failed to specify the proper law of the contract. In both cases, two further steps in the conflict of law rules must be followed to enable the arbitrators to determine the proper law of the contract in order to settle the parties' disputes. They are, namely, the implied test and the "closest and most real" test.

This rule is consistent with the stipulation in Art 3 of the EEC Convention on the Law Applicable to Contractual Obligations (the Rome Convention).[47] In respect of the choice of law rules, the Rome Convention

---

[45] Restatement (Second) Conflict of Laws (1971), s 187.
[46] *Ibid*, s 187(2)(b).
[47] Since 1 April 1990, in the United Kingdom the common law rules concerning choice of law in contract have, to a large extent, been replaced by the rules in the Rome Convention. The Rome Convention has been incorporated into the laws of the United Kingdom by the Contracts (Applicable Law) Act 1990. Although Art 1(2)(d) of the Rome Convention expressly excludes "arbitration agreements and agreements on the choice of courts" from its scope of application, the Convention still governs the choice of law in relation to the main contract. As Anton clearly points out: "the arbitration

provides new rules to be followed by judges and arbitrators sitting in the United Kingdom. Article 3(1) confirms the principle of party autonomy and stipulates: "A contract shall be governed by the law chosen by the parties." The Rome Convention also allows the choice of a foreign law, as Art 3(3) provides that a choice of a foreign law, subject to the mandatory rules[48] and public policy,[49] must be accommodated by the courts of the Contracting States even if all the relevant elements are connected with one country only. This provision is further illustrated:

> "The law chosen need not in principle have any geographical or physical connection with the contract. This approach is in accord with the views expressed by the U.K. negotiators and reflects the practice of the common law. It also appears to be the case that the rules of the Convention are brought into play if the only foreign element in the case is the choice of foreign law to apply to what is otherwise an entirely domestic transaction."[50]

The "implied choice of law" test is also incorporated into the Rome Convention. As Art 3(1) provides: "The choice must be express or demonstrated with reasonable certainty by the terms of the contract or the circumstances of the case." This provision allows judges and arbitrators, taking all the facts into consideration, to decide that the parties have made a choice of law even if this is not expressly stated in the contract.[51] In addition, judges will follow the rules – the closest and most real relationship test, set out in Art 4 – to determine the applicable law in cases where a choice of law has not been made, expressly or implicitly, in the contract itself within the meaning of Art 3 of the Rome Convention.[52]

England

The "implied choice of law" test was upheld in the case of *Rossano v Manufacturers Life Insurance Co*,[53] where the court provided guidance on inferring the proper law of the contract when no expressed choice was made by the parties in their contract. Accepting the "implied choice of

---

agreement is excluded from the operation of the Convention and remains subject to the common law rules. ... This does not mean that an arbiter (or judge) is not bound to apply the rules of the Convention to the substantive issues of choice of law which may arise in the course of the arbitration or litigation. It merely means that issues relating to the validity, interpretation, and effect of the arbitration or choice of court agreement are not governed by the choice of law rules established by the Convention." See Anton, *Private International Law*, p 360.

[48] Articles 3(3), 5(2), 6(1) and 7(2).
[49] Article 16.
[50] *Scottish Current Law Statutes*, Chap 36, p 19.
[51] Giuliano-Lagarde Report, p 17.
[52] As set out in Art 4.
[53] [1962] 2 All ER 214.

law" test set out in the cases of *Re United Railways of the Havana and Regla Warehouses Ltd*[54] and *Bonython v Commonwealth of Australia*,[55] the court indicated: "The parties not having expressly chosen the proper law or stated their intention in terms the court must act on the evidence before it and fix the presumed intentions of the parties as best it can."[56] A more specific explanation was provided in *Whitworth Street Estates (Manchester) Ltd v James Miller*,[57] in which Lord Reid said:

> "Two slightly different tests have been formulated: 'the system of law by reference to which the contract was made or that with which the transaction has its closest and most real connextion' (*Bonython Case* [1951] AC 201, 209) and 'with what country has the transaction the closest and most real connection' (*In Re United Railways of Havana* [1961] AC 1007, 1068). It has become common merely to refer to the system of law but I think that the two tests must be combined for all are agreed that the place of performance is a relevant and may be the decisive factor, and it is only in a loose sense that the place of performance can be equated to the system of law prevailing there."[58]

Indications for the "implied choice of law" test

Place of performance With the "implied choice of law" test, different criteria have been applied in different cases. Among these different criteria, the law of the place of performance (*lex loci solutionis*) has attracted a great deal of attention as the basis for inferring the proper law of the contract.[59] In the 19th century, the place of performance was regarded as a strong factor for a judge or an arbitrator to infer that the proper law of the contract from the terms and nature of the contract and the general circumstances of the case.[60]

The significance of the place of performance may be based on the fact that it would be easier for the arbitrators and the judges to inspect the performance of the work from which the dispute arises. This idea is supported by a number of cases which conclude that the place of performance is a good factor from which to infer the proper law the parties intended. With respect to the cases where more than one place of performance is involved, the "primary place" test is applied. For instance, in the case of *Re United Railways of Havana*,[61] the judge decided that, where

---

[54] [1960] Ch 52 at 94.
[55] [1951] AC 201.
[56] [1962] 2 All ER 214 at 219.
[57] [1970] AC 583.
[58] *Ibid* at 603–604.
[59] *The Assunzione* [1954] AC 224 at 240.
[60] *Fergusson v Fyffe* (1841) 2 Rob 267; *Williamson v Taylor* (1845) 8 D 156; *Scottish Provident Institution v Cohen & Co* (1888) 16 R 112.
[61] *Re United Railways of Havana and Regla Warehouses Ltd* [1961] AC 1007.

there are several places of performance, the law chosen is that of the country which the court finds to be the "primary" place.

Nevertheless, the predominance of the place of performance test was questioned by some judges. For instance, Bowen LJ argued that the court will not normally be able to attach much significance to the place of performance if the parties have to perform their obligations in different countries, especially when the same quality and quantity of the construction works are carried out in the individual different countries.[62] Furthermore, the strength of the *lex loci solutionis* is not absolute, and must "give way to any inference that can legitimately be drawn from the character of the contract and the nature of the transaction".[63] The reason why the place of performance has lost its importance in determining the proper law of the contract[64] may be the fast development of the modern facilities for travelling and communications, and the realisation that disputes may arise from any part of the contract, not just from the performance.

Other indications Apart from the place of performance, the currency of a given country mentioned in the contract,[65] the use of a particular language[66] or a specific legal term[67] and so on, may also give guidance to arbitrators inferring the proper law from the relevant circumstances of the case. However, the use of a particular language in the contract has been rejected as a strong indication of choice of the proper law of the contract.[68] This has been illustrated in a number of cases where the language of English was used in the contracts. It was suggested that the parties, perhaps, would not mean to have their contract governed by English law simply because English was the language of the contract. The use of English language may simply be due to the fact that English is an international language which has been commonly used in international contracts. Therefore, in England, the courts will not regard the use of English in the contract as a strong indication of the proper law unless there is further connection with England.[69]

---

[62] *Jacobs v Credit Lyonnais* (1884) 112 QBD 589 (CA) at 600.
[63] *Ibid.*
[64] *NV Kwik Hoo Tong Handel Maatschappij v James Finlay and Co Ltd* [1927] AC 604.
[65] *The Assunzione* [1954] P 150 (CA); *Re United Railways of Havana and Regla Warehouses Ltd* [1961] AC 1007; *Re Helbert Wagg & Co Ltd* [1956] Ch 323; *NV Handel Maatschappij J Smits v English Exports (London) Ltd* [1955] 2 Lloyd's Rep 69 at 72.
[66] *The Industrie* [1894] PD 58 (CA); *The Adriatic* [1931] PD 241; *The Njegos* [1936] PD 90 at 101.
[67] *R v International Trustee for Protection of Bondholders AG* [1937] AC 500.
[68] *The Metamorphosis* [1953] 1 WLR 543 at 549; *Compagnie Tunisienne de Navigation SA v Compagnie d'Armement Maritime SA* [1971] AC 572 at 583 and 594.
[69] *Atlantic Underwriting Agencies v Compagnia di Assicurazione di Milano SpA* [1979] 2 Lloyd's Rep 240.

In relation to whether the use of a marine policy which is held in a particular country constitutes an implied choice of the proper law, a positive answer was offered by the English Court of Appeal. In *Amin Rasheed Shipping Corp v Kuwait Insurance Co*,[70] the court was unanimous in reaching the conclusion that using a policy governed by the Marine Insurance Act 1906 implies English law as the governing law of the contract. The court believed that the interpretation of the policy would not be comprehensible without reference to the Marine Insurance Act 1906 and that constituted a strong indication of the implied proper law of the contract.

Furthermore, in this case, Lord Diplock firmly stated the importance of the localisation of the proper law of the contract. If you wish to ascertain the proper law of the contract you have "to identify a particular system of law as being that in accordance with which the parties to it intended a contact to be interpreted",[71] or you have "to see whether the parties have by its express terms or by necessary implication from the language evinced a common intention as to the system of law by reference to which their mutual rights and obligations are to be ascertained".[72] As he said:

> "[T]he purpose of entering into a contract being to create legal rights and obligations between the parties to it, interpretation of the contract involves determining what are the legal rights and obligations to which the words used in it give rise. This is not possible except by reference to the system of law by which the legal consequences that follow from the use of those words is to be ascertained."[73]

In addition:

> "[C]ontracts are incapable of existing in a legal vacuum. They are mere pieces of paper devoid of all legal effect unless they were made by reference to some system of private law which defines the obligations assumed by the parties to the contract by their use of particular forms of words and prescribes the remedies enforceable in a court of justice for failure to perform any of those obligations ..."[74]

The "closest and most real" test

In international commercial arbitration, the choice of law issue can be more complicated than the parties might have expected, especially when no expressed choice of law is found in the arbitration agreement, or the arbitrators experience difficulties in inferring the implied choice

---

[70] [1984] AC 50.
[71] *Amin Rasheed Shipping Corp v Kuwait Insurance Co* [1984] AC 50 at 61, [1983] 3 WLR 241 (HL) at 245.
[72] [1984] AC 50 at 62.
[73] *Ibid* at 60.
[74] *Ibid* at 65.

of law. In most international commercial arbitrations, the parties have different nationalities or have offices situated in different countries, and where the contractual obligations are performed in different countries. This makes the choice of the proper law a difficult task. Traditionally, in this kind of situation, arbitrators are expected to refer this issue to the conflict of laws rules of the arbitral *situs*; in most jurisdictions, the closest and most real relationship test will be applied. An objective scrutiny of every term of the contract, every detail affecting its formation and performance, and every fact of the case will be conducted in order to ascertain the proper law. This approach in arbitration has been adopted by some international Conventions or treaties.[75] For instance, Art 4(1) of the European Convention on the Law Applicable to Contractual Obligations (the Rome Convention)[76] provides: "To the extent that the law applicable to the contract has not been chosen in accordance with Art 3, the contract shall be governed by the law of the country with which it is most closely connected."[77] Similar provisions also appear in the United Nations Convention on Contracts for the International Sale of Goods,[78] Art 33 of the UNCITRAL Arbitration Rules, Art 17(1) of the ICC Rules and Art 28(1) of the AAA International Rules.

England

In accordance with the "closest and most real relationship" test, in international commercial arbitration the law of the place of arbitration used to be regarded as a significant indication for both the procedural law and the proper law of the contract. In relation to the proper law of contract, the significance of the place of arbitration was illustrated in a number of cases. For instance, in *Hamlyn v Talisker Distillery*,[79] the proper law of the contract was held to be the law of the place of the arbitral *situs*, since the

---

[75] Born, *International Commercial Arbitration in the United States*, p 101. He said: "In practice, however, the New York Convention and most other multilateral agreements, seldom address the conflict of laws rules applicable to the substantive law governing arbitrable disputes. One exception to this is the 1961 European Convention on International Commercial Arbitration, which provides in Art VII that the parties 'shall be free to determine, by agreement, the law to be applied by the arbitrators to the substance of the dispute', and, failing any agreement, that the dispute will be governed by the proper law under the rules of conflict that the arbitrators deem applicable." Another exception is the International Convention for the Settlement of Disputes, Art 42 of which provides for the application of international law and the law of the host state.
[76] (1981) OJ L266/1. The Rome Convention specifically excludes "arbitration agreements" from its coverage. Article 1(2)(d) of the Convention does apply, however, to the underlying contractual dispute that is the subject of the arbitration agreement.
[77] ICC case no 6379 (1990). However, the Rome Convention imposes certain limitations on this issue.
[78] ICC case no 2930 (1982).
[79] [1894] AC 202.

parties agreed that the arbitration should take place in this given country. Later, the case of *Tzortzis v Monark Line A/B*[80] went further than *Hamlyn*. In this case, Sweden was the country where the contract for the sale of a ship by Swedish sellers to Greek buyers was made. The court decided that the proper law of the contract was English law, even though there was no connection with England at all. The only reason for this choice was that the City of London was the place of arbitration. In addition, in the case of *Norske Atlas Co Ltd v London General Insurance Co Ltd*,[81] where a dispute arose from a reinsurance contract between the parties, MacKinnon J said that the proper law of the contract was Norwegian law since arbitration was to be held in Norway.[82]

The compulsory application of the proper law of the place of arbitration was rejected by the House of Lords in the case of *Compagnie Tunisienne de Navigation SA v Compagnie d'Armement Maritime SA*.[83] In this case, London was expressed as the place of arbitration in the arbitration clause. Rejecting the older case law, the House of Lords decided that French law was the proper law of the contract since the contract had no connection with any other system of law other than French law. In addition, Lord Wilberforce said: "An arbitration clause must be treated as an indication, to be considered together with the rest of the contract and relevant surrounding facts."[84]

USA

Similar to England, the United States courts also supported the idea that the parties' choice of the place of arbitration was a strong indication for the arbitrators to apply the proper law of the arbitral *situs* to settle the disputes.[85] As Ehrenzweig states: "It is widely held that the parties who have chosen a place of arbitration have thus impliedly agreed on the applicability of both the procedural and substantive law of that place."[86] This idea is also stated in the *Restatement*:[87]

> "Provision by the parties in a contract that arbitration shall take place in a certain state may provide some evidence of an intention on their part that the local law of this state should govern the contract as a whole. This is true not only because the provision shows that the parties had this particular state in mind, it is also true because the parties must presumably have

---

[80] [1968] 1 WLR 406 (CA).
[81] [1927] 2 Lloyd's Rep 104.
[82] The reason for the application of Norwegian law was also to be found in the fact that the arbitrators' meeting place was Christiania.
[83] *Compagnie Tunisienne de Navigation SA v Compagnie d'Armement Maritime SA* [1971] AC 572 at 589, 597–598, 605–607.
[84] *Ibid* at 600.
[85] Restatement (Second) Conflict of Laws (1971), s 218, comment b.
[86] A Ehrenzweig, *Conflict of Laws* (1962), p 540.
[87] Restatement (Second) Conflict of Laws (1971), s 218, comment b.

recognised that arbitrators sitting in that state would have a natural tendency to apply its local law."

Moreover, in the case of *Scherk v Alberto-Culver Co*,[88] the plaintiff, an American Corporation, purchased three interrelated business enterprises from the German defendant. As far as the issue of the proper law was concerned, Mr Justice Stewart said: "Under some circumstances, the designation of arbitration in a certain place might also be viewed as implicitly selecting the law of that place to apply to that transaction."[89]

Nevertheless, this traditional idea that supports the application of the arbitral *situs*'s substantive rules has been under serious attack in recent years. It has been criticised by some commentators[90] who believe that the idea is outdated. For instance, Lew explains that of course it may be that "the parties will choose the arbitration forum and intend its law to apply; but then again that intention might equally not exist".[91] Other commentators even argue that the changes have been an almost total abandonment of the rules of the arbitral *situs*.[92] They also believe that it is a fallacy to compare a seat of arbitration with a judicial forum, because "an arbitrator does not exercise public or constitutional power in the name of the State".[93]

Three-step or two-step choice of law rules?

International commercial arbitration has seen some changes in the method of choosing the proper law. Some discussion has centred on whether the implied choice of law test and the closest and most real test are in fact the same test leading to the same conclusion. Accordingly, under the implied choice of law test, the proper law of the contract can only be decided if

---

[88] US 506 (1974) at 519, n 13.
[89] *Splosna Plovba of Piran v Agrelak Steamship Corp*, 381 F Supp 1368 at 1370 (SDNY 1974); *In re Application of Doughboy Indus Inc*, 233 NYS 2d 488 (1962); and *Konkar Indomitable Corp v Fritzen Schiffsagentur und Bereederungs GmbH*, 80 Civ 3230 (SDNY) (1981), where "Selection of an arbitration forum may also be viewed as but one factor in determining a contract's 'centre of gravity' for choice of law purposes".
[90] Eg D Collins, "Arbitration clauses and forum selection clauses in the conflict of laws: some recent developments in England" (1971) 2 JMarL & Com 363; L Kopelmanas, "The settlement of disputes in international trade" (1961) 51 ColumLR 384; Lew, *Applicable Law in International Commercial Arbitration*, pp 190 and 204; B Rubino-Sammartino, *International Arbitration Law* (1990), p 256; *Dicey and Morris on the Conflict of Laws*, p 1183; and Born, *International Commercial Arbitration in the United States – Commentary & Materials*, p 111.
[91] Lew, *Applicable Law in International Commercial Arbitration*, pp 190 and 204.
[92] Goldman, "La *Lex mercatoria* dans les contrats et l'arbitrage international" (1956) NethInt'lLRev 220 at 226; cited in Born, *International Commercial Arbitration in the United States – Commentary & Materials*, p 104.
[93] W Craig, W Park and J Paulsson, *International Chamber of Commerce Arbitration* (2nd edn, 1990), p 285.

this implied choice is demonstrated with reasonable certainty from the terms of the contract or the circumstances of the case. Arbitrators, by putting themselves in the position of the parties, are required to look at this issue from the standings of the parties and try to infer which law the parties intended. As to the "closest and most real relationship" test, it claims to be a more objective test which requires the arbitrators to "impute an intention or to determine for the parties what is the proper law, which, as just and reasonable persons, they ought to or would have intended if they had thought about the question when they made the contract".[94] Contrary to the "implied choice of law" test attempting to ascertain the intention of the parties, the arbitrators are meant to put themselves in the position of "reasonable men" and determine the objective proper law of the contract. However, while the outcome of the application of these twin tests is frequently the same, a question that has to be asked is whether "putting arbitrators into the parties' position", as required by the "implied choice" test, can be clearly distinguished from "putting arbitrators in the place of reasonable men", as required by the closest and most real relationship test?

Three steps

In the *Whitworth* case,[95] Viscount Dilhorne expressly points out that the "implied choice" test and the "closest and most real" test are, in fact, two distinct stages by referring to the judgment of Widgery LJ in the Court of Appeal:[96]

> "To solve a problem such as arises in this case one looks first at the express terms of the contract to see whether that intention is there to be found. If it is not, then in my judgment the next step is to consider the conduct of the parties to see whether that conduct shows that a decision in regard to the proper law of the contract can be inferred from it. ... Finally, if one fails in this inquiry also and is driven to the conclusion that the parties never applied their minds to the question at all, then one has to go to the third stage and see what is the proper law of the contract by considering what system of law is the one with which the transaction has its closest and most real connection."[97]

Two steps

The issues are whether "the standings of the parties" and "a reasonable man" are leading to the same conclusion since the arbitrators, in general, decide the applicable law on a reasonable basis, as well as whether the

---

[94] *Mount Albert Borough Council* [1938] AC 224 (PC) at 240.
[95] [1970] AC 583.
[96] *Whitworth Street Estates Ltd v James Miller* [1969] 1 WLR 377 (CA).
[97] *Ibid* at 383 (CA); also quoted by Viscount Dilhorne in [1970] AC 583 (HL) at 611.

proper law should be determined in accordance with a more objective test which considers the relevant factors of the case and connections the contract has with a particular system of law. In fact, some countries and arbitration institutions have replaced the traditional three-step choice of law rule with a two-step rule. For instance, in Sweden, party autonomy is still the primary principle of conflict of law rules in relation to contracts; however, in the absence of an express choice, Swedish courts are ready to apply the "centre of gravity" test, which allows the judges and arbitrators "to apply the law with which the contract in question has its closest connection, or where its centre of gravity lies".[98] This test was applied in the landmark case of *Försäkringsaktiebolaget Skandia* v *Riksgäldskontoret*,[99] handed down by the Swedish Supreme Court in 1937. Hobér pointed out that the "centre of gravity" test replaced the "implied choice" test, and stated:

> "The *Skandia* case was a landmark case in that it replaced the previously existing theory of the hypothetical will of the parties. The underlying philosophy of this theory was the attempt to establish the will of the parties, as if they had thought of the question of applicable law when they entered into the contract. The search for the hypothetical will of the parties was thus a subjective method. By contrast, the centre of gravity test represents a move away from the subjective approach and introduces an objective approach, in that it prescribes the weighing of all objective elements of a legal relationship with a view to finding the law of the country with which the relationship has its closest connection."[100]

Apart from Sweden, a similar change can also be found in the French Code of Civil Procedure 1981,[101] the Netherlands Arbitration Act 1986[102] and the Swiss Private International Law Act 1987,[103] which provides: "The arbitrator shall decide the dispute according to the rule of law chosen by the parties; in the absence of such a choice, he shall decide according to the rule he deems appropriate."

---

[98] K Hobér, "In search for the centre of gravity-applicable law in international arbitration in Sweden" (1994) Swedish and International Arbitration 7 at 8.

[99] *Ibid*.

[100] *Ibid* at 9. While Hobér distinguishes these two tests, however, he stresses that the difference between them should not be exaggerated as far as the result is concerned, since the hypothetical will of the parties would typically, in most cases, coincide with the law of the country with which the contract has its closest connection.

[101] Article 1496 of the French Code of Civil Procedure, Book IV, 14 May 1981 provides: "The arbitrator shall decide the dispute in accordance with the rules of the law chosen by the parties or, in the absence of such choice, in accordance with the rules of the law he considers appropriate."

[102] Article 1054(2) of the Netherlands Arbitration Act 1986 provides: "If a choice of law is made by the parties, the arbitral tribunal shall make its award in accordance with the rules of law chosen by the parties. Failing such choice of law the arbitral tribunal shall make its award in accordance with the rules of law which it considers appropriate."

[103] Federal Statute of Private International Law, Chapter 12, 1 January 1988, Art 187(1).

TYPES OF PROPER LAW

National laws or a-national principles?

It is acknowledged that most contracts are governed by a national law due to its connection with the parties or the performance of the contract. However, such a choice of national law is frequently pointed out as unsuitable for the needs of international commerce. As Redfern and Hunter pointed out: "In an ideal world, almost any national system of law should be suitable, so long as that law had been drawn up, or has developed, in a manner which suits the requirements of modern commerce. In the real world, some national systems of law will be found to contain outdated laws and regulations which make them unsuitable for use in international contracts."[104] They even claim that, sometimes, well developed and modern codes of law may not suit the needs of international commerce due to its own domestic, social, economic, cultural and political considerations.[105] Consequently, it is not surprising to know that parties to major international contracts may venture out to choose non-national law to govern their contract. While "arbitrators in international commercial arbitrations have shown a growing desire to throw off the shackles of private international law and to avoid dependence, or exclusive dependence, on any particular national law",[106] another trend in the choice of law is the application of a-national principles as the proper law of the contract in international commercial arbitration. A study of recent arbitral awards showed that arbitrators have frequently moved away from the traditional choice of law rules and chosen the proper law of the contract from the category of a-national principles, such as a new *lex mercatoria*, amiable composition and the general principles of law, to govern the main contract.

This trend is also incorporated in r 47 of the Scottish Arbitration Rules. It reads:

> "When deciding the dispute, the tribunal must have regard to –
> (a) the provisions of any contract relating to the substance of the dispute,
> (b) the normal commercial or trade usage of any undefined terms in the provisions of any such contract,
> (c) any established commercial or trade customs or practices relevant to the substance of the dispute, and
> (d) any other matter which the parties agree is relevant in the circumstances."

---

[104] A Redfern, M Hunter, N Blackaby and C Parasides, *Redfern and Hunter on International Arbitration* (5th edn, 2009), para 3.112.
[105] *Ibid* at para 2.42.
[106] R Goode, "Usage and Its Reception in Transnational Commercial" (1997) 46 ICLQ 1 at 6.

General principles of law

The application of the general principles of law has found acceptance first in international arbitral awards. Instead of determining which national law ought to be applied, in some cases international arbitrators deliberately leave this question unanswered and simply apply the general principles of law, claiming that by doing so they are acting in accordance with the will of the parties. Influenced by the idea that such practice is well-suited to the particular needs of international trade, some national courts[107] have shown a relaxed attitude towards it, occasionally setting aside some of their rules (the *lex fori*) in order to correspond with such practice.

From a number of *ad hoc* arbitrations reported, it can be seen that the general principles of law have often been chosen to govern state contracts. With respect to the source of the general principles of law, Art 38 of the International Court of Justice Statute has provided some clues as follows:

> "1. The Court, whose function is to decide in accordance with international law such disputes as are submitted to it, shall apply;
>   (a) international conventions, whether general or particular, establishing rules expressly recognised by the contracting states;
>   (b) international custom, as evidence of a general practice accepted as law;
>   (c) the general principles of law recognised by civilised nations;
>   (d) subject to the provisions of Art 59 (concerning the relative effects of judgments), judicial decisions and the teachings of the most highly qualified publicists of the various nations, as subsidiary means for the determination of rules of law.
> 2. This provision shall not prejudice the power of the Court to decide a case *ex aequo et bono*, if the parties agree thereto."

After World War II, in the sunset of the colonial era, many new countries were founded. In order to build up the political and economic strength of these countries, a number of opportunities were offered to western businessmen to enter into contracts of investment, concession or economic development with the state governments. This type of contract, which involved both a state or state enterprise and a private party, is termed a "state contract". Due to the special nature of state contracts, such as the instability of governments, unequal bargaining power between the parties, frequent changes to legislation in the host country, and so on, it is not surprising that disputes arise from time to time. Among the different dispute settlement mechanisms, arbitration is regarded as the most suitable choice for resolving disputes arising from a state contract.

---

[107] Such as France: see the new French Civil Code of Procedure 1981.

While arbitration has frequently dealt with disputes arising from a state contract, as far as the choice of the proper law in state contracts is concerned, parties shied away from the choice of national laws due to distrust and hostility towards the other party's judicial system. Under these circumstances, a law with a neutral character appears to be more desirable. As a result, the choice of a-national principles or a complex amalgam of national and a-national principles is often selected to be the proper law of the contract by the parties or the arbitrators. A number of international arbitral awards have been decided on such a basis, especially those arising from major international state contracts, for example, oil concession or mining agreements.

Opinions against the application of international law as the proper law of a contract

Not every jurist or practitioner is in favour of the application of the general principles of law as the proper law of the contract. In fact, the application of the general principles of law in international commercial arbitration has been criticised by two schools of thought, and from different angles.

Following the traditional idea that the subject of international law is a state, one school of thought argues that international law cannot be the governing law of a contract between two individuals even though one of them is a sovereign state. The critics insist that international law is solely designed to govern the relationship between states. Moreover, private individuals should not fall into the ambit of international law.[108] This opinion is upheld in the *Serbian Loans* case,[109] where the court first rejected the idea of elevating a foreign investment transaction to the status of a treaty.[110] Second, the court decided that it was inappropriate to apply international law to govern disputes arising from a foreign investment contract between a sovereign state and a private party. Finally, it ruled that this type of relationship can only be governed by the municipal legal systems.

This group also questions whether a foreign or multinational corporation as a party to a state contract has sufficient personality to enjoy the protection provided by international law. They argue that it is very difficult to establish a logical basis for such a situation. The same question is raised in the Draft Code of Conduct for Multinational Corporations, whose purpose is to provide guidelines for a multinational corporation conducting business in a host state, rather than providing an argument for conferring a special personality on such kind of corporation.[111] The

---

[108] M Sornarajah, "The Climate of International Arbitration" (1991) 8(2) JIA 47 at 53.
[109] [1929] *PCIJ Series A*, no 14, p 5, 11 WC 340 (1929).
[110] The idea of elevating a foreign investment transaction to a treaty was applied in the *Wimbledon* case: [1926] *PCIJ Series A*, no 1, p 25.
[111] Sornarajah, above, n 108, at 55.

committee suggested that there was a lack of consideration of the interest of the host states and it criticised the arbitral awards which were made in favour of the application of international law by considering only the interests of the foreign investors. In the committee's opinion, these arbitrators looked at only the possibility that the law of the host state would cause bias against the investors; however, they ignored the fact that an investment contract does not always bring good things to the host state (for instance, the influx of capital may damage the economy of the host state under an investment contract).

Another group of commentators found their argument on the basis of wavier of sovereign immunity. They maintain that a contract, regardless of whether it is between two private parties or a private party and a sovereign state, should be governed by only private laws. They believe that the sovereign immunity of the state involved in a state contract has been waived when the state agrees to refer the dispute to arbitration. This idea is strongly invoked by Luzzatto. He maintains that a contract between a state party and a private party should be regarded as a contract between two private parties, and the dispute arising from this kind of contract should be governed by private laws. He explains:

> "In principle, there can be little doubt, if any, that international arbitrations arising from a dispute between States and foreign subjects, under a contractual relationship between the parties, should be put on the same level as arbitrations between two private parties, and not as arbitrations between States which are governed as such by public international law."[112]

The reasons behind this theory are twofold. First, from a theoretical point of view, it is a fallacy to assume that, through a state contract, a foreign private party can enjoy the same rights and obligations under international law as a state. Based on the same argument, it is similarly fallacious to presume that the international responsibilities of a state can be imposed upon a foreign corporation or an individual private investor. Second, from a practical viewpoint, it is argued that the content of international law is not comprehensive enough to cope with complicated international commercial disputes. This is because international law does not contain rules that are applicable to private contractual relationships. As explained by Sornarajah in an article:

> "The idea that international law could apply to such a contract would have sounded odd as a proposition simply because international law did not contain and does not contain any rules which give validity to such contracts and did not contain any rules of substantive law relating such contracts."[113]

---

[112] R Luzzatto, "International Commercial Arbitration and the Municipal Law of States" (1977) 157 Rec des Cour 87.
[113] Sornarajah, above, n 108, at 53.

In fact, international law has not been provided with an opportunity to develop a set of detailed contractual rules to govern commercial disputes, such as breach or frustration of the contract.[114] Furthermore, in their opinion, such rules simply do not exist in international law at all.[115] As a scholar commented: "Public international law neither aims nor is equipped to regulate the commercial relations and activities of private individuals and organisations in the international arena."[116]

Application of general principles of law in ad hoc arbitration

Despite the objections outlined above, in a number of major international commercial arbitrations the general principles of law have been chosen as the proper law. This practice has attracted a great deal of attention and controversy after a series of arbitral awards were made to settle disputes arising from oil concession agreements, especially a number of cases where the Libyan Government was involved during the period 1971–73.

Sapphire case

The award made in the *Sapphire* case was the first award to give full support to the application of international law and exclude the municipal law of the host country. In this case, a dispute arose from an oil concession agreement between Sapphire and the National Iranian Oil Company, which was a state agent of the Iranian Government. There was no express choice of law clause in the contract. However, a choice of law clause was found in similar concession agreements previously made by the National Iranian Oil Company as follows:

> "[I]t [the agreement] shall be governed by and interpreted and applied in accordance with the principles of law common to Iran and the several nations in which the other parties to this Agreement are incorporated, and in the absence of such common principles then by and in accordance with principles of law recognised by civilised nations in general, including such of those principles as may have been applied by international tribunals."[117]

The arbitrator, Mr Cavin, decided that the proper law applicable to the interpretation and performance of the concession agreement was

---

[114] K Lipstein, "International Arbitration between Individuals and Governments and Conflict of Laws" in B Cheng and E Brown (eds), *Contemporary Problems of International Law: Essays in Honour of George Schwarzenberger on his Eightieth Birthday* (1988), pp 180 and 183; J Lew, *Applicable Law in International Commercial Arbitration* (1986), p 403; and C Amerasinghe, "State breaches of contracts with alien and international law" (1964) 2 AmJIntLaw 58 at 81.

[115] *Ibid.*

[116] Lew, *Applicable Law in International Commercial Arbitration*, p 403.

[117] *Sapphire International Petroleums Ltd v National Iranian Oil Company*, arbitral award made on 15 March 1963, (1968) 35 ILR 136.

the principles of law generally recognised by civilised nations. First, he denied that the parties had an intention to apply Iranian law to the agreement. Second, he stated that the parties could not be presumed to have agreed upon the choice of law by their common choice of the forum of the arbitration. As he said:

> "[I]n the view of some eminent specialists in Private International Law, since the arbitrator has been invested with his powers as a result of the common intention of the parties he is not bound by the rules of conflict in force at the forum of the arbitration. Contrary to a State judge, who is bound to conform to the conflict law rules of the State in whose name he metes out justice, the arbitrator is not bound by such rules. He must look for the common intention of the parties, use the connecting factors generally used in doctrine and in case law and must disregard national peculiarities. This consideration carries particular weight in the present case ..."[118]

Given that the agreements offered *Sapphire* the rights of possession and, to a certain extent control of the territory, the contract in dispute was regarded as one with a particular character which partly existed in public law and partly in private law.[119] Third, considering the decision in the *Lena Goldfield Arbitration*,[120] Mr Cavin agreed that it would be more appropriate to call for the application of the general principles of law based upon reason and upon the common practice of civilised countries to decide the case. This has been expressly recognised in other cases.[121] As he observed:

> "a reference to rules of good faith, together with the absence of any reference to a national system of law, leads the judge to determine, according to the spirit of the agreement, what meaning he can reasonably give to a provision of the agreement which is in dispute. It is therefore perfectly legitimate to find in such a clause evidence of the intention of the parties not to apply the strict rules of a particular system but, rather, to rely upon the rules of law, based upon reason, which are common to civilised nations".[122]

Finally, with reference to Art 38 of the Statute of the International Court of Justice, Mr Cavin decided that the application of the general principles of law to the contract was justified in this case where a State organ and a foreign company were involved.[123]

---

[118] (1968) 35 ILR 136 at 170.
[119] *Ibid* at 171.
[120] Discussed in (1950–51) 36 *Cornell LQ* 31 at 36–37.
[121] Such as *Petroleum Developments Ltd v Ruler of Abu Dhabi* (1951) 18 ILR 141; and *Ruler of Qatar v International Marine Oil Co Ltd* (1953) 20 ILR 534.
[122] *Sapphire International Petroleums Ltd v National Iranian Oil Company*, Arbitral Award 15 March 1963, (1968) 35 ILR 136 at 173.
[123] *Ibid* at 175.

ARAMCO case

In the *ARAMCO* case, a dispute between the Kingdom of Saudi Arabia and the Arabian American Oil Company (ARAMCO) was submitted to an *ad hoc* arbitration held in Geneva in 1955. The facts of the case are as follows: in 1933, the Kingdom of Saudi Arabia granted an oil concession agreement, which gave ARAMCO an exclusive right to transport the oil extracted from the concession area. Nevertheless, in 1954, the Government of Saudi Arabia granted Mr Onassis and his company, Saudi Arabian Maritime Tankers Ltd, the rights to transport Saudi Arabian oil for 30 years. The latter agreement was in conflict with the agreement which granted ARAMCO the right to transport the oil extracted from the concession area.

The arbitral tribunal decided that the choice of the applicable principles would be made by resorting to the worldwide custom and practice in the oil business and industry; failing such custom and practice, the Tribunal will be influenced by the world case law and doctrine and by pure jurisprudence.[124] The tribunal addressed the issue of the proper law in the following terms:

> "[P]ublic international law should be applied to the effects of the Concession, when objective reasons lead it to be concluded that certain matters cannot be governed by any rule of the municipal law of any State, as is the case in all matters relating to transport by sea, to the sovereignty of the State on its territorial waters and to the responsibility of States for the violation of its international obligations."[125]

British Petroleum (Libya) Ltd v Government of the Libyan Arab Republic case

In *British Petroleum Co Ltd* v *Government of the Libyan Arab Republic*[126] the dispute arose from a nationalisation ordered by the Libyan Government. On 18 December 1957, Libya granted in a Deed of Concession, designated as Concession 65, to Mr Hunt (a citizen of the United States) an exclusive right for 50 years to search for and extract petroleum within a designated area in the Sarir Desert of Libya. By an agreement dated 24 June 1960, Mr Hunt assigned to BP an undivided one-half interest in Concession 65 and this was approved by the Libyan Government. Nevertheless, on 7 December 1970, Libya passed the Nationalisation Law (Law No 115), which nationalised the operations of BP in Concession 65. On 11 December 1971, BP instituted arbitration against Libya.

---

[124] *Saudi Arabia* v *Arabian American Oil Company* (1960) 27 ILR 117 at 171.
[125] *Ibid* at 172.
[126] *British Petroleum Co Ltd* v *Government of the Libyan Arab Republic* (1979) 46 ILR 297; reprinted in (1980) V YBCA 143.

A choice of proper law clause was found in para 7 of cl 28 of the Concession, which provided:

> "This Concession shall be governed by and interpreted in accordance with the principles of law of Libya common to the principles of international law and in the absence of such common principles then by and in accordance with the general principles of law, including such of those principles as may have been applied by international tribunals."

In accordance with the clause, the arbitrator decided that "the provision generates practical difficulties in its implementation, it offers guidance in a negative sense by excluding the relevance of any single municipal legal system as such".[127] Therefore, the Tribunal should apply the clause according to its clear and apparent meaning to the extent possible.

Meanwhile, BP made two submissions that the Concession should be governed by international law alone. First, BP maintained that the acceptance of a general principle must be supported by both Libyan and international law if they were to apply to the Concession. Therefore, if the conduct of a party to the Concession could not be justified by the principles of both Libyan law and international law, it was not justifiable under the Concession. In other words, the conduct was justifiable only when the principles of both systems of law – Libyan and international – supported it. Second, BP argued that, in this case, public international law should be the only system of law left since the parties had expressly excluded the direct and the sole application of Libyan law, and had made reference to the general principles of law.[128]

Nevertheless, both arguments were rejected by the arbitrator. In relation to BP's first submission, the arbitrator commented:

> "[S]ince it entirely leaves out of the picture the direction which follows from paragraph 7 of Clause 28 that conduct etc. in the last analysis should be tested by reference to the general principles of law. It is not correct to say that 'a principle must be supported by both Libyan law and international law in order to be justifiable under the concession' and that conduct 'is justifiable only if principles of both systems of law – Libyan and international – support it'. The principle may still be acceptable, and the conduct justifiable, if supported by the general principles of law."[129]

And:

> "If a particular action by a party amounts to breach of contract under one system but not under the other, the issue is one which can only be decided by reference to the general principles of law. Thus, the first part of the Claimant's argument must be rejected. It is not sufficient for the Claimant

---

[127] (1979) 46 ILR 297 at 327.
[128] Ibid at 328.
[129] Ibid.

to show that the conduct of the Respondent is a breach of international law as a basis for maintaining a claim based on breach of contract. In the event that international law and Libyan law conflict on that issue, the question is to be resolved by the application of the general principles of law."[130]

In relation to the second submission, the arbitrator stated:

"The Tribunal cannot accept the submission that public international law applies for paragraph 7 of Clause 28 does not so stipulate. Nor does the BP Concession itself constitute the sole source of law controlling the relationship between the Parties. The governing system of law is what that clause expressly provides, viz. in the absence of principles of law, including such of those principles as may have been applied by international tribunals."[131]

The arbitrator interpreted the choice of law clause as follows: (1) the law of Libya was the proper law of the concession, but only to the extent that it was consistent with the principles of international law; and (2) in the event of inconsistency between these two legal systems, the general principles of law would prevail. Nevertheless, the arbitrator stated that he was unable to find any principles of the Libyan law common to principles of international law pursuant to which the BP Concession would be valid and subsisting and the remedy of restitution available to the Claimant. Hence, in accordance with para 7 of cl 28, the tribunal decided to consider the issue in the light of the general principles of law. Finally, the arbitrator decided that a nationalisation in breach of the concession agreement amounted to an illegality and, similar to a treaty, the foreign investment agreement should act as a fetter on the sovereignty of the host state while it was valid.

TEXACO *case*

As with other nationalisation disputes arising between the Libyan Government and foreign companies, the TEXACO arbitration dealt with another oil concession agreement. In this case,[132] during the period between 1955 and 1968, 14 Deeds of Concession were concluded between the Libyan Government and two American companies, the Texas Overseas Petroleum Company and the California Asiatic Oil Company. Similar to what had happened in the *BP* case, despite the concession agreements, Libya unilaterally ordered nationalisation on 1 September 1974. After the dispute arose, the companies notified the Libyan Government that

---

[130] (1979) 46 ILR 297.
[131] *Ibid* at 329.
[132] *Texaco Overseas Petroleum Co and California Asiatic Co v Government of the Libyan Arab Republic* (1978) 17 ILM 3. (Award on the merits, 19 January 1977; R Depury was the sole arbitrator.)

recourse had been made to arbitration in accordance with cl 28 of the Deeds of Concession.

After deciding that the arbitration procedures should be governed by public international law,[133] the arbitrator went on to discuss the issue of the proper law of the contract. On the issue concerning the proper law of the contract, the arbitrator referred to cl 28. It reads:

> "This concession shall be governed by and interpreted in accordance with the principles of the law of Libya common to the principles of international law and in the absence of such common principles then by and in accordance with the general principles of law, including such of those principles as may have been applied by international tribunals."

This choice of law clause was interpreted as a "two-tier system" by the arbitrator. He explained that, in accordance with this clause, the principles of Libyan law were applicable to the extent that such principles were common to the principles of international law, and, in the absence of such conformity, reference was to be made to general principles of law.[134]

Following such a conclusion, the arbitrator said that under a new concept, contracts between states and foreign private persons could be "internationalised" in the sense of being subjected to public international law. Therefore, under certain conditions, the arbitrator could regard contracts between states and private individuals as coming within the ambit of a particular and new branch of international law – the international law of contracts.[135]

Accordingly, the arbitrator not only chose international law as the proper law but also referred to international law as a means of empowering him to choose this two-tier system. In particular, the application of *the principles of Libyan law* did not rule out the application of *the principles of*

---

[133] As far as the dispute about the law governing the arbitration is concerned, the arbitrator found sufficient reasons to adopt the solution used in the *ARAMCO* case: as the arbitration was to take place outside the host country, the parties had intended to secure the guarantee of a neutral judge. Moreover, the jurisdictional immunity of states excludes the possibility, for the judicial authorities of the country of the seat, of exercising their right of supervision and interference in arbitral proceedings. Under the principle of jurisdictional immunity of foreign states the arbitrator was unable to hold that one state could be subject to the law of another state. The arbitrator still had other reasons for holding international law to govern the arbitration. One of these was the provision in cl 28 to the effect that, failing agreement of the parties, the President of the ICJ should appoint the arbitrator. Furthermore, the Rules of Procedure, adopted by the arbitrator in the first hearing on 24 February 1975, declared in Art 1, para 2 (after having fixed, in para 1, Geneva as the seat of the arbitral tribunal) that "the arbitration shall be governed by these Rules of Procedure to the exclusion of local law".

[134] *Texaco Overseas Petroleum Co and California Asiatic Oil Co v Government of the Libyan Arab Republic* (1978) 17 ILM 3, at 11; reprinted in (1979) IX YBCA 177.

[135] (1978) 17 ILM 3 at 13.

international law. In fact, it was a combination of these two sets of principles in verifying the conformity of the Libyan law with international law. As he explained in the following terms:

> "In the present dispute, general principles of law have a subsidiary role in the governing law clause and apply in the case of lack of conformity between the principles of Libyan law and the principles of international law; ... Now, these principles of international law must, in the present case, be the standard for the application of Libyan law since it is only if Libyan law is in conformity with international law that it should be applied. Therefore, the reference that is made mainly to the principles of international law and secondarily, to the general principles of law must have as a consequence the application of international law to the legal relations between the parties."[136]

Finally, after consulting the principles of international law and the nature of the contract, the arbitrator stated that the contract involved was internationalised and governed by the general principles of law.

LIAMCO case

The third case involving a dispute arising from an oil concession agreement between the Libyan Government and a foreign investor is *Libyan American Oil Company (LIAMCO) v Government of the Libyan Arab Republic.*[137] On 1 September 1969, the Libyan Government nationalised 51 per cent of the concession rights of a number of companies including LIAMCO. Later, the remaining 49 per cent of the LIAMCO concession was also nationalised. After the second nationalisation, LIAMCO referred the dispute to arbitration.

A choice of law clause was found in cl 28, para 7 of the Concession Agreement, which read: "This concession shall be governed and interpreted in accordance with the principles of law of Libya common to the principles of international law, and in the absence of such common principles then by and in accordance with the general principles of law as may have been applied by international tribunals."

In the arbitral award, the arbitrator considered the choice of law contained in cl 28, para 7 of the LIAMCO Concession Agreement valid and stated that "it is an accepted universal principle of both domestic and international laws that the parties to a mixed public and private contract are free to select in their contract the law to govern their contractual relationship". Furthermore, the arbitrator analysed the choice of law clause by stating:

---

[136] (1978) 17 ILM 3 at 15.
[137] *Libyan American Oil Company (LIAMCO) v Government of the Libyan Arab Republic* (1982) 62 ILR 140; reprinted in (1981) VI YBCA 89.

"The proper law governing LIAMCO's concession agreement as set forth in the amended version of said Clause 28, para 7, is in the first place the law of Libya when consistent with international law, and subsidiarily the general principles of law. Hence, the principal proper law of the contract in said Concessions is Libyan domestic law. But it is specified in the Agreements that this covers only 'the principles of law of Libya common to the principles of international law'. Thus, it excludes any part of Libyan law that is in conflict with the principles of international law."[138]

In relation to the argument that the application of international law might contradict Libyan law, the arbitrator commented:

"It is relevant to note that the other subsidiary legal sources mentioned in said Art 1 of the Libyan Civil Code, namely custom and natural law and equity, are also in harmony with the Islamic legal system itself. As a matter of fact, in the absence of contrary legal text based on the Holy Koran or the Traditions of the Prophet, Islamic law considers custom as a source of law and as complementary to and explanatory of the contents of contracts, especially in commercial transactions."[139]

Moreover,

"It is very relevant in this connection to point out that Islamic law treats international law as an imperative compendium forming part of the general positive law, and that the principles of that part are very similar to those adopted by modern international legal theory.

Thus it has been pointed out that Libyan law in general and Islamic law in particular have common rules and principles with international law, and provide for the application of custom and equity as subsidiary sources.

...

These general principles are usually embodied in most recognised legal systems, and particularly in Libyan legislation, including its modern codes and Islamic law. They are applied by municipal courts and are mainly referred to international and arbitral case-law."[140]

Finally, the arbitrator concluded that the Concession agreements were governed by, in the first place, the law of Libya when consistent with international law, and subsequently, the general principles of law.

AMINOIL case[141]

This case involved a dispute arising from a concession agreement between Aminoil and the Kuwaiti government. Aminoil was granted a Concession

---

[138] (1982) 62 ILR 140 at 173.
[139] Ibid at 174; reprinted in (1981) VI YBCA 89 at 93–94.
[140] (1982) 62 ILR 140 at 175; and (1981) VI YBCA 89 at 94.
[141] *American Independent Oil Co Inc (AMINOIL) v Government of the State of Kuwait International* (1982) 21 ILM 976; reprinted in (1984) IX YBCA 71.

by the Rulers of Kuwait for the exploration of petroleum and natural gas in the Kuwait "Neutral Zone" in 1948. However, on 19 September 1977, the Government of Kuwait issued Decree Law No 124 to terminate the concession agreement between the parties. All assets and interests of the Company were nationalised by Kuwait. Article III of the Concession Agreement contained a choice of law clause. As far as the proper law was concerned, Art III(2) of the agreement provided:

> "The law governing the substantive issues between the parties shall be determined by the Tribunal, having regard to the quality of the Parties, the transnational character of their relations and the principles of law and practice prevailing in the modern world."

The arbitrator commented on the choice of law clause and stated that Art III(2):

> "[M]akes it clear that Kuwait is a sovereign state entrusted with the interests of a national community, the law of which constitutes an essential part of intra-community relations with the state. At the same time, by referring to the transnational character of relations with the concessionaire, and to the general principles of law, this Article brings out the wealth and fertility of the set of legal rules that the Tribunal is called upon to apply."[142]

The arbitrator also stressed that the different sources of law to be applied in this case were not contradictory with each other. He said:

> "The different sources of the law thus to be applied are not – at least in the present case – in contradiction with one another. Indeed if, as recalled above, international law constitutes an integral part of the law of Kuwait, the general principles of law correspondingly recognise the rights of the State in its capacity of supreme protector of the general interest. If the different legal elements involved do not always and everywhere blend as successfully as in the present case, it is nevertheless on taking advantage of their resources, and encouraging their trend towards unification, that the future of a truly international economic order in the investment field will depend."[143]

SPP case[144]

This case involved a dispute arising from a construction agreement in relation to a tourist village made between SPP, the Ministry of Tourism of

---

[142] (1982) 21 ILM 976 at 1001.
[143] *Ibid*; reprinted in (1984) IX YBCA. 71 at 72.
[144] *SPP (Middle East) Ltd, Hong Kong and Southern Pacific Properties Ltd, Hong Kong v Arab Republic of Egypt and Egyptian General Company for Tourism and Hotels*, ICC case no 3493, made on 16 February 1983; the facts and the award were published in (1983) 22 ILM 752. The challenge was published in (1984) 23 ILM 1048; reprinted in (1984) IX YBCA 111 at 116–118.

Egypt and EGOTH. This agreement was followed by a second agreement on 12 December 1974, between EGOTH and SPP. The words "approved, agreed and ratified by the Minister of Tourism" and the signature of the Minister appeared on the agreement. However, the project was objected to by the People's Assembly at a later stage. The project was eventually cancelled by several Decrees issued by the Government. An arbitration clause was found in the second agreement. In accordance with the arbitration clause, SPP initiated the arbitration with the ICC. With respect to the issue of the proper law, the arbitral tribunal stated:

> "The Agreements do not provide specially for the law which is to govern the contract. The parties have fully debated this issue coming to conclusions which only partially diverge. They both agree that in view of the circumstances of the case the relevant domestic law is that of Egypt. The Claimants, however, contend that no rules and/or principles drawn from the body of domestic Egyptian law should be allowed to override the principles of international law applicable to international investment projects of this kind."

The arbitral tribunal affirmed the idea that a state and a private person to a state contract can be removed, to a certain extent, from the jurisdiction of the domestic law and be subject to international rules.[145] Regarding the issue of the proper law, the tribunal decided that the Egyptian law was the governing law but within the scope of the general principles of international law. After considering the opinions of some Egyptian law specialists, the tribunal found that the Egyptian law must be construed so as to include such principles of international law as may be applicable. Moreover, the national laws of Egypt can be relied upon only in as much as they do not contravene the principles of international law. While being required to take the provisions of the contract and the relevant trade usages into account, the tribunal stated:

> "International Law Principles such as '*Pacta Sunt Servanda*' and '*Just compensation for expropriatory measures*' can be deemed as part of Egyptian Law. The adherence to the ICSID Convention should then be treated as conclusive evidence of Egypt's declared intent to abide by these principles, which indeed represent the basic philosophy adopted by the Convention's drafters."[146]

The new *lex mercatoria*

Schmitthoff suggested that the sources of a new *lex mercatoria* can be found in (a) international rules of commerce; (b) applicable state law;

---

[145] (1983) 22 ILM 752 at 769.
[146] *Ibid* at 771.

and (c) trade usages in each branch of commerce.[147] Influenced by this statement, the new *lex mercatoria* has frequently been chosen by arbitrators to be the proper law governing the substantive disputes between parties, particularly in the European Continent.[148] The most frequent choices of the new *lex mercatoria* include the UNIDROIT Principles of International Commercial Law ("the UNIDROIT Principles"), the 1998 Principles of European Contract Law, the United Nations Convention on Contracts for the International Sale of Goods 1980 ("the Vienna Convention" or "the CISG"), trade usages, the ICC Uniform Customs and Practice for Documentary Credits 2007 ("the UCP 600"), INCOTERMS 2010. Apart from these usual choices, both the English High Court and the Court of Appeal also upheld the choices of Shari'ah law[149] and Jewish law[150] as valid applicable substantive laws to govern contracts under s 46(1)(b) of the (English) Arbitration Act 1996.

Analysis of arbitral awards made during the past 30 years shows that a substantial number were made on the basis of the new *lex mercatoria*. The choice of the new *lex mercatoria* can be made in two ways: either by the parties' expressed choice provided in the choice of law clause in the arbitration agreement or in the contract, or by the arbitrator's decision in the absence of express choice from the parties.

With increasing international commercial activities conducted between parties from different countries, the need for fair and suitable norms has increased.[151] Under these circumstances, the practice of applying the new *lex mercatoria* has been invoked by some scholars. They have suggested that the national law regimes and the conventional choice of law rules to find the proper law of the contract within the scope of national laws should be modified.

In their opinion, in the absence of an express choice of law, the traditional choice of law rules appear to be inadequate in providing certainty for international business people to predict which law will govern the disputes between them. Searching within national laws,

---

[147] C Schmitthoff, "The unification of the law of international trade" in B Cheng (ed), *Schmitthoff's Select Essays on International Trade Law* (1988) at p 170.

[148] According to Mr Lando, the arbitrators from Europe more frequently apply the *lex mercatoria* to disputes arising from international contracts than those from other countries, especially disputes arising from contracts between a government or government enterprise and a private company. With the fear of potential bias, the private party will not wish to have the dispute governed by the laws of the foreign government, and vice versa. Besides the state contracts, this application is also very popular among the private enterprises engaged in international trade. The application of the *lex mercatoria* in an international contract as the proper law has been generally accepted in Austria and France.

[149] *Musawi v R E International (UK) Ltd & Others* [2007] EWHC 2981.

[150] *Halpern v Halpern* [2007] EWCA Civ 291.

[151] K C Randall and J E Norris, "A New Paradigm for International Business Transactions" (1993) 71 WashULQ 599 at 607.

the business people may be forced to have their contract governed by a law they never expected, or they may be disadvantaged by their lack of language skills or difficulty in discovering the relevant regulations of the applicable laws. As Redfern and Hunter commented: "It is sometimes suggested, however, that this search for the proper law is out of touch with the realities of international trade; and that what is needed is not a particular national system of law, but a modern law merchant."[152]

Second, the proponents of the new *lex mercatoria* point out the inadequacy of municipal laws in coping with the complexities of disputes arising from international commerce. They maintain that municipal laws are inadequate for the needs of international trade because the legislative mechanism of states has demonstrated slow progress in amending the laws to cope with the fast development of international commerce. Even if a state is capable of catching up with the fast changes of commerce, the question is how far and how fast a society can afford to change its domestic legislation in order to cope with the rapidly expanding development of economic life.[153]

Recognising that keeping the commercial laws up to date and developing unified international rules can be beneficial to the development of international commercial arbitration, some jurists and merchants believe that it would be desirable to develop a set of universal rules to be applied to all international commercial activities worldwide. Responding to these demands, the concept of the new *lex mercatoria* has been invoked and has attracted a great deal of attention because it is regarded as a device that meets the real needs of the international commercial communities.

Definition of the new lex mercatoria

Since no codified rules are provided, different definitions have been suggested in legal literature on this subject.[154] Primarily, these various definitions can be categorised as two different types. One is autonomism, which regards the new *lex mercatoria* as an autonomous body of law which is self-contained and independent from any national legal system. The other group supports the idea of positivism, that the new *lex mercatoria* is supplementary to the national law and the conflict of laws rules.

As far as autonomism is concerned, Berman, Goldman and Fouchard are the scholars often associated with the idea that the new

---

[152] A Redfern and M Hunter, *Law and Practice of International Commercial Arbitration* (2nd edn, 1991), at p 117.
[153] A Goldstājn, "The new law merchant reconsidered" in C Schmitthoff (ed), *Commercial Law in a Changing Economic Climate* (1981) at p 175.
[154] C W O Stoecker, "The *lex mercatoria*: to what extent does it exist?" (1990) 7(1) JIA 101 at 105.

lex mercatoria is a self-contained autonomous body of law. Berman believes that the new *lex mercatoria* is completely disconnected to any municipal legal system. In his opinion, the new *lex mercatoria* is a body of autonomous law for international commercial transactions based upon the rule-creating power of the mercantile community. In addition, the new *lex mercatoria* is a principal source of the law governing export and import transactions which is founded on the universal practice of international business and on the common sense of business people in all parts of the globe; therefore, it should be regarded as binding upon national courts.[155]

Apart from Professor Berman, a number of jurists also share the same view. For instance, according to Professor Goldman, the new *lex mercatoria* is a collection of general principles and customary legal rules,[156] which are spontaneously created by the merchant community within the framework of international trade; furthermore, the new *lex mercatoria* can fulfil the functions of a legal system or even serve alternative choice-of-law theory[157] without reference to a particular national system of law.[158]

Other jurists define the new *lex mercatoria* as:

"An international body of law, founded on commercial understandings and contract practices of an international community composed principally of mercantile, shipping, insurance and banking enterprises of all countries."[159]

"The body of rules governing commercial relationships of a private law nature involving different countries."[160]

"The customs of the business community may combine all general principles of law to create a principle of commercial self-determination."[161]

This autonomous definition caused controversy and a group of positivists have taken a different view on this issue. This group of scholars deny the idea that the new *lex mercatoria* is a self-contained system. They

---

[155] H J Berman, *Law and Revolution: the Formation of the Western Legal Tradition* (1983), p 302.
[156] B Goldman, *Lex Mercatoria* (1983), p 6. Also see K P Berger, *International Economic Arbitration*, (1993), Vol 9, pp 526–527.
[157] Goldman and Fouchard believe that this choice of law theory allows the application of the new *lex mercatoria* as a legal system; as a result, the national laws are excluded.
[158] B Goldman, "The applicable law: general principles of the law – the *lex mercatoria*" in J Lew (ed), *Contemporary Problems in International Arbitration* (1986), at p 116.
[159] H J Berman and C Kaufmann, "The law of international commercial transactions" (1978) HarvInt'lLJ 221 at 273.
[160] Goldstâjn, above n 153, at p 171.
[161] W Craig, W Park, and J Paulsson, *International Chamber of Commerce Arbitration* (1986), para 35.02.

believe that the new *lex mercatoria* plays a supplementary role to the national law and the conflict of laws rules. It is only valid as far as it is expressly adopted by the individual state.[162] Schmitthoff is one of the jurists associated with this view. According to him, the new *lex mercatoria* is a group of "common principles in the law relating to international commercial transactions"[163] and "uniform rules accepted in all countries".[164] Furthermore, the sources of the new *lex mercatoria* are the international legislation and international customs which are formulated by an international agency and adopted by the parties to the contract.

Another supporter of the positivism of the new *lex mercatoria* is Lowenfeld, who said:

> "My concept of *lex mercatoria*, is not that of a self-contained system covering all aspects of international commercial law to the exclusion of national law, but rather as a source of law made up of custom, practice, convention, precedent, and many national laws. Thus *lex mercatoria* as I see it can furnish an alternative to a conflict of laws search which is often artificial and inconclusive, and a way out of applying rules that are inconsistent with the needs and usages of international commerce and that were adopted by individual states with internal, not international, transactions in mind."[165]

In addition, Professor Lando is another advocate for the supplementary role of the new *lex mercatoria*. He defines the new *lex mercatoria* as the "rules of law which are common to all or most of the States engaged in international trade or to those States that are connected with the dispute, and if not ascertainable, then the rules which appear to be the most appropriate and equitable".[166] This view is also held by Langen, who suggests that the new *lex mercatoria* is "[t]he rules of the game of international trade"[167] and the collection of all these rules is stipulated

---

[162] Schmitthoff, "The unification of the law of international trade" in Cheng (ed), *Schmitthoff's Select Essays on International Trade Law*, at pp 171–172; C Schmitthoff, "Nature and evolution of the transnational law of commercial transactions" in Horn and Schmitthoff (eds), *The Transnational Law of International Commercial Transactions* (1982), at pp 23–24.
[163] C Schmitthoff, "Nature and evolution of the transnational law of commercial transactions" in Horn and Schmitthoff (eds), *The Transnational Law of International Commercial Transactions* (1982), at p 19.
[164] C Schmitthoff, *Commercial Law in a Changing Economic Climate* (2nd edn, 1981), p 20.
[165] A F Lowenfeld, "*Lex mercatoria*: an arbitrator's view" (1990) 6(2) Arbitration Int 133 at 145.
[166] O Lando, "The *lex mercatoria* in international commercial arbitration" (1985) 34 ICLQ 747 at 747.
[167] E Langen, *Transnational Commercial Law* (1973), p 21.

"in the same or a similar way for a given concrete legal situation in two or more spheres of national jurisdiction".[168]

Additionally, Goldstäjn proposes a rather broad definition of the new *lex mercatoria*, which includes custom and other rules that do not necessarily reflect business conduct. As he explained:

> "Usages of trade constitute the most important part of the *lex mercatoria*. National laws and multilateral conventions explicitly emphasised usages of trade. This, however, does not exhaust the content of *lex mercatoria*. Along with usages of trade, all other phenomenal forms of business practice must be taken into account, ... commercial practices in international trade in general, and, in particular, general conditions, standard clauses, standard contracts as well as general principles of law and codes of conduct which have recently been drafted with the intention of contributing to the formation of fair-play rules."[169]

Despite all the different suggestions concerning the definition of the new *lex mercatoria*, unfortunately no one definition is recognised and accepted universally. Under these circumstances, the reality of the new *lex mercatoria* can be seen in one of Lando's speeches, as he said:

> "An arbitrator applying the *lex mercatoria* will act as an inventor more often than one who applies national law. Faced with the restricted legal material which the law merchant offers, he must often seek guidance elsewhere. His main source is the various legal systems. Applying the *lex mercatoria*, arbitrators may take advantage of their freedom to select the better rule of law which courts sometimes miss."[170]

As a result of its ambiguous nature, the new *lex mercatoria* has been debated over a few decades. In the next section of the study, opinions for and against the application of the new *lex mercatoria* will be highlighted.

The opinions against the application of the new **lex mercatoria**

While a definition of the new *lex mercatoria* has been discussed, a group of international practitioners, such as Mann,[171] Mustill,[172]

---

[168] Langen, above, n 167, p 33.
[169] A Goldstäjn, *Usages of Trade and Other Autonomous Rules of International Trade According to the UN* (1980), pp 71–72.
[170] Lando, "The *lex mercatoria* in international commercial arbitration" (1985) ICLQ 747.
[171] F Mann, "England rejects 'delocalised' contracts and arbitration" (1984) 33 ICLQ 193 at 196–197; "Private arbitration and public policy" (1985) 4 Civil JustQ 257 at 264; "*Lex Facit Arbitrum*" in P Sanders (ed), *Liber Amicorum for Martin Domke* (1967), p 157; "Introduction" in T E Carbonneau (ed), *Lex Mercatoria and Arbitration: A discussion of the New Merchant* (1997/98).
[172] M Mustill, "The new *lex mercatoria*: the first 25 years" in M Bos and I Brownlie (eds), *Liber Amicorum for the Right Honourable Lord Wilberforce* (1987); "Contemporary problems in international commercial arbitration: a response" (1989) 17 Int'lBusL 161.

Delaume[173] and Boyd,[174] have expressed some doubts as to the practical usefulness of the new *lex mercatoria*.[175] They oppose the concept of the new *lex mercatoria* for its lack of precision and predictability, failing to meet the requirement of law and lacking in precedent.

First, in their opinion, the new *lex mercatoria* is not comprehensive enough to resolve the complicated disputes arising from international commercial transactions. Although the sources and the rules of the new *lex mercatoria* have been suggested by some jurists, there has been no consistent and systematic research allowing the practitioners to understand the rules of the new *lex mercatoria*.[176] Lack of a clear definition and detailed rules is the main deficiency criticised by this school of thought. They are convinced that without clear indications of the scope of the new *lex mercatoria*, the results of arbitration will be unpredictable.

They also believe that the lack of precise rules may lead the arbitrators to render an award of what they deem fair and reasonable even though the parties never authorised them to decide the case *ex aequo et bono*. As a result, through the application of the new *lex mercatoria*, the parties will not have any control over the choice of law proceedings since the *lex mercatoria* gives the arbitrator a practically unbridled discretion. Eventually, they argue, the application of the new *lex mercatoria* will distort the purpose of the choice of laws rules in international business contracts.[177]

Second, they do not regard the new *lex mercatoria* as a legitimate source of law because it does not meet the definition of "law". In their opinion, law is a system of written rules that a state develops over time and enacted by the legislature in order to deal with business agreements, social relationships, crime and other aspects of people's daily life. Such a description does not correspond with the new *lex mercatoria*, which draws its source from unwritten practices and trade usages common to business transactions. Consequently, any awards made on such a basis

---

[173] G R Delaume, "State contracts and transnational arbitration" (1981) 75 AmJIntLaw 784.
[174] M Mustill and C S Boyd, *The Law and Practice of Commercial Arbitration in England* (2nd edn, 1989), p 81.
[175] The French authorities opposing the application of the new *lex mercatoria* include Rogers, Kassis, Lagarde and Khan. For reservations against the practicability of the *lex mercatoria* concept, see M Sornarajah, *International Commercial Arbitration* (1992), pp 116 *et seq*; A van den Berg, *New York Convention* (1984), p 200; G R Delaume, (1988) ICSID Rev 79 at 105; and S T Toope, *Mixed International Arbitration* (1990), p 95.
[176] C M Gertz, "The selection of choice of law provisions in international commercial arbitration: a case for contractual depeçage" (1991) 12 NorthwestJInt'lL & Bus 163 at 176.
[177] *Ibid* at 177.

may not provide a solid basis upon which a national jurisdiction can recognise or enforce them.[178]

The final point of attack by this group of jurists is the lack of a source of precedent within the new *lex mercatoria*. Without any precedents, the level of predictability of the result can be seriously affected. As Messrs Randall and Norris commented:

> "[E]ven if arbitral decisions were made public, their value is slight because lengthy explications of the ruling are not required and the decisions analyse few written rules. So the *lex mercatoria* again is not positivistic, but rather more akin to customary international law. More precise precedent would be far more helpful in this context, particularly where unique or complex deals are involved."[179]

Lord Mustill also strongly opposed the notion of the new *lex mercatoria*. He dismissed the argument that the new *lex mercatoria* can fill a gap left by the municipal laws on the ground that the new *lex mercatoria* is nowhere to be found in an explicit form. It must be culled by the individual arbitrator from whatever sources he may find to be fruitful: such as, the writings of scholars and the common features of various systems of municipal law. Moreover, since no codified rules are provided, the parties will be left in an uncertain position until the arbitrators render the awards.[180] Lord Mustill has further indicated that it is not a simple task to codify these common trade usages:[181]

> "The proponents of the *lex mercatoria* claim it to be the law of the international business community, which must mean the law unanimously adopted by all countries engaged upon two centuries ago. But the international business community is now immeasurably enlarged. What principles of trade law, apart from those which are so general as to be useless, are common to the legal systems of the members of such a community? How could the arbitrators amass the necessary materials on the laws of, say, Brazil, China, the Soviet Union, Australia, Nigeria, and Iraq?"[182]

Opinions in favour of the application of the new **lex mercatoria**

After a serious debate about the new *lex mercatoria* among international practitioners, the opinion in favour of the application of the new

---

[178] G R Delaume, "Comparative analysis as a basis of law in state contracts: the myth of the *lex mercatoria*" (1989) 63 TulLRev 575.

[179] Randall and Norris, "A New Paradigm for International Business Transactions" (1993) 71 WashULQ 599 at 611.

[180] M Mustill, "Transnational Arbitration in English Law" (1984) 33 CurrLPr 133 at 150.

[181] M Mustill, "The New *Lex Mercatoria*" (1988) 4 International Arbitration 86.

[182] *Ibid* at 89, 92–93.

lex mercatoria has prevailed. The proponents of the new *lex mercatoria* include Lando,[183] Goldman,[184] Lew,[185] Schmitthoff,[186] Lowenfeld,[187] Carbonneau,[188] Berman[189] and Dasser.[190] They maintain that the new *lex mercatoria* is a kind of independent legal order, being separated from any national laws, and suitable to settle the disputes arising from the international merchant community.

The proponents also argue that, from the parties' viewpoint, the new *lex mercatoria* provides business people with an alternative choice to free themselves from the strict application of national laws and subject themselves to a more flexible legal system. They also argue that business people frequently wish their disputes to be given a solution other than that which would be given by national laws.[191] On the other hand, from the arbitrator's point of view, the flexibility of the new *lex mercatoria* will enable arbitrators to meet the legitimate expectations of parties and apply the most up-to-date rules and reasoning to resolve any kind of dispute arising from international commercial transactions.

The supporters of the new *lex mercatoria* also believe that international business people with common interests should be able to organise a community with its own legal system that does not derive its authority from any municipal laws. Within this community, arbitrators play a similar role to the judges from national courts. Consequently, with the freedom to find better rules of law which the national judges may not be able to apply, arbitrators should be regarded as the inventors when they apply the new *lex mercatoria* as the proper law of the contract.[192]

Furthermore, they maintain that the popularity of the new *lex mercatoria* within the international commercial community is caused by the fact

---

[183] Lando, "The *lex mercatoria* in international commercial arbitration" (1985) 34 ICLQ 747; *Conflict of Law Rules for Arbitrators in Festschrift für Konard Zweigert* (1981). The French authorities include Fouchard, Francescakis, Oppetit and Robert.

[184] Goldman, "The applicable law: general principles of law – the *lex mercatoria*" in Lew (ed), *Contemporary Problems in International Arbitration*, p 113; Carbonneau (ed), "Introduction" I in *Lex Mercatoria and Arbitration* (1990).

[185] Lew, *The Applicable Law in International Commercial Arbitration*, 436–437; Lew (ed), *Contemporary Problems in International Commercial Arbitration*.

[186] C Schmitthoff, "The law of international trade, its growth, formulation and operation" in Schmitthoff (ed), *Sources of the Law of International Trade* (1964), p 3; *Commercial Law in a Changing Economic Climate; Export Trade* (5th edn, 1990), pp 655–656.

[187] Lowenfeld, "Lex mercatoria: an arbitrator's view" (1990) 6(2) Arbitration Int 133.

[188] T Carbonneau, "The Remaking of Arbitration: Design and Destiny" in Carbonneau (ed), *Lex Mercatoria and Arbitration* (1990), at p 1; and *Alternative Dispute Resolution* (1989), pp 59–104.

[189] Berman, *Law and Revolution: the Formation of the Western Legal Tradition*, pp 339–340.

[190] T Carbonneau, "The 'New' Law Merchant and the 'Old' Source, Content and Legitimacy" in Carbonneau (ed), *Lex Mercatoria and Arbitration* (1990), at p 21.

[191] R David, *Arbitration in International Trade* (1985), p 16.

[192] Lando, "The *lex mercatoria* in international commercial arbitration" (1985) 34 ICLQ 747 at 754.

that the new *lex mercatoria* can provide equity which may be ignored by applying national laws. An example of late delivery of goods is used by Professor Lando to illustrate this point. Lando uses Danish law as an example. In the case of the late delivery of goods, buyers are required to send an immediate notice to the seller under the Danish law. Nonetheless, some doubts would arise as to whether it is more reasonable for the Danish courts to reduce the demands put on buyers who are foreign subjects and who failed to send an immediate notice to the seller when goods were delivered late as required under the Danish law. He argues:

> "By choosing the *lex mercatoria* the parties oust the technicalities of national legal systems and they avoid rules which are unfit for international contracts. Thus they escape peculiar formalities, brief cut-off periods, and some of the difficulties created by domestic laws which are unknown in other countries such as the common law rules on consideration and *privity* of contract. Furthermore, those involved in the proceedings – parties, counsel and arbitrators – plead and argue on an equal footing; nobody has the handicap of seeing it governed by a foreign law."[193]

Moreover,

> "the binding force of the *lex mercatoria* does not depend on the fact that it is made and promulgated by State authorities but that it is recognised as an autonomous norm system by the business community and by State authorities".[194]

The same opinion is expressed by Thomas, who agrees that, in terms of the parties' intention, an award made under the new *lex mercatoria* may be different from a judgment made by the court which can apply only national laws to decide the disputes. His point is expressed in the following terms:

> "When the issue is looked at reasonably and practically to release commercial arbitrators from the obligations to apply the law is to enable arbitrators to act in a manner the parties to the agreement wish them to act, and in a manner in which commercial judges frequently wish they themselves could act. Thereunder it would be open to arbitrators to construe commercial agreements according to the prevailing commercial understanding of their effect; give effect to invalid agreements when it is clear that the parties intended to be in honour bound by such an agreement; take a liberal view of the effect of illegality on contracts; adopt an approach to the categorisation of contractual terms which would foster certainty; apply a commercial understanding of the doctrine of frustration; ignore technical defences which are unworthy and shamefaced; and so on. All these decisions would entail the arbitral forum arriving at a decision

---

[193] Lando, above, n 192, at 748.
[194] *Ibid* at 752.

different from that of a court of law faced with similar facts. This difference does not however, inevitably lead to a qualitative difference. Justice according to law is but one manifestation of justice; justice according to an arbitral scheme established by parties in dispute is another. The error of the prevailing policy, as Lord Devlin has so perceptively observed, is its adherence to the belief that beyond justice according to law there is nothing other than injustice."[195]

While the debates over the new *lex mercatoria* continue, in practice the new *lex mercatoria* has frequently been applied to decide the disputes in international commercial contracts. The issue may be what Delaume describes as no longer being whether transnational contract fitted well within the framework of the national private laws but which law can provide answers to the parties' disputes. He states:

"Today, a number of contractual relationships involve both subjects of private and public international law, and, with increasing frequency, a plurality of parties whose combined efforts are required for the carrying out of a single venture. Neither traditional domestic law rules nor, to the extent that they can be identified with sufficient precision, international law norms necessarily provide adequate answers to problems that they were not designed to meet in the first place."[196]

The new lex mercatoria *in international Conventions and international arbitration rules*

Although no conclusive agreement has been reached as to the definition and applicability of the new *lex mercatoria*, this concept is adopted by some international Conventions and the international arbitration rules. In relation to international Conventions, Art VII(1) of the European Convention on International Commercial Arbitration provides:

"[T]he parties shall be free to determine, by agreement, the law to be applied by the arbitrators to the substance of the dispute. Failing any indication by the parties as to the applicable law, the arbitrator shall apply the proper law under the rule of conflict that the arbitrators deem applicable. In both cases the arbitrators shall take account of the terms of the contract and trade usage."

In accordance with this provision, first, parties are allowed to choose the new *lex mercatoria* to govern the substantive disputes of the contract. Second, in the case where the choice of the proper law is referred to a

---

[195] D R Thomas, "Commercial arbitration – justice according to law" (1983) 2 Civil JustQ 166 at 182.
[196] Delaume, "State contracts and transnational arbitration" (1981) 75 AmJIntLaw 784; Berger, *International Economic Arbitration*, Vol 9, p 532.

national law, arbitrators are still required to pay attention to the relevant trade usage.[197]

Apart from international Conventions, an arbitrator is offered a greater power than that of judges to apply the law he regards as appropriate.[198] Instead of explicitly mentioning the new *lex mercatoria*, the words "take into account the usage of the trade" or "take account of ... the relevant trade usages" have been mentioned in various arbitration rules, such as Art 28(4) of the UNCITRAL Model Law, Art 33(3) of the UNCITRAL Arbitration Rules, Art 33(1) of the Iran–US Claims Tribunal Rules, and Art 17(1) and (2) of the ICC Rules. While international Conventions and international arbitration rules have adopted the notion of the new *lex mercatoria*, the most important legal materials illustrating the acceptance of the new *lex mercatoria* in practice are arbitral awards. The following study will highlight the practice of applying the new *lex mercatoria* in arbitration.

Application of the new lex mercatoria in international arbitral awards[199]

The new *lex mercatoria* has been applied in a number of arbitral awards, both *ad hoc* and institutional arbitration. In an *ad hoc* arbitration where an English company and a Belgian company were involved, the dispute arose from a concession agreement which included an exclusive distributorship contract. The parties did not specify the proper law; however, an arbitration clause contained in the concession contract empowered the arbitrators to decide the case as *amiables compositeurs*.[200]

The arbitrators first allocated the dispute under a national law framework. In accordance with the Belgian choice of law rules, English law would be the proper law of the contract by applying the objective test.

---

[197] The answer to the question whether the "trade usage" mentioned in Art VII(1) means the new *lex mercatoria* should be postive. Primarily, trade usage is one of the sources of the new *lex mercatoria*. Nonetheless, from the previous sections of this chapter, it should be noted that the jurists do not strictly distinguish trade usage from the new *lex mercatoria*. At times, they are interchangeable. This situation is evident, for instance, when Lord Mustill used the term "trade usage" when he pointed out the difficulties in codifying the new *lex mercatoria*. (See Mustill, "The New *Lex Mercatoria*" (1988) 4 International Arbitration 86.) In the present writer's opinion, trade usage, as used in Art VII(1), is a reference to the new *lex mercatoria*.

[198] UNCITRAL Model Law, Art 28(2); UNCITRAL Arbitration Rules, Art 33(1); ICC Rules, Art 17.

[199] Due to a difficulty in obtaining arbitral awards, this part of the study will primarily be based on the ICC awards and those published in the *Yearbook of Commercial Arbitration*.

[200] This award was enforced in Belgium by a decision of the Court of First Instance of Brussels, 12 December 1978 and confirmed by the Court of Appeal of Brussels on 14 October 1980.

However, they found that the English law did not agree with the notion of amiable composition under its legal system. Under these circumstances, the arbitrators tried to confirm the real intention of the parties on the issue of the choice of law. Then, they decided that the parties indeed sought to give amiable composition an extremely comprehensive meaning and sought to help possible litigations escape from any national law.

After ascertaining the parties' intention, the arbitrators exercised the power of amiable composition to choose the new *lex mercatoria* as the proper law of the contract on the ground that arbitrators are not necessarily obliged to determine a national law applicable to the substance. As they held:

> "Having established that the character of the contract, and the place where it has its effect, necessarily exclude an obligatory application of either Belgian or English law, it is for the above-mentioned reasons that the arbitrators will abide by the '*lex mercatoria*' in the exercise of their power as *amiables compositeurs*."[201]

The new *lex mercatoria* is a not unfamiliar phenomenon in ICC arbitration. In fact, it has been applied in a large number of cases. For instance, the new *lex mercatoria* was applied in a case where the dispute arose from a construction contract involving a project in the USSR between a French enterprise and a Yugoslav subcontractor.[202] The dispute was referred to the ICC in accordance with the arbitration clause in which no proper law was expressed. The arbitration was held in Geneva, the procedure was subject to the law of the Canton of Geneva, that is, the Swiss Concordat on Arbitration, subsidiarily to the law of the Canton of Geneva for all matters not regulated in the Arbitration Rules of the ICC. In accordance with Art 13(4) of the ICC Arbitration Rules, the arbitrators were to decide the case as *amiables compositeurs*.

After agreeing to decide as *amiables compositeurs*, the arbitrators tried to decide the proper law of the contract according to the choice of laws rules. The arbitrators regarded Yugoslav law – the law of the habitual residence of the builder – as the proper law in accordance with the choice of laws of the *lex fori*, that is, Swiss private international law. However, this choice was dismissed because neither party had invoked the application of the Yugoslav law. Later, Russian law, the law of the place of performance, was considered as the proper law in accordance with French private international law. However, this possibility was also dismissed on the same ground.

---

[201] *Mechema Ltd v SA Mines, Minerais et Metaux*, Ad hoc Arbitration, Award of 3 November 1977; reprinted in (1982) VII YBCA 77 at 79.
[202] ICC case no 3540, 3 October 1980, reprinted in *Collection of ICC Awards 1974–1985*, pp 105–115.

The arbitrators decided to avoid the choice of laws rules on the ground that "in this field the most recent and authoritative doctrine as well as the jurisprudence of arbitrators, especially that of the ICC, acknowledge that in determining the substantive law arbitrators may avoid the rules of conflict of the forum if they have the power of *amiables compositeurs*".[203] Finally, the arbitrators decided to apply the "direct approach" and base their decision uniquely on the contract and the general and common legal principles. According to these principles, the new *lex mercatoria* was chosen as the proper law of the contract.

The second award made on the basis of the new *lex mercatoria* was *Pabalk Ticaret Ltd Sirketi v Norsolor*.[204] In this case, in the absence of any reference to a given law and clear indication to reveal the common intention of the parties, the arbitrators decided the substantive disputes should be governed by the new *lex mercatoria*. As they explained:

> "Faced with the difficulty of choosing a national law the application of which is sufficiently compelling, the Tribunal considered that it was appropriate, given the international nature of the agreement, to leave aside any compelling reference to a specific legislation, be it Turkish or French, and to apply the international *lex mercatoria*."[205]

In another case, the dispute arose from a construction contract between a Mexican construction company and a Belgian company.[206] According to the contract, the arbitrators were offered the powers to act as *amiables compositeurs*; however, no choice of proper law was made. The arbitrators decided to apply the new *lex mercatoria* to resolve the disputes between the parties. The arbitrators tried to justify their choice by stating:

> "In the first award, the arbitral tribunal decided to determine the issue under generally accepted legal principles governing international commercial relations, without specific reference to a particular system of law, which was qualified by a learned commentator[207] as a reference to *lex mercatoria*. In the second phase of this arbitration neither of the parties did require the application of any particular system of law, nor did they rely on any specific provision of any municipal system. The arbitral tribunal sees no reason therefore, to depart from the view expressed in its first award on this aspect of the cases. Indeed, as it will appear later, all legal issues in this arbitration depend on the construction and system of the contractual documents."[208]

---

[203] ICC case no 3540, above, n 202, at p 109.
[204] ICC case no 3131, 26 October 1979, reprinted in *Collection of ICC Awards 1974–1985*, pp 122–124.
[205] *Ibid* at pp 123–124.
[206] Final award of case no 3267, 28 March 1984, reprinted in *Collection of the ICC Arbitral Awards 1986–1990*, pp 43–52.
[207] Yves Derains, "Chronique des sentences arbitrales" (1980) JDI 961 at 966–969.
[208] Final award of case no 3267, 28 March 1984, reprinted in *Collection of the ICC Arbitral Awards 1986–1990*, pp 43–52 (at p 45).

In this case, the other issue connected with the application of the general principles of international commercial law or the new *lex mercatoria* was the question of the nature and extent of the powers of arbitrators acting as *amiables compositeurs*. In other words, in addition to the new *lex mercatoria*, whether the power to act as *amiables compositeurs* entitled the arbitrators to modify or disregard the provisions of the contract. The arbitrators were convinced that this question should be answered on a case-by-case basis. As they explained:

> "As a matter of principle, the arbitral tribunal does not reject the view that an *amiable compositeur* may go beyond certain solutions deriving from the normally applicable legal rules, be they those of a municipal legal system or those of *lex mercatoria*. The question however is how far he can go, especially when faced with specific provisions of a contract. A further question is whether the individual situation and circumstances justify his making use of such power. These two questions shall be dealt with when examining the specific claims in connection therewith."[209]

The new *lex mercatoria* has also been applied in conjunction with a municipal law by the ICC arbitrators. A dispute between Italian and Libyan parties was referred to the ICC.[210] The dispute arose out of a contract for building and civil engineering works in Libya. In the partial award made with the parties' consent, the arbitral tribunal held that the Libyan law was the primarily applicable law. Recognising that, in principle, the Libyan law was the proper law, the tribunal also added that the Libyan law would be supplemented by the new *lex mercatoria* and the general principles of law where Libyan law was not proved or was incomplete.[211]

However, not every ICC arbitrator feels completely comfortable with the application of the new *lex mercatoria*. For instance, in a 1986 ICC case, the tribunal had been given broad discretion concerning the issue of choice of law, even to the extent that the arbitrators were allowed to act as *amiables compositeurs*. The three members of the tribunal, implicitly rejecting any resort to a delocalised law merchant, chose to apply national choice of law rules to determine the proper law from national law regimes. This case is evidence that the concept of the new *lex mercatoria* is not shared by all arbitrators in practice.

In another case concerning a dispute between a Syrian enterprise and a Ghanaian enterprise, the arbitrator refused to apply the *lex mercatoria* as the proper law. In relation to the issue of the proper law, he stated:[212]

---

[209] ICC case no 3267, above, n 208, at pp 45–46.
[210] ICC case no 4761 (1987), reprinted in *Collection of the ICC Arbitral Awards 1986–1990*, pp 519–525.
[211] *Ibid* at p 521.
[212] Malmberg, Loek, J was the arbitrator.

"It is argued in literature that international arbitrators should, to the extent possible, apply the *lex mercatoria*. Leaving aside that its contents are not easy to determine, neither party has argued that a *lex mercatoria* should be applied. Rather, each party strenuously argued on the basis of a national law, i.e., Syrian and Ghanaian/English law respectively. Accordingly, the Arbitrator shall follow the implied desire of the parties to apply national law ... Ghanaian law would in principle be applicable."[213]

England

The new *lex mercatoria* was first accepted in an earlier case: *Deutsche- und Tiefbohrgesellschaft v Ras Al Khaimah National Oil Co and Shell International Petroleum Co Ltd (DST v Rakoil)*.[214] An agreement for the exploration of oil contained a clause providing for the settlement of all disputes by three arbitrators appointed in Geneva under the rules of the ICC, and the determination of the proper law to be applied to the contract was left to the arbitrators. The arbitrators decided to choose "internationally accepted principles of law governing contractual relations" as the proper law and made the final award in favour of the plaintiffs. The losing party argued before the Court of Appeal that the enforcement of the award would be against English public policy because the award was not decided on the basis of any national law. The Court of Appeal dismissed the defendants' appeal concerning the proper law and upheld the arbitrators' choice of "internationally accepted principles of law" to govern contractual relations between the parties, since it did not lead to the conclusion that the parties did not intend to create legally enforceable rights and obligations. Accordingly, such a choice did not affect the validity of the award under Swiss law, which was the procedural law of the arbitration and the law governing the arbitration agreement; moreover, the enforcement of the award would not be contrary to English public policy. With regard to public policy, Sir John Donaldson MR suggested that as long as the parties intended to create legally enforceable rights and obligations, a request for enforcement of an arbitral award made on the basis of a system of law which was not that of England or of any other state or was a serious modification of such a law would be granted.[215] As he stated:

"Considerations of public policy can never be exhaustively defined, but they should be approached with extreme caution. ... It has to be shown that there is some element of illegality or that the enforcement of the award would be clearly injurious to the public good or, possibly, that

---

[213] ICC case no 4237 (1984), reprinted in *Collection of ICC Arbitral Awards 1974–1985*, p 167 (at pp 170–171).
[214] [1987] 3 WLR 1023.
[215] [1990] 1 AC 295 at 315–316, [1987] 3 WLR 1023 at 1035–1036.

enforcement would be wholly offensive to the ordinary reasonable and fully informed member of the public on whose behalf the powers of the state are exercised."[216]

And:

"Asking myself these questions, I am left in no doubt that the parties intended to create legally enforceable rights and liabilities and that the enforcement of the award would not be contrary to public policy."[217]

Furthermore, it is followed by a discussion on the certainty of the clause of choice of law:

"By choosing to arbitrate under the Rules of the ICC and, in particular, art. 13.3, the parties have left the proper law to be decided by the arbitrators and have not in terms confined the choice to national systems of law. I can see no basis for concluding that the arbitrators' choice of proper law, a common denominator or principles underlying the laws of the various nations governing contractual relations, is outwith the scope of the choice which the parties left to the arbitrators."[218]

This case also provides a positive answer to the question of whether the English courts hold a similar attitude towards cases where the application of the new *lex mercatoria* is on the arbitrators' own initiative rather than on the basis of the parties' agreement.

Later, Lord Mustill expressed a more understanding view about the application of the new *lex mercatoria* in the *Channel Tunnel* case. He said that, under the special circumstances and needs of the Channel Tunnel venture, it may be the right choice for the parties to choose an indeterminate "law" to govern their substantive rights. Also, he concluded that no matter whether this choice of law was right or wrong, it was the choice which the parties had made; moreover, he believed that ordering an injunction in this case would be to act contrary both to the general tenor of the construction contract and to the spirit of international arbitration, though the courts could and should, in the right case, provide reinforcement of the arbitral process.[219] Furthermore, the court simply directed the parties to resolve their disputes by means of arbitration without expressing any objection about the potential application of the new *lex mercatoria*, that is, the general principles of international trade law. Finally, the application of the new *lex mercatoria* is formally given statutory force by s 46(1)(b) of the (English) Arbitration Act 1996.

---

[216] [1987] 3 WLR 1023 at 1035.
[217] *Ibid* at 1035.
[218] *Ibid*.
[219] [1992] IQB 656; *Channel Tunnel Group Ltd v Balfour Beatty Construction Ltd* [1993] AC 334 at 363, [1993] 2 WLR 262 at 291.

Amiables composition/*ex aequo et bono*

Rule 47 of the Scottish Arbitration Rules adapts such international practice. Accordingly, an arbitrator is allowed to disregard the law and rely solely on what he considers to be fair and equitable only if that is expressly authorised by the law or the agreement between the parties.[220]

Historically, amiable[221] composition was a concept which developed widely in France and other civil law countries.[222] The notion of amiable composition was first developed in the Code Napoléon and the French Code of Civil Procedure of 1806,[223] with the intention of restoring harmony between the parties and to work out a new kind of legal relationship between them.[224] Today, the notion and function of amiable composition remain the same. In international commercial arbitration, from the parties' point of view, the application of rules of law to determine the dispute cannot completely satisfy their particular needs. Under these circumstances, international arbitrators are frequently empowered to act as *amiables compositeurs* to determine the dispute on the basis of equity. Such power, which enables arbitrators to deviate from the application of law and decide the case on the basis of what is fair and reasonable according to their personal sense of equity, is commonly conferred by the so-called "equity clause".[225]

Opinions against the application of amiable composition

There is a fear that the arbitrator's power may be open to abuse by means of amiable composition. In common with the new *lex mercatoria*, the concept of amiable composition is also not shared by all jurisdictions, especially those which insist on the application of strict rules of law to determine the substantive issues. If the awards fail to comply this requirement, they may be challenged on the grounds of mandatory rules and public policy.

Objections to amiable composition are especially notable among English lawyers. Due to unfamiliarity with the concept of amiable composition, English lawyers tend to treat it as an unknown object and dismiss any possible use in arbitration. In their opinion, arbitrators, empowered as

---

[220] Paragraph 121 of the Consultation Paper. It also stated that "[t]he technical expressions arbitration '*ex bono et aequo*' and 'amiable compositeur' have not been used for reasons of comprehensibility".

[221] Sometimes, this is written as "amicable".

[222] Born, *International Commercial Arbitration in the United States – Commentary & Materials* (1994), p 135.

[223] Above, n 93, at p 310.

[224] David, *Arbitration in International Trade*, pp 334–335.

[225] Although amiable composition is included in the types of equity clause listed by Sir Michael Kerr, he states that the English meaning of "amiable composition" is far from clear. See M Kerr, "Equity arbitration in England" (1993) 2(4) The American Review of International Arbitration 377.

amiables compositeurs, are analogous only to conciliators or mediators who guide the parties towards a compromise settlement of their dispute. Such function is, they argue, contradictory to that of arbitrators whose decision is to have the force of law. As Sir Michael Kerr argues:

> "If the function of an *amiable compositeur* is merely to mediate and conciliate, then he is not an arbitrator. If his function includes the powers to impose a compromise settlement upon the parties as a binding decision which disregards the legal position, then he would equally not be acting as an arbitrator according to law, and his 'award' would risk being set aside."[226]

He concludes that a reference to amiable composition is a sequential action, "whereby mediation/conciliation are tried first and are followed by an arbitration if they fail. In effect, therefore, the reference to arbitration would then not operate as an equity clause at all".[227]

Opinions in favour of the application of amiable composition

Although there is dispute surrounding the concept of amiable composition, the opinion in favour of its application prevails in practice. Jurists who are in favour of the notion of amiable composition are divided into two camps. One group of jurists contends that an arbitrator's power to decide the dispute as an *amiable compositeur* should be accessory to law, or, to be precise, such power should supplement the deficiency in the particular rule of law. In accordance with their opinion, while exercising the power of amiable composition, arbitrators should consider not only the international law but also the municipal laws which are relevant to the case. Furthermore, the municipal laws should be disregarded only if they are contrary to the general principles of law.

Nevertheless, the other faction within the jurists upholds a more liberal attitude towards the notion of amiable composition. This group of jurists argues that, in the case where the law is contrary to the principles of justice, arbitrators only have to consider the principles of international justice when they are empowered to decide the case *ex aequo et bono* or act as *amiables compositeurs*. One commentator has asserted that "in the most extreme sense, an arbitrator is under no obligation to observe the rules of law".[228] This group of jurists believes that the power to decide a matter *ex aequo et bono* allows an international arbitrator to base his decision exclusively on considerations of equity in the sense of general justice and to disregard the rights and obligations in force in so far as their application would lead to an inequitable solution.[229] Moreover, they

---

[226] Kerr, above, n 225, at 383–384.
[227] *Ibid* at 384.
[228] Mustill and Boyd, *The Law and Practice of Commercial Arbitration in England* at p 77.
[229] M Habicht, *The Power of the International Judge to Give A Decision "Ex Aequo Et Bono"* (1935), p 2.

maintain that "considerations of equity are applied in an *ex aequo et bono* decision not only to supplement the law, but also to overrule it, if the application of the law would cause an inequitable result".[230]

Following extensive debate on this subject, the group in favour of the idea that both international law and municipal law may be ignored if they are in conflict with the general principles of justice and amiable composition has prevailed. This idea was applied in a decision made by an American–Norwegian Arbitral Tribunal in 1922. As the tribunal opined: "The Tribunal cannot ignore the municipal law of the Parties, unless that law is contrary to ... the principles of justice."[231] According to this judgment, the formula "principles of law and equity" permits the arbitrators to disregard the relevant positive law if it is contrary to the general principles of justice.

Nevertheless, it is worth noting that such a clause does not confer an unlimited freedom upon them. To a certain extent, such a clause may allow arbitrators to escape from the restraints of the national laws; however, they are still bound by the general principles of justice and by generally recognised standards of international relations. In other words, a clause of amiable composition does not give arbitrators a "blank cheque" or unfettered discretionary power. After all, a decision made by *amiables compositeurs* is still an arbitral decision pronounced with binding force and it must, by definition, follow general principles and standards.

Amiable composition/ex aequo et bono *in international* Conventions, arbitration rules and domestic laws

The notion of amiable composition has been adopted by various international Conventions, arbitration rules and some domestic laws. In the case of international Conventions, the concept of amiable composition can be seen in Art VII(2) of the European Convention on International Commercial Arbitration, which stipulates: "The arbitrators shall act as amiables compositeurs if the parties so decide and they may do so under the law applicable to the arbitration."[232] A similar passage is also found in Art 55(2) of ICSID Facility; Schedule C: Arbitration, Art 42(3) of the ICSID Convention; Art 30 of the Permanent Court of Arbitration Rules of Arbitration and Conciliation for Settlement of International Disputes between Two Parties of Which Only One is a State.

Although different opinions are held towards the application of amiable composition in international commercial arbitration, such power has also been adopted in various international arbitration rules. The concept of amiable composition has been adopted by the major international arbitration rules. For instance, the phrase "the arbitrators shall assume

---

[230] Habicht, above, n 229.
[231] A decision made by the American–Norwegian Tribunal 1922.
[232] The term *"amiables compositeurs"* is used in this chapter.

the powers of an *amiable compositeur* if the parties are agreed to give him such powers", has been incorporated in Art 17(3) of the ICC Arbitration Rules,[233] Art 28 of the American Arbitration Association International Rules, Art 33(2) of the UNCITRAL Arbitration Rules[234] and Art 33(2) of the Iran–US Claims Tribunal Rules.

Apart from international Conventions and arbitration rules, in order to keep up with the trend in international commercial arbitration, some jurisdictions also incorporate the concept of amiable composition into their domestic legislation. For instance, Art 1497 of the French Code of Civil Procedure allows arbitrators to be empowered as *amiables compositeurs*, as it provides: "The arbitrator shall decide as *amiable compositeur* if the parties' agreement conferred this authority upon him." An identical provision can also be seen in Art 1054(3) of the Netherlands Arbitration Act 1986. Although using the term "*ex aequo et bono*", Art 187(2) of the Swiss Private International Law Act 1987 upholds such an application by stipulating that "The parties may authorise the arbitral tribunal to decide *ex aequo et bono*". Section 46(1)(b) of the (English) Arbitration Act 1996 provides that the arbitral tribunal shall decide the dispute, if the parties so agree, in accordance with such other considerations as are agreed by them or determined by the tribunal.

Application of amiable composition/ex aequo et bono in international arbitral awards

Despite all the objections, amiable composition has been applied to decide the dispute between the parties in a number of international arbitral awards. It is especially the case in ICC arbitration whose rules expressly permit such practice. For instance, in an ICC arbitration, a dispute concerning non-payment by one of the parties arose from a construction contract for a sugar plant. The arbitration was held in Zurich. The arbitral tribunal decided that the legal problems arising from this contract should be settled in accordance with the rules of Swiss law, which gave the tribunal the power of amiable composition. Acting as *amiables compositeurs*, the tribunal decided to rule on the case on the basis of equity according to the terms of Art 19(3) of the Rules of Conciliation and Arbitration. As to the issue of the proper law, the tribunal held that "according to general principles, the arbitral tribunal is not authorised to take a decision contrary to an absolutely constraining law, particularly the rules concerning public order or morals."[235]

---

[233] The term "*amiables compositeurs*" is also used in this article.
[234] The provision is as follows: "The arbitral tribunal shall decide as *amiable compositeur* or *ex aequo et bono* only if the parties have expressly authorised the arbitral tribunal to do so and if the law applicable to the arbitral procedure permits such arbitration."
[235] ICC case no 1677 (1975), reprinted in *Collection of ICC Arbitral Awards 1974–1985*, p 20.

The power of amiable composition was, again, exercised in another case where the general principle governing commercial international law was applied to decide the substantive issues. In June 1976, a Saudi Arabian state entity entered into a construction contract with a Belgian company, which later subcontracted part of this project to a Mexican company. However, due to the difficulties between the Belgian (claimant) and Mexican (defendant) parties, the Belgian company terminated the subcontract in 1977. The issue of whether it was a legal termination was instituted in ICC. In the arbitration agreement, no choice of law was mentioned. However, the claimant submitted that the legal issues arising from the subcontract should be resolved with reference to general principles of commercial law, whereas the defendant did not specify which law should be applied.

Based on the indication to a specific legal system contained in the (claimant's) initial brief, which referred to Belgian law in connection with the applicability of amiable composition, the arbitral tribunal decided that they were empowered to act as *amiables compositeurs*.[236] Furthermore, regarding the issue of the proper law, based upon the power of *amiables compositeurs*, the tribunal decided to apply the general principles of international commercial law. It stated:

> "[W]hen the authority is granted to it [the tribunal] to act as *amiable compositeur*, as specified in the Contract and in the Term of Reference, the Arbitral Tribunal needs not to decide which specific law governs the contractual relationship between the parties.
> On the basis of foregoing, ... the Arbitral Tribunal will apply the widely accepted general principle governing commercial international law with no specific reference to a particular system of law."[237]

Moreover, on the issue of payments, the tribunal maintained that the agreement between the parties should be taken into account. As the tribunal held:

> "[I]t is a generally accepted principle in international arbitration that the paramount duty of the arbitrator, even as '*amiable compositeur*', is to apply the contract of the parties, unless it is shown that the provisions relied on are clearly against the true intent of the parties, or violate a basic commonly accepted principle of public policy."[238]

Furthermore,

> "In addition to the power to decide on the dispute before him on the basis of generally accepted legal principles, without being deterred by

---

[236] ICC case no 3267 (1979), reprinted in *Collection of ICC Arbitral Awards 1974–1985*, pp 76–87 (at p 78).
[237] *Ibid.*
[238] *Ibid* at p 85.

the technicalities of a particular legal system, the arbitrator sitting as *'amiable compositeur'* is entitled to disregard legal or contractual rights of party when the insistence on such right amounts to an abuse thereof."[239]

In another case, the disputes arose from a contract between an Italian company (claimant) and a Syrian company (defendant).[240] The choice of law clause appeared in two individual articles of the contract. According to Art 19.6 of the contract, "arbitration shall be held at Geneva (Switzerland) and shall judge according to the general principles of law and justice", whereas Art 25 provided that "this agreement shall be subject to and constructed in accordance with the Law of Syria". The words "shall judge according to the general principles of law and justice" were handwritten, and replaced the printed words *"ex aequo et bono"*.

According to the claimant, the dispute should be resolved by the arbitrators acting as *amiables compositeurs*. However, the defendant argued that amiable composition should not be allowed and the general principles referred to in Art 19.6 were legal principles which should at least be common to the two systems involved, Syrian and Italian. Faced with this complicated situation, the tribunal decided to take into account both Arts 25 and 19.6. Finally, the arbitral tribunal decided that the power of deciding *ex aequo et bono* should be exercised together with the application of Syrian law. The tribunal ruled that "the contract is governed by and should be interpreted in accordance with Syrian law in its entirety without any restrictions, under reservations of the 'general principles of law and justice', according to which the arbitrators have to decide under Art 19.6".[241]

England

In England, the application of amiable composition was eventually confirmed as a valid choice of proper law by the enactment of the Arbitration Act 1996. Section 46 makes provision for the rules applicable to the substance of the dispute. In accordance with s 46(1)(b), "the arbitral tribunal shall decide the dispute if the parties so agree, in accordance with such other considerations as are agreed by them or determined by the tribunal". This section can be construed in favour of the notion of "amiable composition". It is suggested that this section means that "the parties might want their dispute decided not under a recognised system of law but under what are often referred to as 'equity clauses', which is not uncommon in international commercial contracts".[242] The reason

---

[239] ICC case no 3267, above, n 236, at p 86.
[240] ICC case no 3380, 29 November 1980, reprinted in *Collection of ICC Arbitral Awards 1974–1985*, pp 96–100.
[241] *Ibid* at p 100.

why the term "amiable composition" or deciding the case "*ex aequo et bono*" is not used is because "the expressions do not derive from English law or arbitration practice and it was felt inappropriate to incorporate them into the Act, all the more so since Latin and French phrases have been studiously avoided in the Act in the interests of simplicity and understandability".[243]

---

[242] M Rutherford and J Sims, *Arbitration Act 1996: A Practical Guide* (1996), para 46.4.
[243] *Ibid* at para 46.5.

CHAPTER 10

ARBITRAL PROCEEDINGS

PART 4 OF THE SCOTTISH ARBITRATION RULES

The limitation of the Scottish arbitration laws before the Arbitration (Scotland) Act 2010 was highlighted by the draftsmen during the enactment process for the new Act, The specific limitations pointed out were the lack of power to award damage, expenses or interests and the absence of powers allowing arbitrators to move arbitration forward without undue delay.[1] Part 4 of the Rules – all default rules – are introduced to remedy this by providing a fall-back system to ensure the smooth operation of arbitration proceedings.

PROCEDURE AND EVIDENCE – r 28

Unless modified or disapplied by the parties' agreement, r 28 (a default rule) offers the arbitrator the power to decide the procedure to be followed and also evidential matters.[2] For the evidential matters, the tribunal may determine the admissibility, relevance, materiality and weight of any evidence. For instance, the tribunal may determine whether, and, if so, to what extent, the tribunal should take the initiative in ascertaining the facts and the law,[3] and whether to apply rules of evidence used in legal proceedings or any other rules of evidence.[4] Regarding the procedures, r 28(2) provides "an illustrative, but not exhaustive"[5] list of the powers. For example, the tribunal may decide:

– when and where the arbitration is to be conducted;[6]

---

[1] Policy Memorandum 29 January 2009, para 160.
[2] Scottish Arbitration Rules, r 28(1).
[3] *Ibid*, r 28(2)(e).
[4] *Ibid*, r 28(2)(h).
[5] Revised Explanatory Notes 2009, para 152.
[6] Scottish Arbitration Rules, r 28(2)(a).

- whether parties are to submit claims or defences and, if so, when they should do so and the extent to which claims or defences may be amended;[7]
- whether any documents or other evidence should be disclosed by or to any party and, if so, when such disclosures are to be made and to whom copies of disclosed documents and information are to be given;[8]
- whether any and, if so, what questions are to be put to and answered by the parties;[9]
- the extent to which the arbitration is to proceed by way of –
    (i) hearings for the questioning of parties;
    (ii) written or oral argument;
    (iii) presentation or inspection of documents or other evidence; or
    (iv) submission of documents or other evidence;[10] and
- the language to be used in the arbitration (and whether a party is to supply translations of any document or other evidence).[11]

While a similar list can be seen in s 34 of the (English) Arbitration Act 1996 and a more general provision appearing in Arts 15 and 25(6) of the UNCITRAL Arbitration Rules, a much more concise provision is contained in Art 19 of the UNCITRAL Model Law. It reads:

> "(1) Subject to the provisions of this Law, the parties are free to agree on the procedure to be followed by the arbitral tribunal in conducting the proceedings.
> (2) Failing such agreement, the arbitral tribunal may, subject to the provisions of this Law, conduct the arbitration in such manner as it considers appropriate. The power conferred upon the arbitral tribunal includes the power to determine the admissibility, relevance, materiality and weight of any evidence."

The latest international development on taking evidence is the adoption of the resolution of IBA Rules on the Taking of Evidence in International Arbitration on 29 May 2010 (IBA Rules of Evidence). Reflecting the procedures used in different jurisdictions, the purpose of the IBA Rules of Evidence is to provide the stakeholders of arbitration with "an efficient, economical and fair process for the taking of evidence in international arbitration".[12] The areas covered by the Rules include presentation of documents, witnesses of fact and expert witnesses

---

[7] Scottish Arbitration Rules, r 28(2)(b).
[8] Ibid, r 28(2)(c).
[9] Ibid, r 28(2)(d).
[10] Ibid, r 28(2)(f).
[11] Ibid, r 28(2)(g).
[12] IBA Rules of Evidence 2010, p 10. http://www.ibanet.org/Publications/publications_IBA_guides_and_free_materials.aspx.

and inspections, as well as the conduct of evidentiary hearings. As the Rules do not have mandatory effect, they are "designed to be used in conjunction with, and adopted together with, institutional, ad hoc or other rules or procedures governing international arbitrations".[13] The relevant provisions include:

"**Article 2 Consultation on Evidentiary Issues**

1. The Arbitral Tribunal shall consult the Parties at the earliest appropriate time in the proceedings and invite them to consult each other with a view to agreeing on an efficient, economical and fair process for the taking of evidence.

Article 3 Documents

1. Within the time ordered by the Arbitral Tribunal, each Party shall submit to the Arbitral Tribunal and to the other Parties all Documents available to it on which it relies, including public Documents and those in the public domain, except for any

   documents that have already been submitted by another Party.

   ...

5. If the Party to whom the Request to Produce is addressed has an objection to some or all of the documents requested, it shall state the objection in writing to the Arbitral Tribunal and the other Parties within the time ordered by the Arbitral Tribunal.

   The reasons for such objection shall be any of those set forth in Article 9.2 or a failure to satisfy any of the requirements of Article 3.3.

6. Upon receipt of any such objection, the Arbitral Tribunal may invite the relevant Parties to consult with each other with a view to resolving the objection.

   ...

10. At any time before the arbitration is concluded, the Arbitral Tribunal may (i) request any Party to produce Documents, (ii) request any Party to use its best efforts to take or (iii) itself take, any step that it considers appropriate to obtain Documents from any person or organisation. A Party to whom such a request for Documents is addressed may object to the request for any of the reasons set forth in Article 9.2. In such cases, Article 3.4 to Article 3.8 shall apply correspondingly.

Article 7 Inspection

Subject to the provisions of Article 9.2, the Arbitral Tribunal may, at the request of a Party or on its own motion, inspect or require the inspection by a Tribunal-Appointed Expert or a Party-Appointed Expert of any site, property, machinery or any other goods, samples, systems, processes or Documents, as it deems appropriate. The Arbitral Tribunal shall, in consultation with the Parties, determine the timing and arrangement for

---

[13] IBA Rules of Evidence 2010, above, n 12.

the inspection. The Parties and their representatives shall have the right to attend any such inspection

Article 9 Admissibility and Assessment of Evidence
1. The Arbitral Tribunal shall determine the admissibility, relevance, materiality and weight of evidence."

PLACE OF ARBITRATION – r 29

Subject to parties' agreement, the tribunal may meet and otherwise conduct the arbitration, anywhere it chooses.[14] This place of arbitration can be in or outwith Scotland. The similar power in choosing the place of arbitration is also provided in Art 20 of the UNCITRAL Model Law which provides:

> "(1) The parties are free to agree on the place of arbitration. Failing such agreement, the place of arbitration shall be determined by the arbitral tribunal having regard to the circumstances of the case, including the convenience of the parties.
>
> (2) Notwithstanding the provisions of paragraph (1) of this article, the arbitral tribunal may, unless otherwise agreed by the parties, meet at any place it considers appropriate for consultation among its members, for hearing witnesses, experts or the parties, or for inspection of goods, other property or documents."

Art 16 of the UNCITRAL Arbitration Rules contains a general provision on the choice of the place of arbitration.

> "Article 16
> 1. Unless the parties have agreed upon the place where the arbitration is to be held, such place shall be determined by the arbitral tribunal, having regard to the circumstances of the arbitration.
> 2. The arbitral tribunal may determine the locale of the arbitration within the country agreed upon by the parties. It may hear witnesses and hold meetings for consultation among its members at any place it deems appropriate, having regard to the circumstances of the arbitration.
> 3. The arbitral tribunal may meet at any place it deems appropriate for the inspection of goods, other property or documents. The parties shall be given sufficient notice to enable them to be present at such inspection.
> 4. The award shall be made at the place of arbitration."

TRIBUNAL'S DECISIONS AND DIRECTIONS – rr 30 and 31

In the absence of agreement between the parties, r 30(1) provides that decisions, orders and awards can be made by all or a majority of the

---

[14] Scottish Arbitration Rules, r 29.

arbitrators if no unanimous decision can be reached.[15] If there is no animity or majority decision, the chairman shall make the casting vote.[16] In a case where no chairman is appointed, the decision will be made by the last arbitrator appointed if the tribunal consists of three arbitrators,[17] or by an umpire if the tribunal consists of two arbitrators.[18]

Rule 30 gives the tribunal the power to give directions to the parties for the purposes of conducting the arbitration proceedings as it considers appropriate.[19] Once the directions are given, the parties must comply with the directions.[20]

POWER TO APPOINT CLERKS, AGENTS OR EMPLOYEES ETC – r 32

Subject to parties' agreement, the tribunal has the power to appoint clerks, agents, employees and other persons as it thinks fit to assist in the arbitration.[21] However, the parties' consent is required if significant expenses are expected to incur in such appointment.[22] This is because under r 24(1)(c) the tribunal owes the parties a general duty to avoid unnecessary delay and costs to conduct arbitration. The draftsman also points out that the potential argument about "significant" can be decided by taxation or by the auditor of court.[23]

PARTY REPRESENTATIVES – r 33

A party can choose to be represented by a lawyer or any other person chosen by the party. Any representation of the parties must be communicated to the tribunal and to the other party at the beginning of the arbitration proceedings, or as soon as such person carries out the representation.[24] Similar provision regarding representation can be observed in s 36 of the Arbitration Act 1996, however, no requirement is imposed on the party to communicate the representation to the tribunal. Likewise, Art 4 of the UNCITRAL Arbitration Rules only requires the appointing party to communicate the name and address of the representative to the other party. This communication must be made in writing and specify whether the appointment is being made for the purposes of representation or assistance.

---

[15] Scottish Arbitration Rules, r 30(1).
[16] Ibid, r 30(2)(a).
[17] Ibid, r 30(2)(b)(i).
[18] Ibid, r 30(2)(b)(ii).
[19] Ibid, r 31(1).
[20] Ibid, r 31(2).
[21] Ibid, r 32(1).
[22] Ibid, r 32(2).
[23] Revised Explanatory Notes 2009, para 157.
[24] Scottish Arbitration Rules, r 33(2).

EXPERTS – r 34

In the absence of the parties' agreement to the contrary, r 34 empowers the tribunal to instruct experts, legal advisers or assessors to assist it to form the opinions on areas outwith the arbitrator's knowledge and specialisation, and to make decisions as a result. If the tribunal decides to appoint experts, the tribunal must ensure that both parties are given a reasonable opportunity to comment on the opinions delivered by the experts. If the opinion is given in a written form, the parties must be given the opportunity to make representations about such written opinions.[25] In the case where the opinion is to be delivered in person during the arbitration proceedings, the tribunal must ensure that the parties have the opportunity to hear any oral expert opinion and to ask questions of the expert giving it.[26] Similar powers are stipulated in s 37(1) of the Arbitration Act 1996, while s 37(2) requires the parties to be responsible for experts' fees in the form of arbitration expenses. Under the UNCITRAL Model Law, the tribunal is also allowed to appoint an expert in assisting the tribunal.[27] However, the appointed expert is required, after delivery of his written or oral report, to participate in a hearing where the parties have the opportunity to put questions to him and to present expert witnesses in order to testify on the points at issue.[28]

Similar but much detailed provision is given in Art 27 of the UNCITRAL Arbitration Rules. It provides:

> "1. The arbitral tribunal may appoint one or more experts to report to it, in writing, on specific issues to be determined by the tribunal. A copy of the expert's terms of reference, established by the arbitral tribunal, shall be communicated to the parties.
> 2. The parties shall give the expert any relevant information or produce for his inspection any relevant documents or goods that he may require of them. Any dispute between a party and such expert as to the relevance of the required information or production shall be referred to the arbitral tribunal for decision.
> 3. Upon receipt of the expert's report, the arbitral tribunal shall communicate a copy of the report to the parties who shall be given the opportunity to express, in writing, their opinion on the report. A party shall be entitled to examine any document on which the expert has relied in his report.
> 4. At the request of either party the expert, after delivery of the report, may be heard at a hearing where the parties shall have the opportunity to be present and to interrogate the expert. At this hearing either party may present expert witnesses in order to testify on the points at issue. The provisions of article 25 shall be applicable to such proceedings."

---

[25] Scottish Arbitration Rules, r 34(2)(a).
[26] *Ibid*, r 34(2)(b).
[27] UNCITRAL Model Law, Art 26(1).
[28] *Ibid*, Art 26(2).

The IBA Rules of Evidence also have a detailed provision on the tribunal-appointed experts.

"**Article 6   Tribunal-Appointed Experts**

1. The Arbitral Tribunal, after consulting with the Parties, may appoint one or more independent Tribunal-Appointed Experts to report to it on specific issues designated by the Arbitral Tribunal. The Arbitral Tribunal shall establish the terms of reference for any Tribunal-Appointed Expert Report after consulting with the Parties. A copy of the final terms of reference shall be sent by the Arbitral Tribunal to the Parties.

2. The Tribunal-Appointed Expert shall, before accepting appointment, submit to the Arbitral Tribunal and to the Parties a description of his or her qualifications and a statement of his or her independence from the Parties, their legal advisors and the Arbitral Tribunal. Within the time ordered by the Arbitral Tribunal, the Parties shall inform the Arbitral Tribunal whether they have any objections as to the Tribunal-Appointed Expert's qualifications and independence. The Arbitral Tribunal shall decide promptly whether to accept any such objection. After the appointment of a Tribunal-Appointed Expert, a Party may object to the expert's qualifications or independence only if the objection is for reasons of which the Party becomes aware after the appointment has been made. The Arbitral Tribunal shall decide promptly what, if any, action to take.

3. Subject to the provisions of Article 9.2, the Tribunal- Appointed Expert may request a Party to provide any information or to provide access to any documents, goods, samples, property, machinery, systems, processes or site for inspection, to the extent relevant to the case and material to its outcome. The authority of a Tribunal-Appointed Expert to request such information or access shall be the same as the authority of the Arbitral Tribunal. The Parties and their representatives shall have the right to receive any such information and to attend any such inspection. Any disagreement between a Tribunal-Appointed Expert and a Party as to the relevance, materiality or appropriateness of such a request shall be decided by the Arbitral Tribunal, in the manner provided in Articles 3.5 through 3.8. The Tribunal-Appointed Expert shall record in the Expert Report any non-compliance by a Party with an appropriate request or decision by the Arbitral Tribunal and shall describe its effects on the determination of the specific issue.

4. The Tribunal-Appointed Expert shall report in writing to the Arbitral Tribunal in an Expert Report. The Expert Report shall contain:
    (a) the full name and address of the Tribunal-Appointed Expert, and a description of his or her background, qualifications, training and experience;
    (b) a statement of the facts on which he or she is basing his or her expert opinions and conclusions;
    (c) his or her expert opinions and conclusions, including a description of the methods,

evidence and information used in arriving at the conclusions. Documents on which the Tribunal-Appointed Expert relies that have not already been submitted shall be provided;

(d) if the Expert Report has been translated, a statement as to the language in which it was originally prepared, and the language in which the Tribunal-Appointed Expert anticipates giving testimony at the Evidentiary Hearing;

(e) an affirmation of his or her genuine belief in the opinions expressed in the Expert Report;

(f) the signature of the Tribunal-Appointed Expert and its date and place; and

(g) if the Expert Report has been signed by more than one person, an attribution of the entirety or specific parts of the Expert Report to each author.

5. The Arbitral Tribunal shall send a copy of such Expert Report to the Parties. The Parties may examine any information, Documents, goods, samples, property, machinery, systems, processes or site for inspection that the Tribunal-Appointed Expert has examined and any correspondence between the Arbitral Tribunal and the Tribunal-Appointed Expert. Within the time ordered by the Arbitral Tribunal, any Party shall have the opportunity to respond to the Expert Report in a submission by the Party or through a Witness Statement or an Expert Report by a Party-Appointed Expert. The Arbitral Tribunal shall send the submission, Witness Statement or Expert Report to the Tribunal-Appointed Expert and to the other Parties.

6. At the request of a Party or of the Arbitral Tribunal, the Tribunal-Appointed Expert shall be present at an Evidentiary Hearing. The Arbitral Tribunal may question the Tribunal-Appointed Expert, and he or she may be questioned by the Parties or by any Party-Appointed Expert on issues raised in his or her Expert Report, the Parties' submissions or Witness Statement or the Expert Reports made by the Party-Appointed Experts pursuant to Article 6.5.

7. Any Expert Report made by a Tribunal-Appointed Expert and its conclusions shall be assessed by the Arbitral Tribunal with due regard to all circumstances of the case.

8. The fees and expenses of a Tribunal-Appointed Expert, to be funded in a manner determined by the Arbitral Tribunal, shall form part of the costs of the arbitration."

POWERS RELATING TO PROPERTY

Rule 35 of the Scottish Arbitration Rules is a default rule designed to prevent the parties going to the courts to obtain orders by empowering the arbitral tribunal to make protective measures, for example production or preservation relating to property which may constitute evidence in the arbitration to maintain the smooth operation of arbitration proceedings. The necessity of offering such powers to the tribunal is clearly explained in the policy memorandum, which reads:

"The fact that the parties may not agree on the need for such a preservation order should not be able to restrict the power of an arbitrator to make such an order, because a party inclined to action which would frustrate the possible outcome of the arbitration is unlikely to agree (at least once the dispute has arisen) that the arbitrator should have power to make orders which would interfere with such action."[29]

In accordance with r 35, the tribunal may give direction to the parties to allow the tribunal, an expert or another party to inspect, photograph, preserve or take custody of any property which that party owns or possesses which is the subject of the arbitration, or as to which any question arises in the arbitration;[30] or take samples from or conduct an experiment on any such property;[31] or to preserve any document or other evidence which the party possesses or controls.[32]

Apart from the similar powers relating to property offered to the tribunal under s 38(4) and (6) of the Arbitration Act 1996, s 38(3) allows the tribunal to order a claimant to provide security for the costs of the arbitration. However, such power shall not be exercised on the ground that the claimant is an individual ordinarily resident outside the United Kingdom, or a corporation or association incorporated or formed under the law of a country outside the United Kingdom, or whose central management and control is exercised outside the United Kingdom.

Although no dedicated provision relating to the tribunal's power relating to property can be found in the UNCITRAL Arbitration Rules. However, a reading of Art 16(3) which empowers the arbitral tribunal to "meet at any place it deems appropriate for the inspection of goods, other property or documents", makes it clear that such powers are offered under the Rules.

OATHS OR AFFIRMATIONS – r 36

Taking its common law tradition and s 38(5) of the Arbitration Act 1996 into consideration, the tribunal may direct that a party or witness is to be examined on oath or affirmation and administer an oath or affirmation for that purpose.

FAILURE TO SUBMIT CLAIM OR DEFENCE TIMEOUSLY – r 37

To ensure speedy dispute resolution, the arbitral tribunal is empowered to make sanctions to deal with late submission of statements or claim

---

[29] Policy Memorandum, 29 January 2009, para 163.
[30] Scottish Arbitration Rules, r 35(a)(i).
[31] *Ibid*, r 35(a)(ii).
[32] *Ibid*, r 35(b).

counterclaims and defences.[33] If the arbitral tribunal is of the opinion that there is no good reason for the delay and such delay gives rise to a substantial risk that it will not be possible to resolve the issues in that claim fairly; or has caused, or is likely to cause, serious prejudice to the other party, the arbitral tribunal is empowered to end the arbitration in so far as it relates to the subject-matter of the claim. If the tribunal decides to end arbitration under these circumstances, it can make an award or an award on expenses as it considers appropriate in consequence of the claim. Similar situations will allow the tribunal to dismiss the delayed claims under s 41(3) of the Arbitration Act 1996 and Art 25(1) of the UNCITRAL Model Law.

In the event of delay in submitting a defence to the tribunal, the tribunal must proceed with the arbitration if the tribunal is not persuaded by any reason for the delay. The decision to proceed with the arbitration will not treat the delay as an admission of anything.[34] Similar provision is also given in Art 25(b) of the UNCITRAL Model Law.

FAILURE TO ATTEND HEARING OR PROVIDE EVIDENCE – r 38

To ensure the smooth operation of arbitration, any party's failure to attend hearings requested by the tribunal without a reasonable advance notice, or the failure to produce any documents or evidence required by the tribunal, r 38 (a default rule) empowers the tribunal to proceed with the arbitration and make its award in the absence of the party or without considering the documents or evidence required. This provision is similar to s 41(4) of the Arbitration Act 1996 and Art 25(1)(c) of the UNCITRAL Model Law.

FAILURE TO COMPLY WITH TRIBUNAL DIRECTION OR ARBITRATION AGREEMENT – r 39

Under r 39, the arbitral tribunal is empowered to make an order to a party who fails to comply with the direction given by the tribunal or is in breach of the obligations imposed by the arbitration agreement, the Scottish Arbitration Rules, or any agreements between the parties in relation to the conduct of arbitration. The orders a tribunal is empowered to make include:

> "– direct that the party is not entitled to rely on any allegation or material which was the subject-matter of the order,
> – draw adverse inferences from the non-compliance,
> – proceed with the arbitration and make its award,

---

[33] Scottish Arbitration Rules, r 37.
[34] *Ibid*, r 37(2).

— make such provisional award (including an award on expenses) as it considers appropriate in consequence of the non-compliance."[35]

The Arbitration Act 1996 has more detailed provisions in relation to the party's failure to comply with the directions given by the arbitral tribunal. In accordance with s 41(5), (6) and (7):

> "(5) If without showing sufficient cause a party fails to comply with any order or directions of the tribunal, the tribunal may make a peremptory order to the same effect, prescribing such time for compliance with it as the tribunal considers appropriate.
> (6) If a claimant fails to comply with a peremptory order of the tribunal to provide security for costs, the tribunal may make an award dismissing his claim.
> (7) If a party fails to comply with any other kind of peremptory order, then, without prejudice to section 42 (enforcement by court of tribunal's peremptory orders), the tribunal may do any of the following –
> (a) direct that the party in default shall not be entitled to rely upon any allegation or material which was the subject matter of the order;
> (b) draw such adverse inferences from the act of non-compliance as the circumstances justify;
> (c) proceed to an award on the basis of such materials as have been properly provided to it;
> (d) make such order as it thinks fit as to the payment of costs of the arbitration incurred in consequence of the non-compliance."

The provision empowering an arbitral tribunal to order interim measures can also be seen in Art 22(1) of the Vienna Rules which reads:

> "Unless otherwise agreed by the parties, the sole arbitrator (arbitral tribunal) may, at the request of a party order any party, after hearing such party, to take such interim measure of protection as the sole arbitrator (arbitral tribunal) may consider necessary in respect of the subject matter of the dispute, as otherwise the enforcement of the claim would be frustrated or considerably impeded or there is a danger of irreparable harm. The sole arbitrator (arbitral tribunal) may require any party to provide appropriate security in connection with such measure. The parties are obliged to comply with such orders, whether or not they are enforceable by State courts."

With its 2006 amendment, the UNCITRAL Model Law produced a much elaborated provision dealing with the issues of interim measures and preliminary orders. Art 17 provides:

> *"Article 17. Power of arbitral tribunal to order interim measures*
> (1) Unless otherwise agreed by the parties, the arbitral tribunal may, at the request of a party, grant interim measures.

---

[35] Scottish Arbitration Rules, r 39(2)(a)–(d).

(2) ... , the arbitral tribunal orders a party to:
   (a) Maintain or restore the status quo pending determination of the dispute;
   (b) Take action that would prevent, or refrain from taking action that is likely to cause, current or imminent harm or prejudice to the arbitral process itself;
   (c) Provide a means of preserving assets out of which a subsequent award may be satisfied; or
   (d) Preserve evidence that may be relevant and material to the resolution of the dispute.

Article 17 A.   Conditions for granting interim measures
(1) The party requesting an interim measure under article 17(2)(a), (b) and (c) shall satisfy the arbitral tribunal that:
   (a) Harm not adequately reparable by an award of damages is likely to result if the measure is not ordered, and such harm substantially outweighs the harm that is likely to result to the party against whom the measure is directed if the measure is granted; and
   (b) There is a reasonable possibility that the requesting party will succeed on the merits of the claim. The determination on this possibility shall not affect the discretion of the arbitral tribunal in making any subsequent determination.
(2) With regard to a request for an interim measure under article 17(2)(d), the requirements in paragraphs (1)(a) and (b) of this article shall apply only to the extent the arbitral tribunal considers appropriate.

Article 17 B.   Applications for preliminary orders and conditions for granting preliminary orders
(1) Unless otherwise agreed by the parties, a party may, without notice to any other party, make a request for an interim measure together with an application for a preliminary order directing a party not to frustrate the purpose of the interim measure requested.
   ...

Article 17 E.   Provision of security
(1) The arbitral tribunal may require the party requesting an interim measure to provide appropriate security in connection with the measure.
(2) The arbitral tribunal shall require the party applying for a preliminary order to provide security in connection with the order unless the arbitral tribunal considers it inappropriate or unnecessary to do so."

CONSOLIDATION OF PROCEEDINGS – r 40

In commercial arbitration, it is not uncommon to have two or more arbitrations involving the same disputes and the same issues among different parties. This situation can easily lead to conflicting arbitral awards which are very undesirable in maintaining the stability of arbitration. This is especially acute in construction arbitration and has been the concerns of practitioners.

Following the passing of the Arbitration Act 1996[36] and in line with international trends, r 40(1) stipulates that the parties may agree to consolidate the arbitration with another arbitration or to hold concurrent hearings. However, an arbitral tribunal must obtain the parties' authorisation before ordering consolidation of different arbitrations or holding concurrent hearings.[37]

---

[36] (English) Arbitration Act, s 35.
[37] Scottish Arbitration Rules, r 40(2).

CHAPTER 11

THE RELATIONSHIP BETWEEN THE COURTS AND ARBITRATION

GENERAL

Arbitration is a legal procedure whereby the parties submit their disputes to an arbitral tribunal for resolution. Strictly speaking, arbitration is not a self-contained mechanism, as the tribunal does not have power to force the parties, or third parties, either to take part in the arbitration proceedings or to carry out the award if they do not wish to do so. When an arbitral tribunal faces unwilling or unco-operative parties, it becomes essential for the courts to provide assistance to both the parties and the tribunal to ensure the smooth operation of arbitration and the successful enforcement of the arbitral awards. The national courts used to be overzealous in their assisting and supervisory roles. However, the current trend is to have limited judicial intervention, which allows the tribunal to have more power in managing arbitration proceedings. This can be seen in one of the founding principles listed in s 1 of the Arbitration (Scotland) Act 2010 which stipulates that "the court should not intervene in an arbitration except as provided by this Act".[1] Despite its intention to reduce court intervention to a minimum, the draftsman still felt the need to specify the powers of the court in relation to arbitral proceedings in the issues of referral on a point of law; variation of time limits set by parties; ordering attendance of witnesses; ordering disclosure of evidence; and others. Nevertheless, it is worthwhile noting that all these powers, provided in Pt 5 of the Scottish Arbitration Rules, can be exercised only on the application of the parties.

POWER TO DETERMINE POINTS OF SCOTS LAW – rr 41 and 42

Following tradition and s 45(1) of the (English) Arbitration Act 1996, r 41 expressly offers the Outer House the power to determine any points

---

[1] Arbitration (Sc) Act 2010, s 1(c).

of Scots law arising in arbitration. This power found its origin in the infamous English practice of the stated case procedure which also applied in Scotland via the introduction of s 3 of the Administration of Justice (Scotland) Act 1972. This provision allowed the parties to appeal an arbitral award on a question of law at any stage of the arbitration. This practice can trace its roots to *Mitchell v Cable*,[2] which concerned whether the arbiter had vitiated the whole proceedings in hearing evidence in the absence of one of the parties. Lord Jeffrey famously stated:

> "On every matter touching the merits of the case, the judgement of the arbiter is beyond question or cavil. He may believe what nobody else believes, and he may disbelieve what all the world believes. He may overlook or flagrantly misapply the most ordinary principles of law, and there is no appeal for those who have chosen to subject themselves to his despotic power."[3]

Although the Arbitration (Scotland) Act 2010 maintains the practice of allowing the parties to apply to the Outer House to determine any point of Scots law arising in the arbitration,[4] such practice is restricted under r 42 of the Scottish Arbitration Rules. In accordance with r 42, the stated case application is valid only if the parties have agreed that the application may be made;[5] or have consented to it being made and the court is satisfied that determining the question is likely to produce substantial savings in expenses; the application was made without delay; and there is a good reason why the question should be determined by the court.[6] To avoid the possibility of using the stated case procedure as a delaying tactic, r 42(3) allows the tribunal to continue with the arbitration when the application is pending in the court. The Outer House's decision on a point of Scots law is final.[7] However, it is important to point out that r 41 is a default rule; therefore the courts will not be able to exercise the power on referral of a point of law if the parties agree to exclude the application of r 41.

The other issue concerning the stated case procedure is that the new Act allows "legal error appeal". According to r 69, a party may appeal to the Outer House against the tribunal's award on the ground that the tribunal erred on a point of Scots law. With this rule, the arbitral tribunal may not be the "final judge of fact and law"[8] as most jurisdictions allow it to be. This will be discussed in detail in Chapter 12 on the recognition and enforcement of arbitral awards.

---

[2] (1848) 10 D 1297.
[3] *Ibid* at 1309.
[4] Scottish Arbitration Rules, r 41.
[5] *Ibid*, r 42(2)(a).
[6] *Ibid*, r 42(2)(b)(i)–(iii).
[7] *Ibid*, r 42(4).
[8] F Davidson, *Arbitration* (2000), p 269.

POWERS TO VARY TIME LIMITS SET BY PARTIES – rr 43 and 44

By submitting their disputes to arbitration, parties usually agree between them the time limits for different aspects of arbitration proceedings, such as the time limit for submitting claims, a defence or counterclaims; submitting evidence or documents; or time limits for arbitration proceedings themselves, in their arbitration agreement or any other agreement between them. As was pointed out in the Policy Memorandum, generally speaking, Scots arbitration law has no specific time limits which must be applied. Under the Act, an arbitral tribunal is empowered to set time limits for the completion of particular stages of arbitration proceedings but not to vary the time limits agreed between the parties.[9]

To ensure that justice can be successfully carried out in arbitration, upon any party's or the tribunal's application, the court is allowed to exercise power to vary the time limits agreed between the parties[10] if it is satisfied that the parties have exhausted the arbitration proceedings on this issue or no arbitral process for varying the time limit is available,[11] and if a person would suffer a substantial injustice if no variation was made.[12] To avoid unnecessary delay in arbitration proceedings, the arbitral tribunal may continue with the arbitration pending the final decision of the application. The effect of the court's decision on the issue of variation of the time limit is final and the courts are required to determine whether a variation will be made; and, if so, the courts also have to decide the extent of the variation.

POWER TO ORDER ATTENDANCE OF WITNESSES AND DISCLOSURE OF EVIDENCE – r 45

Differing from other default provisions on the powers of the court in relation to arbitration provided in Pt 5, r 45 is a mandatory provision to allow the court, upon the application made by the tribunal or the parties, to order the attendance of a witness or the taking of evidence on commission. As the tribunal does not possess coercive powers over any third parties who are not the parties to an arbitration agreement, its power to order attendance of witnesses and disclosure of evidence is essential to ensure that the parties and the tribunal are given the opportunities to present or hear all important evidence before any decisions are reached. Such powers allow the courts to order any person to attend a hearing to give evidence to the tribunal, or to disclose documents or other material evidence to the tribunal.[13] However, such power is restricted if the person

---

[9] Policy Memorandum, 29 January 2009, para 168.
[10] Scottish Arbitration Rules, r 43(a)–(b).
[11] Ibid, r 44(2)(a).
[12] Ibid, r 44(2)(b).
[13] Ibid, r 45(1)(a)–(b).

or evidence concerned in the application is entitled to refuse to give or disclose in civil proceedings.[14] As in other applications to the courts, the court's decision on this issue is final, subject to no appeal or review,[15] and the arbitral tribunal may continue with the arbitration proceedings pending determination of the application.[16]

Such a power is also provided in s 43 of the (English) Arbitration Act 1996, however, this is subject to more restrictions then those listed in r 45(2). In accordance with s 43(2), the application to the court to order the attendance of witnesses or disclosure of evidence or documents can be made only with the permission of the tribunal or the agreement of the other parties. Furthermore, s 43(3) stipulates that such court proceedings may be used only if the witness is in the United Kingdom and the arbitral proceedings are being conducted in England and Wales or, as the case may be, Northern Ireland.

OTHER POWERS IN RELATION TO ARBITRATION – r 46

Subject to parties' agreement to disapply or modify r 46, the court has the same power in arbitration proceedings as it would have in ordinary civil proceedings. The purpose of this provision is to retain the existing law and specify a list of powers exercisable by the court to assist the relevant arbitration proceedings. A list of powers is as follows:

- to appoint a person to safeguard the interests of any party lacking capacity;[17]
- to order the sale of any property in dispute in the arbitration;[18]
- to make an order securing any amount in dispute in the arbitration;[19]
- to make an order under s 1 of the Administration of Justice (Scotland) Act 1972;[20]
- to grant warrant for arrestment or inhibition;[21]
- to grant interdict (or interim interdict);[22] or
- to grant any other interim or permanent order.[23]

However, to exercise such powers, the court must ensure that the application has been submitted by any party and the application is made

---

[14] Scottish Arbitration Rules, r 45(2).
[15] Ibid, r 45(4).
[16] Ibid, r 45(3).
[17] Ibid, r 46(1)(a).
[18] Ibid, r 46(1)(b).
[19] Ibid, r 46(1)(c).
[20] Ibid, r 46(1)(d).
[21] Ibid, r 46(1)(e).
[22] Ibid, r 46(1)(f).
[23] Ibid, r 46(1)(g).

with the tribunal's consent[24] and it is a matter of urgency[25] for the court to exercise such powers. This rule applies to arbitrations which have begun[26] or where the court is satisfied that a dispute has arisen or might arise,[27] and that an arbitration agreement provides that such a dispute is to be resolved by arbitration.[28] While the court is dealing with the application, the tribunal may continue with the arbitration pending determination of the application.[29] The application of r 46 does not affect any other powers which the court has under any enactment or rule of law in relation to arbitrations,[30] or any powers possessed by the tribunal.[31]

Certain issues may arise from the tribunal's powers to award interim measures. For instance, can parties go to national courts to seek interim measures if disputes are submitted to an arbitral tribunal? This issue was left undecided in the amended UNCITRAL Model Law 2006 due to a wide split between the countries which are in favour of offering tribunals the powers to award interim measures and those which believe that national courts are best positioned to grant interim measures by taking the issue of enforcement into consideration. This issue is further complicated by the question whether arbitral tribunal should be allowed to grant *ex parte* interim measures. Among the countries participating in the amendments, England and France were of the opinion that against *ex parte* interim measures should be awarded by national courts rather than the tribunals. On the other hand, Switzerland was keen to have such issues decided by the tribunals and expressed reluctance to allow Swiss taxpayers' money to be used in such way by allowing the parties who have no connection with Switzerland to seek interim measures from the Swiss courts. The final compromise was that *ex parte* interim measures made by the tribunals should be limited to a period of 48 hours.

As the benefit of interim measures relies on the national courts' coercive powers to enforce them, the other issue raised was whether the tribunal's power awarding interim measures may amount to an empty power if the parties refuse to comply with them. Observing recent practice, the consensus appears to be that most parties would comply with the interim measures made by the tribunals as the parties may not want to upset the tribunal as well as consider the ongoing commercial relationship between them. For instance, if a dispute arises at an early stage of a 20-year crude oil supply contract, it would make commercial sense for the parties to the

---

[24] Scottish Arbitration Rules, r 46(2)(b)(i).
[25] Ibid, r 46(2)(b)(ii).
[26] Ibid, r 46(4)(a).
[27] Ibid, r 46(4)(b)(i).
[28] Ibid, r 46(4)(b)(ii).
[29] Ibid, r 46(3).
[30] Ibid, r 46(5)(a).
[31] Ibid, r 46(5)(b).

dispute to comply with the interim measures with a view to resolving the dispute in order to perform the rest of the contract.

Another issue which is worth considering in practice is whether the interim measures made by the tribunals are indeed classified as "awards" or "orders" under the different domestic arbitration laws. Less difficulty will arise from the enforcement stage if the interim measures made by the tribunal are accepted as awards by the national courts of the place of enforcement. However, such "awards" may not be enforced if they are defined as "orders" at a place of enforcement for such interim measures.

CHAPTER 12

ARBITRAL AWARDS

GENERAL

Most, if not all, arbitrating parties choosing arbitration as the means of resolving their disputes want a speedy and an efficient way to reach a binding decision between them and, ultimately, to have an enforceable arbitral award. To ensure the enforceability of an arbitral award, it is important to make sure that: (1) procedural formalities required in the relevant arbitration laws are fulfilled; (2) the award does not fall into the grounds for setting aside; and/or (3) the recognition and enforcement procedures are fulfilled under the New York Convention 1958. All these three aspects are covered in Pt 6 of the Scottish Arbitration Rules, ss 11–15 and ss 18–22 of the Arbitration (Scotland) Act 2010 respectively, and will be discussed below.

PROCEDURAL FORMALITY REQUIRED IN MAKING AN AWARD

Law applied to make an award

As discussed in Chapter 9, the tribunal is required to apply the substantive law agreed by the parties to determine the merits of the dispute when making an award in order to decide the rights and obligations of the parties involved in the dispute. In the absence of agreement on the substantive law, the default rule is that the tribunal shall take commercial or trade usage, custom or practices into consideration and apply the law which appears to be the most appropriate.[1] Rule 47 of the Scottish Arbitration Rules provides that an arbitrator is to apply the substantive law agreed by the parties (either by expression or implication) to the merits of the dispute. In the absence of parties' agreement on this issue, the default

---

[1] Scottish Arbitration Rules, r 47(1)–(2). Similar provision can be seen in s 46(1) and (3) of the (English) Arbitration Act 1996.

rule is that the arbitrator should apply such law, or laws, as appear to the arbitrator to be appropriate. Commercial and trade usage, custom or practices should also be taken into account.[2] Rule 47(2) stipulates that the tribunal can only decide the disputes "*ex aequo et bono*" or act as "*amiable compositeur*" if it is incorporated into the law concerned or the parties have given express authorisation to do so.

Remedies awarded in the award

Prior to the enactment of the Arbitration (Scotland) Act 2010, the arbitral tribunal had no power to award damages. There was also no expressed power for the arbitral tribunal to award expenses. Such a power to award expenses was regarded as customary and implied into the mandate of the tribunal in the case *Pollich v Heatley*, where Lord President Dunedin stated: "The matter of expenses is incidental to the conduct of the case, and there is an inherent power in the tribunal to grant them."[3] Later, it was determined that the tribunal's power to award expenses had to be construed in accordance with the parties' arbitration agreement.[4] Similar reasoning in relation to the issue of the tribunal's power to award interest can also be seen in *Farrans (Construction) Ltd v Dunfermline District Council*,[5] where Lord Justice Clerk Ross stated that the tribunal's power to award interest must be found in the deed of submission.

However, this is changed in r 48(1) of the Scottish Arbitration Rules. Rule 48(1) provides a mandatory provision granting the tribunal the power to order the payment of a sum of money as well as a sum in damages. The currency of the sum ordered by the tribunal has to be the one agreed between the parties or, in the absence of such agreement, in such a currency as the tribunal considers appropriate.[6] Other remedies available to the tribunal, though, which can be modified or disapplied by the parties' agreement, include a declaratory award, an award ordering a party to do or refrain from doing something or an award ordering the rectification or reduction of any deed or other document allowed by the applicable laws.[7] However, if a court decree is involved in the decision-making process, it is not possible for the tribunal to reduce a court decree.

---

[2] Scottish Arbitration Rules, r 47(3).
[3] 1910 SC 469 at 482.
[4] *Grampian Regional Council v John G McGregor (Construction) Ltd* 1994 SLT 133.
[5] 1988 SC 120.
[6] Scottish Arbitration Rules, r 48(2). Similar provision can be seen in s 48(4) of the (English) Arbitration Act 1996.
[7] Scottish Arbitration Rules, r 49(a)–(c). Similar provision can be seen in s 48(5) of the (English) Arbitration Act 1996.

Rule 50 clarifies the situation concerning the issue of awarding interest in arbitration in Scotland and offers the tribunal the mandatory power to make an award including interest payments. It is stipulated that the tribunal can order interest payment for pre-award[8] and post-award periods.[9] In the award, the tribunal must specify the interest rate awarded[10] as well as the period for which the interest is payable.[11] The award shall also specify the manner in which interest is calculated according to the parties' agreement or, in the absence of such agreement, the manners applied by the tribunal. Moreover, the tribunal is allowed to make provision for different interest rates in respect of different amounts awarded.[12]

Format of award

As a default rule, r 51 provides that an award must be signed by all arbitrators or all those assenting to the award.[13] This provision corresponds with international practice. The award must state the seat of the arbitration in order to ascertain the juridical seat of the arbitration.[14] In order to work out the time limitation which allows the parties to appeal against an award, the award shall also contain the information concerning when the award is made and when it shall take effect.[15] Although there is international debate between common law and civil law countries on whether an award shall contain reasons, the Scottish Arbitration Rules stipulate that an award shall contain reasons and, if there are any other provisional or partial awards in relation to the particular arbitration, these shall also be stated in an award.[16] Once an award is made, it has to be in writing and delivered (by hand, post, electronic transmissions, or any other methods).[17] To avoid issues similar to those which occurred in *Hiscox* v *Outhwaite*[18] where the arbitration was conducted in London but the award was signed in Paris, r 52 makes it clear that, subject to parties' agreement, as long as the seat of arbitration is in Scotland, an award is to be treated as having been made in Scotland even if the award is signed outwith Scotland.

---

[8] Scottish Arbitration Rules, r 50(1)(a)–(b). Similar provision can be seen in s 49 of the (English) Arbitration Act 1996.
[9] Scottish Arbitration Rules, r 50(1)(c).
[10] *Ibid*, r 50(2)(a).
[11] *Ibid*, r 50(2)(b).
[12] *Ibid*, r 50(3).
[13] *Ibid*, r 51(1). Relevant provision on the writing requirement can be seen in s 52 of the (English) Arbitration Act 1996.
[14] Scottish Arbitration Rules, r 51(2)(a).
[15] *Ibid*, r 51(2)(b).
[16] *Ibid*, r 51(2)(c)–(d).
[17] *Ibid*, rr 51(3) and 83 in relation to formal communication.
[18] [1992] AC 562.

Types of award

Under the Arbitration (Scotland) Act 2010, arbitrators are allowed to make different types of award, such as provisional awards, partial awards, draft awards and final awards in order to dispose of all the issues submitted to the tribunal and complete the arbitration process.

Regarding provisional awards, in order to avoid the need to seek an interdict from the court and prolonging the arbitration process, as a default rule, r 53 allows the tribunal to make provisional awards for relief on a provisional basis which it has the power to grant permanently later in the final award.

Differing from the default rule on making a provisional award, the arbitral tribunal has the mandatory power to make different partial awards disposing of different aspects of the disputes during arbitration proceedings. This so-called partial award known in international commercial arbitration is termed a "part award" in the Arbitration (Scotland) Act 2010. A partial award is defined as an award which decides some, but not all, of the matters which the tribunal is to decide in the arbitration.[19] It is mandatory for the tribunal to state clearly the matters to which the part award relates.

Subject to the parties' agreement to the contrary, interestingly the arbitral tribunal can elect to send a draft of the proposed award to the parties. This type of award is termed as "draft award" in the Scottish Arbitration Rules.[20] If the tribunal sends a draft award to the parties, then it is bound to consider any representations made by the parties in relation to the draft award before making the final award.[21] Although the draftsmen acknowledged that this practice is not common internationally due to time restraint, and it will not always be possible for the tribunal to adopt it, they are convinced that "[i]t is thought to be good practice for arbitrators to issue awards in draft form to the parties who will therefore have an opportunity to comment and point out any errors, ambiguity, etc".[22]

Correction of awards

From time to time, arbitral tribunals may make some clerical, typographical or accidental errors or omission in the awards. To invalidate an award on such ground is not cost efficient for the arbitrating parties

---

[19] Scottish Arbitration Rules, r 54(2). Similar provision can be seen in s 47 of the (English) Arbitration Act 1996.
[20] Scottish Arbitration Rules, r 55(a). There is no such provision in the (English) Arbitration Act 1996; however, s 55 of the Act contained provision concerning notification of awards.
[21] Scottish Arbitration Rules, r 55(b).
[22] Revised Explanatory Notes (2009), para 192.

and administrating justice in general. Instead of invalidating such awards, r 58 of the Scottish Arbitration Rules, a default rule, allows the tribunal to correct such errors or omissions in order to clarify or remove any ambiguity in the awards.[23] Such correction can be carried out on the tribunal's initiative or on any party's application.[24] A party's application for correction is valid only if a copy of the application is sent to the other party,[25] and should be made within 28 days of the award being made available to the parties,[26] or by a later date specified by the Outer House or the sheriff.[27] The tribunal must give both parties a reasonable opportunity to make representations about the proposed forms if the correction is necessary and proposed by the tribunal. In the case where the correction is applied for by one of the parties, a reasonable opportunity must be given to the other party to make representations.[28] Tribunals will have 28 days from the date of making the award or from the date of application to make such corrections.[29] Consequential correction may be made if a correction affects another part of the corrected award[30] or any other award[31] made by the tribunal. A corrected award is to be treated as if it had been in corrected form on the date it first took effect.[32]

Withholding an award for non-payment

To ensure the consistency with modern arbitration practice in most international arbitration institutions, r 56 provides the tribunal a mandatory power to withhold an award until all the fees and expenses incurred by the tribunal have been paid in full.[33] To balance such power with the parties' rights, the rule allows the parties to appeal against or request for a review of the amount of the fees and expenses within the arbitration proceedings. If the parties have exhausted any available arbitral process of appeal or review of the amount of the fees and expenses demanded by the tribunal which has refused to deliver

---

[23] Scottish Arbitration Rules, r 58(1). Similar provision can be seen in s 57(3) of the (English) Arbitration Act 1996.
[24] Scottish Arbitration Rules, r 58(2).
[25] Ibid, r 58(3).
[26] Ibid, r 58(4)(a). Similar provision can be seen in s 57(4) of the (English) Arbitration Act 1996.
[27] Scottish Arbitration Rules, r 58(4)(b).
[28] Ibid, r 58(5).
[29] Ibid, r 58(6). Similar provision can be seen in s 57(5) of the (English) Arbitration Act 1996.
[30] Scottish Arbitration Rules, r 58(7)(a).
[31] Ibid, r 58(7)(b).
[32] Ibid, r 58(8).
[33] Ibid, r 56(1). Similar provision can be seen in s 56 of the (English) Arbitration Act 1996.

the award concerned,[34] on the application by any party, the court may order the tribunal to deliver the award if the applicant paid the fees and expenses in full[35] and as properly payable.[36] If there is any balance left, then the balance is to be repaid to the party which applied for the appeal or the review.[37]

Arbitration ends when the tribunal delivers the last and final award.[38] However, sometimes arbitration may end prematurely if the tribunal determines to end the arbitration if a justified objection to its jurisdiction[39] is made, or parties fail to submit a claim or defence for the tribunal to consider the disputes submitted.[40] Arbitration may also be brought to an end by the parties if an early settlement is reached between them.[41] In the case of a settlement, the parties can request the tribunal to make a final and binding award recording the terms of the settlement.[42] However, it is important to point out that the relevant Scottish Arbitration Rules still apply to matters connected with the arbitration even if there is an early termination of arbitration proceedings.

ENFORCEMENT AND CHALLENGE OF ARBITRAL AWARDS – ss 11–15 OF THE ARBITRATION (SCOTLAND) ACT 2010

In general

To ensure that arbitration remains a speedy and efficient method of alternative dispute resolution, it is essential for an arbitral award to be final and binding on the arbitrating parties and be capable of being recognised or enforced. Consequently, s 11(1) of the Arbitration (Scotland) Act 2010 states: "A tribunal's award is final and binding on the parties and any person claiming through or under them." However, there are a few exceptions contained in s 11(1) that should be mentioned. Due to privity, an arbitral award has no binding effect on any third party. Also, an award dealing with any issues arising from rectification or reduction of a deed or other document does not affect the interests of any third party who acts in good faith.[43]

---

[34] Scottish Arbitration Rules, r 56(3).
[35] Ibid, r 56(2)(a).
[36] Ibid, r 56(2)(b).
[37] Ibid, r 56(2)(c).
[38] Ibid, r 57(1).
[39] Ibid, rr 57(2) and 20(3).
[40] Ibid, rr 57(2) and 37(1).
[41] Ibid, r 57(3). Similar provision can be seen in s 51 of the (English) Arbitration Act 1996.
[42] Scottish Arbitration Rules, r 57(4).
[43] Arbitration (Sc) Act 2010, s 11(2). Similar provision can be seen in s 58(1) of the (English) Arbitration Act 1996.

Challenging arbitral awards

The finality of an arbitral award does not mean that the arbitrating parties must carry out the award according to the tribunal's decision immediately if substantial injustice has been caused because the arbitrators or oversmen have failed in their duty towards the parties. Taking this possibility into consideration, the draftsmen felt that it is essential to provide a remedy for the parties who have suffered injustice during the arbitration proceedings. To eliminate unnecessary vexatious or frivolous challenges which may be deployed as a delaying tactic, the challenge procedures available in the Act are limited to the grounds of lack of substantive jurisdiction, serious irregularity or legal errors.[44] The draftsmen also made it clear that the court's task is to review the process on how the arbitrator came to a decision, rather than review the merits of the award. Furthermore, a challenge on these grounds is competent only if the applicant party has exhausted any available arbitral process of appeal or review of the award,[45] and made the application within 28 days after the award, the correction or review of the award was made available.[46] The right to challenge the tribunal's awards can be seen in Pt 8 of the Scottish Arbitration Rules, which will be discussed below.

Challenge based on lack of substantive jurisdiction

It is internationally accepted that the validity of an award made by a tribunal which does not have jurisdiction over the parties or the disputes can be thrown into doubt. A party who wishes to challenge the tribunal's award on the grounds of lack of jurisdiction may appeal to the Outer House against such an award.[47] Upon receiving the application, the Outer House may decide to confirm, vary or set aside the award (or part of it).[48] If the Outer House decides to vary the award, then its decision has the same effect as part of the tribunal's award.[49] If the Outer House is satisfied that a proposed appeal against its decision on the issue of substantive jurisdiction would raise an important point of principle or practice or there is a compelling reason for the Inner House to consider the appeal, the Outer House may grant a leave of appeal to allow an appeal to be made to the Inner House.[50]

---

[44] Arbitration (Sc) Act 2010, s 11(3). Similar provision can be seen in s 58(2) of the (English) Arbitration Act 1996.
[45] Scottish Arbitration Rules, r 71(2). Similar provision can be seen in s 70(2) of the (English) Arbitration Act 1996.
[46] Scottish Arbitration Rules, r 71(4). Similar provision can be seen in s 70(3) of the (English) Arbitration Act 1996.
[47] Scottish Arbitration Rules, r 67(1). Similar provision can be seen in s 67 of the (English) Arbitration Act 1996.
[48] Scottish Arbitration Rules, r 67(2).
[49] *Ibid*, r 67(3).
[50] *Ibid*, r 67(4) and (5).

Challenge based on serious irregularities

If a party can prove and satisfy the Outer House that substantial injustice[51] has been caused by the tribunal's failure to conduct the arbitration in accordance with the arbitration agreement, the applicable Scottish Arbitration Rules or any agreed conduct of the arbitration between the parties, the affected party may appeal to the Outer House against the award on the basis of serious irregularity contained in r 68(1) of the Scottish Arbitration Rules. Other grounds which allow the parties to appeal against an award for serious irregularities include exceeding jurisdiction, failure to deal with all the issues submitted to the tribunal, exceeding powers conferred by the parties, uncertainty or ambiguity of an award, lack of impartiality or independence, breach of due process or public policy, lack of ability or qualification of arbitrators, or any other irregularity in the conduct of the arbitration.[52]

Legal error appeal

A party may appeal to the Outer House against the tribunal's award on the grounds that the tribunal erred on a point of Scots law.[53] According to the draftsmen, this type of challenge is limited to the error of Scots law on the basis of the findings of fact in the award, including facts which the tribunal treated as established for the purpose of deciding the points concerned.[54]

Enforcement of arbitral awards

Generally speaking, once a party receiving an award in his favour applies to the sheriff courts or the Court of Session[55] in Scotland, the courts have the discretion to order the enforcement of an arbitral award made by a tribunal as if it were an extract registered decree bearing a warrant for execution granted by the court.[56] However, the courts will not exercise such discretion if it is clear to them that the award concerned is subject to an appeal under Pt 8 of the Scottish Arbitration Rules,[57] an appeal or review during the arbitral process[58] or a correction process under r 58 of the Scottish Arbitration Rules.[59] No order will be made if the courts

---

[51] Scottish Arbitration Rules, r 68(2)(a). Similar provision can be seen in s 68 of the (English) Arbitration Act 1996.
[52] Scottish Arbitration Rules, r 68(2)(b)–(k).
[53] Ibid, r 69(1).
[54] Revised Explanatory Notes (2009), para 224.
[55] Arbitration (Sc) Act 2010, s 12(8).
[56] Ibid, s 12(1). Similar provision can be seen in s 66 of the (English) Arbitration Act 1996.
[57] Arbitration (Sc) Act 2010, s 12(2)(a).
[58] Ibid, s 12(2)(b).
[59] Ibid, s 12(2)(c).

are convinced that the tribunal making the award concerned does not have jurisdiction to do so.[60] Providing no such situations existing and no parties' agreement to the contrary, the courts will allow a tribunal's award to be registered for execution in the Books of Council and Session or in the sheriff court books.[61] Such enforcement procedures apply to both awards whose juridical seat is in Scotland or in other jurisdictions.[62]

Corresponding with the founding principle in s 1(c) which limits court intervention to a minimum, s 13(1) does not allow legal proceedings initiated in the courts in respect of the tribunal's award or any other acts or omissions by a tribunal when conducting an arbitration other than those provided for in the Scottish Arbitration Rules or in any other provision of the Act.[63] However, it is also stated that other recourse to the courts available to the arbitrating parties under their existing powers in relation to arbitration are not undermined by s 13(1). The principle of limited court intervention also applies to non-review of the merits of an arbitral award, with the exceptions of lack of substantive jurisdiction, serious irregularity, or legal errors, listed in Pt 8 of the Scottish Arbitration Rules.[64] Under s 13(3) of the Act, jurisdictional issues can only be raised in the courts in relation to an objection to an order being made under s 12(3) or an appeal against a tribunal's ruling on its jurisdiction,[65] referral of point of jurisdiction,[66] and challenge to a tribunal's substantive jurisdiction.[67] In the case where the parties agree to the application of the UNCITRAL Model Law to their arbitration, the court or other authority is allowed to provide assistance or supervision for the functions of arbitration under Arts 6 (courts' assistance and supervision) and 11(2)–(5) (appointment of arbitrators) of the UNCITRAL Model Law.[68]

To maintain a balance between limited judicial intervention and judicial assistance or supervision, the draftsmen of the Act pointed out that:

> "To ensure that the courts have jurisdiction where necessary under the Bill, and that the Scottish Arbitration Rules are not only a matter of private right between individuals, it is also made clear that while court interference with a tribunal's award or any other act or omission by a tribunal in conducting the arbitration is prohibited, the courts do have jurisdiction on those matters where the Scottish Arbitration Rules or the Bill so permitted."[69]

---

[60] Arbitration (Sc) Act 2010, s 12(3).
[61] Ibid, s 12(5).
[62] Ibid, s 12(6).
[63] Ibid, s 13(1).
[64] Ibid, s 13(2).
[65] Scottish Arbitration Rules, r 21. Relevant provision can be seen in s 30(2) of the (English) Arbitration Act 1996.
[66] Scottish Arbitration Rules, r 22.
[67] Ibid, r 67.
[68] Arbitration (Sc) Act 2010, s 13(4).
[69] Revised Explanatory Notes (2009), para 53.

While the finality of an award is supported in s 11, the Act also sets out to protect the rights of those who are alleged to be a party to the arbitration, but decide not to take part in the arbitration proceedings due to the issues of the validity of the arbitration agreement, the constitution of the tribunal or the scope of submission. In accordance with s 14(1) of the Act, such a person can initiate court proceedings to challenge the tribunal's jurisdiction and ask the courts to make a declaration, interdict or other remedy to decide whether there is a valid arbitration agreement,[70] whether the tribunal is properly constituted[71] or whether the disputes submitted to the tribunal fall within the scope of the arbitration agreement.[72] Such an alleged party's right to appeal against any award made in the arbitration in relation to the issues of jurisdiction or serious irregularities is equally protected and not affected by the lack of participation during the arbitration proceedings.[73] Furthermore, the requirement of exhausting arbitral procedures within the arbitration is not imposed upon such a party.

To avoid the characteristics of confidentiality being undermined during the court proceedings, the Arbitration (Scotland) Act 2010 allows parties to request anonymity in the court legal proceedings. However, such anonymity only applies to the identity of the parties, not the contents of the court judgment. To ensure fairness to the winning party in the arbitration, anonymity will not be granted to the party who fails to carry out the arbitral awards voluntarily.[74] This is because the draftsmen believe that a party who fails to comply with an arbitral award should not be allowed to "hide behind confidentiality".[75] Once the application for anonymity has been made, the court must grant a final order[76] unless the court is satisfied that the disclosure is required for the following reasons: (a) for the proper performance of the discloser's public functions[77] or in order to enable any public body or office holder to perform public functions properly,[78] (b) such disclosure can reasonably be considered as being needed to protect a party's lawful interest,[79] (c) such disclosure is in the public interest,[80] or (d) such disclosure would be necessary in the

---

[70] Arbitration (Sc) Act 2010, s 14(1)(a). Similar provision can be seen in s 72(1) of the (English) Arbitration Act 1996.
[71] Arbitration (Sc) Act 2010, s 14(1)(b).
[72] Ibid, s 14(1)(c).
[73] Ibid, s 14(2). Similar provision can be seen in s 72(2) of the (English) Arbitration Act 1996.
[74] Arbitration (Sc) Act 2010, s 15(1).
[75] Revised Explanatory Notes (2009), para 58.
[76] Arbitration (Sc) Act 2010, s 15(3).
[77] Ibid, s 15(2)(a)(i).
[78] Ibid, s 15(2)(a)(ii).
[79] Ibid, s 15(2)(b).
[80] Ibid, s 15(2)(c).

interests of justice.[81] All these factors to be considered by the courts are similar to some of the exceptions to the duty of confidentiality imposed upon the tribunal members and the arbitrating parties contained in r 26(1) of the Scottish Arbitration Rules.[82]

RECOGNITION AND ENFORCEMENT OF NEW YORK CONVENTION AWARDS – ss 18–22 OF THE ARBITRATION (SCOTLAND) ACT 2010

In general

The United Kingdom ratified and acceded to the Convention on the Recognition and Enforcement of Foreign Arbitral Awards 1958 (the New York Convention) on 24 September 1975. The New York Convention came into force in Scotland by the enactment of the Arbitration Act 1975 to provide legal basis for the recognition and enforcement of New York Convention awards which are made in pursuance of a written arbitration agreement within a territory of a signatory state of the New York Convention.[83] As the Arbitration Act 1975 was repealed by the Arbitration (Scotland) Act 2010,[84] ss 18–22 of the Arbitration (Scotland) Act 2010 are enacted to provide special enforcement procedures for the New York Convention awards as well as maintain the position whereby the New York Convention awards will be recognised and enforced in Scotland.[85]

To avoid the potential complications and potential difficulties experienced in distinguishing the place of arbitration and the place where the award was signed, s 18(2) expressly provides that such an award is to be treated as made at the seat of arbitration, irrespective of "where it was signed, dispatched or delivered to any of the parties".[86] Therefore, if an arbitration had all its hearings held in a non-signatory country but the parties, the tribunal or any authorised third party decided that the juridical seat of the arbitration is in a signatory country of the New York Convention, then the award will be regarded as a Convention award and the request for recognition or enforcement of the award will have to be proceeded under the relevant provisions of the New York Convention as stipulated in ss 18–22 of the Arbitration (Scotland) Act 2010.

The issue of whether a state is a party to the New York Convention is determined by a declaration made by her Majesty by Order in Council

---

[81] Arbitration (Sc) Act 2010, s 15(2)(d).
[82] Scottish Arbitration Rules, r 26(1)(c), (d), (e) and (f).
[83] Arbitration (Sc) Act 2010, s 18(1). Similar provision can be seen in s 100 of the (English) Arbitration Act 1996.
[84] Arbitration (Sc) Act 2010, s 29.
[85] Policy Memorandum (29 January 2009), para 98.
[86] Revised Explanatory Notes (2009), para 67.

(subject to negative resolution procedure in the Scottish Parliament)[87] and such declaration is conclusive evidence of that fact. This is intended to bring the Act in line with Art XI of the Convention which allows an acceding state to declare that the Convention shall be extended to all or any of the territories for the international relations of which it is responsible.[88]

Binding force of New York Convention awards

Section 19(1) of the Arbitration (Scotland) Act 2010 provides that New York Convention awards are to be recognised as binding on the arbitrating parties following Art III of the New York Convention which states:

> "Each Contracting State shall recognize arbitral awards as binding and enforce them in accordance with the rules of procedure of the territory where the award is relied upon, under the conditions laid down in the following articles. There shall not be imposed substantially more onerous conditions or higher fees or charges on the recognition or enforcement of arbitral awards to which this Convention applies than are imposed on the recognition or enforcement of domestic arbitral awards."

The winning arbitrating party to such an award will be able to rely on it and seek recognition and enforcement in the Scottish courts. Provided the usual requirements and formalities are met, the Scottish courts are empowered to make an order by summary diligence to enforce the award concerned in the same manner as a judgment or order of the court to the same effect.[89]

Requirements and formalities required for the recognition or enforcement of New York Convention awards

Following Art IV of the New York Convention, s 21 lists the evidence which the enforcing party is required to produce to seek the recognition or enforcement of an award in the Scottish court. The evidence required includes the duly authenticated original award or a duly certified copy of the award and the original agreement or a duly certified copy of it. If the award or agreement concerned is not made in an official language of the country in which the award is relied upon, the applicant party must produce a translation of these documents. In the case of Scotland, it is English. The translation must be certified by an official or a sworn translator or by a diplomatic or a consular agent.

---

[87] Revised Explanatory Notes (2009), para 68.
[88] Policy Memorandum (29 January 2009), para 100.
[89] Arbitration (Sc) Act 2010, s 19(2). Similar provision can be seen in s 101 of the (English) Arbitration Act 1996.

Grounds for refusal of recognition or enforcement of New York Convention awards

Generally speaking, providing the arbitral award was made in a state which is a signatory country to the New York Convention, such an award can be relied upon by the arbitrating parties as a defence, set-off or in any other way in any legal proceedings in Scotland. To ensure that the arbitration proceedings are properly carried out by the tribunal, modelling on s 103 of the (English) Arbitration Act 1996, s 20 of the Arbitration (Scotland) Act 2010 sets out six grounds allowing the court passively to refuse the recognition or enforcement of the award on the party's application. It also provides two other grounds enabling the court actively to exercise discretion to recognise or enforce New York Convention awards.

On parties' application

Section 20(2) of the Arbitration (Scotland) Act 2010 prescribes the detailed circumstances in which the recognition or enforcement of a New York Convention award may be refused, as long as the party against whom it is invoked proves the following facts.

Incapacity of the parties

In accordance with s 20(2)(a) of the Arbitration (Scotland) Act 2010, the application for recognition or enforcement of a New York Convention award may be refused if the party against whom it is invoked proves that a party was under some incapacity under the law applicable to the party. The law applicable to the parties will depend on the legal status of the parties involved in the arbitration. For a natural person, his capacity to enter into an arbitration agreement will depend on the law of his domicile under private international law. For a legal person, the capacity issue will be decided according to the law of the place of registration or incorporation. This provision is enacted to maintain consistency with Art V(1)(a) of the New York Convention.

Invalidity of arbitration agreements

In line with Art V(1)(a) of the New York Convention, the request for the recognition or enforcement may be refused by the Scottish court if the arbitration agreement concerned is invalid under the law governing the issue of validity, either under the parties' agreed choice of law or, in the absence of such a choice, under the law of the country where the award was made.[90]

---

[90] Arbitration (Sc) Act 2010, s 20(2)(b). Similar provision can be seen in s 103 of the (English) Arbitration Act 1996.

Breach of due process during arbitration proceedings

Although arbitration is a form of private alternative dispute resolution outside the national court system, the Scottish law still requires due process to be properly carried out during the arbitration proceedings. The validity of an award made in breach of due process will be called into question. Hence s 20(2)(c) of the Arbitration (Scotland) Act 2010 empowers the court to refuse a Convention award if the party against whom it is invoked proves that the party was not given proper notice of the arbitral process or of the appointment of the tribunal,[91] or was not given a fair opportunity to present his case.[92] A similar provision can also be seen in Art V(1)(b) of the New York Convention.

Constitution of arbitral tribunal and arbitral process[93]

Similarly, recognition or enforcement of a Convention award may be refused if the party can prove that the arbitration proceedings or, the composition of the tribunal were not carried out according to the parties' agreement,[94] or, failing such an agreement, the law of the country where the arbitration took place.[95]

Award dealing with issues outside the scope of submission[96]

The tribunal is required to make an award to dispose of all the disputes submitted by the parties. No more, no less. If the tribunal's award purports to decide matters which were not submitted to arbitration by the parties, upon the party's application, the court may refuse to recognise or enforce such an award. As s 20(3)(a) and (b) provides: "Recognition or enforcement of a Convention award may also be refused if the person against whom it is invoked proves that the award (a) deals with a dispute not contemplated by or not falling within the submission to arbitration, (b) contains decisions on matters beyond the scope of that submission". While this provision is modelled on Art V(1)(c) of the New York Convention, interestingly, s 20(3)(a) and (b) did not incorporate the second half of Art V(1)(c) containing the phrase "provided that, if the decisions on matters submitted to arbitration can be separated from those not so submitted, that part of the award which contains decisions on matters submitted to arbitration may be recognized and enforced". However, it must be borne in mind that the Act has no intention to refuse the recognition and enforcement of other parts of the same awards, or other

---

[91] Arbitration (Sc) Act 2010, s 20(2)(c)(i).
[92] Ibid, s 20(2)(c)(ii).
[93] New York Convention 1958, Art V(1)(d).
[94] Arbitration (Sc) Act 2010, s 20(2)(d)(i).
[95] Ibid, s 20(2)(d)(ii).
[96] New York Convention 1958, Art V(1)(c).

awards, which properly dealt with the disputes falling within the scope of the submission. This can be seen in s 20(5) of the Act and its Explanatory Notes which point out: "If an award purports to decide matters which were not submitted to arbitration as well as those which were properly so submitted the court is able to recognise or enforce those parts which were properly submitted so long as these can be separated from those which exceeded the jurisdiction of the arbitrator."[97]

Non-binding force, setting aside or suspension of the award[98]

Another ground listed in s 20 of the Arbitration Act 2010 which allows the parties to apply to the Scottish courts for refusal of the recognition or enforcement of an award is that the award has not yet become binding upon the person[99] or the award has been set aside or suspended by a competent authority.[100] The so-called "competent authority" is clearly defined as "a person who has authority to set aside or suspend the Convention award concerned in the country in which, or under the law of which, the Convention award concerned was made".[101] The phrase "the country in which the Convention award concerned was made" indicates the seat of arbitration. Therefore German courts will be regarded as the competent authority for the purposes of s 20(3)(d) if the juridical seat of the arbitration is within the territory of Germany. In the latter case, French courts will be regarded as the competent authority if the award was made and governed according to the law of France.

If an application for setting aside or suspension of a Convention award was already made to the competent authority of the country in which, or under the law of which, the Convention award was made, in order to avoid conflicting judgments on the same issue, the Scottish courts are given the power to suspend the relevant court proceedings in relation to the recognition and enforcement of the award concerned.[102] In this case, the Scottish courts also have the power to order the party against whom recognition or enforcement is sought to provide appropriate security.[103]

Court's discretion to refuse the recognition or enforcement of awards

In contrast to the grounds listed in s 20(2) and (3) of the Arbitration (Scotland) Act 2010, which require the relevant party to apply and prove to the courts the grounds for a refusal, s 20(4) provides the Scottish courts with discretion, on their own initiative, to refuse the recognition

---

[97] Revised Explanatory Notes (2009), para. 71.
[98] New York Convention 1958, Art V(1)(e).
[99] Arbitration (Sc) Act 2010, s 20(3)(c).
[100] Ibid, s 20(3)(d).
[101] Ibid, s 20(7).
[102] Ibid, s 20(6)(a).
[103] Ibid, s 20(6)(b).

or enforcement of an award if it relates to a matter which is not capable of being settled by arbitration (arbitrability) or the recognition or enforcement of such an award would be contrary to public policy.

Other basis of recognition or enforcement of New York Convention awards

An enforcing party to a New York Convention award can also rely upon other procedures available to him, such as common law, to seek recognition or enforcement of a New York Convention award in the Scottish courts.[104]

INTERNATIONAL PRACTICE – ARTS I, V(1)(e) AND VII OF THE NEW YORK CONVENTION

Internationally, the issue of whether the enforcing courts must follow Art V(1)(e) to refuse the recognition or enforcement of an arbitral award which has not yet become binding on the parties, or has been set aside or suspended by a competent authority of the country in which, or under the law of which, that award was made, has been raised and discussed for a few decades. The discussion on this issue can be analysed from the aspects of Arts I, V(1)(e) and VII.

Argument under Art I – linking arbitral awards to the place of arbitration

It is widely acknowledged that the success and popularity enjoyed by international commercial arbitration lies in Art I of the New York Convention 1958 (hereinafter "the Convention"), which establishes a framework of recognition and enforcement of arbitral awards among the signatory countries and imposes upon them an obligation to recognise and enforce the arbitral awards made in another signatory country. It reads:

> "This Convention shall apply to the recognition and enforcement of arbitral awards made in the territory of a State other than the State where the recognition and enforcement of such awards are sought, and arising out of differences between persons, whether physical or legal. It shall also apply to arbitral awards not considered as domestic awards in the State where their recognition and enforcement are sought."

The wording *"made in the territory of a State"* shows a clear intention to anchor international commercial arbitration to the place where arbitration

---

[104] Arbitration (Sc) Act 2010, s 22. Similar provision can be seen in s 104 of the (English) Arbitration Act 1996.

is held. In 1958 the delegates agreed to use this limited notion to slow down the progressive idea of truly international arbitral awards. Since then, this limited notion has had a strong dominant force among practitioners and academics during five decades while the importance of the involvement of national law has always been stressed. For instance, supporting the territorial link between arbitration and states in geographical terms, van der Berg stated that:

> "[A]rbitration, international as it may be, needs at least a supporting judicial authority (*autroité d'appui*), which is, failing an international authority competent in this respect, necessarily a national court. For example, the assistance of a national court may be needed for the appointment, replacement or challenge of an arbitrator."[105]

He also directly pointed out that such a link shall exist between arbitration and the country where the arbitration is held because "it is a generally accepted principle of the international division of judicial competence that the court of the country under the arbitration law of which the arbitration is to take, is taking or took place, is the competent judicial authority in relation to arbitration. If the applicability of an arbitration law is excluded, it will be difficult to find such court".[106]

By saying "... it is to be noted that none of the arbitral institutions which are specialised in international commercial arbitrations provide that the arbitrations conducted under their Arbitration Rules are entirely detached from the ambit of any national arbitration law",[107] he dismissed the argument invoking the idea that the avenue of "internationalised" arbitration was opened by arbitration rules of arbitral institutions.

Furthermore, using Art 1(2) of the UNCITRAL Arbitration Rules (Arbitration Rules of 1976 of the United Nations Commission on International Trade Law (UNCITRAL)) and the ICC Rules (Arbitration Rules of the International Chamber of Commerce) as examples, he concluded that the concept of internationalisation of such rules goes only as far as is permitted by the non-stringent rules of the applicable arbitration law. He stated:

> "The opinion that under the ICC Arbitration Rules an arbitration can be 'de-nationalised' is, in my opinion, incorrect. Although the ICC Arbitration Rules, too, must be deemed to be basically governed by the law of the place of arbitration or, theoretically, the different arbitration law chosen by the parties or the arbitrator.
>
> The crucial point is that an arbitration procedure – and award – can be considered to be 'de-nationalised' really only if the mandatory provision of

---

[105] A van der Berg, *The New York Arbitration Convention of 1958: Towards a Uniform Judicial Interpretation* (1981), p 30.
[106] *Ibid*.
[107] *Ibid*, p 31.

national arbitration laws are made inapplicable. The ICC Rules cannot be deemed to have gone to such extent."[108]

Following this argument, he refused the applicability of the New York Convention to the so-called "a-national awards" or "floating award". Failing to find any expressed provisions stating that the award made in another Contracting State must be subject to a national arbitration law, he indicated that the combination of Arts I and V implied that a-national awards do not fall into the field of application of the Convention on the grounds that "the Convention is built on the presumption that the award is governed by a national arbitration law since the setting aside of an award belongs to the exclusive jurisdiction of the court under whose arbitration law the award is made".[109]

Argument under Art V(1)(e) – the validity of the award "may" or "may not" be linked to the country of origin

By linking Art I with Art V(1)(e) of the New York Convention, the proponents of the territorial link between arbitration and the country of origin have religiously applied Art V(1)(e) and refused recognition or enforcement of any arbitral awards which were set aside by the court of the country where the arbitration was held. Although this school of thought recognises the arbitrators' freedom in choosing the applicable law in the case where no expressed choice is made by the parties, the extent of this freedom is only limited to the substantive law of the contract, rather than the procedural law. Therefore, without a procedural law being specified, it would be compulsory for the arbitrators to refer to the law of the place where arbitration is held to decide the appropriate procedures they should follow. The basis of their argument is the denial of the existence of "international" commercial arbitration as we discussed in Chapter 8 on Procedural Law.

Taking England as an example, a jurisdiction against the idea of delocalisation theory, supposing a dispute concerning whether the goods delivered were defective or not was submitted to an arbitral tribunal sitting in London. No applicable law was mentioned in the arbitration agreement. According to the traditional approach, first of all the arbitral tribunal has to refer to the (English) Arbitration Act 1996 to examine the questions of jurisdiction of the tribunal and the validity of the arbitration agreement, and so on. Second, if the submission is valid, the English law will govern the arbitration procedures. Third, the tribunal is required to apply the English conflict of laws rules to decide the substantive law of the contract. Failing any clear indications of the choice of law, either express

---

[108] van der Berg, above, n 105, pp 32–33.
[109] Ibid, p 37.

or implied, the law which has the most real and closest connection with the case will be chosen by the tribunal. Failure to do so will mean that the validity of the award can be in doubt and challenged in the country where the award is made, that is, England, or where the recognition or enforcement of the award is sought. This is stipulated in s 2(1) of the (English) Arbitration Act 1996, which expressed the necessities of such linkage. It reads: "The provisions of this Part apply where the seat of the arbitration is in England and Wales or Northern Ireland." To emphasise the link between arbitration and the country of origin further, the control exercised by the jurisdiction of the place of arbitration is introduced in s 4(1) of the Act, which stipulates: "The mandatory provisions of this Part are listed in Schedule 1 and have effect notwithstanding any agreement to the contrary."

However, this strong support of the territorial link between arbitration and the country of origin believed by the territorialists has been questioned by the supporters of the delocalisation theory which invoked the idea of detaching arbitration from the country of origin. First of all, they root the justification of their arguments in Art V(1)(e) itself. After examining the wordings used in the Article, they point out and distinguish the permissive words "may be refused" in Art V(1)(e) and "shall" used in Arts II and III. As Paulsson stated:

> "The conditional 'may' leaps out at any lawyer, since it necessarily contemplates 'or may not'. There is no other guidance in the text of the Convention. One therefore, may fairly conclude that enforcement notwithstanding annulment elsewhere is a matter left to the States parties to the Convention. If such a State incorporates the rules of the Convention into its own law without alteration or qualification, the same discretionary freedom is passed on to the judge."[110]

They argue that the word "may" contrasts with the word "shall" used in Arts II and III. Articles II and III require that Contracting States "shall" recognise an agreement in writing under which the parties undertake to submit to arbitration and that the Contracting State shall recognise arbitral awards as binding and enforce them in accordance with the rules of procedure of the territory where the award is relied upon and the Convention "shall not" impose substantially more onerous conditions or higher fees or charges on the recognition or enforcement of arbitral awards than those imposed on the domestic arbitral awards. Consequently, they believe that the draftsmen of the Convention did intend to leave the discretion to the enforcing courts to decide whether to refuse the recognition or enforcement of Conventional arbitral awards.

---

[110] J Paulsson, "Enforcing arbitral awards notwithstanding a local standard annulment (LSA)" (1998) 9/N1 May, *The ICC International Court of Arbitration Bulletin* 14 at 17.

The other basis for their arguments is the use of delocalisation theory to minimise the territorial link between arbitration and the place of arbitration as discussed in Chapter 8. To summarise, in their opinion, the application of the delocalisation theory can successfully avoid the uncertainty caused by the application of the mandatory rules and public policy exceptions of the relevant laws. Using the different nature of a national court's judge from a private arbitrator as one of the foundations of their arguments, they claim that arbitrators are under no duty to apply the *lex loci arbitri* to the arbitration. Paulsson once expressed:

> "The international arbitrator is in a fundamentally different position. Whatever one might think of the contractual source of an arbitral tribunal's authority as a purely internal matter, it is difficult to consider the international arbitrator as a manifestation of the power of a State. His mission, conferred by the parties' consent, is one of a private nature, and it would be a rather artificial interpretation to deem his power to be derived, and very indirectly at that, from a tolerance of the State of the place of arbitration."[111]

Following the suggestion that arbitrators do not have to follow the *lex loci arbitri*, it is therefore unnecessary for them to consider the mandatory rules of the *lex loci arbitri* when they deal with an international commercial dispute. They recommend that the supervisory powers should only be exercised by the courts where the recognition or enforcement is sought. Paulsson points out that the purpose of this theory is not to try to escape from the national court's control, but rather to promote the acceptance of delocalised arbitral awards. In other words, "[t]o seek completely to avoid national jurisdictions would be misguided. Indeed, the international arbitral system would ultimately break down if no national jurisdiction could be called upon to recognise and enforce awards".[112] Furthermore, "the delocalised award is not thought to be independent of any legal order. Rather, the point is that a delocalised award may be accepted by the legal order of an enforcement jurisdiction although it is independent from the legal order of its country of origin".[113]

Arguments under Art VII

The delocalisation theory not only has strong influence on the legislation of a handful of European jurisdictions, such as France, Belgium and Switzerland, but also paves the way for a number of court judgments

---

[111] J Paulsson, "Arbitration unbound: award detached from the law of its country of origin" (1981) 30 ICLQ 358 at 362.
[112] J Paulsson, "Delocalisation of international commercial arbitration: when and why it matters" (1983) 32 ICLQ 53 at 54.
[113] *Ibid* at 57.

recognising and enforcing awards which were set aside by the courts of the place of arbitration.

France

As early as 1981, France enacted a Decree on arbitration. Titles V and VI of the Decree (Arts 1492–1507) deal with the recognition and enforcement of arbitral awards and awards rendered in international arbitration in France. The spirit of the delocalisation theory can be found in Art 1502 of the French New Code of Civil Procedure 1981 (NCPC), which reads:

> "An appeal against a decision granting recognition or enforcement may be brought only in the following cases:
> 1. If the arbitrator decided in the absence of an arbitration agreement on the basis of a void or expired agreement;
> 2. If the arbitral tribunal was irregularly composed or the sole arbitrator irregularly appointed;
> 3. If the arbitrator decided in a manner incompatible with the mission conferred upon him;
> 4. Whenever due process has not been respected;
> 5. If the recognition or enforcement is contrary to international public policy (*ordre public*)."

From this provision, it is clear that France has gone in a different direction from Art V(1)(e) of the New York Convention by removing the ground for refusal of enforcement of the annulment of the award by a court in the country of origin.

Belgium

Belgium has taken a step further than France by limiting court intervention in the arbitration result to an extreme extent. Article 1717 of the Belgian Judicial Code expresses its position in non-interference of arbitral awards affecting the interests of non-Belgian nationals if the parties so agree. It reads:

> "The parties may, by an express statement in the arbitration agreement or by a later agreement, exclude any application for the setting aside of an arbitral award, in case none of them is a physical person of Belgian nationality or a physical person having his normal residence in Belgium or a legal person having its principal office or a branch office in Belgium."[114]

---

[114] Judicial Code, Sixth Part: Arbitration (adopted 4 July 1972 and last amended on 19 May 1998).

Switzerland

Instead of compulsory non-interference as in the Belgian Judicial Code, Switzerland introduced Art 192 of the Swiss Private International Law Act in 1987, which provides that Swiss courts will not deal with any arbitral awards if an exclusion agreement was reached between the parties involved in arbitration. It states:

> "1. Where none of the parties has its domicile, its habitual residence, or a business establishment in Switzerland, they may, by an express statement in the arbitration agreement or by a subsequent agreement in writing, exclude all setting aside proceedings, or they may limit such proceedings to one or several of the grounds [for annulment] listed in Art 190(2).
>
> 2. Where the parties have excluded all setting aside proceedings and where the awards are to be enforced in Switzerland, the New York Convention of 10 June 1958 on the recognition and enforcement of Foreign Arbitral Awards shall apply by analogy."

Court decisions – Hilmarton, Chromalloy *and* Putrabali *cases*

Linking the permissive language used in Art V(1)(e) and the cases of SEEE,[115] *Götaverken Arendal AB*[116] and *Norsolor*,[117] discussed in Chapter 8, the message was that it is not compulsory for the enforcing courts of the signatory countries to follow the strict and narrow interpretation of Art V(1)(e) of the Convention and grant an automatic refusal of recognition or enforcement of the arbitral awards once they have been set aside in their country of origin. To take their argument further, while Paulsson maintained that "an arbitral award may indeed "drift', but of course it is ultimately subject to the post facto control of the execution jurisdiction(s)",[118] Gaillard predicted that "in so doing the ruling opened the door by applying the more favourable right principle to the recognition in France of an award set aside in the country of origin".[119] This is what happened in the *Hilmarton* and *Chromalloy* cases, which explored the impact Art VII has on Art V(1)(e).

---

[115] *Société Européene d'Etudes et d'Entreprise (SEEE)* v *Yugoslavia* (1959) JDI 1074; a detailed discussion is contained in J Paulsson, "The extent of independence of international arbitration from the law of the *situs*" in J Lew (ed), *Contemporary Problems in International Commercial Arbitration* (1986), at pp 142–146.

[116] Paris, 21 February 1980: (1980) JDI 660.

[117] Decision of the Court of Appeal is discussed in (1986) XI YBCA 484; decision of the Supreme Court of Austria is discussed in (1984) IX YBCA 159.

[118] Above, n 111, at 368.

[119] E Gaillard, " Enforcement of awards set aside in the country of origin: the French experience" in ICCA Congress Series, *Improving the Efficiency of Arbitration Agreements and Awards – 40 Years of Application of the New York Convention* (1999) at p 16.

Hilmarton case

This case concerned the payment of a commission by OTV, a French company, to Hilmarton, an English company, for securing a contract in Algeria. Based on the grounds that commission payment is an absolute prohibition under Algerian law, the sole arbitrator decided that the commission was not due in this case. In November 1989, Hilmarton brought an action in Switzerland to have the award set aside and the Court of Justice of the Canton of Geneva set aside the award, which was also affirmed by the Swiss Federal Tribunal in April 1990. However, OTV's petition to have the first award recognised and enforced was granted by the Tribunal de Grande Instance of Paris in February 1990. Dealing with the question whether to enforce an award which has been set aside in its country of origin, the Cour d'appel in Paris, in December 1991, decided to affirm the leave of enforcement granted by the Tribunal de Grande Instance of Paris. The Court held that, according to Art VII(1) of the Convention, the judge may not refuse to enforce the award unless the national law so authorises, as well as the provisions of the Convention do not deprive a party of the right it may have to avail itself of an arbitral award in the manner and to the extent allowed by the law of the country where such award is sought to be relied upon. Based on Art VII, the Court decided to uphold the more favourable right principle under Art VII of the Convention and recognised the award, as the ground listed in Art V(1)(e) of the Convention did not exist in Art 1502 of the NCPC. The Court ruled:

> "Considering that French law on international arbitration does not oblige a French judge to take into account an annulment decision on the award given within the framework of the foreign internal order, and that, hence the incorporation in the French legal order of an award which was rendered in international arbitration and which was annulled abroad on the basis of local law, is not contrary to international public policy within the meaning of Art 1520(5) of the New Code of Civil Procedure."

Chromalloy case

The French decision discussed above was regarded as one of the rare cases and it was believed that France was one of the very few countries which have shown interests in combining the delocalisation theory with the country's own arbitration practice. As a result, the delocalisation theory was dismissed as a fallacy which was invoked by a small group of French jurists. As van der Berg commented:

> "The main reason for which no effect needs to be given in France to an annulment of an award by a court in the country of origin seems to be the view that in international arbitration an arbitral award is not incorporated in the legal order of the country where the award is merely located geographically. The French system for the recognition and enforcement of

arbitral awards made in another country is a so-called unilateral system. The incorporation of the arbitral award into the French legal order is defined by French law only. These rules are territorial in nature. As is characteristic of the unilateral approach, these rules are not concerned with the incorporation of an award in a foreign legal order, even if the latter is the place where the award has been made. The question of whether the arbitral award is incorporated in another legal system does not play any role. The rationale of this system is that an arbitral award which is acceptable to a French judge should not be refused force and effect because a foreign judge has different ideas about its acceptability. Furthermore, in France, the notion of the nationality of an award does not exist."[120]

It was not until 1996, when the US District of Columbia enforced the *Chromalloy* award, that the whole debate surrounding the delocalisation theory and the relationship between arbitration and the country of origin once again revived. The case of *Chromalloy Aeroservices Inc v Arab Republic of Egypt*[121] concerned an arbitration between Chromalloy Aeroservices, a US company, and the Arab Republic of Egypt which took place in Cairo; it is regarded as the strongest ever support for minimising the link between arbitration and the place of origin. In this arbitration an award was made in 1994 against Arab Republic of Egypt. Republic of Egypt later applied to the Court of Appeal in Cairo for annulment of the award by claiming that an action for annulment is permissible "if the arbitral award excluded the application of the law agreed upon by the parties to govern the subject matter of the dispute" and that the "arbitral tribunal had wrongly failed to apply Egyptian administrative law". The Court of Appeal in Cairo agreed with the arguments raised by the Egyptian Government and annulled the validity of the award.

Later, Chromalloy sought recognition of the award in both the USA and France. The action brought to the Cour d'appel in Paris was granted an exequatur in May 1995 and the exequatur was enforced in 1997 despite that the award was already annulled by the Court of Appeal in Cairo. Following the same line of argument given in the *Hilmarton* case resorting to Art VII of the Convention and Art 1502 of the NCPC, the court expressed that the winning party in this case was entitled to avail itself of the more favourable right principle for enforcement in the domestic law (according to Art VII of the Convention) and that the annulment of the award in its country of origin is not regarded as one of the grounds for non-recognition or enforcement in France under Art 1502 of the NCPC.

Adopting the similar attitude to the French court, the US District Court, District of Columbia, granted the recognition of the award in July 1996,

---

[120] A van der Berg, "Annulment of awards in international arbitration" in Richard B Lillich and Charles N Brower (eds), *International Arbitration: In the 21st Century: towards "judicialization" and uniformity? Twelfth Sokol Colloquium* (1996), at pp 151–152.

[121] 939 F Supp 907 (DDC 1996); (2003) 19 *Arbitration International* 424; 12(4) *International Arbitration Report* B-1.

despite the fact that the award was annulled in the country of origin. According to the court, its decision was supported by three pillars. The court first of all established the need to protect the winning party's rights in seeking recognition and enforcement under the domestic law regime. Second, the reason for setting the award aside in Cairo was not one of the grounds for the refusal of recognition and enforcement of arbitral awards under the US domestic law. Consequently, the decision made by the Egyptian court was not regarded as a good foreign court judgment by the US court and should not have binding force in the US courts. Finally, the court believed that Art VII of the Convention allows the winning party to rely on the application of domestic laws that are more favourable to the recognition of foreign awards than those established under the Convention regime because:

> "While Art V provides a discretionary standard, Art VII of the Convention requires that, "The provisions of the present Convention shall not ... deprive any interested party of any right he shall have to avail himself of an arbitral award in the manner and to the extent allowed by the law ... of the country where such award is sought to be relied upon.' In other words, under the Convention, CAS maintains all rights to enforcement of this arbitral award that it would have had in the absence of the Convention."[122]

Putrabali *case*

Later on, in 2007, the French Cour de Cassation enforced an award which was partially set aside by the High Court of London and was replaced by another award issued by the same arbitral tribunal in *Société PT Putrabali Adyamulia v Société Rena Holding et Société Mnogutia Est Epices*,[123] which involved a dispute arising from breach of contract due to a failure to make payment. The first award, made on 10 April 2001, denied Putrabali's request for payment. However, the High Court of London partially set aside the award and decided that Rena's failure to make payment constituted breach of contract. Later, Rena was ordered to make payment in the second award, made on 21 August 2001. After the second award, despite the first award being partially set aside by the English court, Rena applied to the French lower court and the Cour d'appel to recognise and enforce the first award and the application was granted. Putrabali appealed against the court decisions and argued that there was no binding force in the first award because it was removed by the arbitral tribunal and had been replaced by another award in order to satisfy the parties' agreement

---

[122] 939 F Supp 907 at 909–910.
[123] (2007) *Revue de l'Arbitrage* 507; English translation in Bertrand Derains and Yves Derains, "29 June 2007 Cour de cassation – Première chambre civile Cour de cassation – Première chambre civile 29 June 2007", available at http://www.kluwerarbitration.com/document.aspx?id=ipn80892&query=content%3A%22putrabali%22.

in relation to the procedural rules to be followed. Consequently, Rena's request for recognition and enforcement of the award should be rejected. Not surprisingly, the Cour de Cassation denied Putrabali's appeal and ruled that the validity of an international award shall be decided by the enforcing court. It stated:

> "[A]n international award, which is not integrated in any national legal system, is an international judicial decision whose regularity is reviewed in compliance with the applicable rules in the country where recognition and enforcement is requested ; pursuant to Art VII of the New York Convention of April 10, 1958, Rena Holding's request in France for recognition of [the award] was admissible and it could rely on the French rules of international arbitration which do not include a foreign setting aside of the award among the cases of denial of recognition."

Accordingly, the *Hilmarton*, *Chromalloy* and *Putrabali* cases made a substantial link between Art V(1)(e) and Art VII of the Convention. Not only did they endorse the concept of delocalisation theory applied in *SEEE*, *Götaverken* and *Norsolor*, but they also stressed the significance of the "more favourable right principle" established in Art VII of the Convention and its interplay with Art V(1)(e). It was believed that the language used in Art VII was intended to facilitate the development of international commercial arbitration, rather than placing obstacles in its path. Additionally, due to the lack of negative language in Art VII, they argued that the draftsmen did not exclude the possibility of using Art VII as the basis for recognising or enforcing an award which has been set aside in its country of origin. Furthermore, this particular provision allowed the parties to rely on more favourable domestic law as the basis for the recognition or enforcement of Conventional arbitral awards.

Doubts over Chromalloy case

One of the major reasons why these three cases attracted so much attention is due to the very real fear among the traditionalists that different judgments or different arbitral results involving the same issue, same facts and same parties can produce more conflicting decisions and place international commercial arbitration in an unstable framework. This is exactly what happened in the *Hilmarton* case, where the second arbitrator was appointed to reopen the case under the Swiss law after the first award was set aside by the court in Switzerland. The second arbitrator decided against the Algerian law and awarded a sum in favour of Hilmarton, which brought the award to the French court and asked for recognition of the award. Surprisingly, undeterred by the previous judgment, the French court accepted Hilmarton's arguments and granted recognition of the award. Consequently, a situation arose with the creation of two conflicting but enforceable awards.

Instead of celebrating the refocusing of the delocalisation theory, this development opened the door to its weakness and put the proponents of the delocalisation theory into a defending position, while negative concerns were expressed over the *Chromalloy* case. Concerning the possible instability arising from these conflicting judgments on the same matter under the Convention framework, Carbonneau criticised the *Chromalloy* decision handed down by the US court in the following terms:

> "The exercise of would-be discretion under Art V could destabilise the transborder framework for enforcement established by the Convention. Moreover, the meaning and effect that the court affixes to the language of Art VII could not have been part of the intent of the drafters of the Convention and has not been part of the contemporary decisional practice under the Convention. Evaluated from the standard point of the orderliness and stability of governing norms, the court's tendencious interpretative pragmatism renders the Convention framework chaotic."[124]

Similar doubts were also expressed by Gharavi, who believed that *Hilmarton* exposed the weakness of the delocalisation theory as difficulties can arise when annulment is not effective in the country of enforcement because "enforcing set aside awards may result in coexistence of two conflicting awards concerning the same issues between the same parties, and thus violate the intended uniformity of the convention and damage the image of international commercial arbitration".[125]

Van der Berg used to argue for the extra-territorial effect of the award which has been annulled by the courts in the country on the basis of its exclusive jurisdiction over an action for annulment of an award. Following this development, he decided to revise his opinions by stating that "having reflected further on this question, I have come to the conclusion that I should revise my opinion. It can indeed be argued that the Convention confers upon a court the discretionary power to recognise and enforce an a-national award under the Convention".[126] However, he remained cautious about such development and its possible effects on arbitration. Acknowledging that an enforcing court does have residual discretionary power to decide whether it has to refuse the recognition or enforcement of the awards if one of the grounds for refusal stated in Art V of the Convention is present, he stated that such discretionary power can be exercised if the respondent invoking the ground for refusal can be deemed to be estopped from invoking the ground, the defect is insignificant, or it would not have led to a different result. However, he believed that such kind of results should not be

---

[124] T Carbonneau, "Debating the proper role of national law under the New York Arbitration Convention" (1998) 6 TJICL 277 at 279.
[125] H Gharavi, "*Chromalloy*: another view" (1997) 12(1) Intl Arb Rep 21.
[126] Above, n 120, at p 28.

overrated, and, "I should add that I believe that it is neither advisable nor necessary for parties to agree to "de-nationalised' arbitration in most cases at present".[127]

Not only receiving attacks from the academics, the proponents of the delocalisation theory also received further qualifications over such a development from the US courts. After the *Chromalloy* case, two cases decided by the Second Circuit and the court of Southern District of New York respectively have added further qualifications to the *Chromalloy* case. The first case was *Baker Marine (Nig) Ltd* v *Chevron (Nig) Ltd*, which involved no United States citizens and in which no intention was found of making US arbitration law the governing law of the arbitration. Based on these two factors, the court pointed out that, unlike the arbitration agreement in *Chromalloy*, there was no contractual promise not to appeal against the award in this case. Moreover, the fact that the awards had been appealed (and set aside) in the Nigerian court was not a breach of US public policy to uphold the agreements of the parties. The court also found that, similar to one of the reasons given in *Götaverken,* there was nothing to indicate that either party had intended the domestic US arbitration law to govern their disputes and therefore the application of that law via Art VII would frustrate US public policy.[128]

The second case, *Spier* v *Calzaturificio Tecnica*, involved a US citizen (Spier) who tried to enforce an award handed down in Italy but which had been set aside by the Italian courts. Relying on *Chromalloy's* decision on the "more favourable right" established in Art VII of the Convention, Spier asked the US court to enforce the award. However, this petition was rejected on the grounds that the court "precluded the effort" of introducing domestic law through the vehicle of Art VII of the Convention.[129] In addition, the fact that there was no evidence to suggest that the parties contemplated that US law would govern their disputes and there was nothing in the arbitration agreement that amounted to a contractual promise not to appeal the award, meant that Spier had shown no adequate reason for refusing to recognise the judgments of the Italian courts.[130]

It is clear that *Baker Marine (Nig) Ltd* v *Chevron (Nig) Ltd* and *Spier* v *Calzaturificio Tecnica* established three further qualifications than the *Chromalloy* case. They are: providing US public policy is respected, any petition based on Art VII of the Convention may be upheld if there has been a breach of a clear contractual promise between the parties not to appeal the award, or there has been an involvement of US citizens.

---

[127] Above, n 120, at p 28.
[128] 91 F 3d 194 (2nd Cir 1999) at 197 n 3.
[129] 71 F Supp 2d 279, 77 F Supp 2d 405 (SDNY 1999) at 288.
[130] *Ibid.*

Furthermore, there must be a clear intention of the parties to have US domestic arbitration law to govern the disputes.

CONTRACTUALLY RESTRICTING OR EXPANDING THE GROUNDS FOR REFUSAL OF ARBITRAL AWARDS[131]

The issue of whether the parties can contractually expand or restrict the grounds for refusal of recognition of arbitral awards is another subject of discussion. In this section, examination will be centred on the practices of Belgium, Switzerland and the USA.

Can parties contractually agree to restrict the grounds for setting aside arbitral awards? Belgian and Swiss perspectives

Belgium

As discussed in Chapter 8, with an intention to attract more revenue generated from arbitration to Belgium, the Belgian Judicial Code famously excluded all grounds for challenging the awards for non-Belgian nationals as early as 19 May 1985. Article 1717(4) stated: "The Belgian Court can take cognizance of an application to set aside only if at least one of the parties to the dispute decided in the arbitral award is either a physical person having Belgian nationality or residing in Belgium, or a legal person formed in Belgium or having a branch (*une succursale*), or some seat of operation (*un siège quelconque d'opération*) there."

However, such support for ensuring the finality of arbitral awards by means of removing all challenging avenues not only backfired, but also caused an outcry among international businessmen worrying about the lack of challenging procedures in the case of substantial injustice, especially those who chose Brussels as the place of arbitration in their arbitration agreements before the provision came into force. Consequently, for over a decade, the Belgian government saw a significantly decreased number of arbitration cases choosing Brussels as the place of arbitration. This situation prompted the amendment to Art 1717(4) once again in 1998. Instead of mandatorily removing challenging avenues from non-Belgian nationals who arbitrate in Belgium, the amended Art 1717(4) offers the parties the freedom to choose to rule out the jurisdiction of the Belgian courts. However, to protect the rights of the parties, such a choice

---

[131] See discussions in F Grizel, "Control of awards and re-centralisation of international commercial arbitration" (2006) 25 CJQ 166; RM Dickson and D Donovan, "US: parties' ability to expand the scope of judicial review of an arbitral award" (2002) 5(6) Int ALR N58; M Ball, "The Revised Uniform Arbitration Act in the United States: state law in a complex federal system" (2002) 5(2) Int ALR 56; and RC Corn, "Recent Development: *LaPine Technology Corp v Kyocera Corp*" (1997–1998) 13 Ohio St J on Disp Resol 1085.

cannot be implied and must be made in an express statement between the parties.

Switzerland

Belgium apart, the Swiss law has been another subject of discussion in relation to exclusive agreements or waivers contained in arbitration clauses. Article 190(2) of the Swiss Private International Law Act 1987 (PILA) sets out five grounds, allowing the parties to challenge an award if: (a) the sole arbitrator has been incorrectly appointed or where the arbitral tribunal has been incorrectly constituted, (b) the arbitral tribunal has wrongly declared itself to have or not to have jurisdiction, (c) the award has gone beyond the claims submitted to the arbitral tribunal, or failed to decide one of the claims, (d) the principle of equal treatment of the parties or their right to be heard in adversarial procedure has not been observed, or (e) the award is incompatible with public policy.[132]

Apart from disallowing any judicial review on the merits of arbitral awards, the Swiss law allows the exclusion of all forms of recourse against arbitral awards.[133] Article 192(1) allows the parties who have no link with Switzerland to waive their rights to challenge the award under Art 192(1) of PILA. Article 192(1) reads:

> "Where none of the parties has its domicile, its habitual residence, or a business establishment in Switzerland, they may, by an express statement in the arbitration agreement or by a subsequent agreement in writing, exclude all setting aside proceedings, or they may limit such proceedings to one or several of the grounds listed in Art 190, para 2."

This provision applies to parties who have no domicile, habitual residence or business establishment within Switzerland. It is enacted to provide protection to parties who may not be familiar with Swiss law when drafting the arbitration clause.[134] Such parties are allowed to partially or completely exclude or waive the grounds listed in Art 190(2) of PILA to set aside the award. To take advantage of this right, the parties must have a written agreement to that effect. The written requirement is intended to "protect the parties from ill-considered waivers and their far-reaching consequences. It therefore leaves no room for an implied waiver".[135] This requirement was also upheld by the Swiss Federal Court in an earlier case handed down in 1997.[136]

---

[132] PILA, Art 190(2).
[133] D Baizeau, "Waiving the right to challenge an arbitral award rendered in Switzerland: caveats and drafting considerations for foreign parties" (2005) 8(3) Int ALR 69.
[134] *Ibid* at 71.
[135] PM Patocchi and C Jermini, "Arbitration" in SV Berti (ed), *International Arbitration in Switzerland* (2000), at Art 192, para 2; above n 133, at 71.
[136] Decision of the Swiss Federal Court (4P 265/1996), (1997) *ASA Bulletin* 494.

It is worth noting that, according to Baizeau, the parties' agreement that the award shall be rendered without reasons or parties' agreement to arbitrate pursuant to arbitration rules in general terms, does not amount to a valid exclusion agreement to exclude the right to challenge the awards. However, an express and specific reference in the agreement to the arbitration rule containing the waiver is regarded as a valid exclusion clause.[137] The latter category was reviewed the first time by the Swiss court in 2005. The court applied Art 192(1) and upheld the parties' right to exclude the jurisdiction of the Swiss court in relation to the challenge of the award.[138] The parties to this case expressly agreed that: "All and any awards or other decisions of the Arbitral Tribunal shall be made in accordance with the UNCITRAL Rules and shall be final and binding on the parties who exclude all and any rights of appeal from all and any awards insofar as such exclusion can validly be made." The Swiss Federal Court decided:

> "[F]or an exclusion agreement to be deemed valid, an express waiver of Art190 PILA, although being recommended, was by no means mandatory. Indeed, the Court ruled that it is not sustainable to overlook a clear manifestation of the parties' mutual assent to waive their right to file an appeal against an arbitration award, based solely on the lack of express mention of a provision of which non-Swiss parties are often not even aware."[139]

However, this decision does not affect the view that reference to a set of arbitration rules in general terms[140] does not constitute a valid exclusion agreement.

After the landmark decision in 2005, the Swiss Federal Supreme Court once again confirmed the application of Art 192(1) of PILA in a case involving a partial exclusion agreement to the effect that the parties waived their right to challenge the award on the grounds of jurisdiction.[141] Motorola and Uzan (Turkish company) agreed to a partial exclusion agreement. The plaintiff challenged the award and claimed that the exclusion agreement was contrary to Turkish public policy. The Turkish party claimed that the Turkish law should be considered due to its relevance. The Swiss court

---

[137] Above, n 133, at 71.
[138] Bundesgericht (4P 236/2004) (unreported, 4 February 2005), discussed in L Levy and V Sieber, "Switzerland: A valid waiver of the right to file an appeal" (2005) 8(3) Int ALR N32; M Scherer, "Switzerland: No challenge of award in case of an exclusion agreement" (2005) 8(2) Int ALR 2005 N27.
[139] L Levy and V Sieber, "Switzerland: A valid waiver of the right to file an appeal" (2005) 8(3) Int ALR N32 at 33.
[140] Eg ICC Rules, Art 28(6).
[141] Bundesgericht (*Motorola Credit Corp v Uzan*) (4P 198/2005) (unreported, 31 October 2005), discussed in M Scherer, "Switzerland: Waiver of remedies against arbitral awards" (2006) 9(4) Int ALR N47.

ruled that it was not against public policy to limit or exclude appeals under the Swiss law and the scope of Art 192 of PILA is a matter of Swiss law; and whether the exclusion was compatible with Turkish public policy was left open since foreign laws, whether mandatory or not, could not be considered under Art 192 of PILA. Therefore, the exclusion agreement was held to be valid. The court also pointed out that the exclusion agreement does not affect other remedies available to the parties if they apply for recognition and enforcement in Switzerland and the judge would hold the award to the standards provided in the New York Convention.

Can parties contractually agree to expand the grounds for setting aside? US perspectives

Legal framework

Instead of excluding the grounds for challenging awards, the issue of whether the grounds for setting aside can be expanded by parties' agreement was discussed in the US Federal Circuit courts and the Supreme Court. The legal framework for judicial review to confirm, vacate or modify an award is stipulated in §§ 9–11 of the Federal Arbitration Act (FAA), 9 USC. Under § 9, a court "must" confirm an award "unless" it is vacated, modified or corrected "as prescribed" in §§ 10 and 11. The grounds listed in § 10 for vacating an award include: (1) awards procured by corruption, fraud, or undue means; (2) cases in which the arbitrators are obviously partial or corrupt; (3) where there is misbehaviour prejudicing a party's rights; and (4) where the arbitrators exceeded their power, or so imperfectly executed their power that no "mutual, final, and definite award" was made. Under § 11, the grounds for modifying or correcting an award include "evident material miscalculation", "evident material mistake" and "imperfect[ions] in [a] matter of form not affecting the merits".

Split in the Federal Courts of Appeals

The issue whether the parties can expand the grounds of judicial review of the arbitral awards caused a split in the US Federal Courts of Appeals over the exclusiveness of the statutory grounds listed in the FAA to confirm, vacate or modify an award. The Ninth and Tenth Circuits are of the opinion that the recitations are exclusive, and the First, Third, Fifth and Sixth Circuits decided that the statutory grounds are mere threshold provisions and they are open to expansion by parties' agreement.

The Ninth and Tenth Circuits have held that parties may not contract for expanded judicial review. This view was agreed in dicta delivered by the Eighth Circuit.[142] In the case of the Ninth Circuit, changing from its

---

[142] *UHC Management Co v Computer Sciences Corp*, 148 F 3d 992 (1998) at 997–998.

original position in *LaPine Technology Corp* v *Kyocera Corp*[143] that "Federal courts can expand their review of an arbitration award beyond the FAA's grounds, when … the parties have so agreed",[144] it decided that a direct and prompt examination of the award depended on the FAA and the much discussed expanded-review provision was unenforceable in *Kyocera Corp* v *Prudential-Bache Trade Services, Inc*,[145] as well as that review of the original award was allowed only if the district court determined that the award should be vacated on the grounds allowable under 9 USC, § 10, or modified or corrected under the grounds allowable under 9 USC, § 11. It ruled:

> "We agree with the Seventh, Eighth, and Tenth Circuits that private parties have no power to determine the rules by which federal courts proceed, especially when Congress has explicitly prescribed those standards. Pursuant to *Volt*, parties have complete freedom to contractually modify the arbitration process by designing whatever procedures and systems they think will best meet their needs — including review by one or more appellate arbitration panels. Once a case reaches the federal courts, however, the private arbitration process is complete, and because Congress has specified standards for confirming an arbitration award, federal courts must act pursuant to those standards and no others. Private parties' freedom to fashion their own arbitration process has no bearing whatsoever on their inability to amend the statutorily prescribed standards governing federal court review. Even when Congress is silent on the matter, private parties lack the power to dictate *how* the federal courts conduct the business of resolving disputes."[146]

A similar line is also held by the Tenth Circuit in *Bowen* v *Amoco Pipeline Co*,[147] where the Court stated:

> "Although the Court has emphasized that parties may 'specify by contract the rules under which arbitration will be conducted',[148] it has never said parties are free to interfere with the judicial process. … To the contrary, through the FAA Congress has provided explicit guidance regarding judicial standards of review of arbitration awards. … Moreover, if parties desire broader appellate review, 'they can contract for an appellate arbitration panel to review the arbitrator's award'.[149] The decisions directing courts

---

[143] 130 F 3d 884 (9th Cir 1997) at 887.
[144] *Ibid*. The parties agreed that a review is allowed if the arbitrators' findings of fact were not supported by substantial evidence or their conclusions of law were "erroneous" (at 887).
[145] 341 F 3d 987 (CA9 2003).
[146] *Ibid* at 1000.
[147] 254 F 3d 925 (CA10 2001) at 936.
[148] *Volt Info Sciences, Inc* v *Stanford University*, 489 US 468 at 479.
[149] *Chicago Typographical Union* v *Chicago Sun-Times, Inc*, 935 F 2d 1501 (7th Cir 1991) at 1504.

to honour parties' agreements and to resolve close questions in favour of arbitration simply do not dictate that courts submit to varying standards of review imposed by private contract."[150]

...

"Contractually expanded standards, particularly those that allow for factual review, clearly threaten to undermine the independence of the arbitration process and dilute the finality of arbitration awards because, in order for arbitration awards to be effective, courts must not only enforce the agreements to arbitrate but also enforce the resulting arbitration awards."[151]

On the other hand, joined by an unpublished opinion delivered by the Fourth Circuit,[152] the First, Third, Fifth and Sixth Circuits stood firm in the other camp which allowed additional grounds for review if the parties so contract. For instance, in *Gateway Technologies, Inc v MCI Telecommunications Corp*,[153] the Fifth Circuit reasoned:

"[T]he FAA's pro-arbitration policy does not operate without regard to the wishes of the contracting parties. ... [I]t does not follow that the FAA prevents the enforcement of agreements to arbitrate under different rules than those set forth in the Act itself. Indeed, such a result would be quite inimical to the FAA's purpose of ensuring that private agreements to arbitrate are enforced according to their terms. Arbitration under the Act is a matter of consent, not coercion, and parties are generally free to structure their arbitration agreements as they see fit. Just as they may limit by contract the issues which they will arbitrate, so too may they specify by contract the rules under which that arbitration will be conducted. ... When, as here, the parties agree contractually to subject an arbitration award to expanded judicial review, federal arbitration policy demands that the court conduct its review according to the terms of the arbitration contract."[154]

Getting in line with the US Supreme Court – Hall Street v Mattel[155]

The split among the Federal Circuit courts was finally resolved in *Hall Street* v *Mattel*. This case involved a dispute arising from a property lease between Hall Street (landlord) and Mattel (tenant). The parties agreed to arbitrate after the dispute was referred to the Federal Court. The

---

[150] *Bowen* v *Amoco Pipeline Co*, 254 F 3d 925 at 934.
[151] *Ibid* at 935.
[152] *Syncor Int'l Corp* v *McLeland*, 120 F 3d 262 (1997).
[153] 64 F 3d 993 (CA5 1995) at 997. Also see *Puerto Rico Tel Co* v *US Phone Mfg Corp*, 427 F 3d 21 (CA1 2005) at 31; *Jacada (Europe), Ltd* v *International Marketing Strategies, Inc*, 401 F 3d 701 (CA6 2005) at 710; *Roadway Package System, Inc* v *Kayser*, 257 F 3d 287 (CA3 2001) at 288.
[154] 64 F 3d 993 at 996.
[155] *Hall Street Associates, LLC* v *Mattel, Inc*, 128 SCt 1396, 552 US 576 (2008).

parties' arbitration agreement provided for a wider scope of review of the arbitrator's award. On the appeal to the Ninth Circuit, following the case of *Kyocera Corp v Prudential-Bache Trade Services Inc*, the court reversed the district court's decision and vacated the arbitral award on the basis of unenforceability of the arbitration agreement, which expanded the grounds of review listed in the FAA.[156] Hall Street filed a petition for writ of *certiorari* to the US Supreme Court after the Ninth Circuit refused to grant *en banc* review of its decision.

When the case reached the US Supreme Court, the Court, first of all, dismissed Hall Street's argument that expandable judicial review authority has been accepted as the law since *Wilko v Swan*[157] and pointed out that Hall Street had misunderstood the meaning of the case. It stated that "[q]uite apart from its leap from a supposed judicial expansion by interpretation to a private expansion by contract ... We, when speaking as a Court, have merely taken the *Wilko* language as we found it, without embellishment".[158]

The Supreme Court further expressed its disagreement with Hall Street's second argument that the agreement to review for legal error ought to prevail simply because arbitration is a creature of a contract, and the FAA is "motivated, first and foremost, by a congressional desire to enforce agreements into which parties have entered".[159] It stated:

> "[T]he FAA lets parties tailor some, even many features of arbitration by contract, including the way arbitrators are chosen, what their qualifications should be, which issues are arbitrable, along with procedure and choice of substantive law. But to rest this case on the general policy of treating arbitration agreements as enforceable as such would be to beg the question, which is whether the FAA has textual features at odds with enforcing a contract to expand judicial review following the arbitration. To that particular question we think the answer is yes, that the text compels a reading of the §§ 10 and 11 categories as exclusive."[160]

Furthermore, citing *Kyocera*, the Supreme Court explained:

---

[156] US Federal Arbitration Act, § 10 sets the following limited grounds for the review of an award: (1) where the award was procured by corruption, fraud, or undue means; (2) where there was evident partiality or corruption in the arbitrators, or either of them; (3) where the arbitrators were guilty of misconduct in refusing to postpone the hearing, upon sufficient cause shown, or in refusing to hear evidence pertinent and material to the controversy; or of any other misbehaviour by which the rights of any party have been prejudiced; (4) or where the arbitrators exceeded their powers, or so imperfectly executed them that a mutual, final, and definite award upon the subject matter submitted was not made.
[157] *Wilko v Swan*, 346 US 427 (1953).
[158] 552 US 576 (2008) at 585.
[159] *Dean Witter Reynolds Inc v Byrd*, 470 US 213 (1985) at 220.
[160] 552 US 576 (2008) at 586.

"Instead of fighting the text, it makes more sense to see the three provisions, §§ 9–11, as substantiating a national policy favouring arbitration with just the limited review needed to maintain arbitration's essential virtue of resolving disputes straightaway. Any other reading opens the door to the full-bore legal and evidentiary appeals that can rende[r] informal arbitration merely a prelude to a more cumbersome and time-consuming judicial review process and bring arbitration theory to grief in post-arbitration process."[161]

While the Supreme Court agreed with the Ninth Circuit that the FAA confines its expedited judicial review to the grounds listed in 9 USC, §§ 10 and 11 and vacated the judgment and remanded the case for proceedings consistent with this opinion, the Court did not rule out possible reviews based on authority outside the statute. It stated:

"In holding that §§ 10 and 11 provide exclusive regimes for the review provided by the statute, we do not purport to say that they exclude more searching review based on authority outside the statute as well. The FAA is not the only way into court for parties wanting review of arbitration awards: they may contemplate enforcement under state statutory or common law, for example, where judicial review of different scope is arguable. But here we speak only to the scope of the expeditious judicial review under §§ 9, 10, and 11, deciding nothing about other possible avenues for judicial enforcement of arbitration awards."[162]

---

[161] 552 US 576 (2008) at 588 and *Kyocera*, 341 F 3d at 998.
[162] 552 US 576 (2008) at 590.

CHAPTER 13

ARBITRATION EXPENSES

The Scottish Arbitration Rules contained eight provisions in Pt 7 to regulate the issues which may arise from arbitration fees and expenses. The purpose of Pt 7 is to clarify the definitions of fees and expenses incurred in arbitration and determine who is responsible for paying such fees and expenses to protect arbitrators. To protect the parties, the Rules also contain provisions for liability for recoverable arbitration expenses.

ARBITRATION EXPENSES – r 59

Rule 59 contains a default provision defining the term "arbitration expenses" incurred in arbitration proceedings. In accordance with r 59, "arbitration expenses" means the arbitrators' fees and expenses for which the parties are liable under r 60;[1] any expenses incurred by the tribunal when conducting the arbitration for which the parties are liable under r 60;[2] the parties' legal and other expenses;[3] and the fees and expenses of any arbitral appointments referee, and any other third party to whom the parties give powers in relation to the arbitration for which the parties are liable under r 60.[4] It is pointed out that this provision also applies to any fees and expenses incurred by an arbitral appointment referee and arbitration institutions in connection with the arbitration.[5]

Section 59 of the Arbitration Act 1996 also contains a similar definition of arbitration costs. Accordingly, the costs of arbitration include the arbitrators' fees and expenses, the fees and expenses of any arbitral institution concerned, the legal or other costs of the parties and any incidental costs to any proceedings to determine the amount of the recoverable costs of the arbitration under s 63.

---

[1] Scottish Arbitration Rules, r 59(a).
[2] Ibid, r 59(b).
[3] Ibid, r 59(c).
[4] Ibid, r 59(d)(i)–(ii).
[5] Policy Memorandum, 29 January 2009, para 179; Scottish Arbitration Rules, r 60(2).

ARBITRATORS' FEES AND EXPENSES – r 60

To protect the arbitrators' entitlements to payment, r 58 is a mandatory rule stipulating that the parties are severally liable to pay the arbitrators their fees and any expenses incurred by the tribunal when conducting the arbitration.[6] The fees and expenses which the parties severally liable to pay to the arbitrators are further defined in r 60(1)(a) and (b) include the arbitrators' fees for conducting the arbitration;[7] any expenses incurred personally by the arbitrators when conducting the arbitration;[8] and expenses incurred by the tribunal when conducting the arbitration.[9]

Arbitrators' fees are the daily fees and commitment fees chargeable by the arbitrator when he accepts the appointment. The English case of *K/S Norjarl A/S v Hyundai Heavy Industries Co Ltd*[10] concerning an issue whether the agreement between the arbitrators and one of the parties constituted misconduct, the proper conduct of an arbitration pending between the parties, the issue of arbitrators' was also examined. In that case, Leggatt LJ confirmed that an implied contract was formed to pay arbitrator's fees when the appointment was made by the parties. He stated:

> "By accepting appointment in this case the arbitrators by implication undertook to conduct the arbitration with due diligence and at a reasonable fee. The commitment subsequently sought by the parties was of such an extent as, in my judgment, justified a request by the arbitrators to the parties to consider the payment of a commitment fee, and so did not of itself amount to misconduct - still less did it warrant removal. Because no agreement was concluded by Norjarl to pay any fees to its arbitrator or to the third arbitrator, no misconduct has occurred on that account."[11]

The expenses incurred personally by the arbitrators for conducting the arbitration may include the transportation costs, accommodation costs or fees of the arbitrator's clerks, employees and agents incurred for the purpose of conducting the arbitration. The parties are also liable to pay any expenses incurred by the tribunal when conducting the arbitration. These may include the fees and expenses of any clerk, agent, employee or other person appointed by the tribunal to assist it in conducting the arbitration;[12] the fees and expenses of any expert from whom the tribunal obtains an opinion;[13] any expenses in respect of meeting and

---

[6] Scottish Arbitration Rules, r 60(1).
[7] *Ibid*, r 60(1)(a)(i).
[8] *Ibid*, r 60(1)(a)(ii).
[9] *Ibid*, r 60(1)(b).
[10] [1992] QB 863.
[11] *Ibid*, at 877.
[12] Scottish Arbitration Rules, r 60(1)(b)(i).
[13] *Ibid*, r 60(1)(b)(ii).

hearing facilities;[14] and any expenses incurred in determining recoverable arbitration expenses.[15]

The amounts of the fees and expenses payable shall be agreed between the parties and the arbitrators, or the arbitral appointment referee or other third party.[16] In the absence of any agreement, the level of the fees and expenses shall be decided by the Auditor of the Court of Session.[17] Unless the Auditor of the Court of Session decides otherwise, the amount of any fee is to be determined by the Auditor on the basis of a reasonable commercial rate of charge.[18] The amount of any expenses is to be determined by the Auditor on the basis that a reasonable amount is to be allowed in respect of all reasonably incurred expenses.[19] Once the application to the Auditor is made, the Auditor of the Court of Session may order the arbitrators to repay any excessive fees and expenses already paid by the parties.[20] Such an order made by the Auditor has the same effect as an order made by the court.

However, it is worth noting that r 60 does not affect the parties' liability for fees and expenses regarded as recoverable arbitration expenses under r 62 or limitation of such expenses under r 65,[21] and the Outer House's power to make an order relating to expenses in cases of arbitrator's resignation or removal.[22]

Similar provisions can also be seen in s 28 of the Arbitration Act 1996 which renders the parties jointly and severally liable to pay to the arbitrators such reasonable fees and expenses (if any) as are appropriate in the circumstances. Upon notice to the other party and to the arbitrators, any party may apply to the court for adjustment of the amounts of the arbitrator's fees and expenses.[23]

RECOVERABLE ARBITRATION EXPENSES – r 61

Going further than is stipulated in r 59 regarding the parties' liability for the arbitrators' fees and expenses, r 61 provides a list of arbitration expenses which may be recoverable. They are: the arbitrators' fees and expenses for which the parties are liable under r 60;[24] any expenses incurred by the tribunal when conducting the arbitration for which the

---

[14] Scottish Arbitration Rules, r 60(1)(b)(iii).
[15] Ibid, r 60(1)(b)(iv).
[16] Ibid, r 60(3)(a).
[17] Ibid, r 60(3)(b).
[18] Ibid, r 60(4)(a).
[19] Ibid, r 60(4)(b).
[20] Ibid, r 60(5).
[21] Ibid, r 60(6)(a).
[22] Ibid, r 60(6)(b).
[23] (English) Arbitration Act 1996, s 28(2).
[24] Scottish Arbitration Rules, r 61(1)(a).

parties are liable under r 60;[25] and the fees and expenses of any arbitral appointments referee (or any other third party to whom the parties give powers in relation to the arbitration) for which the parties are liable under r 60.[26]

It is the arbitral tribunal's task to determine the amount of the other arbitration expenses which are recoverable.[27] The arbitral tribunal can also seek assistance from the Auditor of the Court of Session to determine the amount to be recovered.[28] To maintain equality and avoid an imbalance of power between the parties and arbitrators, the tribunal or the Auditor of the Court Session must determine the amount of the other arbitration expenses which are recoverable on the basis that a reasonable amount is to be allowed in respect of all reasonably incurred expenses.[29] Any doubts as to whether expenses were reasonably incurred or are reasonable in amount is to be resolved in favour of the person liable to pay the expenses.[30]

For recoverable arbitration expenses, the arbitral tribunal may allocate the amount of total or part of expenses between the parties in an award.[31] Such an award can be made in the final award or separately from an award on the substantive issues.[32] The arbitral tribunal must follow the principle that expenses should follow a decision made in favour of a party except where this would be inappropriate in the circumstances.[33] Unless such an award is made or the arbitral tribunal chooses not to make such an award, each party is jointly liable for any such expenses for which the parties are liable under r 60,[34] and their own legal and other expenses.[35]

It is important to note that r 62 does not affect the parties' equal liability for fees and expenses under r 60,[36] or the liability of any party to any other third party.[37] Furthermore, similar to s 56 of the Arbitration Act 1996, the arbitral tribunal has a mandatory power to withhold its award if the parties failed to pay for any fees and expenses in full.[38] It is also mandatory to prohibit any pre-dispute agreements allocating the parties' liability between themselves for any or all of the arbitration expenses. Such pre-dispute agreements have no effect if they are entered into before the

---

[25] Scottish Arbitration Rules, r 61(1)(b).
[26] Ibid, r 61(1)(c).
[27] Ibid, r 61(2)(a).
[28] Ibid, r 61(2)(b).
[29] Ibid, r 61(3)(a).
[30] Ibid, r 61(3)(b).
[31] Ibid, r 62(1).
[32] Ibid, r 66.
[33] Ibid, r 62(2).
[34] Ibid, r 62(3)(a).
[35] Ibid, r 62(3)(b).
[36] Ibid, r 62(4)(a).
[37] Ibid, r 62(4)(b).
[38] Ibid, r 56(1).

dispute being arbitrated has arisen.[39] The tribunal also has power to order the claimant to provide security for recoverable arbitration expenses or any part of them.[40] If the claimant fails to comply with the security order for expenses, the tribunal has the power to dismiss the claim.[41] However, this kind of order cannot be made on the grounds that the party is an individual who ordinarily resides outwith the United Kingdom;[42] or is a body which is incorporated or formed under the law of a country outwith the United Kingdom, or managed or controlled from outwith the United Kingdom.[43]

To avoid the recoverable arbitration expenses being escalated to an unreasonable amount, it is also possible for the arbitral tribunal to limit the recoverable amount in a provisional award.[44] However, such an award must be made well in advance of the expenses being incurred or any arrangements being made.[45]

Similarly, s 61 of the (English) Arbitration Act 1996 allows the tribunal to make an award allocating the costs of the arbitration between the parties. Any agreement as to how the costs of arbitration are to be borne or allocated between the parties extends only to recoverable costs.[46] Subject to parties' agreement, the recoverable costs of the arbitration are to be determined by the tribunal on such basis as it thinks fit. However, the tribunal must specify the basis on which it has acted,[47] and the items of recoverable costs and the amount referable to each.[48] If no recoverable costs are determined by the tribunal, any party to the arbitral proceedings may apply to the court and ask the court to determine the recoverable costs of the arbitration on such basis as it thinks fit,[49] or order that they shall be determined by such means and upon such terms as it may specify.[50]

The Arbitration Act 1996 distinguishes recoverable fees and expenses of arbitration from the fees and costs of arbitrators in s 64. Only reasonable fees and expenses can be included in the recoverable costs of arbitrators.[51] If there are any doubts, any of the parties can apply to the

---

[39] Scottish Arbitration Rules, r 63. This provision is similar to s 60 of the Arbitration Act 1996 which provides "An agreement which has the effect that a party is to pay the whole or part of the costs of the arbitration in any event is only valid if made after the dispute in question has arisen".
[40] Scottish Arbitration Rules, r 64(1)(a).
[41] *Ibid*, r 64(1)(b).
[42] *Ibid*, r 64(2)(a).
[43] *Ibid*, r 64(2)(b).
[44] *Ibid*, r 65(1). See (English) Arbitration Act 1996, s 65(1).
[45] Scottish Arbitration Rules, r 65(2). See (English) Arbitration Act 1996, s 65(2).
[46] (English) Arbitration Act 1996, s 62.
[47] *Ibid*, s 63(3)(a).
[48] *Ibid*, s 63(3)(b).
[49] *Ibid*, s 63(4)(a).
[50] *Ibid*, s 63(4)(b).
[51] *Ibid*, s 64(1).

courts to determine the amount of reasonable fees and expenses that are appropriate in the circumstances.[52]

INTERNATIONAL PRACTICE

It is common for the parties to agree and include "expenses cap provisions" in the appointment agreements. If the tribunal accepts the appointment, he will have to accept that his fees and expenses will be capped at an agreed level between the parties. If no such provisions agreed before the appointment, it is up to the tribunal to determine the reasonable amount with the parties' consent. The problem may arising from this situation is that a party who contemplates the possibility of losing the case may challenge the so-called "reasonable amount" decided by the tribunal. For instance, in an English case the losing party to the arbitration was ordered by the court to pay all the costs despite his objections to the different hourly rates charged by the three different arbitrators appointed. The court pointed out that the parties could have agreed to a ceiling cost to be imposed upon the tribunal. Failing such arrangements, the losing party had to pay.

The other point worth noting is that an arbitrator may run the risk of being removed by the parties if he insists on re-negotiating the fees once the fees and expenses are agreed between the parties and the members of the tribunal. For instance, an Australian retired judge was removed by the parties because he insisted on having his agreed fees raised from $1,000 to $1,500 per day after realising that the other two members of the tribunal had their fees set at $1,200 per day.

On the other hand, in the case of institutional arbitrations, the costs of arbitration are stipulated in details in various institutional arbitration rules. Taking the ICC as an example, the ICC requires an advance on the costs of the arbitration. According to its Rules, to initiate a request for arbitration with the ICC, the requesting party shall make an advance payment of US $3,000 on the administrative expenses.[53] Once the request is received, the ICC Secretary General may request the Claimant to pay a provisional advance in an amount intended to cover the costs of arbitration.[54] After that, The ICC Court shall fix the advance on costs in an amount to cover the fees and expenses of the arbitrators and the ICC administrative costs for the claims and counterclaims which have been referred to it by the parties. This amount may be subject to re-adjustment at any time during the arbitration.[55] Both the claimant and the respondent must share equally the shares of the advance on costs

---

[52] (English) Arbitration Act 1996, s 64(2).
[53] Rules of Arbitration of the International Chamber of Commerce, Appendix Three: Costs and Expenses, Art 1.
[54] Ibid, Art 30(1).
[55] Ibid, Art 30(2).

fixed by the court.[56] Without payment being made, and after consultation with the arbitral tribunal, the Secretary General may direct the arbitral tribunal to suspend its work and set a time limit of no less than 15 days for payment to be made. On the expiry of the time limit, the relevant claims or counterclaims shall be considered as withdrawn.[57]

According to Art 31(1) of the ICC Rules, "the costs of the arbitration shall include the fees and expenses of the arbitrators and the ICC administrative expenses fixed by the Court, in accordance with the scale in force at the time of the commencement of the arbitral proceedings, as well as the fees and expenses of any experts appointed by the Arbitral Tribunal and the reasonable legal and other costs incurred by the parties for the arbitration". Regarding the arbitrator's fees, in exceptional circumstances, the Court has the discretion to fix the fees at a figure higher or lower than the figures on the scales.[58] The arbitral tribunal is required to determine the final costs of the arbitration and the proportions to be borne by the parties.[59]

ICC arbitration

Below is the scale used by the ICC to determine the costs of arbitration, effective as at 1 May 2010:

A. ADMINISTRATIVE EXPENSES

Sum in dispute (in US $)	Administrative expenses(*)
up to 50,000	$3,000
from 50,001 to 100,000	4.73%
from 100,001 to 200,000	2.53%
from 200,001 to 500,000	2.09%
from 500,001 to 1,000,000	1.51%
from 1,000,001 to 2,000,000	0.95%
from 2,000,001 to 5,000,000	0.46%
from 5,000,001 to 10,000,000	0.25%
from 10,000,001 to 30,000,000	0.10%
from 30,000,001 to 50,000,000	0.09%
from 50,000,001 to 80,000,000	0.01%
from 80,000,001 to 500,000,000	0.0035%
over 500,000,000	$113,215

(*) For illustrative purposes only, the last table below indicates the resulting administrative expenses in US$ when the proper calculations have been made.

---

[56] Rules of Arbitration of the International Chamber of Commerce, Appendix Three: Costs and Expenses, Art 30(3).
[57] Ibid, Art 30(4).
[58] Ibid, Art 31(2).
[59] Ibid, Art 31(3).

B. ARBITRATOR'S FEES

Sum in dispute (in US $)	Fees(**)	
	minimum	maximum
up to 50,000	$ 3,000	18.0200%
from 50,001 to 100,000	2.6500%	13.5680%
from 100,001 to 200,000	1.4310%	7.6850%
from 200,001 to 500,000	1.3670%	6.8370%
from 500,001 to 1,000,000	0.9540%	4.0280%
from 1,000,001 to 2,000,000	0.6890%	3.6040%
from 2,000,001 to 5,000,000	0.3750%	1.3910%
from 5,000,001 to 10,000,000	0.1280%	0.9100%
from 10,000,001 to 30,000,000	0.0640%	0.2410%
from 30,000,001 to 50,000,000	0.0590%	0.2280%
from 50,000,001 to 80,000,000	0.0330%	0.1570%
from 80,000,001 to 100,000,000	0.0210%	0.1150%
from 100,000,001 to 500,000,000	0.0110%	0.0580%
over 500,000,000	0.0100%	0.0400%

(**) For illustrative purposes only, the table below indicates the resulting range of fees when the proper calculations have been made.

Sum in dispute (in US $)	A. Administrative Expenses (*) (in US $)	B. Arbitrator's Fees (**) (in US $)	
		Minimum	Maximum
up to 50,000	3,000	3,000	18,0200% of amount in dispute
from 50,001 to 100,000	3,000 + 4.73% of amt over 50,000	3,000 + 2.6500% of amt over 50,000	9,010 + 13.5680% of amt over 50,000
from 100,001 to 200,000	5,365 + 2.53% of amt over 100,000	4,325 + 1.4310% of amt over 100,000	15,794 + 7.6850% of amt over 100,000
from 200,001 to 500,000	7,895 + 2.09% of amt over 200,000	5,756 + 1.3670% of amt over 200,000	23,479 + 6.8370% of amt over 200,000
from 500,001 to 1,000,000	14,165 + 1.51% of amt over 500,000	9,857 + 0.9540% of amt over 500,000	43,990 + 4.0280% of amt over 500,000

Sum in dispute (in US $)	A. Administrative Expenses (*) (in US $)	B. Arbitrator's Fees (**) (in US $)	
		Minimum	Maximum
from 1,000,001 to 2,000,000	21,715 + 0.95% of amt over 1,000,000	14,627 + 0.6890% of amt over 1,000,000	64,130 + 3.6040% of amt over 1,000,000
from 2,000,001 to 5,000,000	31,215 + 0.46% of amt over 2,000,000	21,517 + 0.3750% of amt over 2,000,000	100,170 + 1.3910% of amt over 2,000,000
from 5,000,001 to 10,000,000	45,015 + 0.25% of amt over 5,000,000	32,767 + 0.1280% of amt over 5,000,000	141,900 + 0.9100% of amt over 5,000,000
from 10,000,001 to 30,000,000	57,515 + 0.10% of amt over 10,000,000	39,167 + 0.0640% of amt over 10,000,000	187,400 + 0.2410% of amt over 10,000,000
from 30,000,001 to 50,000,000	77,515 + 0.09% of amt over 30,000,000	51,967 + 0.0590% of amt over 30,000,000	235,600 + 0.2280% of amt over 30,000,000
from 50,000,001 to 80,000,000	95,515 + 0.01% of amt over 50,000,000	63,767 + 0.0330% of amt over 50,000,000	281,200 + 0.1570% of amt over 50,000,000
from 80,000,001 to 100,000,000	98,515 + 0.0035% of amt over 80,000,000	73,667 + 0.0210% of amt over 80,000,000	328,300 + 0.1150% of amt over 80,000,000
from 100,000,01 to 500,000,000	99,215 + 0.0035% of amt over 100,000,000	77,867 + 0.0110% of amt over 100,000,000	351,300 + 0.0580% of amt over 100,000,000
over 500,000,000	113,215	121,867 + 0.0100% of amt over 500,000,000	583,300 + 0.0400% of amt over 500,000,000

LCIA arbitration

Similar rules are also provided in the LCIA Arbitration Rules. The costs of the arbitration (other than the legal or other costs incurred by the parties themselves) are to be determined by the LCIA Court in accordance with the Schedule of Costs. Similarly, the parties are to be jointly and severally liable to the Arbitral Tribunal and the LCIA for such arbitration costs.[60] In the award, the arbitral tribunal must consider the parties' relative success

---

[60] LCIA Arbitration Rules, Art 28.1.

and failure in the award or arbitration[61] and specify the total amount of the costs of the arbitration and the proportions to be borne by the parties.[62]

Below is the breakdown of the costs chargeable.

SCHEDULE OF ARBITRATION COSTS (effective as at 1 June 2010)

For all arbitrations in which the LCIA provides services, whether as administrator, or as appointing authority only, and whether under the LCIA Rules, UNCITRAL Rules or other, *ad hoc*, rules or procedures agreed by the parties to the arbitration.

1. Administrative charges under LCIA Rules, UNCITRAL Rules, or other, *ad hoc*, rules or procedures*

1(a) Registration Fee (payable in advance with Request for Arbitration non-refundable) £1,500

1(b) Time spent** by the Secretariat of the LCIA in the administration of the arbitration.***

Registrar / Deputy Registrar / Counsel	**£225 per hour**
Other Secretariat personnel depending on activity	**£100 or £150 per hour**

1(c) Time spent by members of the LCIA Court in carrying out their functions in deciding any challenge brought under the applicable rules.***

at hourly rates advised by members of the LCIA Court

1(d) A sum equivalent to 5% of the fees of the Tribunal (excluding expenses) in respect of the LCIA's general overhead.***

1(e) Expenses incurred by the Secretariat and by members of the LCIA Court, in connection with the arbitration (such as postage, telephone, facsimile, travel etc.), and additional arbitration support services, whether provided by the Secretariat or the members of the LCIA Court from their own resources or otherwise.***

at applicable hourly rates or at cost

1(f) The LCIA's fees and expenses will be invoiced in sterling, but may be paid in other convertible currencies, at rates prevailing at the time of payment, provided that any transfer and/or currency exchange charges shall be borne by the payer.

2. Request to act as Appointing Authority only*

2(a) Appointment Fee (payable in advance with request – non-refundable). £1,000

2(b) As for 1(b) and 1(e), above.

---

[61] LCIA Arbitration Rules, Art 28.4.
[62] *Ibid*, Art 28.2.

3. **Request to act in deciding challenges to arbitrators in non-LCIA arbitrations***

3(a) As for 2(a) and 2(b), above; plus

3(b) Time spent by members of the LCIA Court in carrying out their functions in deciding the challenges.

at hourly rates advised by members of the LCIA Court

4. **Fees and expenses of the Tribunal***

4(a) The Tribunal's fees will be calculated by reference to work done by its members in connection with the arbitration and will be charged at rates appropriate to the particular circumstances of the case, including its complexity and the special qualifications of the arbitrators. The Tribunal shall agree in writing upon fee rates conforming to this Schedule of Arbitration Costs prior to its appointment by the LCIA Court. The rates will be advised by the Registrar to the parties at the time of the appointment of the Tribunal, but may be reviewed annually if the duration of the arbitration requires.

Fees shall be at hourly rates **not exceeding £400**.

However, in exceptional cases, the rate may be higher provided that, in such cases, (a) the fees of the Tribunal shall be fixed by the LCIA Court on the recommendation of the Registrar, following consultations with the arbitrator(s), and (b) the fees shall be agreed expressly by all parties.

* Charges may be subject to Value Added Tax at the prevailing rate.
** Minimum unit of time in all cases: 15 minutes.
*** Items 1(b), 1(c), 1(d) and 1(e) above, are payable on interim invoice; with the award, or as directed by the LCIA Court under Article 24.1 of the Rules.

Vienna Arbitration Rules

On filing the claims or counterclaims, the relevant parties are to make a payment of EUR 2,000 as the registration fees. On filing the claim (counterclaim), the claimant (counterclaimant) shall pay into the cover, the costs up to the submission of the files to a sole arbitrator or an arbitral tribunal. If a higher outlay is incurred, an additional sum may be required.[63] The parties are also responsible for the costs of the proceedings which include the costs of arbitration (administrative costs), arbitrators' fees plus any value added tax and cash outlay (such as travel and subsistence expenses of arbitrators, costs of service of documents, rent, costs of simple minuting); and the costs of the parties (their representation and other outlay related to the arbitration proceedings).[64] In the award, upon application by the party, the arbitrator or the arbitral tribunal shall state

---

[63] Rules of Arbitration and Conciliation of the International Arbitral Centre of the Austrian Federal Economic Chamber (VIAC), Art 33(1).
[64] *Ibid*, Art 32.

the details of the costs of arbitration fixed by the Secretary General, the costs of the parties and the proportions to be borne by the parties.[65]

Schedule of arbitration costs[66]

Registration fee: EUR 2,000

Administrative Charges			
Amount in dispute in euros		Rate in euros	
from	to		
0	100,000	3,000	
100,001	200,000	3,000 + 1.5% of excess over	100,000
200,001	500,000	4,500 + 1% of excess over	200,000
500,001	1,000,000	7,500 + 0.7% of excess over	500,000
1,000,001	2,000,000	11,000 + 0.4% of excess over	1,000,000
2,000,001	5,000,000	15,000 + 0.1% of excess over	2,000,000
5,000,001	10,000,000	18,000 + 0.05% of excess over	5,000,000
over 10,000,000		20,500 + 0.01% of excess over	10,000,000

Fees for sole arbitrators

Amount in dispute in euros		Rate in euros	
from	to		
0	100,000	6% – minimum fee:	1,000
100,001	200,000	6,000 + 3% of excess over	100,000
200,001	500,000	9,000 + 2.5% of excess over	200,000
500,001	1,000,000	16,500 + 2% of excess over	500,000
1,000,001	2,000,000	26,500 + 1% of excess over	1,000,000
2,000,001	5,000,000	36,500 + 0.6% of excess over	2,000,000
5,000,001	10,000,000	54,500 + 0.4% of excess over	5,000,000
10,000,001	20,000,000	74,500 + 0.2% of excess over	10,000,000
20,000,001	100,000,000	94,500 + 0.1% of excess over	20,000,000
Over 100,000,000		174,500 + 0.01% of excess over	100,000,000

---

[65] Rules of Arbitration and Conciliation of the International Arbitral Centre of the Austrian Federal Economic Chamber (VIAC), Art 31.
[66] Further details can be obtained from http://portal.wko.at/wk/format_detail.wk?angid =1&stid=323813&dstid=8459#schedule [accessed on 1 September 2010].

APPENDIX

ARBITRATION (SCOTLAND) ACT 2010
2010 asp 1

CONTENTS

SECTION

Introductory

1 Founding principles
2 Key terms
3 Seat of arbitration

Arbitration agreements

4 Arbitration agreement
5 Separability
6 Law governing arbitration agreement

Scottish Arbitration Rules

7 Scottish Arbitration Rules
8 Mandatory rules
9 Default rules

Suspension of legal proceedings

10 Suspension of legal proceedings

Enforcing and challenging arbitral awards etc

11 Arbitral award to be final and binding on parties
12 Enforcement of arbitral awards
13 Court intervention in arbitrations
14 Persons who take no part in arbitral proceedings
15 Anonymity in legal proceedings

Statutory arbitration

16 Statutory arbitration: special provisions
17 Power to adapt enactments providing for statutory arbitration

Recognition and enforcement of New York Convention awards

18 New York Convention awards
19 Recognition and enforcement of New York Convention awards
20 Refusal of recognition or enforcement
21 Evidence to be produced when seeking recognition or enforcement
22 Saving for other bases of recognition or enforcement

Supplementary

23 Prescription and limitation
24 Arbitral appointments referee
25 Power of judge to act as arbitrator or umpire
26 Amendments to UNCITRAL Model Law or Rules or New York Convention
27 Amendment of Conveyancing (Scotland) Act 1924 (c.27)
28 Articles of Regulation 1695
29 Repeals
30 Arbitrability of disputes

Final provisions

31 Interpretation
32 Ancillary provision
33 Orders
34 Crown application
35 Commencement
36 Transitional provisions
37 Short title

Schedule 1—Scottish Arbitration Rules

  Part 1—Commencement and constitution of tribunal etc

  Rule 1   Commencement of arbitration   **D**
  Rule 2   Appointment of tribunal   **D**
  Rule 3   Arbitrator to be an individual   **M**
  Rule 4   Eligibility to act as arbitrator   **M**
  Rule 5   Number of arbitrators   **D**
  Rule 6   Method of appointment   **D**
  Rule 7   Failure of appointment procedure   **M**
  Rule 8   Duty to disclose any conflict of interests   **M**
  Rule 9   Arbitrator's tenure   **D**

Rule 10 Challenge to appointment of arbitrator **D**
Rule 11 Removal of arbitrator by parties **D**
Rule 12 Removal of arbitrator by court **M**
Rule 13 Dismissal of tribunal by court **M**
Rule 14 Removal and dismissal by court: supplementary **M**
Rule 15 Resignation of arbitrator **M**
Rule 16 Liability etc of arbitrator when tenure ends **M**
Rule 17 Reconstitution of tribunal **D**
Rule 18 Arbitrators nominated in arbitration agreements **D**

Part 2—Jurisdiction of tribunal

Rule 19 Power of tribunal to rule on own jurisdiction **M**
Rule 20 Objections to tribunal's jurisdiction **M**
Rule 21 Appeal against tribunal's ruling on jurisdictional objection **M**
Rule 22 Referral of point of jurisdiction **D**
Rule 23 Jurisdiction referral: procedure etc **M**

Part 3—General duties

Rule 24 General duty of the tribunal **M**
Rule 25 General duty of the parties **M**
Rule 26 Confidentiality **D**
Rule 27 Tribunal deliberations **D**

Part 4—Arbitral proceedings

Rule 28 Procedure and evidence **D**
Rule 29 Place of arbitration **D**
Rule 30 Tribunal decisions **D**
Rule 31 Tribunal directions **D**
Rule 32 Power to appoint clerk, agents or employees etc **D**
Rule 33 Party representatives **D**
Rule 34 Experts **D**
Rule 35 Powers relating to property **D**
Rule 36 Oaths or affirmations **D**
Rule 37 Failure to submit claim or defence timeously **D**
Rule 38 Failure to attend hearing or provide evidence **D**
Rule 39 Failure to comply with tribunal direction or arbitration agreement **D**
Rule 40 Consolidation of proceedings **D**

Part 5—Powers of court in relation to arbitral proceedings

Rule 41 Referral of point of law **D**
Rule 42 Point of law referral: procedure etc **M**
Rule 43 Variation of time limits set by parties **D**
Rule 44 Time limit variation: procedure etc **M**

Rule 45   Court's power to order attendance of witnesses and
           disclosure of evidence   **M**
Rule 46   Court's other powers in relation to arbitration   **D**

Part 6—Awards

Rule 47   Rules applicable to the substance of the dispute   **D**
Rule 48   Power to award payment and damages   **M**
Rule 49   Other remedies available to tribunal   **D**
Rule 50   Interest   **M**
Rule 51   Form of award   **D**
Rule 52   Award treated as made in Scotland   **D**
Rule 53   Provisional awards   **D**
Rule 54   Part awards   **M**
Rule 55   Draft awards   **D**
Rule 56   Power to withhold award on non-payment of fees or
           expenses   **M**
Rule 57   Arbitration to end on last award or early settlement   **D**
Rule 58   Correcting an award   **D**

Part 7—Arbitration expenses

Rule 59   Arbitration expenses   **D**
Rule 60   Arbitrators' fees and expenses   **M**
Rule 61   Recoverable arbitration expenses   **D**
Rule 62   Liability for recoverable arbitration expenses   **D**
Rule 63   Ban on pre-dispute agreements about liability for
           arbitration expenses   **M**
Rule 64   Security for expenses   **D**
Rule 65   Limitation of recoverable arbitration expenses   **D**
Rule 66   Awards on recoverable arbitration expenses   **D**

Part 8—Challenging awards

Rule 67   Challenging an award: substantive jurisdiction   **M**
Rule 68   Challenging an award: serious irregularity   **M**
Rule 69   Challenging an award: legal error   **D**
Rule 70   Legal error appeals: procedure etc   **M**
Rule 71   Challenging an award: supplementary   **M**
Rule 72   Reconsideration by tribunal   **M**

Part 9—Miscellaneous

Rule 73   Immunity of tribunal etc   **M**
Rule 74   Immunity of appointing arbitral institution etc   **M**
Rule 75   Immunity of experts, witnesses and legal
           representatives   **M**
Rule 76   Loss of right to object   **M**
Rule 77   Independence of arbitrator   **M**

Rule 78   Consideration where arbitrator judged not to be impartial and independent   **D**
Rule 79   Death of arbitrator   **M**
Rule 80   Death of party   **D**
Rule 81   Unfair treatment   **D**
Rule 82   Rules applicable to umpires   **M**
Rule 83   Formal communications   **D**
Rule 84   Periods of time   **D**

Index

Schedule 2—Repeals

ARBITRATION (SCOTLAND) ACT 2010
2010 asp 1

The Bill for this Act of the Scottish Parliament was passed by the Parliament on 18th November 2009 and received Royal Assent on 5th January 2010

An Act of the Scottish Parliament to make provision about arbitration.

Introductory

1 Founding principles

The founding principles of this Act are—
(a) that the object of arbitration is to resolve disputes fairly, impartially and without unnecessary delay or expense,
(b) that parties should be free to agree how to resolve disputes subject only to such safeguards as are necessary in the public interest,
(c) that the court should not intervene in an arbitration except as provided by this Act.

Anyone construing this Act must have regard to the founding principles when doing so.

2 Key terms

(1) In this Act, unless the contrary intention appears—
"arbitration" includes—
(a) domestic arbitration,
(b) arbitration between parties residing, or carrying on business, anywhere in the United Kingdom, and
(c) international arbitration,
"arbitrator" means a sole arbitrator or a member of a tribunal,
"dispute" includes—
(a) any refusal to accept a claim, and
(b) any other difference (whether contractual or not),
"party" means a party to an arbitration,
"rules" means the Scottish Arbitration Rules (see section 7), and
"tribunal" means a sole arbitrator or panel of arbitrators.

(2) References in this Act to "an arbitration", "the arbitration" or "arbitrations" are references to a particular arbitration process or, as the case may be, to particular arbitration processes.

(3) References in this Act to a tribunal conducting an arbitration are references to the tribunal doing anything in relation to the arbitration, including—
   (a) making a decision about procedure or evidence, and
   (b) making an award.

3   **Seat of arbitration**

(1) An arbitration is "seated in Scotland" if—
   (a) Scotland is designated as the juridical seat of the arbitration—
      (i) by the parties,
      (ii) by any third party to whom the parties give power to so designate, or
      (iii) where the parties fail to designate or so authorise a third party, by the tribunal, or
   (b) in the absence of any such designation, the court determines that Scotland is to be the juridical seat of the arbitration.

(2) The fact that an arbitration is seated in Scotland does not affect the substantive law to be used to decide the dispute.

Arbitration agreements

4   **Arbitration agreement**

An "arbitration agreement" is an agreement to submit a present or future dispute to arbitration (including any agreement which provides for arbitration in accordance with arbitration provisions contained in a separate document).

5   **Separability**

(1) An arbitration agreement which forms (or was intended to form) part only of an agreement is to be treated as a distinct agreement.

(2) An arbitration agreement is not void, voidable or otherwise unenforceable only because the agreement of which it forms part is void, voidable or otherwise unenforceable.

(3) A dispute about the validity of an agreement which includes an arbitration agreement may be arbitrated in accordance with that arbitration agreement.

6   **Law governing arbitration agreement**

Where—
   (a) the parties to an arbitration agreement agree that an arbitration under that agreement is to be seated in Scotland, but

(b) the arbitration agreement does not specify the law which is to govern it, then, unless the parties otherwise agree, the arbitration agreement is to be governed by Scots law.

Scottish Arbitration Rules

7   **Scottish Arbitration Rules**

The Scottish Arbitration Rules set out in schedule 1 are to govern every arbitration seated in Scotland (unless, in the case of a default rule, the parties otherwise agree).

8   **Mandatory rules**

The following rules, called "mandatory rules", cannot be modified or disapplied (by an arbitration agreement, by any other agreement between the parties or by any other means) in relation to any arbitration seated in Scotland—

rule 3 (arbitrator to be an individual)
rule 4 (eligibility to act as an arbitrator)
rule 7 (failure of appointment procedure)
rule 8 (duty to disclose any conflict of interests)
rules 12 to 16 (removal or resignation of arbitrator or dismissal of tribunal)
rules 19 to 21 and 23 (jurisdiction of tribunal)
rules 24 and 25 (general duties of tribunal and parties)
rule 42 (point of law referral: procedure etc)
rule 44 (time limit variation: procedure etc)
rule 45 (securing attendance of witnesses and disclosure of evidence)
rule 48 (power to award payment and damages)
rule 50 (interest)
rule 54 (part awards)
rule 56 (power to withhold award if fees or expenses not paid)
rule 60 (arbitrators' fees and expenses)
rule 63 (ban on pre-dispute agreements about liability for arbitration expenses)
rules 67, 68, 70, 71 and 72 (challenging awards)
rules 73 to 75 (immunity)
rule 76 (loss of right to object)
rule 77 (independence of arbitrator)
rule 79 (death of arbitrator)
rule 82 (rules applicable to umpires)

9 Default rules

(1) The non-mandatory rules are called the "default rules".

(2) A default rule applies in relation to an arbitration seated in Scotland only in so far as the parties have not agreed to modify or disapply that rule (or any part of it) in relation to that arbitration.

(3) Parties may so agree—
   (a) in the arbitration agreement, or
   (b) by any other means at any time before or after the arbitration begins.

(4) Parties are to be treated as having agreed to modify or disapply a default rule—
   (a) if or to the extent that the rule is inconsistent with or disapplied by—
       (i) the arbitration agreement,
       (ii) any arbitration rules or other document (for example, the UNCITRAL Model Law, the UNCITRAL Arbitration Rules or other institutional rules) which the parties agree are to govern the arbitration, or
       (iii) anything done with the agreement of the parties, or
   (b) if they choose a law other than Scots law as the applicable law in respect of the rule's subject matter.

This subsection does not affect the generality of subsections (2) and (3).

Suspension of legal proceedings

10 Suspension of legal proceedings

(1) The court must, on an application by a party to legal proceedings concerning any matter under dispute, sist those proceedings in so far as they concern that matter if—
   (a) an arbitration agreement provides that a dispute on the matter is to be resolved by arbitration (immediately or after the exhaustion of other dispute resolution procedures),
   (b) the applicant is a party to the arbitration agreement (or is claiming through or under such a party),
   (c) notice of the application has been given to the other parties to the legal proceedings,
   (d) the applicant has not—
       (i) taken any step in the legal proceedings to answer any substantive claim against the applicant, or
       (ii) otherwise acted since bringing the legal proceedings in a manner indicating a desire to have the dispute resolved by the legal proceedings rather than byarbitration, and

(e) nothing has caused the court to be satisfied that the arbitration agreement concerned is void, inoperative or incapable of being performed.

(2) Any provision in an arbitration agreement which prevents the bringing of the legal proceedings is void in relation to any proceedings which the court refuses to sist.

This subsection does not apply to statutory arbitrations.

(3) This section applies regardless of whether the arbitration concerned is to be seated in Scotland.

Enforcing and challenging arbitral awards etc

11 Arbitral award to be final and binding on parties

(1) A tribunal's award is final and binding on the parties and any person claiming through or under them (but does not of itself bind any third party).

(2) In particular, an award ordering the rectification or reduction of a deed or other document is of no effect in so far as it would adversely affect the interests of any third party acting in good faith.

(3) This section does not affect the right of any person to challenge the award—
(a) under Part 8 of the Scottish Arbitration Rules, or
(b) by any available arbitral process of appeal or review.

(4) This section does not apply in relation to a provisional award (see rule 53), such an award not being final and being binding only—
(a) to the extent specified in the award, or
(b) until it is superseded by a subsequent award.

12 Enforcement of arbitral awards

(1) The court may, on an application by any party, order that a tribunal's award may be enforced as if it were an extract registered decree bearing a warrant for execution granted by the court.

(2) No such order may be made if the court is satisfied that the award is the subject of—
(a) an appeal under Part 8 of the Scottish Arbitration Rules,
(b) an arbitral process of appeal or review, or
(c) a process of correction under rule 58 of the Scottish Arbitration Rules, which has not been finally determined.

(3) No such order may be made if the court is satisfied that the tribunal which made the award did not have jurisdiction to do so (and the court may restrict the extent of its order if satisfied that the tribunal did not have jurisdiction to make a part of the award).

(4) But a party may not object on the ground that the tribunal did not have jurisdiction if the party has lost the right to raise that objection by virtue of the Scottish Arbitration Rules (see rule 76).

(5) Unless the parties otherwise agree, a tribunal's award may be registered for execution in the Books of Council and Session or in the sheriff court books (provided that the arbitration agreement is itself so registered).

(6) This section applies regardless of whether the arbitration concerned was seated in Scotland.

(7) Nothing in this section or in section 13 affects any other right to rely on or enforce an award in pursuance of—
   (a) sections 19 to 21, or
   (b) any other enactment or rule of law.

(8) In this section, "court" means the sheriff or the Court of Session.

13   Court intervention in arbitrations

(1) Legal proceedings are competent in respect of—
   (a) a tribunal's award, or
   (b) any other act or omission by a tribunal when conducting an arbitration,
   only as provided for in the Scottish Arbitration Rules (in so far as they apply to that arbitration) or in any other provision of this Act.

(2) In particular, a tribunal's award is not subject to review or appeal in any legal proceedings except as provided for in Part 8 of the Scottish Arbitration Rules.

(3) It is not competent for a party to raise the question of a tribunal's jurisdiction with the court except—
   (a) where objecting to an order being made under section 12, or
   (b) as provided for in the Scottish Arbitration Rules (see rules 21, 22 and 67).

(4) Where the parties agree that the UNCITRAL Model Law is to apply to an arbitration, articles 6 and 11(2) to (5) of that Law are to have the force of law in Scotland in relation to that arbitration (as if article 6 specified the Court of Session and any sheriff court having jurisdiction).

14   Persons who take no part in arbitral proceedings

(1) A person alleged to be a party to an arbitration but who takes no part in the arbitration may, by court proceedings, question—
   (a) whether there is a valid arbitration agreement (or, in the case of a statutory arbitration, whether the enactment providing for arbitration applies to the dispute),

(b) whether the tribunal is properly constituted, or
(c) what matters have been submitted to arbitration in accordance with the arbitration agreement, and the court may determine such a question by making such declaration, or by granting such interdict or other remedy, as it thinks appropriate.

(2) Such a person has the same right as a party who participates in the arbitration to appeal against any award made in the arbitration under rule 67 or 68 (jurisdictional and serious irregularity appeals) and rule 71(2) does not apply to such an appeal.

15   Anonymity in legal proceedings

(1) A party to any civil proceedings relating to an arbitration (other than proceedings under section 12) may apply to the court for an order prohibiting the disclosure of the identity of a party to the arbitration in any report of the proceedings.

(2) On such an application, the court must grant the order unless satisfied that disclosure—
   (a) is required—
      (i) for the proper performance of the discloser's public functions, or
      (ii) in order to enable any public body or office-holder to perform public functions properly,
   (b) can reasonably be considered as being needed to protect a party's lawful interests,
   (c) would be in the public interest, or
   (d) would be necessary in the interests of justice.

(3) The court's determination of an application for an order is final.

Statutory arbitration

16   Statutory arbitration: special provisions

(1) "Statutory arbitration" is arbitration pursuant to an enactment which provides for a dispute to be submitted to arbitration.

(2) References in the Scottish Arbitration Rules (or in any other provision of this Act) to an arbitration agreement are, in the case of a statutory arbitration, references to the enactment which provides for a dispute to be resolved by arbitration.

(3) None of the Scottish Arbitration Rules (or other provisions of this Act) apply to a statutory arbitration if or to the extent that they are excluded by, or are inconsistent with, any provision made by virtue of any other enactment relating to the arbitration.

(4) Every statutory arbitration is to be taken to be seated in Scotland.

(5) The following rules do not apply in relation to statutory arbitration—

rule 43 (extension of time limits)
rule 71(9) (power to declare provision of arbitration agreement void)
rule 80 (death of party)

(6) Despite rule 40, parties to a statutory arbitration may not agree to—
   (a) consolidate the arbitration with another arbitration,
   (b) hold concurrent hearings, or
   (c) authorise the tribunal to order such consolidation or the holding of concurrent hearings,
   unless the arbitrations or hearings are to be conducted under the same enactment.

17 Power to adapt enactments providing for statutory arbitration

Ministers may by order—
(a) modify any of the Scottish Arbitration Rules, or any other provisions of this Act, in so far as they apply to statutory arbitrations (or to particular statutory arbitrations),
(b) make such modifications of enactments which provide for disputes to be submitted to arbitration as they consider appropriate in consequence of, or in order to give full effect to, any of the Scottish Arbitration Rules or any other provisions of this Act.

Recognition and enforcement of New York Convention awards

18 New York Convention awards

(1) A "Convention award" is an award made in pursuance of a written arbitration agreement in the territory of a state (other than the United Kingdom) which is a party to the New York Convention.

(2) An award is to be treated for the purposes of this section as having been made at the seat of the arbitration.

(3) A declaration by Her Majesty by Order in Council that a state is a party to the Convention (or is a party in respect of any territory) is conclusive evidence of that fact.

19 Recognition and enforcement of New York Convention awards

(1) A Convention award is to be recognised as binding on the persons as between whom it was made (and may accordingly be relied on by those persons in any legal proceedings in Scotland).

(2) The court may order that a Convention award may be enforced as if it were an extract registered decree bearing a warrant for execution granted by the court.

20   Refusal of recognition or enforcement

(1) Recognition or enforcement of a Convention award may be refused only in accordance with this section.

(2) Recognition or enforcement of a Convention award may be refused if the person against whom it is invoked proves—
   (a) that a party was under some incapacity under the law applicable to the party,
   (b) that the arbitration agreement was invalid under the law which the parties agree should govern it (or, failing any indication of that law, under the law of the country where the award was made),
   (c) that the person—
      (i) was not given proper notice of the arbitral process or of the appointment of the tribunal, or
      (ii) was otherwise unable to present the person's case,
   (d) that the tribunal was constituted, or the arbitration was conducted, otherwise than in accordance with—
      (i) the agreement of the parties, or
      (ii) failing such agreement, the law of the country where the arbitration took place.

(3) Recognition or enforcement of a Convention award may also be refused if the person against whom it is invoked proves that the award—
   (a) deals with a dispute not contemplated by or not falling within the submission to arbitration,
   (b) contains decisions on matters beyond the scope of that submission,
   (c) is not yet binding on the person, or
   (d) has been set aside or suspended by a competent authority.

(4) Recognition or enforcement of a Convention award may also be refused if—
   (a) the award relates to a matter which is not capable of being settled by arbitration, or
   (b) to do so would be contrary to public policy.

(5) A Convention award containing decisions on matters not submitted to arbitration may be recognised or enforced to the extent that it contains decisions on matters which were so submitted which are separable from decisions on matters not so submitted.

(6) The court before which a Convention award is sought to be relied on may, if an application for the setting aside or suspension of the award is made to a competent authority—
   (a) sist the decision on recognition or enforcement of the award,
   (b) on the application of the party claiming recognition or enforcement, order the other party to give suitable security.
(7) In this section "competent authority" means a person who has authority to set aside or suspend the Convention award concerned in the country in which (or under the law of which) the Convention award concerned was made.

21 Evidence to be produced when seeking recognition or enforcement

(1) A person seeking recognition or enforcement of a Convention award must produce—
   (a) the duly authenticated original award (or a duly certified copy of it), and
   (b) the original arbitration agreement (or a duly certified copy of it).
(2) Such a person must also produce a translation of any award or agreement which is in a language other than English (certified by an official or sworn translator or by a diplomatic or consular agent).

22 Saving for other bases of recognition or enforcement

Nothing in sections 19 to 21 affects any other right to rely on or enforce a Convention award in pursuance of any other enactment or rule of law.

Supplementary

23 Prescription and limitation

(1) The Prescription and Limitation (Scotland) Act 1973 (c.52) is amended as follows.
(2) In section 4 (positive prescription: interruption)—
   (a) in subsection (2)(b), after "Scotland" insert "in respect of which an arbitrator (or panel of arbitrators) has been appointed",
   (b) in subsection (3)(a), for the words from "and" to "served" substitute ", the date when the arbitration begins",
   (c) for subsection (4) substitute—
   "(4) An arbitration begins for the purposes of this section—
      (a) when the parties to the arbitration agree that it begins, or

(b) in the absence of such agreement, in accordance with rule 1 of the Scottish Arbitration Rules (see section 7 of, and schedule 1 to, the Arbitration (Scotland) Act 2010 (asp 1)).".

(3) In section 9 (negative prescription: interruption)—
   (a) in subsection (3), for the words from "and" to "served" substitute "the date when the arbitration begins",
   (b) in subsection (4), for "preliminary notice" substitute "the date when the arbitration begins".

(4) After section 19C, insert—

"**19D Interruption of limitation period: arbitration**

(1) Any period during which an arbitration is ongoing in relation to a matter is to be disregarded in any computation of the period specified in section 17(2), 18(2), 18A(1) or 18B(2) of this Act in relation to that matter.

(2) In this section, "arbitration" means—
   (a) any arbitration in Scotland,
   (b) any arbitration in a country other than Scotland, being an arbitration an award in which would be enforceable in Scotland.".

(5) In section 22A(4), for the words from "and" to "served" substitute "the date when the arbitration begins (within the meaning of section 4(4) of this Act)".

(6) After section 22C, insert—

"**22CA Interruption of limitation period for 1987 Act actions: arbitration**

(1) Any period during which an arbitration is ongoing in relation to a matter is to be disregarded in any computation of the period specified in section 22B(2) or 22C(2) of this Act in relation to that matter.

(2) In this section, "arbitration" means—
   (a) any arbitration in Scotland,
   (b) any arbitration in a country other than Scotland, being an arbitration an award in which would be enforceable in Scotland.".

24 Arbitral appointments referee

(1) Ministers may, by order, authorise persons or types of person who may act as an arbitral appointments referee for the purposes of the Scottish Arbitration Rules.

(2) Ministers must, when making such an order, have regard to the desirability of ensuring that arbitral appointments referees—
   (a) have experience relevant to making arbitral appointments, and

(b) are able to provide training, and to operate disciplinary procedures, designed to ensure that arbitrators conduct themselves appropriately.

(3) Despite subsection (2)(b), an arbitral appointments referee is not obliged to appoint arbitrators in respect of whom the referee provides training or operates disciplinary procedures.

25 **Power of judge to act as arbitrator or umpire**

(1) A judge may act as an arbitrator or umpire only where—
   (a) the dispute being arbitrated appears to the judge to be of commercial character, and
   (b) the Lord President, having considered the state of Court of Session business, has authorised the judge to so act.

(2) A fee of such amount as Ministers may by order prescribe is payable in the Court of Session for the services of a judge acting as an arbitrator or umpire.

(3) Any jurisdiction exercisable by the Outer House under the Scottish Arbitration Rules (or any other provision of this Act) in relation to—
   (a) a judge acting as a sole arbitrator or umpire, or
   (b) a tribunal which the judge forms part of,
   is to be exercisable instead by the Inner House (and the Inner House's decision on any matter is final).

(4) In this section—
   "judge" means a judge of the Court of Session, and
   "Lord President" means the Lord President of the Court of Session.

26 **Amendments to UNCITRAL Model Law or Rules or New York Convention**

(1) Ministers may by order modify—
   (a) the Scottish Arbitration Rules,
   (b) any other provision of this Act, or
   (c) any enactment which provides for disputes to be resolved by arbitration,
   in such manner as they consider appropriate in consequence of any amendment made to the UNCITRAL Model Law, the UNCITRAL Arbitration Rules or the New York Convention.

(2) Before making such an order, Ministers must consult such persons appearing to them to have an interest in the law of arbitration as they think fit.

27 Amendment of Conveyancing (Scotland) Act 1924 (c.27)

In section 46 of the Conveyancing (Scotland) Act 1924—
(a) in subsection (2), for "This section" substitute "Subsection (1)", and
(b) after subsection (2) insert—
"(3) Where—
    (a) an arbitral award orders the reduction of a deed or other document recorded in the Register of Sasines (or forming a midcouple or link of title in a title recorded in that Register), and
    (b) the court orders that the award may be enforced in accordance with section 12 of the Arbitration (Scotland) Act 2010 (asp 1),
subsection (1) applies to the arbitral award as it applies to a decree of reduction of a deed recorded in the Register of Sasines.".

28 Articles of Regulation 1695

The 25th Act of the Articles of Regulation 1695 does not apply in relation to arbitration.

29 Repeals

The repeals of the enactments specified in column 1 of schedule 2 have effect to the extent specified in column 2.

30 Arbitrability of disputes

Nothing in this Act makes any dispute capable of being arbitrated if, because of its subject-matter, it would not otherwise be capable of being arbitrated.

Final provisions

31 Interpretation

(1) In this Act, unless the contrary intention appears—

"arbitral appointments referee" means a person authorised under section 24,

"arbitration" has the meaning given by section 2,

"arbitration agreement" has the meaning given by section 4,

"arbitrator" has the meaning given by section 2,

"claim" includes counterclaim,

"Convention award" has the meaning given by section 18,

"court" means the Outer House or the sheriff (except in sections 1, 3, 10, 13 and 15, where it means any court), "default rule" has the meaning given by section 9(1),

"dispute" has the meaning given by section 2,

"Inner House" means the Inner House of the Court of Session,

"mandatory rule" has the meaning given by section 8,

"Ministers" means the Scottish Ministers,

"New York Convention" means the Convention on the Recognition and

Enforcement of Foreign Arbitral Awards adopted by the United Nations

Conference on International Commercial Arbitration on 10 June 1958,

"Outer House" means the Outer House of the Court of Session,

"party" is to be construed in accordance with section 2 and subsection (2) below,

"rule" means one of the Scottish Arbitration Rules,

"Scottish Arbitration Rules" means the rules set out in schedule 1,

"seated in Scotland" has the meaning given by section 3,

"statutory arbitration" has the meaning given by section 16(1),

"tribunal" has the meaning given by section 2,

"UNCITRAL Arbitration Rules" means the arbitration rules adopted by

UNCITRAL on 28 April 1976, and

"UNCITRAL Model Law" means the UNCITRAL Model Law on International Commercial Arbitration as adopted by the United Nations Commission on International Trade Law on 21 June 1985 (as amended in 2006).

(2) This Act applies in relation to arbitrations and disputes between three or more parties as it applies in relation to arbitrations and disputes between two parties (with references to both parties being read in such cases as references to all the parties).

32 Ancillary provision

(1) Ministers may by order make any supplementary, incidental, consequential, transitional, transitory or saving provision which they consider appropriate for the purposes of, or in connection with, or for the purposes of giving full effect to, any provision of this Act.

(2) Such an order may modify any enactment, instrument or document.

33 Orders

(1) Any power of Ministers to make orders under this Act—
   (a) is exercisable by statutory instrument, and
   (b) includes power to make—
      (i) any supplementary, incidental, consequential, transitional, transitory or saving provision which Ministers consider appropriate,
      (ii) different provision for different purposes.
(2) A statutory instrument containing such an order (or an Order in Council made under section 18) is subject to annulment in pursuance of a resolution of the Scottish Parliament.
This subsection does not apply—
   (a) to orders made under section 35(2) (commencement orders), or
   (b) where subsection (3) makes contrary provision.
(3) An order—
   (a) under section 17 or 32 which adds to, replaces or omits any text in this or any other Act,
   (b) under section 26, or
   (c) under section 36(4),
may be made only if a draft of the statutory instrument containing the order has been laid before, and approved by resolution of, the Scottish Parliament.

34 Crown application

(1) This Act binds the Crown.
(2) Her Majesty may be represented in any arbitration to which she is a party otherwise than in right of the Crown by such person as she may appoint in writing under the Royal Sign Manual.
(3) The Prince and Steward of Scotland may be represented in any arbitration to which he is a party by such person as he may appoint.
(4) References in this Act to a party to an arbitration are, where subsection (2) or (3) applies, to be read as references to the appointed representative.

35 Commencement

(1) The following provisions come into force on Royal Assent—
   section 2
   sections 31 to 34

this section
section 37
(2) Other provisions come into force on the day Ministers by order appoint.

36 **Transitional provisions**
(1) This Act does not apply to an arbitration begun before commencement.
(2) This Act otherwise applies to an arbitration agreement whether made on, before or after commencement.
(3) Despite subsection (2), this Act does not apply to an arbitration arising under an arbitration agreement (other than an enactment) made before commencement if the parties agree that this Act is not to apply to that arbitration.
(4) Ministers may by order specify any day falling at least 5 years after commencement as the day on which subsection (3) is to cease to have effect.
(5) Before making such an order, Ministers must consult such persons appearing to them to have an interest in the law of arbitration as they think fit.
(6) Any reference to an arbiter in an arbitration agreement made before commencement is to be treated as being a reference to an arbitrator.
(7) Any reference in an enactment to a decree arbitral is to be treated for the purposes of section 12 as being a reference to a tribunal's award.
(8) An express provision in an arbitration agreement made before commencement which disapplies section 3 of the Administration of Justice (Scotland) Act 1972 (c.59) in relation to an arbitration arising under that agreement is, unless the parties otherwise agree, to be treated as being an agreement to disapply rules 41 and 69 in relation to such an arbitration.
(9) In this section, "commencement" means the day on which this section comes into force.

37 **Short title**
This Act is called the Arbitration (Scotland) Act 2010.

SCHEDULE 1
(introduced by section 7)

SCOTTISH ARBITRATION RULES

Mandatory rules are marked "**M**".
Default rules are marked "**D**".

PART 1
COMMENCEMENT AND CONSTITUTION OF TRIBUNAL ETC.

Rule 1   *Commence of arbitration*   **D**

1   An arbitration begins when a party to an arbitration agreement (or any person claiming through or under such a party) gives the other party notice submitting a dispute to arbitration in accordance with the agreement.

Rule 2   *Appointment of tribunal*   **D**

2   An arbitration agreement need not appoint (or provide for appointment of) the tribunal, but if it does so provide it may—
 (a) specify who is to form the tribunal,
 (b) require the parties to appoint the tribunal,
 (c) permit another person to appoint the tribunal, or
 (d) provide for the tribunal to be appointed in any other way.

Rule 3   *Arbitrator to be an individual*   **M**

3   Only an individual may act as an arbitrator.

Rule 4   *Eligibility to act as arbitrator*   **M**

4   An individual is ineligible to act as an arbitrator if the individual is—
 (a) aged under 16, or
 (b) an incapable adult (within the meaning of section 1(6) of the Adults with Incapacity (Scotland) Act 2000 (asp 4)).

Rule 5   *Number of arbitrators*   **D**

5   Where there is no agreement as to the number of arbitrators, the tribunal is to consist of a sole arbitrator.

Rule 6   *Method of appointment*   **D**

6   The tribunal is to be appointed as follows—
 (a) where there is to be a sole arbitrator, the parties must appoint an eligible individual jointly (and must do so within 28 days of either party requesting the other to do so),

(b) where there is to be a tribunal consisting of two or more arbitrators—
  (i) each party must appoint an eligible individual as an arbitrator (and must do so within 28 days of the other party requesting it to do so), and
  (ii) where more arbitrators are to be appointed, the arbitrators appointed by the parties must appoint eligible individuals as the remaining arbitrators.

Rule 7   *Failure of appointment procedure*   **M**

7(1)   This rule applies where a tribunal (or any arbitrator who is to form part of a tribunal) is not, or cannot be, appointed in accordance with—
  (a) any appointment procedure set out in the arbitration agreement (or otherwise agreed between the parties), or
  (b) rule 6.

(2)   Unless the parties otherwise agree, either party may refer the matter to an arbitral appointments referee.

(3)   The referring party must give notice of the reference to the other party.

(4)   That other party may object to the reference within 7 days of notice of reference being given by making an objection to—
  (a) the referring party, and
  (b) the arbitral appointments referee.

(5)   If—
  (a) no such objection is made within that 7-day period, or
  (b) the other party waives the right to object before the end of that period,
  the arbitral appointments referee may make the necessary appointment.

(6)   Where—
  (a) a party objects to the arbitral appointments referee making an appointment,
  (b) an arbitral appointments referee fails to make an appointment within 21 days of the matter being referred, or
  (c) the parties agree not to refer the matter to an arbitral appointments referee, the court may, on an application by any party, make the necessary appointment.

(7)   The court's decision on whom to appoint is final.

(8)   Before making an appointment under this rule, the arbitral appointments referee or, as the case may be, the court must have regard to—
  (a) the nature and subject-matter of the dispute,

  (b) the terms of the arbitration agreement (including, in particular, any terms relating to appointment of arbitrators), and

  (c) the skills, qualifications, knowledge and experience which would make an individual suitable to determine the dispute.

(9) Where an arbitral appointments referee or the court makes an appointment under this rule, the arbitration agreement has effect as if it required that appointment.

Rule 8 *Duty to disclose any conflict of interests* **M**

8(1) This rule applies to—

  (a) arbitrators, and

  (b) individuals who have been asked to be an arbitrator but who have not yet been appointed.

(2) An individual to whom this rule applies must, without delay disclose—

  (a) to the parties, and

  (b) in the case of an individual not yet appointed as an arbitrator, to any arbitral appointments referee, other third party or court considering whether to appoint the individual as an arbitrator,

any circumstances known to the individual (or which become known to the individual before the arbitration ends) which might reasonably be considered relevant when considering whether the individual is impartial and independent.

Rule 9 *Arbitrator's tenure* **D**

9 An arbitrator's tenure ends if—

  (a) the arbitrator becomes ineligible to act as an arbitrator (see rule 4),

  (b) the tribunal revokes the arbitrator's appointment (see rule 10),

  (c) the arbitrator is removed by the parties, a third party or the Outer House (see rules 11 and 12),

  (d) the Outer House dismisses the tribunal of which the arbitrator forms part (see rule 13), or

  (e) the arbitrator resigns (see rule 15) or dies (see rule 79).

Rule 10 *Challenge to appointment of arbitrator* **D**

10(1) A party may object to the tribunal about the appointment of an arbitrator.

(2)   An objection is competent only if—
  (a) it is made on the ground that the arbitrator—
    (i) is not impartial and independent,
    (ii) has not treated the parties fairly, or
    (iii) does not have a qualification which the parties agreed (before the arbitrator's appointment) that the arbitrator must have,
  (b) it states the facts on which it is based,
  (c) it is made within 14 days of the objector becoming aware of those facts, and
  (d) notice of it is given to the other party.
(3)   The tribunal may deal with an objection by confirming or revoking the appointment.
(4)   If the tribunal fails to make a decision within 14 days of a competent objection being made, the appointment is revoked.

Rule 11   *Removal of arbitrator by parties*   **D**

11(1)   An arbitrator may be removed—
  (a) by the parties acting jointly, or
  (b) by any third party to whom the parties give power to remove an arbitrator.
(2)   A removal is effected by notifying the arbitrator.

Rule 12   *Removal of arbitrator by court*   **M**

12   The Outer House may remove an arbitrator if satisfied on the application by any party—
  (a) that the arbitrator is not impartial and independent,
  (b) that the arbitrator has not treated the parties fairly,
  (c) that the arbitrator is incapable of acting as an arbitrator in the arbitration (or that there are justifiable doubts about the arbitrator's ability to so act),
  (d) that the arbitrator does not have a qualification which the parties agreed (before the arbitrator's appointment) that the arbitrator must have,
  (e) that substantial injustice has been or will be caused to that party because the arbitrator has failed to conduct the arbitration in accordance with—
    (i) the arbitration agreement,
    (ii) these rules (in so far as they apply), or
    (iii) any other agreement by the parties relating to conduct of the arbitration.

Rule 13 *Dismissal of tribunal by court* **M**

13 The Outer House may dismiss the tribunal if satisfied on the application by a party that substantial injustice has been or will be caused to that party because the tribunal has failed to conduct the arbitration in accordance with—
(a) the arbitration agreement,
(b) these rules (in so far as they apply), or
(c) any other agreement by the parties relating to conduct of the arbitration.

Rule 14 *Removal and dismissal by court: supplementary* **M**

14(1) The Outer House may remove an arbitrator, or dismiss the tribunal, only if—
(a) the arbitrator or, as the case may be, tribunal has been—
  (i) notified of the application for removal or dismissal, and
  (ii) given the opportunity to make representations, and
(b) the Outer House is satisfied—
  (i) that any recourse available under rule 10 has been exhausted, and
  (ii) that any available recourse to a third party who the parties have agreed is to have power to remove an arbitrator (or dismiss the tribunal) has been exhausted.

(2) A decision of the Outer House under rule 12 or 13 is final.

(3) The tribunal may continue with the arbitration pending the Outer House's decision under rule 12 or 13.

Rule 15 *Resignation of arbitrator* **M**

15(1) An arbitrator may resign (by giving notice of resignation to the parties and any other arbitrators) if—
(a) the parties consent to the resignation,
(b) the arbitrator has a contractual right to resign in the circumstances,
(c) the arbitrator's appointment is challenged under rule 10 or 12,
(d) the parties disapply or modify rule 34(1) (expert opinions) after the arbitrator is appointed, or
(e) the Outer House has authorised the resignation.

(2) The Outer House may authorise a resignation only if satisfied, on an application by the arbitrator, that it is reasonable for the arbitrator to resign.

(3) The Outer House's determination of an application for resignation is final.

Rule 16   Liability etc of arbitrator when tenure ends   **M**

16(1)   Where an arbitrator's tenure ends, the Outer House may, on an application by any party or the arbitrator concerned, make such order as it thinks fit—
  (a) about the arbitrator's entitlement (if any) to fees and expenses,
  (b) about the repaying of fees or expenses already paid to the arbitrator,
  (c) where the arbitrator has resigned, about the arbitrator's liability in respect of acting as an arbitrator.

(2)   The Outer House must, when considering whether to make an order in relation to an arbitrator who has resigned, have particular regard to whether the resignation was made in accordance with rule 15.

(3)   The Outer House's determination of an application for an order is final.

Rule 17   Reconstitution of tribunal   **D**

17(1)   Where an arbitrator's tenure ends, the tribunal must be reconstituted—
  (a) in accordance with the procedure used to constitute the original tribunal, or
  (b) where that procedure fails, in accordance with rules 6 and 7.

(2)   It is for the reconstituted tribunal to decide the extent, if any, to which previous proceedings (including any award made, appointment by or other act done by the previous tribunal) should stand.

(3)   The reconstituted tribunal's decision does not affect a party's right to object or appeal on any ground which arose before the tribunal made its decision.

Rule 18   Arbitrators nominated in arbitration agreements   **D**

18   Any provision in an arbitration agreement which specifies who is to be an arbitrator ceases to have effect in relation to an arbitration when the specified individual's tenure as an arbitrator for that arbitration ends.

PART 2
JURISDICTION OF TRIBUNAL

Rule 19   Power of tribunal to rule on own jurisdiction   **M**

19   The tribunal may rule on—

(a) whether there is a valid arbitration agreement (or, in the case of a statutory arbitration, whether the enactment providing for arbitration applies to the dispute),
(b) whether the tribunal is properly constituted, and
(c) what matters have been submitted to arbitration in accordance with the arbitration agreement.

Rule 20   Objections to tribunal's jurisdiction   **M**

20(1)   Any party may object to the tribunal on the ground that the tribunal does not have, or has exceeded, its jurisdiction in relation to any matter.

(2)   An objection must be made—
(a) before, or as soon as is reasonably practicable after, the matter to which the objection relates is first raised in the arbitration, or
(b) where the tribunal considers that circumstances justify a later objection, by such later time as it may allow,
but, in any case, an objection may not be made after the tribunal makes its last award.

(3)   If the tribunal upholds an objection it must—
(a) end the arbitration in so far as it relates to a matter over which the tribunal has ruled it does not have jurisdiction, and
(b) set aside any provisional or part award already made in so far as the award relates to such a matter.

(4)   The tribunal may—
(a) rule on an objection independently from dealing with the subject-matter of the dispute, or
(b) delay ruling on an objection until it makes its award on the merits of the dispute (and include its ruling in that award),
but, where the parties agree which of these courses the tribunal should take, the tribunal must proceed accordingly.

Rule 21   Appeal against tribunal's ruling on jurisdictional objection   **M**

21(1)   A party may, no later than 14 days after the tribunal's decision on an objection under rule 20, appeal to the Outer House against the decision.

(2)   The tribunal may continue with the arbitration pending determination of the appeal.

(3)   The Outer House's decision on the appeal is final.

Rule 22   Referral of point of jurisdiction   **D**

22   The Outer House may, on an application by any party, determine any question as to the tribunal's jurisdiction.

Rule 23 Jurisdiction referral: procedure etc **M**

23(1)   This rule applies only where an application is made under rule 22.

(2)   Such an application is valid only if—
(a) the parties have agreed that it may be made, or
(b) the tribunal has consented to it being made and the court is satisfied—
   (i) that determining the question is likely to produce substantial savings in expenses,
   (ii) that the application was made without delay, and
   (iii) that there is a good reason why the question should be determined by the court.

(3)   The tribunal may continue with the arbitration pending determination of an application.

(4)   The Outer House's determination of the question is final (as is any decision by the Outer House as to whether an application is valid).

PART 3
GENERAL DUTIES

Rule 24 General duty of the tribunal **M**

24(1)   The tribunal must—
(a) be impartial and independent,
(b) treat the parties fairly, and
(c) conduct the arbitration—
   (i) without unnecessary delay, and
   (ii) without incurring unnecessary expense.

(2)   Treating the parties fairly includes giving each party a reasonable opportunity to put its case and to deal with the other party's case.

Rule 25 General duty of the parties **M**

25   The parties must ensure that the arbitration is conducted—
(a) without unnecessary delay, and
(b) without incurring unnecessary expense.

Rule 26 Confidentiality **D**

26(1)   Disclosure by the tribunal, any arbitrator or a party of confidential information relating to the arbitration is to be actionable as a breach of an obligation of confidence unless the disclosure—
(a) is authorised, expressly or impliedly, by the parties (or can reasonably be considered as having been so authorised),

(b) is required by the tribunal or is otherwise made to assist or enable the tribunal to conduct the arbitration,
(c) is required—
   (i) in order to comply with any enactment or rule of law,
   (ii) for the proper performance of the discloser's public functions, or
   (iii) in order to enable any public body or office-holder to perform public functions properly,
(d) can reasonably be considered as being needed to protect a party's lawful interests,
(e) is in the public interest,
(f) is necessary in the interests of justice, or
(g) is made in circumstances in which the discloser would have absolute privilege had the disclosed information been defamatory.

(2) The tribunal and the parties must take reasonable steps to prevent unauthorised disclosure of confidential information by any third party involved in the conduct of the arbitration.

(3) The tribunal must, at the outset of the arbitration, inform the parties of the obligations which this rule imposes on them.

(4) "Confidential information", in relation to an arbitration, means any information relating to—
(a) the dispute,
(b) the arbitral proceedings,
(c) the award, or
(d) any civil proceedings relating to the arbitration in respect of which an order has been granted under section 15 of this Act,
which is not, and has never been, in the public domain.

Rule 27 *Tribunal deliberations* **D**

27(1) The tribunal's deliberations may be undertaken in private and accordingly need not be disclosed to the parties.

(2) But, where an arbitrator fails to participate in any of the tribunal's deliberations, the tribunal must disclose that fact (and the extent of the failure) to the parties.

PART 4
ARBITRAL PROCEEDINGS

Rule 28 *Procedure and evidence* **D**

28(1) It is for the tribunal to determine—
(a) the procedure to be followed in the arbitration, and

(b) the admissibility, relevance, materiality and weight of any evidence.

(2) In particular, the tribunal may determine—
(a) when and where the arbitration is to be conducted,
(b) whether parties are to submit claims or defences and, if so, when they should do so and the extent to which claims or defences may be amended,
(c) whether any documents or other evidence should be disclosed by or to any party and, if so, when such disclosures are to be made and to whom copies of disclosed documents and information are to be given,
(d) whether any and, if so, what questions are to be put to and answered by the parties,
(e) whether and, if so, to what extent the tribunal should take the initiative in ascertaining the facts and the law,
(f) the extent to which the arbitration is to proceed by way of—
  (i) hearings for the questioning of parties,
  (ii) written or oral argument,
  (iii) presentation or inspection of documents or other evidence, or
  (iv) submission of documents or other evidence,
(g) the language to be used in the arbitration (and whether a party is to supply translations of any document or other evidence),
(h) whether to apply rules of evidence used in legal proceedings or any other rules of evidence.

Rule 29 *Place of arbitration* **D**

29 The tribunal may meet, and otherwise conduct the arbitration, anywhere it chooses (in or outwith Scotland).

Rule 30 *Tribunal decisions* **D**

30(1) Where the tribunal is unable to make a decision unanimously (including any decision on an award), a decision made by the majority of the arbitrators is sufficient.

(2) Where there is neither unanimity nor a majority in favour of or opposed to making any decision—
(a) the decision is to be made by the arbitrator nominated to chair the tribunal, or
(b) where no person has been so nominated, the decision is to be made—

(i) where the tribunal consists of 3 or more arbitrators, by the last arbitrator to be appointed, or
(ii) where the tribunal consists of 2 arbitrators, by an umpire appointed by the tribunal or, where the tribunal fails to make an appointment within 14 days of being requested to do so by either party or any arbitrator, by an arbitral appointments referee (at the request of a party or an arbitrator).

Rule 31   Tribunal directions   **D**

31(1)   The tribunal may give such directions to the parties as it considers appropriate for the purposes of conducting the arbitration.

(2)   A party must comply with such a direction by such time as the tribunal specifies.

Rule 32   Power to appoint clerk, agents or employees etc   **D**

32(1)   The tribunal may appoint a clerk (and such other agents, employees or other persons as it thinks fit) to assist it in conducting the arbitration.

(2)   But the parties' consent is required for any appointment in respect of which significant expenses are likely to arise.

Rule 33   Party representatives   **D**

33(1)   A party may be represented in the arbitration by a lawyer or any other person.

(2)   But the party must, before representation begins, give notice of the representative—
(a) to the tribunal, and
(b) to the other party.

Rule 34   Experts   **D**

34(1)   The tribunal may obtain an expert opinion on any matter arising in the arbitration.

(2)   The parties must be given a reasonable opportunity—
(a) to make representations about any written expert opinion, and
(b) to hear any oral expert opinion and to ask questions of the expert giving it.

Rule 35   Powers relating to property   **D**

35   The tribunal may direct a party—
(a) to allow the tribunal, an expert or another party—

              (i) to inspect, photograph, preserve or take custody of any property which that party owns or possesses which is the subject of the arbitration (or as to which any question arises in the arbitration), or
              (ii) to take samples from, or conduct an experiment on, any such property, or
        (b) to preserve any document or other evidence which the party possesses or controls.

Rule 36   Oaths or affirmations   **D**

36   The tribunal may—
          (a) direct that a party or witness is to be examined on oath or affirmation, and
          (b) administer an oath or affirmation for that purpose.

Rule 37   Failure to submit claim or defence timeously   **D**

37(1)   Where—
          (a) a party unnecessarily delays in submitting or in otherwise pursuing a claim,
          (b) the tribunal considers that there is no good reason for the delay, and
          (c) the tribunal is satisfied that the delay—
              (i) gives, or is likely to give, rise to a substantial risk that it will not be possible to resolve the issues in that claim fairly, or
              (ii) has caused, or is likely to cause, serious prejudice to the other party,
          the tribunal must end the arbitration in so far as it relates to the subject-matter of the claim and may make such award (including an award on expenses) as it considers appropriate in consequence of the claim.
    (2)   Where—
          (a) a party unnecessarily delays in submitting a defence to the tribunal, and
          (b) the tribunal considers that there is no good reason for the delay,
          the tribunal must proceed with the arbitration (but the delay is not, in itself, to be treated as an admission of anything).

Rule 38   Failure to attend hearing or provide evidence   **D**

38   Where—
          (a) a party fails—

(i) to attend a hearing which the tribunal requested the party to attend a reasonable period in advance of the hearing, or
(ii) to produce any document or other evidence requested by the tribunal, and
(b) the tribunal considers that there is no good reason for the failure,

the tribunal may proceed with the arbitration, and make its award, on the basis of the evidence (if any) before it.

Rule 39 *Failure to comply with tribunal direction or arbitration agreement* **D**

39(1) Where a party fails to comply with—
(a) any direction made by the tribunal, or
(b) any obligation imposed by—
  (i) the arbitration agreement,
  (ii) these rules (in so far as they apply), or
  (iii) any other agreement by the parties relating to conduct of the arbitration,

the tribunal may order the party to so comply.

(2) Where a party fails to comply with an order made under this rule, the tribunal may do any of the following—
(a) direct that the party is not entitled to rely on any allegation or material which was the subject-matter of the order,
(b) draw adverse inferences from the non-compliance,
(c) proceed with the arbitration and make its award,
(d) make such provisional award (including an award on expenses) as it considers appropriate in consequence of the non-compliance.

Rule 40 *Consolidation of proceedings* **D**

40(1) Parties may agree—
(a) to consolidate the arbitration with another arbitration, or
(b) to hold concurrent hearings.

(2) But the tribunal may not order such consolidation, or the holding of concurrent hearings, on its own initiative.

PART 5
POWERS OF COURT IN RELATION TO ARBITRAL PROCEEDINGS

Rule 41 *Referral of point of law* **D**

41 The Outer House may, on an application by any party, determine any point of Scots law arising in the arbitration.

Rule 42 *Point of law referral: procedure etc* **M**

42(1) This rule applies only where an application is made under rule 41.

(2) Such an application is valid only if—
   (a) the parties have agreed that it may be made, or
   (b) the tribunal has consented to it being made and the court is satisfied—
       (i) that determining the question is likely to produce substantial savings in expenses,
       (ii) that the application was made without delay, and
       (iii) that there is a good reason why the question should be determined by the court.

(3) The tribunal may continue with the arbitration pending determination of the application.

(4) The Outer House's determination of the question is final (as is any decision by the Outer House as to whether an application is valid).

Rule 43 *Variation of time limits set by parties* **D**

43 The court may, on an application by the tribunal or any party, vary any time limit relating to the arbitration which is imposed—
   (a) in the arbitration agreement, or
   (b) by virtue of any other agreement between the parties.

Rule 44 *Time limit variation: procedure etc* **M**

44(1) This rule applies only where an application for variation of time limit is made under rule 43.

(2) Such a variation may be made only if the court is satisfied—
   (a) that no arbitral process for varying the time limit is available, and
   (b) that someone would suffer a substantial injustice if no variation was made.

(3) It is for the court to determine the extent of any variation.

(4) The tribunal may continue with the arbitration pending determination of an application.

(5) The court's decision on whether to make a variation (and, if so, on the extent of the variation) is final.

Rule 45 *Court's power to order attendance of witnesses and disclosure of evidence* **M**

45(1) The court may, on an application by the tribunal or any party, order any person—

(a) to attend a hearing for the purposes of giving evidence to the tribunal, or
(b) to disclose documents or other material evidence to the tribunal.

(2) But the court may not order a person to give any evidence, or to disclose anything, which the person would be entitled to refuse to give or disclose in civil proceedings.

(3) The tribunal may continue with the arbitration pending determination of an application.

(4) The court's decision on whether to make an order is final.

Rule 46 *Court's other powers in relation to arbitration* **D**

46(1) The court has the same power in an arbitration as it has in civil proceedings—
(a) to appoint a person to safeguard the interests of any party lacking capacity,
(b) to order the sale of any property in dispute in the arbitration,
(c) to make an order securing any amount in dispute in the arbitration,
(d) to make an order under section 1 of the Administration of Justice (Scotland) Act 1972 (c.59),
(e) to grant warrant for arrestment or inhibition,
(f) to grant interdict (or interim interdict), or
(g) to grant any other interim or permanent order.

(2) But the court may take such action only—
(a) on an application by any party, and
(b) if the arbitration has begun—
  (i) with the consent of the tribunal, or
  (ii) where the court is satisfied that the case is one of urgency.

(3) The tribunal may continue with the arbitration pending determination of the application.

(4) This rule applies—
(a) to arbitrations which have begun,
(b) where the court is satisfied—
  (i) that a dispute has arisen or might arise, and
  (ii) that an arbitration agreement provides that such a dispute is to be resolved by arbitration.

(5) This rule does not affect—
(a) any other powers which the court has under any enactment or rule of law in relation to arbitrations, or
(b) the tribunal's powers.

PART 6
AWARDS

Rule 47 *Rules applicable to the substance of the dispute* **D**

47(1) The tribunal must decide the dispute in accordance with—
- (a) the law chosen by the parties as applicable to the substance of the dispute, or
- (b) if no such choice is made (or where a purported choice is unlawful), the law determined by the conflict of law rules which the tribunal considers applicable.

(2) Accordingly, the tribunal must not decide the dispute on the basis of general considerations of justice, fairness or equity unless—
- (a) they form part of the law concerned, or
- (b) the parties otherwise agree.

(3) When deciding the dispute, the tribunal must have regard to—
- (a) the provisions of any contract relating to the substance of the dispute,
- (b) the normal commercial or trade usage of any undefined terms in the provisions of any such contract,
- (c) any established commercial or trade customs or practices relevant to the substance of the dispute, and
- (d) any other matter which the parties agree is relevant in the circumstances.

Rule 48 *Power to award payment and damages* **M**

48(1) The tribunal's award may order the payment of a sum of money (including a sum in respect of damages).

(2) Such a sum must be specified—
- (a) in any currency agreed by the parties, or
- (b) the absence of such agreement, in such currency as the tribunal considers appropriate.

Rule 49 *Other remedies available to tribunal* **D**

49 The tribunal's award may—
- (a) be of a declaratory nature,
- (b) order a party to do or refrain from doing something (including ordering the performance of a contractual obligation), or
- (c) order the rectification or reduction of any deed or other document (other than a decree of court) to the extent permitted by the law governing the deed or document.

Rule 50 Interest **M**

50(1)   The tribunal's award may order that interest is to be paid on—
  (a) the whole or part of any amount which the award orders to be paid (or which is payable in consequence of a declaratory award), in respect of any period up to the date of the award,
  (b) the whole or part of any amount which is—
    (i) claimed in the arbitration and outstanding when the arbitration began, but
    (ii) paid before the tribunal made its award,
  in respect of any period up to the date of payment,
  (c) the outstanding amount of any amounts awarded (including any award of arbitration expenses or pre-award interest under paragraph (a) or (b)) in respect of any period from the date of the award up to the date of payment.

(2)   An award ordering payment of interest may, in particular, specify—
  (a) the interest rate,
  (b) the period for which interest is payable (including any rests which the tribunal considers appropriate).

(3)   An award may make different interest provision in respect of different amounts.

(4)   Interest is to be calculated—
  (a) in the manner agreed by the parties, or
  (b) failing such agreement, in such manner as the tribunal determines.

(5)   This rule does not affect any other power of the tribunal to award interest.

Rule 51 Form of award **D**

51(1)   The tribunal's award must be signed by all arbitrators or all those assenting to the award.

(2)   The tribunal's award must state—
  (a) the seat of the arbitration,
  (b) when the award is made and when it takes effect,
  (c) the tribunal's reasons for the award, and
  (d) whether any previous provisional or part award has been made (and the extent to which any previous provisional award is superseded or confirmed).

(3)   The tribunal's award is made by delivering it to each of the parties in accordance with rule 83.

Rule 52   *Award treated as made in Scotland*   **D**

52   An award is to be treated as having been made in Scotland even if it is signed at, or delivered to or from, a place outwith Scotland.

Rule 53   *Provisional awards*   **D**

53   The tribunal may make a provisional award granting any relief on a provisional basis which it has the power to grant permanently.

Rule 54   *Part awards*   **M**

54(1)   The tribunal may make more than one award at different times on different aspects of the matters to be determined.

(2)   A "part award" is an award which decides some (but not all) of the matters which the tribunal is to decide in the arbitration.

(3)   A part award must specify the matters to which it relates.

Rule 55   *Draft awards*   **D**

55   Before making an award, the tribunal—
   (a) may send a draft of its proposed award to the parties, and
   (b) if it does so, must consider any representations from the parties about the draft which the tribunal receives by such time as it specifies.

Rule 56   *Power to withhold award on non-payment of fees or expenses*   **M**

56(1)   The tribunal may refuse to deliver or send its award to the parties if any fees and expenses for which they are liable under rule 60 have not been paid in full.

(2)   Where the tribunal so refuses, the court may (on an application by any party) order—
   (a) that the tribunal must deliver the award on the applicant paying into the court an amount equal to the fees and expenses demanded (or such lesser amount as may be specified in the order),
   (b) that the amount paid into the court is to be used to pay the fees and expenses which the court determines as being properly payable, and
   (c) that the balance (if any) of the amount paid into the court is to be repaid to the applicant.

(3)   The court may make such an order only if the applicant has exhausted any available arbitral process of appeal or review of the amount of the fees and expenses demanded.

(4)   The court's decision on an application under this rule is final.

Rule 57 *Arbitration to end on last award or early settlement* **D**

57(1) An arbitration ends when the last award to be made in the arbitration is made (and no claim, including any claim for expenses or interest, is outstanding).

(2) But this does not prevent the tribunal from ending the arbitration before then under rule 20(3) or 37(1).

(3) The parties may end the arbitration at any time by notifying the tribunal that they have settled the dispute.

(4) On the request of the parties, the tribunal may make an award reflecting the terms of the settlement and these rules (except for rule 51(2)(c) and Part 8) apply to such an award as they apply to any other award.

(5) The fact that the arbitration has ended does not affect the operation of these rules (in so far as they apply) in relation to matters connected with the arbitration.

Rule 58 *Correcting an award* **D**

58(1) The tribunal may correct an award so as to—
 (a) correct a clerical, typographical or other error in the award arising by virtue of accident or omission, or
 (b) clarify or remove any ambiguity in the award.

(2) The tribunal may make such a correction—
 (a) on its own initiative, or
 (b) on an application by any party.

(3) A party making an application under this rule must send a copy of the application to the other party at the same time as the application is made.

(4) Such an application is valid only if made—
 (a) within 28 days of the award concerned, or
 (b) by such later date as the Outer House or the sheriff may, on an application by the party, specify (with any determination by the Outer House or the sheriff being final).

(5) The tribunal must, before deciding whether to correct an award, give—
 (a) where the tribunal proposed the correction, each of the parties,
 (b) where a party application is made, the other party,
 a reasonable opportunity to make representations about the proposed correction.

(6) A correction may be made under this rule only—
 (a) where the tribunal proposed the correction, within 28 days of the award concerned being made, or

(b) where a party application is made, within 28 days of the application being made.
(7) Where a correction affects—
(a) another part of the corrected award, or
(b) any other award made by the tribunal (relating to the substance of the dispute, expenses, interest or any other matter),
the tribunal may make such consequential correction of that other part or award as it considers appropriate.
(8) A corrected award is to be treated as if it was made in its corrected form on the day the award was made.

PART 7
ARBITRATION EXPENSES

Rule 59 Arbitration expenses **D**

59 "Arbitration expenses" means—
(a) the arbitrators' fees and expenses for which the parties are liable under rule 60,
(b) any expenses incurred by the tribunal when conducting the arbitration for which the parties are liable under rule 60,
(c) the parties' legal and other expenses, and
(d) the fees and expenses of—
(i) any arbitral appointments referee, and
(ii) any other third party to whom the parties give powers in relation to the arbitration,
for which the parties are liable under rule 60.

Rule 60 Arbitrators' fees and expenses **M**

60(1) The parties are severally liable to pay to the arbitrators—
(a) the arbitrators' fees and expenses, including—
(i) the arbitrators' fees for conducting the arbitration,
(ii) expenses incurred personally by the arbitrators when conducting the arbitration, and
(b) expenses incurred by the tribunal when conducting the arbitration, including—
(i) the fees and expenses of any clerk, agent, employee or other person appointed by the tribunal to assist it in conducting the arbitration,
(ii) the fees and expenses of any expert from whom the tribunal obtains an opinion,
(iii) any expenses in respect of meeting and hearing facilities, and

(iv) any expenses incurred in determining recoverable arbitration expenses.

(2) The parties are also severally liable to pay the fees and expenses of—
 (a) any arbitral appointments referee, and
 (b) any other third party to whom the parties give powers in relation to the arbitration.

(3) The amount of fees and expenses payable under this rule and the payment terms are—
 (a) to be agreed by the parties and the arbitrators or, as the case may be, the arbitral appointments referee or other third party, or
 (b) failing such agreement, to be determined by the Auditor of the Court of Session.

(4) Unless the Auditor of the Court of Session decides otherwise—
 (a) the amount of any fee is to be determined by the Auditor on the basis of a reasonable commercial rate of charge, and
 (b) the amount of any expenses is to be determined by the Auditor on the basis that a reasonable amount is to be allowed in respect of all reasonably incurred expenses.

(5) The Auditor of the Court of Session may, when determining the amount of fees and expenses, order the repayment of any fees or expenses already paid which the Auditor considers excessive (and such an order has effect as if it was made by the court).

(6) This rule does not affect—
 (a) the parties' liability as between themselves for fees and expenses covered by this rule (see rules 62 and 65), or
 (b) the Outer House's power to make an order under rule 16 (order relating to expenses in cases of arbitrator's resignation or removal).

Rule 61 *Recoverable arbitration expenses* **D**

61(1) The following arbitration expenses are recoverable—
 (a) the arbitrators' fees and expenses for which the parties are liable under rule 60,
 (b) any expenses incurred by the tribunal when conducting the arbitration for which the parties are liable under rule 60, and
 (c) the fees and expenses of any arbitral appointments referee (or any other third party to whom the parties give powers in relation to the arbitration) for which the parties are liable under rule 60.

(2) It is for the tribunal to—
  (a) determine the amount of the other arbitration expenses which are recoverable, or
  (b) arrange for the Auditor of the Court of Session to determine that amount.
(3) Unless the tribunal or, as the case may be, the Auditor decides otherwise—
  (a) the amount of the other arbitration expenses which are recoverable must be determined on the basis that a reasonable amount is to be allowed in respect of all reasonably incurred expenses, and
  (b) any doubt as to whether expenses were reasonably incurred or are reasonable in amount is to be resolved in favour of the person liable to pay the expenses.

Rule 62 *Liability for recoverable arbitration expenses* **D**

62(1) The tribunal may make an award allocating the parties' liability between themselves for the recoverable arbitration expenses (or any part of those expenses).
(2) When making an award under this rule, the tribunal must have regard to the principle that expenses should follow a decision made in favour of a party except where this would be inappropriate in the circumstances.
(3) Until such an award is made (or where the tribunal chooses not to make such an award) in respect of recoverable arbitration expenses (or any part of them), the parties are, as between themselves, each liable—
  (a) for an equal share of any such expenses for which the parties are liable under rule 60, and
  (b) for their own legal and other expenses.
(4) This rule does not affect—
  (a) the parties' several liability for fees and expenses under rule 60, or
  (b) the liability of any party to any other third party.

Rule 63 *Ban on pre-dispute agreements about liability for arbitration expenses* **M**

63 Any agreement allocating the parties' liability between themselves for any or all of the arbitration expenses has no effect if entered into before the dispute being arbitrated has arisen.

Rule 64 *Security for expenses* **D**

64(1) The tribunal may—

(a) order a party making a claim to provide security for the recoverable arbitration expenses or any part of them, and
(b) if that order is not complied with, make an award dismissing any claim made by that party.

(2) But such an order may not be made only on the ground that the party—
(a) is an individual who ordinarily resides outwith the United Kingdom, or
(b) is a body which is—
(i) incorporated or formed under the law of a country outwith the United Kingdom, or
(ii) managed or controlled from outwith the United Kingdom.

Rule 65 *Limitation of recoverable arbitration expenses* **D**

65(1) A provisional or part award may cap a party's liability for the recoverable arbitration expenses at an amount specified in the award.

(2) But an award imposing such a cap must be made sufficiently in advance of the expenses to which the cap relates being incurred, or the taking of any steps in the arbitration which may be affected by the cap, for the parties to take account of it.

Rule 66 *Awards on recoverable arbitration expenses* **D**

66 An expenses award (under rule 62 or 65) may be made together with or separately from an award on the substance of the dispute (and these rules apply in relation to an expenses award as they apply to an award on the substance of the dispute).

PART 8
CHALLENGING AWARDS

Rule 67 *Challenging an award: substantive jurisdiction* **M**

67(1) A party may appeal to the Outer House against the tribunal's award on the ground that the tribunal did not have jurisdiction to make the award (a "jurisdictional appeal").

(2) The Outer House may decide a jurisdictional appeal by—
(a) confirming the award,
(b) varying the award (or part of it), or
(c) setting aside the award (or part of it).

(3) Any variation by the Outer House has effect as part of the tribunal's award.

(4) An appeal may be made to the Inner House against the Outer House's decision on a jurisdictional appeal (but only with the leave of the Outer House).

(5) Leave may be given by the Outer House only where it considers—
- (a) that the proposed appeal would raise an important point of principle or practice, or
- (b) that there is another compelling reason for the Inner House to consider the appeal.

(6) The Outer House's decision on whether to grant such leave is final.

(7) The Inner House's decision on such an appeal is final.

Rule 68   Challenging an award: serious irregularity   **M**

68(1) A party may appeal to the Outer House against the tribunal's award on the ground of serious irregularity (a "serious irregularity appeal").

(2) "Serious irregularity" means an irregularity of any of the following kinds which has caused, or will cause, substantial injustice to the appellant—
- (a) the tribunal failing to conduct the arbitration in accordance with—
  - (i) the arbitration agreement,
  - (ii) these rules (in so far as they apply), or
  - (iii) any other agreement by the parties relating to conduct of the arbitration,
- (b) the tribunal acting outwith its powers (other than by exceeding its jurisdiction),
- (c) the tribunal failing to deal with all the issues that were put to it,
- (d) any arbitral appointments referee or other third party to whom the parties give powers in relation to the arbitration acting outwith powers,
- (e) uncertainty or ambiguity as to the award's effect,
- (f) the award being—
  - (i) contrary to public policy, or
  - (ii) obtained by fraud or in a way which is contrary to public policy,
- (g) an arbitrator having not been impartial and independent,
- (h) an arbitrator having not treated the parties fairly,
- (i) an arbitrator having been incapable of acting as an arbitrator in the arbitration (or there being justifiable doubts about an arbitrator's ability to so act),

(j) an arbitrator not having a qualification which the parties agreed (before the arbitrator's appointment) that the arbitrator must have, or

(k) any other irregularity in the conduct of the arbitration or in the award which is admitted by—

    (i) the tribunal, or

    (ii) any arbitral appointments referee or other third party to whom the parties give powers in relation to the arbitration.

(3) The Outer House may decide a serious irregularity appeal by—

(a) confirming the award,

(b) ordering the tribunal to reconsider the award (or part of it), or

(c) if it considers reconsideration inappropriate, setting aside the award (or part of it).

(4) Where the Outer House decides a serious irregularity appeal (otherwise than by confirming the award) on the ground—

(a) that the tribunal failed to conduct the arbitration in accordance with—

    (i) the arbitration agreement,

    (ii) these rules (in so far as they apply), or

    (iii) any other agreement by the parties relating to conduct of the arbitration,

(b) that an arbitrator has not been impartial and independent, or

(c) that an arbitrator has not treated the parties fairly,

it may also make such order as it thinks fit about any arbitrator's entitlement (if any) to fees and expenses (and such an order may provide for the repayment of fees or expenses already paid to the arbitrator).

(5) An appeal may be made to the Inner House against the Outer House's decision on a serious irregularity appeal (but only with the leave of the Outer House).

(6) Leave may be given by the Outer House only where it considers—

(a) that the proposed appeal would raise an important point of principle or practice, or

(b) that there is another compelling reason for the Inner House to consider the appeal.

(7) The Outer House's decision on whether to grant such leave is final.

(8) The Inner House's decision on such an appeal is final.

Rule 69 Challenging an award: legal error **D**

69(1) A party may appeal to the Outer House against the tribunal's award on the ground that the tribunal erred on a point of Scots law (a "legal error appeal").

(2) An agreement between the parties to disapply rule 51(2)(c) by dispensing with the tribunal's duty to state its reasons for its award is to be treated as an agreement to exclude the court's jurisdiction to consider a legal error appeal.

Rule 70 Legal error appeals: procedure etc **M**

70(1) This rule applies only where rule 69 applies.

(2) A legal error appeal may be made only—
   (a) with the agreement of the parties, or
   (b) with the leave of the Outer House.

(3) Leave to make a legal error appeal may be given only if the Outer House is satisfied—
   (a) that deciding the point will substantially affect a party's rights,
   (b) that the tribunal was asked to decide the point, and
   (c) that, on the basis of the findings of fact in the award (including any facts which the tribunal treated as established for the purpose of deciding the point), the tribunal's decision on the point—
      (i) was obviously wrong, or
      (ii) where the court considers the point to be of general importance, is open to serious doubt.

(4) An application for leave is valid only if it—
   (a) identifies the point of law concerned, and
   (b) states why the applicant considers that leave should be granted.

(5) The Outer House must determine an application for leave without a hearing (unless satisfied that a hearing is required).

(6) The Outer House's determination of an application for leave is final.

(7) Any leave to appeal expires 7 days after it is granted (and so any legal error appeal made after then is accordingly invalid unless made with the agreement of the parties).

(8) The Outer House may decide a legal error appeal by—
   (a) confirming the award,
   (b) ordering the tribunal to reconsider the award (or part of it), or
   (c) if it considers reconsideration inappropriate, setting aside the award (or part of it).

(9) An appeal may be made to the Inner House against the Outer House's decision on a legal error appeal (but only with the leave of the Outer House).

(10) Leave may be given by the Outer House only where it considers—
(a) that the proposed appeal would raise an important point of principle or practice, or
(b) that there is another compelling reason for the Inner House to consider the appeal.

(11) The Outer House's decision on whether to grant such leave is final.

(12) The Inner House's decision on such an appeal is final.

Rule 71 *Challenging an award: supplementary* **M**

71(1) This rule applies to—
(a) jurisdictional appeals,
(b) serious irregularity appeals, and
(c) where rule 69 applies to the arbitration, legal error appeals,
and references to "appeal" are to be construed accordingly.

(2) An appeal is competent only if the appellant has exhausted any available arbitral process of appeal or review (including any recourse available under rule 58).

(3) No appeal may be made against a provisional award.

(4) An appeal must be made no later than 28 days after the later of the following dates—
(a) the date on which the award being appealed against is made,
(b) if the award is subject to a process of correction under rule 58, the date on which the tribunal decides whether to correct the award, or
(c) if there has been an arbitral process of appeal or review, the date on which the appellant was notified of the result of that process.

A legal error appeal is to be treated as having being made for the purposes of this rule if an application for leave is made.

(5) An application for leave to appeal against the Outer House's decision on an appeal must be made no later than 28 days after the date on which the decision is made (and any such leave expires 7 days after it is granted).

(6) An appellant must give notice of an appeal to the other party and the tribunal.

(7) The tribunal may continue with the arbitration pending determination of an appeal against a part award.

(8) The Outer House (or the Inner House in the case of an appeal against the Outer House's decision) may—
   (a) order the tribunal to state its reasons for the award being appealed in sufficient detail to enable the Outer House (or Inner House) to deal with the appeal properly, and
   (b) make any other order it thinks fit with respect to any additional expenses arising from that order.

(9) Where the Outer House (or the Inner House in the case of an appeal against the Outer House's decision) decides an appeal by setting aside the award (or any part of it), it may also order that any provision in an arbitration agreement which prevents the bringing of legal proceedings in relation to the subject-matter of the award (or that part of it) is void.

(10) The Outer House (or the Inner House in the case of an appeal against the Outer House's decision) may—
   (a) order an appellant (or an applicant for leave to appeal) to provide security for the expenses of the appeal (or application), and
   (b) dismiss the appeal (or application) if the order is not complied with.

(11) But such an order may not be made only on the ground that the appellant (or applicant)—
   (a) is an individual who ordinarily resides outwith the United Kingdom, or
   (b) is a body which is—
      (i) incorporated or formed under the law of a country outwith the United Kingdom, or
      (ii) managed or controlled from outwith the United Kingdom.

(12) The Outer House (or the Inner House in the case of an appeal against the Outer House's decision) may—
   (a) order that any amount due under an award being appealed (or any associated provisional award) must be paid into court or otherwise secured pending its decision on the appeal (or the application for leave to appeal), and
   (b) dismiss the appeal (or application) if the order is not complied with.

(13) An appeal to the Inner House against any decision of the Outer House under this rule may be made only with the leave of the Outer House.

(14) An application for leave to appeal against such a decision must be made no later than 28 days after the date on which the decision is made (and any such leave expires 7 days after it is granted).

(15) Leave may be given by the Outer House only where it considers—
(a) that the proposed appeal would raise an important point of principle or practice, or
(b) that there is another compelling reason for the Inner House to consider the appeal.
(16) The Outer House's decision on whether to grant such leave is final.
(17) A decision of the Inner House under this rule (including any decision on an appeal against a decision by the Outer House) is final.

Rule 72   *Reconsideration by tribunal*   **M**

72(1) Where the Outer House or, as the case may be, the Inner House decides a serious irregularity appeal or a legal error appeal by ordering the tribunal to reconsider its award (or any part of it), the tribunal must make a new award in respect of the matter concerned (or confirm its original award) by no later than—
(a) in the case of a decision by the Outer House—
(i) where the decision is appealed, the day falling 3 months after the appeal (or, as the case may be, the application for leave to appeal) is dismissed or abandoned,
(ii) where the decision is not appealed, the day falling 3 months after the decision is made, or
(iii) such other day as the Outer House may specify,
(b) in the case of a decision by the Inner House—
(i) the day falling 3 months after the decision is made, or
(ii) such other day as the Inner House may specify.
(2) These rules apply in relation to the new award as they apply in relation to the appealed award.

PART 9
MISCELLANEOUS

Rule 73   *Immunity of tribunal etc*   **M**

73(1) Neither the tribunal nor any arbitrator is liable for anything done or omitted in the performance, or purported performance, of the tribunal's functions.
(2) This rule does not apply—
(a) if the act or omission is shown to have been in bad faith, or
(b) to any liability arising from an arbitrator's resignation (but see rule 16(1)(c)).

(3) This rule applies to any clerk, agent, employee or other person assisting the tribunal to perform its functions as it applies to the tribunal.

Rule 74 *Immunity of appointing arbitral institution etc* **M**

74(1) An arbitral appointments referee, or other third party who the parties ask to appoint or nominate an arbitrator, is not liable—
(a) for anything done or omitted in the performance, or purported performance, of that function (unless the act or omission is shown to have been in bad faith), or
(b) for the acts or omissions of—
  (i) any arbitrator whom it nominates or appoints, or
  (ii) the tribunal of which such an arbitrator forms part (or any clerk, agent or employee of that tribunal).
(2) This rule applies to an arbitral appointments referee's, or other third party's, agents and employees as it applies to the referee or other third party.

Rule 75 *Immunity of experts, witnesses and legal representatives* **M**

75 Every person who participates in an arbitration as an expert, witness or legal representative has the same immunity in respect of acts or omissions as the person would have if the arbitration were civil proceedings.

Rule 76 *Loss of right to object* **M**

76(1) A party who participates in an arbitration without making a timeous objection on the ground—
(a) that an arbitrator is ineligible to act as an arbitrator,
(b) that an arbitrator is not impartial and independent,
(c) that an arbitrator has not treated the parties fairly,
(d) that the tribunal does not have jurisdiction,
(e) that the arbitration has not been conducted in accordance with—
  (i) the arbitration agreement,
  (ii) these rules (in so far as they apply), or
  (iii) any other agreement by the parties relating to conduct of the arbitration,
(f) that the arbitration has been affected by any other serious irregularity,
may not raise the objection later before the tribunal or the court.
(2) An objection is timeous if it is made—

(a) as soon as reasonably practicable after the circumstances giving rise to the ground for objection first arose,
(b) by such later date as may be allowed by—
  (i) the arbitration agreement,
  (ii) these rules (in so far as they apply),
  (iii) the other party, or
(c) where the tribunal considers that circumstances justify a later objection, by such later date as it may allow.

(3) This rule does not apply where the party shows that it did not object timeously because it—
(a) did not know of the ground for objection, and
(b) could not with reasonable diligence have discovered that ground.

(4) This rule does not allow a party to raise an objection which it is barred from raising for any reason other than failure to object timeously.

Rule 77 *Independence of arbitrator* **M**

77 For the purposes of these rules, an arbitrator is not independent in relation to an arbitration if—
(a) the arbitrator's relationship with any party,
(b) the arbitrator's financial or other commercial interests, or
(c) anything else,
gives rise to justifiable doubts as to the arbitrator's impartiality.

Rule 78 *Consideration where arbitrator judged not to be impartial and independent* **D**

78(1) This rule applies where—
(a) an arbitrator is removed by the Outer House under rule 12 on the ground that the arbitrator is not impartial and independent,
(b) the tribunal is dismissed by the Outer House under rule 13 on the ground that it has failed to comply with its duty to be impartial and independent, or
(c) the tribunal's award (or any part of it) is returned to the tribunal for reconsideration, or is set aside, on either of those grounds (see rule 68).

(2) Where this rule applies, the Outer House must have particular regard to whether an arbitrator has complied with rule 8 when it is considering whether to make an order under rule 16(1) or 68(4) about—
(a) the arbitrator's entitlement (if any) to fees or expenses,
(b) repaying fees or expenses already paid to the arbitrator.

Rule 79   Death of arbitrator   **M**

79   An arbitrator's authority is personal and ceases on death.

Rule 80   Death of party   **D**

80(1)   An arbitration agreement is not discharged by the death of a party and may be enforced by or against the executor or other representative of that party.

(2)   This rule does not affect the operation of any law by virtue of which a substantive right or obligation is extinguished by death.

Rule 81   Unfair treatment   **D**

81   A tribunal (or arbitrator) who treats any party unfairly is, for the purposes of these rules, to be deemed not to have treated the parties fairly.

Rule 82   Rules applicable to umpires   **M**

82(1)   The following rules apply in relation to an umpire appointed under rule 30 (or otherwise with the agreement of the parties) as they apply in relation to an arbitrator or, as the case may be, the tribunal—

rule 4
rule 8
rules 10 to 14
rule 24
rule 26
rules 59, 60 and 61(1)
rule 68
rule 73
rules 76 to 79

(2)   But the parties are, in so far as those rules are not mandatory rules, free to modify or disapply the way in which those rules would otherwise apply to an umpire.

Rule 83   Formal communications   **D**

83(1)   A "formal communication" means any application, award, consent, direction, notice, objection, order, reference, request, requirement or waiver made or given or any document served—

(a) in pursuance of an arbitration agreement,
(b) for the purposes of these rules (in so far as they apply), or
(c) otherwise in relation to an arbitration.

(2) A formal communication must be in writing.
(3) A formal communication is made, given or served if it is—
   (a) hand delivered to the person concerned,
   (b) sent to the person concerned by first class post in a properly addressed envelope or package—
      (i) in the case of an individual, to the individual's principal place of business or usual or last known abode,
      (ii) in the case of a body corporate, to the body's registered or principal office, or
      (iii) in either case, to any postal address designated for the purpose by the intended recipient (such designation to be made by giving notice to the person giving or serving the formal communication), or
   (c) sent to the person concerned in some other way (including by email, fax or other electronic means) which the sender reasonably considers likely to cause it to be delivered on the same or next day.
(4) A formal communication which is sent by email, fax or other electronic means is to be treated as being in writing only if it is legible and capable of being used for subsequent reference.
(5) A formal communication is, unless the contrary is proved, to be treated as having been made, given or served—
   (a) where hand delivered, on the day of delivery,
   (b) where posted, on the day on which it would be delivered in the ordinary course of post, or
   (c) where sent in any other way described above, on the day after it is sent.
(6) The tribunal may determine that a formal communication—
   (a) is to be delivered in such other manner as it may direct, or
   (b) need not be delivered,
   but it may do so only if satisfied that it is not reasonably practicable for the formal communication to be made, given or served in accordance with this rule (or, as the case may be, with any contrary agreement between the parties).
(7) This rule does not apply in relation to any application, order, notice, document or other thing which is made, given or served in or for the purposes of legal proceedings.

Rule 84 *Periods of time* **D**

84 Periods of time are to be calculated for the purposes of an arbitration as follows—
   (a) where any act requires to be done within a specified period after or from a specified date or event, the period begins

immediately after that date or, as the case may be, the date of that event, and
(b) where the period is a period of 7 days or less, the following days are to be ignored—
    (i) Saturdays and Sundays, and
    (ii) any public holidays in the place where the act concerned is to be done.

INDEX

AAA *see* American Arbitration
 Association
ACICA *see* Australian Centre for
 International Arbitration
affirmations, making 233, 325
American Arbitration Association (AAA)
 impartiality of arbitrator 112
 International Arbitration Rules (ICDR
  Rules)
   amiable composition 221
   confidentiality obligations 35
   party autonomy 71, 72
amiable composition
 definition 218
 England, application in 223–224
 favourable opinions on 219–220
 international practice, in
  arbitral awards, in 221–223
  Conventions, rules and domestic
   laws, in 220–221
 opposition to application of 218–219
 Scottish Rules and 172, 218
a-national principles of law 188, 190
anonymity in legal proceedings 304
appointment
 arbitrators, of
  challenging 102–103, 316–317
  eligibility for 107
  failure in procedure 101–102,
   105–106, 315–316
  generally 99–100, 314–315
  mandatory rules on 107–108
  method of 106–107
  time limits for 99–100, 314–315
 clerk, of 324
 tribunal, of 99–100, 314

arbitrability
 EU 63
 France 61
 generally 60–61
 Germany 61–62
 Scotland 61
 USA 62
arbitral appointments referee
 definition 106
 fees and expenses 281
 immunity of
  mandatory rules 94
 referral to 108
 role of 101–102, 308–309
arbitral awards
 see also New York Convention
 amiable composition, application
  of 221–223
 binding force 302
 challenging
  contracting to restrict or expand
   grounds for 273–276, 276–280
  default rules 52, 251, 302
  lack of substantive
   jurisdiction 251, 336–337
  legal error 252, 339, 340
  serious irregularity 252, 337–338
  supplementary rules 340–341
 correction of
  generally 248–249
  Scottish Rules 332–333
 country of origin, validity and
   262–264
 default rules
  challenging awards 52
  generally 51

349

arbitral awards (cont)
　delivery to parties 247
　draft awards 248, 331
　enforcement of see enforcement of
　　awards
　final 248
　format of 247, 330
　generally 245
　interest on
　　Scottish Rules 330, 331
　law applied to make 245–246
　lex mercatoria, new, application
　　of 212–216
　mandatory rules on
　　challenging 90–94
　　generally 88–89
　partial 248, 331
　place of arbitration, linking to
　　260–262
　provisional awards 248, 331
　reasons for, requirements to 247
　recognition of see recognition of
　　awards
　reconsideration following
　　challenge 342
　remedies awarded 246–247
　Scottish Rules 329–333
　signature, significance of place
　　of 247
　types of 248
　withholding for non-payment of fees
　　and expenses 249–250, 331
arbitration
　agreement on see arbitration
　　agreement
　awards in see arbitral awards
　commencement
　　default rules 46–47, 97
　　generally 97–99
　　mandatory rules 97
　costs
　　definition 281
　　international practice 286–292
　courts and, relationship between
　　attendance of witnesses, power to
　　　order 241–242
　　disclosure of evidence, power to
　　　order 241–242
　　generally 239

arbitration
　courts and, relationship between
　　(cont)
　　miscellaneous powers 242–244
　　Scots law, power to determine
　　　points of 239–240
　　time limits set by parties, power to
　　　vary 241
　definition 10
　failure to comply with 326
　generally 299
　law governing 299–300
　separability 299
　types of 10
arbitration agreement
　Arbitration (Sc) Act 2010
　　contents of agreement 45–53
　　definition 40–41
　　format 41–42
　　generally 40
　　law governing 43–44
　　separability 42–43
　　suspension of legal
　　　proceedings 44–45
　failure to comply with
　　sanctions for 234–236
　format
　　England 41
　　New York Convention 41
　　Scotland 41–42
　　UNCITRAL Model Law 42
　generally 39–40
　international perspectives
　　arbitrability 60–63
　　Australia 66
　　England 56–61, 64–65
　　Hong Kong 65–66
　　hostility to 53–54
　　ICC 66
　　multi-party arbitration 63–66
　　Netherlands 65
　　Scotland 55–56, 64
　　separability 59–60
　　USA 54–55
　interpretation 53–66
　multi-party arbitration
　　Australia 66
　　England 64–65
　　generally 63–64

arbitration agreement
  multi-party arbitration (cont)
    Hong Kong 65–66
    ICC 66
    Netherlands 65
    Scotland 64
  separability
    English views on 43, 59–60
    generally 42–43
arbitration clause
  choice of law in 44
  definition 40
Arbitration (Scotland) Act 2010
  anonymity in legal proceedings,
    in 304
  arbitral appointments referee
    308–309
  arbitral awards
    binding force 302
    challenging 302
    enforcement 302–303
  arbitration agreements
    contents of agreement 45–53
    definition 40–41
    format 41–42
    generally 40, 299
    law governing 43–44, 299–300
    separability 42–43, 299
    suspension of legal
      proceedings 44–45
  coming into force 312–313
  contents 293–347
  court intervention in arbitration 303
  Crown application 312
  features 9–18
  founding principles 9–10, 298
  general principles 16–17
  impartiality, on 10
  interpretation 310–311
  limited court intervention, on 10
  judge's power to act as arbitrator or
    umpire 309
  key terms 298–299
  limitation 307–308
  New York Convention
    amendments to 309
    awards 13–14, 305–307
  objectives 1, 4–7
  parliamentary progress 3–4

Arbitration (Scotland) Act 2010 (cont)
  party autonomy, on 10
  persons other than parties 303–304
  pre-Act legal development 1–2
  prescription 307–308
  repeal provisions 14–16
  scope of application 10–11
  seat of arbitration 11–12, 299
  statutory arbitration 12–13, 304–305
  structure 16–18
  suspension of legal proceedings
    301–302
  UNCITRAL Model Law, amendments
    to 309
Arbitration (Scotland) Bills 2002 and
  2009 3–4
arbitrators
  appointment of
    challenging 102–103, 316–317
    eligibility for 83, 107, 314
    failure in procedure 101–102,
      315–316
    generally 99–100, 105–106,
      314–315
    mandatory rules on 107–108
    method of 106–107
    time limits for 99–100, 314–315
  confidentiality, breach of duty of 19,
    20
  conflicts of interest, disclosure of
    101, 316
  death of 96, 133, 345
  definition 105
  dismissal of
    mandatory rules 124, 125–126
  disqualification of 112–113,
    113–123
  duties
    conflict of interest, disclosure of
      108–109
    impartiality 109–123
    independence 109–112
  eligibility as 83, 100, 314
  expenses 90, 131–133, 281,
    282–283, 333–334
  fees 131–133, 281, 282–283
  immunity from liability 133–134
  impartiality 344
  independence 344

arbitrators (cont)
  individuals, to be 314
  liability at tenure's end 319
  nomination 319
  number of 100–101, 107, 314
  procedure, power to decide 225
  removal 103, 124, 125, 317, 318
  resignation 104, 124, 126, 318
  tenure 104, 316
attendance of witnesses
  power to order 241–242
  failure in, sanctions for 234
Australian Centre for International Arbitration (ACICA) Rules
  confidentiality obligations, on 26–27, 28, 30, 35
  multi-party arbitration, on 66
Austria
  confidentiality obligations 28, 30, 37
  mandatory rules, effect of 81–82
autonomy of parties see party autonomy
awards see arbitral awards

Belgian Centre for Mediation and Arbitration (CEPANI)
  confidentiality obligations, rules on 35
Belgium
  see also Belgian Centre for Mediation and Arbitration (CEPANI)
  confidentiality obligations 28, 30, 35
  contracting to restrict grounds for challenging awards 273–274
  delocalisation theory 159–160
  jurisdiction of tribunal 130
  recognition and enforcement of awards 265
  separability 43
Bermuda
  confidentiality obligations 25–26

Canada
  confidentiality obligations 28, 30
"centre of gravity" test 187
CEPANI see Belgian Centre for Mediation and Arbitration

challenging arbitral awards
  contracting to restrict or expand grounds for 273–276, 276–280
  generally 251
  legal error 252, 339, 340
  serious irregularity 252, 337–338
  substantive jurisdiction, lack of 251, 336–337
  supplementary rules 340–341
Chartered Institute of Arbitrators (Scottish Branch) (CIArb(SB))
  Scottish Arbitration Code 1999 3
China
  confidentiality obligations 28, 30–31, 35
choice of law
  arbitration clause, statement in 44
  "centre of gravity" test 187
  "closest and most real" test 178, 182–185
  connection with case, need for 174–176
  express choice by parties 172, 176–178
  freedom of contract and 172, 173–174
  generally 43–44, 169–224
  "implied choice of law" test 178–182
  international practice
    AAA International Arbitration Rules 172
    England 173, 174–175, 179–180
    France 173
    ICC Rules 172, 175–176
    LCIA Rules 172
    Netherlands 187
    Sweden 187
    Switzerland 187
    UNCITRAL Arbitration Rules 172
    USA 174
  limitations on parties' choice 176–178
  party autonomy and 73
  Scottish Rules 171, 172
  seat of arbitration and 11–12, 148
  three-step rules 185–186
  two-step rules 185–186, 186–187

CIArb(SB) *see* Chartered Institute of
    Arbitrators (Scottish Branch)
clerks to tribunal
    appointment 229
    fees and expenses 282–283
    immunity from liability 94, 134
"closest and most real" test (choice of
    law)
    England, practice in 183–184
    generally 178, 182–183
    USA, practice in 184–185
commencement of arbitration
    default rules 46–47, 97–99, 314
    England 98–99
    ICA Rules 98
    LCIA Rules 98
    mandatory rules on 83–86
    Vienna Rules 98
"competence-competence", principle
    of 127
confidential information
    definition 19
    disclosure of, lawful 19–20
    third parties and 20
confidentiality, duty of
    breach of, consequences of 19
    connected arbitrations, in 22
    default rules 47–48
    exceptions 19–20
    expert witnesses 20
    implied obligation, as 21, 26, 27, 28
    interests of justice, in 23–24
    leave of court 24
    international practice, in
        ACICA Rules 35
        Australia 26–27, 28, 30
        Austria 28, 30, 37
        Belgium 28, 30
        Bermuda 25–26
        Canada 28, 30
        CEPANI Rules 35
        China 28, 30–31, 35
        Costa Rica 28, 31
        Denmark 28, 31
        Dominican Republic 29, 31
        Dubai 29, 31, 35
        Ecuador 28, 31–32
        England 20–24, 28, 30
        Finland 28, 32

confidentiality, duty of
    international practice, in (*cont*)
        France 28, 29, 32
        generally 20
        Germany 35
        Hong Kong 28, 29, 32, 35
        ICC Rules 29, 36
        ICDR Rules 35
        ILA report 28–37
        Iran 28, 32, 35, 37
        Ireland 28, 32
        Italy 28, 32–33, 35
        Japan 28, 29, 33, 36
        LCIA Rules 36
        Malaysia 36
        Netherlands 29, 33, 36
        New Zealand 29, 33
        Nicaragua 29, 33
        Norway 28, 33
        Peru 29, 33
        Russian Federation 29, 35–36
        Singapore 24, 28, 34, 36
        Spain 29, 34
        Sweden 27–28, 29, 34, 36
        Switzerland 28, 34, 36
        UNCITRAL Arbitration Rules 29,
            30, 35
        UNCITRAL Model Law 28
        USA 27, 28, 30
        Venezuela 28, 34
        Vienna Rules 37
        WIPO Rules 37
    Scottish Arbitration Rules 19–20, 29,
        34, 321–322
    third parties and 20
conflict of interest, arbitrator's duty to
    disclose 108–109
consolidation of proceedings
    236–237
constitution of tribunal 83–86, 99–103
consumer arbitrations, legislation
    governing 12–13
contractualist theory 39, 68
convention awards *see* New York
    Convention awards
correction of arbitral awards 248–249,
    332–333
Costa Rica
    confidentiality obligations 28, 31

costs of arbitration
  definition 281
  international practice
    generally 286–287
    ICC arbitration 287–289
    LCIA arbitration 289–291
    Vienna Rules 291–292
courts
  powers of, in relation to arbitral proceedings
    evidence, power to order disclosure of 241–242, 327–328
    generally 50, 239, 303
    miscellaneous powers 242–244
    point of law, referral of 239–240, 326–327
    time limits, variation of parties' 241, 327
    witnesses, power to order attendance 241–242, 327–328

damages, power to award 246
death
  arbitrator, of 96, 133, 345
  party, of
    default rules 52–53, 345
    generally 133
    statutory arbitration and 12
decisions of tribunal
  chairman's casting vote 229
  generally 228–229, 323–324
default rules
  arbitral proceedings 48–50
  awards
    challenging 52
    generally 51
  commencement of arbitration 46–47, 97, 98
  composition of tribunal 97
  confidentiality 19, 47–48
  constitution of tribunal 46–47
  death of party 52–53
  definition 17–18, 45–46, 69–70, 301
  deliberations of tribunal 48
  disapplication 46–53, 69–70
  expenses 51–52
  generally 17–18, 148–150, 301
  impartiality 52–53

default rules (cont)
  jurisdiction of tribunal 47
  marking 149
  modification 46–53, 69–70
  powers of court 50
delocalisation theory
  definition 154–155
  generally 154–156, 263, 264
  opinions against 156–157
  opinions for 155–156
  practice, in
    Belgium 159–160
    England 164–168
    France 160–164
    generally 157–159
    ICC arbitrations 157–159
    Switzerland 159
Denmark
  confidentiality obligations 28, 31
DIAC see Dubai International Arbitration Centre
directions of tribunal
  failure to comply with 234–236, 326
  power to give 229, 324
DIS see German Institution of Arbitration
disclosure of evidence, court's power to order 241–242
dismissal of arbitrator 124, 125–126
dispute
  definition 10, 11
  types of 11
disqualification of arbiter 112–113, 113–123
domestic public policy 78
Dominican Republic
  confidentiality obligations 29, 31
draft arbitral awards 248, 331
Dubai
  confidentiality obligations 29, 31, 35
Dubai International Arbitration Centre (DIAC) 35

Ecuador
  confidentiality obligations 28, 31–32
eligibility of arbitrators 100

INDEX

enforcement of awards
  generally
    Belgium 265
    France 265
    Scotland 252–255, 302–303
    Switzerland 266
  New York Convention, under
    formalities 255
    generally 255–256
    refusal of 257–259, 260
England
  amiable composition, application of 223–224
  arbitrator's fees and expenses 131–132
  appointment of arbitrator
    challenge to 102
    time limit for 100
  "closest and most real" test 183–184
  commencement of arbitration 98–99
  confidentiality obligations 20–24, 28, 30
  delocalisation theory 164–168
  disqualification of arbiters, case law on 113–118
  failure to attend hearing or provide evidence 234
  failure to comply with tribunal directions or arbitration agreement 235
  fees and expenses, recoverability of 285–286
  immunity from liability
    case law on 135–138
    statutory provisions 139–140
  "implied choice of law" test 179–182
  jurisdiction 129–130
  late submission of claims or defences 234
  lex mercatoria, new, application of 216–217
  multi-party arbitration 64–65
  party autonomy 72
  procedure, decisions on 226
  removal of arbitrator 103
  resignation of arbitrator 104
  separability 43, 56–61

EU cases
  arbitrability, views on 63
evidence
  disclosure of, court's power to order 241–242
  failure to provide 234, 325–326
  IBA Rules on taking 226–228
  tribunal, before 225–228, 323
ex aequo et bono
  international practice, in arbitral awards, in 221–223
ex aequo et bono (cont)
  Conventions, rules and domestic laws, in 220–221
  Scottish Rules 172, 218
expenses
  arbitral appointments referee 281
  arbitrators' 131–133, 281, 282–283, 333–334
  capping of 286
  default rules 51–52
  definition 281, 333
  international practice 286–292
  mandatory rules 90
  parties' 281
  power to award 246
  pre-dispute agreements on liability for 335
  recoverability 283–286, 334–335, 336
  security for 335–336
  withholding award for non-payment of 249–250
experts
  appointment, tribunal's power of 230
  fees, parties' liability for 230
  immunity from liability 94, 95, 134, 343
  international practice on 230–232
  opinions of
    generally 230, 324
    responding to 230

fees
  arbitral appointments referee 281
  arbitrators 131–133, 281, 282–283
  withholding award for non-payment of 249–250
final awards 248

Finland
  confidentiality obligations 28, 32
formal communications 345–346
founding principles of 2010 Act 9–10, 40, 298
France
  amiable composition, application of 221
  arbitrability 61
  confidentiality obligations 28, 29, 32
  delocalisation theory 160–164
  jurisdiction of tribunal 130
  mandatory rules, effect of 82
  recognition and enforcement of awards 265
freedom of contract
  basis for rules, as 74
  choice of law and 172, 173–174

German Institution of Arbitration (DIS) 35
Germany
  arbitrability 61–62
  confidentiality obligations 35
  separability 43
Green list (conflicts of interest) 110

HKIAC see Hong Kong International Arbitration Centre
Hong Kong
  confidentiality obligations 28, 29, 32, 35
  jurisdiction of tribunal 130–131
  multi-party arbitration 65–66
Hong Kong International Arbitration Centre (HKIAC) 35

IBA Guidelines on Conflicts of Interest in International Commercial Arbitration 2004 110, 112–113
IBA Rules on the Taking of Evidence in International Arbitration
  experts, tribunal-appointed 231–232
  generally 226–228
ICAC see International Arbitration Court of the Chamber of Commerce and Industry of the Russian Federation

ICC see International Chamber of Commerce
ICDR Rules see American Arbitration Association
ILA report on confidentiality obligations 28–37
immunity from liability
  appointing arbitral institution, of 343
  arbitrator, of 133–134
  England
    case law on 135–138
    statutory provisions 139–140
  experts, of 343
  legal representatives, of 94, 95, 134, 343
  Scottish rules 133–134
  tribunal, of 342–343
  USA
    case law 142–146
    generally 141–142
  witnesses, of 343
impartiality of arbitrator
  default rules 52–53
  generally 109–123
  independence contrasted 110–112
  "justifiable doubts" test 111, 112–113
  objections on ground of 95
  2010 objectives on 5–6, 10
"implied choice of law" test
  England, practice in 179–182
  generally 178–179
  indications for 180–182
  place of performance and 180–181
independence of arbitrator
  generally 109–110
  impartiality contrasted 110–112
interest on arbitral awards
  generally 330
  non-payment of 331
  power to award 247
interim measures
  generally 243–244
  UNCITRAL Model Law 235–236
  Vienna Rules 235
International Arbitration Centre of the Austrian Federal Economic Chamber see Vienna Rules

International Arbitration Court of
    the Chamber of Commerce and
    Industry of the Russian Federation
    (ICAC) 29, 35–36
International Chamber of Commerce
    (ICC)
  arbitration rules
    amiable composition 221
    appointment of arbitrator,
        challenge to 103
    arbitrators' fees 288–289
    commencement of arbitration
        98
    confidentiality obligations 29,
        36
    costs 286, 287–289
    impartiality 112
    lex mercatoria, reflecting 212
    multi-party arbitration 66
    party autonomy 70, 71–72
    separability 43
  delocalisation theory, views on
    157–159
  generally 29
  international practice
    amiable composition, application of
        arbitral awards, in 221–223
    Conventions, rules and domestic
        laws, in 220–221
    choice of law, on
      AAA International Arbitration
          Rules 172
      England 173, 174–175, 179–180
      France 173
      ICC Rules 172, 175–176
      LCIA Rules 172
      Netherlands 187
      Sweden 187
      Switzerland 187
      UNCITRAL Arbitration Rules
          172
      USA 174
    confidentiality, on 20–37
    delocalisation theory, on
      Belgium 159–160
      England 164–168
      France 160–164
      generally 157–159
      Switzerland 159

international practice (*cont*)
    ex aequo et bono, application of
        arbitral awards, in 221–223
    Conventions, rules and domestic
        laws, in 220–221
    expenses, on
      generally 286–287
      ICC arbitration 287–289
      LCIA arbitration 289–291
      Vienna Rules 291–292
    jurisdiction, on 129–131
    party autonomy, on 70–73
    pre-2010 Act 2
international public policy 78–80
Iran
    confidentiality obligations 28, 32,
        35, 37
Ireland
    confidentiality obligations 28, 32
Italy
    confidentiality obligations 28,
        32–33, 35
Japan
    confidentiality obligations 28, 29,
        33, 36
Japan Commercial Arbitration
    Association (JCAA) 29, 36
JCAA *see* Japan Commercial Arbitration
    Association
judge's power to act as arbitrator or
    umpire 309
jurisdiction of tribunal
    England 129–130
    generally 127–131, 319–320
    mandatory rules on 86–87
    objections to 320
    referral of point of 320–321
    ruling on own jurisdiction 128
    Switzerland 130
jurisdictional theory 74–75, 77
"justifiable doubts" test 111, 112–113

KLRCA *see* Kuala Lumpur Regional
    Centre for Arbitration
Kuala Lumpur Regional Centre for
    Arbitration (KLRCA) 36

laissez-faire principle 67, 74
LCIA *see* London Court of International
    Arbitration

legal development
  Arbitration (Sc) Act 2010
    objectives 1, 4–7
  Arbitration (Sc) Bills 2002 and
    2009 3–4
  pre-2010 Act 1–2
  Scottish Arbitration Code 1999 2–3
legal error, challenging award on ground
    of 339, 340
legal representatives
  communication of details of 229,
    324
  immunity of 94, 95, 134, 343
legislation
  Arbitration (Sc) Act 2010 9–18,
    293–347
  consumer arbitrations 12–13
lex loci arbitri 75–76, 154, 156, 158,
    264
lex mercatoria, new
  definition 203–206
  favourable opinions on 208–211
  international practice, in
    arbitral awards, in 212–216
    Conventions and rules, in
      211–212
    England 216–217
  opposition to application of
    206–208
  origins 201–203
limited court intervention, principle
    of 10
London Court of International
    Arbitration (LCIA)
  generally 29, 72
  rules of
    appointment of arbitrator,
      challenge to 103
    arbitrators' fees 291
    commencement of arbitration 98
    confidentiality obligations 36
    costs 289–291
    impartiality of arbitrator 112
    party autonomy 70, 72
    removal of arbitrator 103
    separability 43

Malaysia
  confidentiality obligations 36

mandatory rules
  Arbitration (Sc) Act 2010 and
    17–18, 82–83
  arbitrator
    appointment of 107–108
    fees of 282
  awards, on
    challenging 90–94
    generally 88–89
  commencement of arbitration 83–86,
    97
  constitution of tribunal, on 83–86,
    97
  definition 17–18, 45, 81, 300
  expenses, on 90
  general duties, on 87
  generally 17–18, 74–77, 81–82,
    150–154
  jurisdiction, on 86–87
  marking 150
  miscellaneous provisions, on 94–96
  powers of court, on 87–88
multi-party arbitration
  Australia 66
  England 64–65
  generally 63–64
  Hong Kong 65–66
  ICC 66
  Netherlands 65
  Scotland 64

NAI see Netherlands Arbitration
    Institute
Netherlands
  choice of law rules 187
  confidentiality obligations 29, 33, 36
  multi-party arbitration 65
  separability 43
Netherlands Arbitration Institute
    (NAI) 36
New York Convention
  accession by UK 255
  amendments to 309
  Art I argument 260–262
  Art V(1)(e) argument 262–264
  Art VII argument 264–273
  awards under
    Arbitration (Sc) Act 2010 and
      13–14

New York Convention
  awards under (cont)
    binding force of 13, 256
    recognition or enforcement in
      Scotland 13–14, 255–256,
      257–260, 305–307
  choice of law and 76
  format of arbitration agreement 41
  mandatory rules, effect of 81
  parties to 255–256
  place of arbitration 255
  "public policy", meaning of 79
  Scotland, effect in 255–256
  seat of arbitration 255
New Zealand
  confidentiality obligations 29, 33
Nicaragua
  confidentiality obligations 29, 33
Norway
  confidentiality obligations 28, 33
notice of commencement of arbitration,
  service of 97–98
number of arbitrators 100–101, 107

oaths, taking of 233, 325
object, loss of right to 343–344
Orange list (conflicts of interest) 110

partial awards 248, 331
party autonomy
  Arbitration (Sc) Act 2010 69–70
  choice of proper law and 73
  design of proceedings 48
  generally 67, 147
  international practice, in 70–73
  mandatory rules
    Arbitration (Sc) Act 2010 and
      82–83
    awards, on 88–89, 90–94
    commencement, on 83–86
    constitution of tribunal, on
      83–86
    expenses, on 90
    general duties, on 87
    generally 74–77, 81–82
    jurisdiction, on 86–87
    miscellaneous provisions, on
      94–96
    powers of court, on 87–88

party autonomy
  mandatory rules (cont)
    public policy
      domestic 78
      generally 74–77
      international 78–80
      transnational 80–81
    restrictions on 74–96
    theoretical basis 67–68
    2010 Act provision on 10
party to arbitration
  attend hearing, failure to 234,
    325–326
  confidentiality, breach of duty of 19,
    20
  death of 52–53, 133, 345
  evidence, failure to provide 325–326
  expenses 281
  general duty of 321
  representatives of 229, 324
Peru
  confidentiality obligations 29, 33
place of arbitration
  awards, linking to 260–262
  New York Convention 255
  Scottish rules 228, 323
  UNCITRAL practice 228
place of performance
  "implied choice of law" test and
    180
powers of court
  mandatory rules on 87–88
prescription 307–308
procedural law
  default rules 148–150
  generally 147–148
  mandatory rules 150–154
procedure before tribunal
  generally 225–228
  Scottish Rules 225, 322–323
proper law
  a-national principles of law and 188,
    190
  choice of
    "centre of gravity" test 187
    "closest and most real" test 178,
      182–185
    connection with case, need
      for 174–176

proper law
  choice of (cont)
    express choice by parties 172, 176–178
    generally 169–224
    "implied choice of law" test 178–182
    international practice 172–187
    limitations on parties' choice 176–178
    Scottish Rules 171, 172
    three-step rules 185–186
    two-step rules 185–186, 186–187
  determining 170–187
  general principles of law, application of 189–190, 192–201
  importance of 169–170
  international law, application of 190–192
  types of 188–224
property, tribunal's powers relating to 232–233, 324–325
provisional arbitral awards 248, 331
public policy
  domestic 78
  generally 74–77
  international 78–80
  meaning of 79–80
  transnational 80–81

"reasonable necessity" rule on disclosure of confidential material 21, 22
reasons for awards, requirements to 247
recognition of awards
  generally
    Belgium 265
    France 265
    Switzerland 266
  New York Convention, under
    formalities 255
    generally 255–256
    refusal of
      discretion in 257–259, 260
reconsideration of award following challenge 342
reconstitution of tribunal 104, 319
recoverability of expenses 283–286

Red list (conflicts of interest) 110
removal of arbitrators
  court, by 317, 318
  generally 103
  mandatory rules 124, 125
  parties, by 316
resignation of arbitrator
  generally 104
  mandatory rules 124, 126
Russian Federation
  confidentiality obligations 29, 35–36
SCC see Stockholm Chamber of Commerce
SCIA see Scottish Council for International Arbitration
Scotland
  see also Arbitration (Scotland) Act 2010; Scottish Arbitration Rules
  legal development in 1–7
Scots law, forum's power to determine points of 87, 239–240
Scottish Arbitration Code 1999 2–3
Scottish Arbitration Rules
  amiable composition 172, 218
  appointment
    arbitrators, of 314–315
    challenging 316–317
    failure in procedure 315–316
    tribunal, of 314
  arbitrability 61
  arbitration agreements, failure to comply with 326
  arbitrators
    appointment 314–315
    challenging appointment 316–317
    conflicts of interest 316
    death of 345
    eligibility as 314
    fees and expenses 132–133, 333–334
    impartiality 344
    independence 344
    individuals, to be 314
    liability at tenure's end 319
    nomination 319
    number of 314
    removal 317, 318

Scottish Arbitration Rules
  arbitrators (*cont*)
    resignation 318
    tenure 104, 316
  awards
    challenging 336–342
    generally 329–333
  choice of law 171–172
  commencement of arbitration 314
  confidentiality obligations 19–20, 29, 34, 321–322
  contents of 17–18
  court intervention in arbitration 326–328
  default rules 17–18, 301
  design of 45
  ex aequo et bono 172
  expenses
    arbitrators' 132–133, 333–334
    definition 333
    pre-dispute agreements on liability for 335
    recoverable 334–335, 336
    security for 335–336
  experts
    immunity of 343
    opinions of 324
  fees 132–133, 333–334
  formal communications 345–346
  immunity from liability
    appointing arbitral institution, of 343
    experts, of 133–134, 343
    tribunal, of 342–343
    witnesses, of 133–134, 343
  mandatory rules
    appointment of tribunal 83–84
    awards 88–89
    commencement of arbitration 83
    conflicts of interest, disclosure of 84–85
    court powers in relation to arbitration 87–88
    dismissal of tribunal 85
    generally 17–18, 300
    impartiality 87
    jurisdiction of tribunal 86–87
    generally 82–83

Scottish Arbitration Rules
  mandatory rules (*cont*)
    removal of arbitrator 85
    resignation of arbitrator 85–86
  multi-party arbitration 64
  object, loss of right to 343–344
  parties
    attend hearing, failure to 325–326
    death of 345
    evidence, failure to provide 325–326
    general duty of 321
    representatives of 324
  place of arbitration 323
  procedure 225
  proper law, choice of 171–172
  time, calculation of periods of 346–347
  tribunal
    appointment of 314
    clerk, appointment of 324
    consolidation of proceedings 326
    decisions 323–324
    delay in claim or defence 325
    deliberations 322
    directions 324, 326
    dismissal by court 318
    evidence 323, 325–326
    general duty 321
    immunity of 342–343
    jurisdiction 319–321
    oaths or affirmations 325
    procedure 322–323
    property, powers relating to 324–325
    reconsideration of case by 342
    reconstitution 319
  umpires 345
  unfair treatment 345
  witnesses
    attendance of, power to order 88, 241–242, 327–328
    immunity of 94, 95, 134, 343
Scottish Council for International Arbitration (SCIA) 3
seat of arbitration
  choice of proper law and 11–12, 148

seat of arbitration (*cont*)
  generally 11–12, 148, 299
  New York Convention 255
  specification in award 247
security for expenses 335–336
separability
  English views on 56–61
  generally 42–43
  Scottish Rules 299
  Switzerland 43
  UNCITRAL Model Law 43
serious irregularity
  challenging award on ground of 337–338
SIAC *see* Singapore International Arbitration Centre
Singapore International Arbitration Centre (SIAC)
  confidentiality obligations, rules on 24, 28, 34, 36
Spain
  confidentiality obligations 29, 34
statutory arbitration 12–13 304–305
Stockholm Chamber of Commerce (SCC)
  see also Sweden
  generally 29
  rules of
    confidentiality obligations, on 36
    impartiality, on 112
submission clause 40
substantive jurisdiction
  challenging award on ground of 336–337
substantive law *see* proper law
suspension of legal proceedings 301–302
Sweden
  choice of law rules 187
  confidentiality obligations 27–28, 29, 34, 36
  party autonomy 72
Switzerland
  choice of law rules 187
  confidentiality obligations 28, 34, 36
  contracting to restrict grounds for challenging awards 274–276
  delocalisation theory 159
  jurisdiction of tribunal 130

Switzerland (*cont*)
  mandatory rules, effect of 82
  recognition and enforcement of awards 266
  separability 43

Tehran Regional Arbitration Centre (TRAC) 37
tenure of arbitrators 104, 316
time, calculation of periods of 346–347
time limits
  extension of, statutory arbitration and 12
  parties', court's power to vary 87–88, 241
  submission of claims or defences, for, failure to observe 233–234
TRAC *see* Tehran Regional Arbitration Centre
transnational public policy 80–81
tribunal
  appointment of 99–100, 314
  clerks, agents or employees, power of appointment 229, 324
  composition of 97, 124
  consolidation of proceedings 326
  constitution 46–47, 99–103
  decisions of
    chairman's casting vote 229
    deliberation on 131
    generally 228–229, 323–324
  delay in claim or defence 325
  deliberations 48, 322
  directions
    failure to comply with 234–236, 326
    power to give 229, 324
  dismissal by court 318
  evidence 323, 325–326
  experts, power to appoint 230
  general duty 321
  immunity of 342–343
  jurisdiction
    default rules 47, 319–320
    generally 127–131
    objections to 320
    referral of point of 320–321
    ruling on own 128

tribunal (cont)
  oaths or affirmations 325
  procedure
    generally 322–323
    power to decide 225–226
  property, powers relating to 324–325
  reconsideration of award by 342
  reconstitution 104, 127, 319

umpires
  immunity from liability 133–134
  mandatory rules 96
UNCITRAL Arbitration Rules
  amiable composition 221
  appointment of arbitrators
    challenge to 102
    time limit for 100
  commencement of arbitration 98
  confidentiality obligations 29, 30, 35
  experts, appointment of 230
  legal representatives 229
  lex mercatoria, reflecting 212
  party autonomy 70, 71
  place of arbitration 228
  procedure 226
  property, tribunal's powers relating to 233
UNCITRAL Model Law
  appointment of arbitrators
    challenge to 102
    time limit for 100
  amendments to 309
  commencement of arbitration 98
  confidentiality 28
  experts, appointment of 230
  failure to attend hearing or provide evidence 234
  format of arbitration agreement 42
  impartiality, on 109, 111
  independence, on 109–110, 111
  interim measures 235–236, 243
  jurisdiction, on 130–131
  late submission of claims or defences 234
  lex mercatoria, reflecting 212

UNCITRAL Model Law (cont)
  party autonomy 70, 71
  place of arbitration 228
  pre-2010 Act status in Scotland 2
  procedure 226
  repeal for Scotland 7, 14–16
  separability 43
  status post-2010 Act 16
United States of America
  see also American Arbitration Association
  arbitrability 62
  "closest and most real" test 184–185
  confidentiality obligations 27, 28, 30
  contracting to expand grounds for challenging awards 276–280
  disqualification of arbiters, case law on 118–123

Venezuela
  confidentiality obligations 28, 34
Vienna Rules
  appointment of arbitrator, challenge to 103
  arbitrators' fees 292
  commencement of arbitration 98
  confidentiality obligations 37
  costs 291–292
  interim measures 235
  removal of arbitrator 103
void, power to declare provisions 12

WIPO *see* World Intellectual Property Organization
withholding of arbitral awards 249–250, 331
witnesses
  attendance of, court's power to order 88, 241–242, 327–328
  expert 20
  immunity from liability 94, 95, 134, 343
World Intellectual Property Organization (WIPO)
  confidentiality obligations, rules on 37